ARE RACISTS CRAZY?

BIOPOLITICS: MEDICINE, TECHNOSCIENCE, AND HEALTH IN THE 21ST CENTURY

General Editors: Monica J. Casper and Lisa Jean Moore

Are Racists Crazy?

How Prejudice, Racism, and Antisemitism
Became Markers of Insanity

Sander L. Gilman and James M. Thomas

NEW YORK UNIVERSITY PRESS

New York

NEW YORK UNIVERSITY PRESS
New York
www.nyupress.org

References to Internet websites (URLs) were accurate at the time of writing. Neither the author nor New York University Press is responsible for URLs that may have expired or changed since the manuscript was prepared.

Library of Congress Cataloging-in-Publication Data
Names: Gilman, Sander L., author. | Thomas, James M., 1982– author.
Title: Are racists crazy? : how prejudice, racism, and antisemitism became markers of insanity / Sander L. Gilman and James M. Thomas.
Description: New York : New York University Press, [2016] | Series: Biopolitics: medicine, technoscience, and health in the 21st century | Includes bibliographical references and index.
Identifiers: LCCN 2016023905 | ISBN 978-1-4798-5612-1 (cl : alk. paper)
Subjects: LCSH: Prejudices—Psychological aspects. | Racism—Psychological aspects. | Antisemitism—Psychological aspects. | Mental illness.
Classification: LCC BF575.P9 G55 2016 | DDC 303.3/85—dc23
LC record available at https://lccn.loc.gov/2016023905

New York University Press books are printed on acid-free paper, and their binding materials are chosen for strength and durability. We strive to use environmentally responsible suppliers and materials to the greatest extent possible in publishing our books.

Manufactured in the United States of America

10 9 8 7 6 5 4 3 2 1

Also available as an ebook

CONTENTS

PREFACE AND ACKNOWLEDGMENTS

This book arose out of a car trip. Sander Gilman was invited to come to the University of Mississippi to speak on "race and madness" as part of the University of Mississippi Critical Race Studies Group's Fall Symposium on the intertwining legacies of Jews and black Americans. One of the Critical Race Studies Group's members, James "JT" Thomas, was designated to pick him up at Memphis and drive him the hour to Oxford. On the way, as they chatted about a number of things, the topic of the afternoon talk arose and both were pleased to note that despite very different disciplinary directions, Gilman as a cultural historian and Thomas as a sociologist, they shared a deep interest in the difficulty and complexity of thinking about race and psychopathology as a cultural problem, indeed as a litmus test for our complicated understanding of race, racism, and mental illness. A joint project description arose after the visit. Ilene Kalish of New York University Press and the editors of its series Biopolitics: Medicine, Technoscience, and Health in the Twenty-First Century, Monica J. Casper and Lisa Jean Moore, encouraged the writing of the volume.

Given the authors' different disciplinary backgrounds, the work on the manuscript was from the beginning clearly divided. However, each read and commented on the other's work in a critical and productive way. The end result is an overview of a complex topic with which we hope to spur interest in the difficulties of writing and thinking across disciplines and, in this case, the broad historical span from the mid-nineteenth century to the present. Because this is an overview, much relevant material has been omitted, as the topic of each subchapter merits (and in some cases has received) its own monograph. But the question of the implications of considering group hatred as a psychopathology, spurred on by twenty-first-century claims ranging from a pill for prejudice to a test to identify the perpetrators of genocide in advance of their acts, seemed to us to warrant our strongly comparative approach.

We are grateful to the anonymous reviewers of both our proposal and the finished manuscript for a range of suggestions, most of which found their way into this book. We are also grateful to Kate Epstein for critically editing our text. We are also happy to acknowledge our students at the University of Mississippi and Emory University for their collaboration in the classes we have held on this and related topics. Living scholarship demands critical interaction and this we found in our classrooms. The readings for these classes and the discussion in them helped shape our argument. We are also grateful to Caelyn Cobb at New York University Press for shepherding the project. A special thanks is extended to the University of Mississippi Critical Race Studies Group, and in particular Willa Johnson, for helping to plant the seeds that would become this finished manuscript. Finally, a warm thanks to our families and loved ones, whose support and encouragement prove invaluable to our professional activities.

Introduction

The Problem Limited

In February 2012, an interdisciplinary team of scientists at Oxford University performed a randomized, double-blind experiment whereby the researchers administered a beta-blocker commonly used to treat heart medication to one group of subjects, while giving the other a placebo.[1] The research team then subjected both groups to a standard implicit association test (IAT), and recorded each group's scores on an implicit bias scale.[2] The IAT is a social psychological instrument used to measure the strength of associations between concepts (e.g., women, white people, lesbians) and evaluations (e.g., good, bad, healthy, diseased) or stereotypes (e.g., emotional, intelligent, bossy). The IAT score refers to how fast a person matches certain words or images to evaluative concepts (e.g., white people/good, black people/bad). A person, for example, who is faster to categorize words or images when "white people" and "good" and "black people" and "bad" are grouped together than when the groupings are reversed would be said to have an implicit preference for white people relative to black people.[3]

In the aforementioned experiment, subjects in both groups were shown images of people of different races, alongside words with positive and negative meanings. They were then asked to rate how "warm" their feelings were toward different groups. Results showed that participants taking the beta-blocker scored significantly lower on the IAT, indicating they held lower levels of subconscious racial bias. Measures of explicit racial prejudice, however, were unaffected by the administering of the beta-blocker. One of the lead researchers, in a press release, stated, "Such research raises the *tantalising* possibility that our unconscious racial attitudes could be modulated using drugs" (emphasis ours).[4]

The study quickly gained mass media attention, with its results, comments from the researchers, and editorials about the clinical trial published in outlets across the ideological spectrum, including the *Huff-*

ington Post, Time, and the London-based *Daily Telegraph, Sun*, and *Daily Mirror*. The study's resonance was global, reaching from the *Province* in British Columbia to the *Cape Times* in South Africa. With the exception of one editorial in *Time*, the mass media framed the topic as a question of when and how a medical "cure" for racism would be available, and largely eschewed discussion about whether the study had appropriately conceptualized racism's scope and scale. That same year, the *Oxford Handbook of Personality Disorders* included a chapter on identifying and assessing what the psychologists Carl Bell and Edward Dunbar refer to as "pathological bias," a form of racism identified as having psychopathological origins and leading to extreme violence. Symptoms associated with this proposed disorder include feelings of persecution by out-groups, fantasies of violence against those who are culturally different, recurring fears of racial and ethnic others who reside in close proximity, paranoia toward non-English speakers, and denigration of out-groups seen as unclean, criminal, and less than human.[5]

The question of what exactly was being modified in the Oxford study was raised recently with the publication of a Dutch study. In it, researchers claimed to have removed phobic responses—in this case to spiders—not through long-term desensitization, the common intervention, but by giving participants in a double-blind and placebo-controlled experiment a single dose of the same beta-blocker. Analogous to the Oxford study, the "fear response" (rather than racism) had been measured before and after by "behavioral approach tests . . . [that] were used to assess the degree of fear while being exposed to a spider as well as overt approach behavior toward spiders."[6] The researchers claimed the technique was effective in reducing patients' phobic responses to real spiders even while noting that "people tend to fear objects and situations that they have never really experienced."[7] The study claimed that the combination of the exposure to the drug as well as the subsequent reexposure to the real, rather than imagined spiders (the agent that had triggered the phobia) caused a radical reduction in anxiety and a virtual elimination of the phobic response. But are arachnophobes the same as racists? Is racism merely uncontrolled anxiety triggered by a specific cause, whether experienced or imagined? Indeed should the overall claim of the Oxford study now be understood as arguing that racism is really merely a phobic response to an imagined terror that can be cured through the application of a drug and reexposure to its cause? Or is racism beyond such definition and such treatment?

Research like the Oxford University study in many ways simply reified the general claims of the times that the potential for asocial or violent behavior could be identified through genetic or psychological testing even before such actions took place.[8] The focus of the public seemed to be on the development of specific medical interventions to prevent them. The perfect preventative state would be free of even the potential for such activities as racist acts through the employment of a public health model that targeted antisocial behavior as it had targeted infectious diseases. Since the beginning of the twenty-first century a new field of ethics, labeled neuroethics, has been making claims about the efficacy of such interventions as well as providing a critical examination of the arguments behind them.[9] A split vision—are such interventions in the public good possible and desirable, or do they violate human autonomy—is reflected in the underlying claims of the Oxford study.

That the medical and psychological sciences reconstruct previously defined social problems as medical and mental problems is, of course, not a new phenomenon. However, what is significant is how these reconstructions have, over time, influenced public opinion and policy, in addition to weaving their way into the fabric of some of our most important and influential institutions. As early as 2005, for example, inmates within the California state prison system were being administered antipsychotic drugs to combat what the divisional chief psychologist for the California Department of Corrections identified as the "delusional disorders" of racism and homophobia, despite the inmates not having a diagnosis recognized by the American Psychiatric Association.[10]

If this example appears as an anomaly, or too convenient to draw conclusions from, consider that the U.S. criminal justice system already has had, for over thirty years, legal precedent for recognizing racism as a delusional disorder, allowing perpetrators of racially targeted violence to evade punitive justice for their actions. In May 1981, an elderly white man, Anthony Simon, shot his Chinese American neighbor, Steffen Wong, as Wong was entering his own home. Claiming he was afraid of Wong due to a belief that Wong knew martial arts, and fearful that more "Orientals" were moving into the neighborhood, Simon was ultimately acquitted on two accounts of aggravated assault. An important part of the defense's case was the testimony of a clinical psychologist who stated Simon's mental condition "permitted him to misjudge reality and see himself [as] under attack." Put differently, it was claimed Simon suffered from "anxiety neurosis." Later, the Kansas Supreme Court, in *State v. Simon*, while acknowledging the trial court's instruction to the jury was improper, denied a challenge to the acquittal on the grounds of double jeopardy.[11]

What is the relationship, historically, between race, racism, and mental illness? How did race, once considered an unquestionable ontological category, and significant marker of psychosis, become redefined as a social construct? And how was it made possible that, almost concurrently, racism became reimagined as mental illness? Importantly, what are the implications of this reimagining? Was Glenn Miller, the ex-Klansman responsible for the shooting spree that left three individuals dead at a synagogue in Overland Park, Kansas, in 2013, simply suffering from an extreme mental illness? Is the recent finding by sociologists at Portland State University that Portland drivers show racial bias against pedestrians of color a mental health matter?[12] Is the backward slide toward resegregated public schools throughout the United States indicative of some massive psychosocial disorder?[13] These are the questions that structure the nature of the investigation in this book.

While we question the construction of racism as a psychological disorder, we do not question the fact that individuals suffering from acute mental illnesses fixate on images such as race as a symptom of their illness. Rather, as with many symptoms of mental illness, this fixation is culturally defined, rather than springing from an autonomous mental illness. These are cases of individuals with particular symptoms, not classifications of mental illness that seek to explain manifestations of racism.[14] Thus the case of Anthony Simon mentioned above hovered between the poles of explanation. Was he a mentally ill individual who fixated on the race of his neighbor or did he suffer from a debilitating mental illness called "racism"? When we examine the question of racism's definition and subsequent treatment as a psychopathology, we are looking at what Stephen Bartlett calls "the social consequences of disease labeling."[15] We are not arguing that mental illness is a purely social construction but that its reality is embedded within historical, social, and cultural forces in a complex way. Racism, too, as a broad social phe-

nomenon, is real, but it is a political category, not a psychopathological
one, even if racism can manifest itself as a symptom of an individual's
disease process.

As we will show in this book, the rendering of difference *through*
disease and illness would become central during the mid- to late nineteenth century, and up through the early part of the twentieth century,
as the development of modern medicine produced new ways to distinguish racial groups from one another. The cultural historian Robert
Young correctly demonstrates that during this period, race was being
fashioned within laboratories and classrooms of early biomedical practitioners, and gained currency through the frequent borrowing of biomedical terminology among anthropologists and early sociologists.[16]
Yet, by the end of World War II, within the medical, psychological, and
even social sciences, a shift occurs whereby disease becomes a descriptor
of *racism*. To put another way, if the nineteenth-century Jew and black
American bore the mark of insanity, by the end of World War II that
mark would be placed upon those whose hatred targeted the Jew and
black American.

We are not interested in teasing out the multiple classifications of race
that evolve from the eighteenth century to the present, though we are
certainly aware that, especially with the rise of modern genetics, these
become ever more problematic in the fixed boundaries that they create
between groups. Thus the parallel distinctions between forms of race
hatred based on such classifications during this period—antisemitism or
anti-Judaism; racial prejudice against Africans, within and beyond that
continent, and black Americans; race hatred aimed at Native Americans
or the Chinese and other Asian ethnic groups—are of importance in the
political implications of their application. We shall show that the ideas
race hatred developed using one or the other group slides easily into
categorizing other groups. Indeed, the very artificial construction of the
boundaries of race makes this possible even within the claims of the sciences we are examining.[17]

Certainly the question of how race in its broadest sense was made
into a pathological condition has been explored through numerous academic articles and books. For example, there is a sustained discussion of
the debates about race and mental illness in the analyses offered by Martin Summers, Dennis Doyle, and Jonathan Metzl on the history of race

and American psychiatry (and perhaps some of the literature on mid-twentieth-century colonial psychiatry); Natalia Molina, Samuel Roberts, and Keith Wailoo on race and the foundations of modern public health; and Jonathan Holloway, Darryl Scott, and others on the history of race and urban social science.[18] One of the present authors has written extensively on the idea of race and self-hatred.[19] His work has had many echoes as well as rebuttals.[20] However, the shift toward pathologizing *racism*, and demonstrating the relationship of this shift to the previous *pathologization* of race, has not been documented to the degree that the present study undertakes.

As Sander L. Gilman has argued, for the targets of prejudice, self-hatred is one of many reactions to exposure to hate.[21] We often see complex and dynamic human responses to such circumstances. As we shall see in detail in Chapter Three, Anna Freud outlined in her *The Ego and Mechanisms of Defense* (1936) that the defenses of the ego under such circumstances can take the form of repression, displacement, denial, projection, reaction formation, intellectualization, rationalization, undoing, and sublimation as well as identification with the aggressor or self-hatred. In that context, prejudice has been defined as the cause of the latter.[22] But resilience and rebellion are also possible reactions. Self-hatred may exist in individuals, but not in classes of individuals, and it can lead to both repression and sublimation. Repressed self-hatred can be corrosive and lead to forms of mental illness; sublimated self-hatred can be the wellspring of creative, if not always pleasant, forms of externalization.

Having gotten that out of the way, let us turn not to racism as psychopathology but to its primary predecessor and the claims that later structure this view. In the era of both the biologization of difference as "race" and the rise of a biologically driven definition of mental illness, it was of little surprise that madness came to be seen as a quality of specific races. As early as the Enlightenment, race was considered a precipitating factor in defining the etiology of mental illness, but almost exclusively in the "inferior races": blacks in the United States, the Irish in Great Britain, and Jews in Western and Central Europe. The development of the scientific perspective on "race" emerged alongside the epistemological shift within Western European society from religious doctrine to scientific doctrine, whereby authority was relocated from the church to the laboratory, with the scientist as an independent and unbiased observer of nature.

The Enlightenment, and the subsequent emergence of scientific knowledge as an authoritative regime, helped to create clearly defined biological categories of "mankind" perceived to be independent of any political definition of difference, but nevertheless used to reinforce such political categories as slavery or social exclusion. The *Oxford English Dictionary* traces "race"'s meaning ("a tribe, nation, or people, regarded as of common stock, and, in early use, frequently with modifying adjective, as British race, Roman race") through citations from 1572, where race is a collective—"The Englishe race ouerrunne and daily spoiled"—to 1612, where race's association with color functions as an index of biology: "He is a white man and of the Race of the Tartares." By 1775, the scientific study of races was prevalent, with German researcher J. F. Blumenbach and his *De Generis Humani Varietati Nativa* cited as using race as "more or less formal systems of classification: any of the major groupings of mankind, having in common distinct physical features or having a similar ethnic background." In 1795, the *OED* notes the popular acceptance of this view: "These Tartar tribes, which he supposes to be of the Red Race, distinct from the European White Race." Race in its nonmetaphoric sense had become a reflex of the *science* of biology, not merely pseudoscience.

Karl Popper's principle of "demarcation" between science and pseudoscience as stated in his 1935 *Logik der Forschung* (*The Logic of Scientific Discovery*) distinguished them through the claims of the falsifiability of science.[23] Popper's work was temporally parallel to the debates about racial predisposition to specific forms of mental illness, although his example of pseudoscience was psychoanalysis, not race science. Given that Popper was an acculturated Austrian Jew, this was more than merely an oversight. Contesting racial science meant contesting science itself. For at that time "race science" was so integrated into all aspects of the human sciences and medicine as to be inseparable from them. Science was, as George Herbert Mead put it, a systematized form of knowledge: "Knowledge is never a mere contact of our organisms with other objects. It always takes on a universal character. If we know a thing, explain it, we always put it into a texture of uniformities. There must be some reason for it, some law expressed in it. That is the fundamental assumption of science."[24] For the science of race, as understood in all of the human sciences during that first age of positivistic and empirical science, knowledge of the "laws" governing racial differences and distinctions was not only universal, but also systematized into every field of inquiry dealing with human populations.

"The meaning of race," as Michael Omi and Howard Winant suggested over twenty years ago, "is defined and contested in both collective action and personal practice."[25] Through this process, they argue, "racial categories themselves are formed, transformed, destroyed and re-formed."[26] Racial formation, then, is the process of investing meaning in racial categories—"the extension of racial meaning to relationships, social practices, or groups" previously understood in nonracial terms.[27] Thus the very absence or presence of racial categories reflects absolute boundaries of biologically fixed groups whose character is as radically circumscribed as its biology.[28] Make no mistake, we are not arguing here for a concretization of racial categories or racial differences. Rather, like Omi and Winant we argue racial formation is a process of investing meaning in racial categories. Where we differ from Omi and Winant, however, is that we claim this process and its extension through modern science, rather than the state, continues to be a major driving force behind contemporary racial projects.

Racial meaning, for Omi and Winant, also "is constructed and transformed sociohistorically through competing political projects, through the necessary and ineluctable link between the structural and cultural dimensions of race."[29] In their account, "competing political projects" have primarily been theorized as a dynamic and contested relationship between the state and movements on the ground. The dialectic interplay between the two is understood as responsible for the meanings of race, and racism, within any given sociohistorical context. Though quite useful for considering the political dimensions of race's history, Omi and Winant's framework is not as useful for identifying the epistemic cultural history of race and racial meaning.

Though race scholars to date have identified the role "race science" played in eighteenth- and nineteenth-century constructions of human difference, much of this literature frames the role of "race science" as subservient to state power.[30] This approach rightfully identifies the structural dimension of race. Yet, though this approach gives mention to the imbrication between this dimension and a cultural one, it neverthe-less undersells it.[31] In her book, *Epistemic Cultures*, Karin Knorr Cetina writes, "A knowledge society is not simply a society of more experts. . . . It is a society permeated with knowledge cultures, the whole set of struc-tures and mechanisms that serve knowledge and unfold with its articu-lation."[32] One feature to our approach we hope readers find useful is our historical and sociological analysis of the *epistemic culture* of race, and racism.[33] That is, in the dialectic encounter between structural and cultural forces identified by Omi and Winant in the production of race's meaning, we aim to show how the relationship of an "expert system" of race science permeates Western society's production of racial meaning.[34]

This is not to suggest the state has no role to play here; rather, the role of the state in the production of racial meaning has been overde-termined. The investing of meaning into the supposed reality of racial categories, and into analyzing human affairs in terms of racial differ-ences, emerged and was supported within laboratories, classrooms, conferences, and writings of early biomedical practitioners, not among politicians. This meaning was further invested when biomedical termi-nology began to diffuse among nonmedical scientists, as well as public policymakers.[35] Policy, as an extension of state power, required scientific authority for its legitimation. This was evident, as we shall show, in some of the most influential Supreme Court cases concerning the significance of race, including *Plessy v. Ferguson*, *Buck v. Bell*, and *Brown v. Board of Education*. In fact, scientific rationality was instrumental, and contin-ues to be instrumental, in the redesigning and reimagining of nearly all state-based apparatuses, including public education, public health, law, the economy, and the military.

Race and Difference in This Book

We find it prudent to state up front our approach to the concept "race," and how it may differ from its use among other scholars of history and the social sciences. Throughout this book, we treat race as a set of histor-ical and discursive practices that, in various forms, tether constructions of madness, disease, illness, and, fundamentally, *difference* to certain bodies. These practices are, of course, ideologically driven. However, we are hesitant to claim, as some have, that ideologies necessarily *drive* practices. As we show in this book, for example, ideologies about innate racial differences both produce, and importantly, are produced by, the authority of medical, behavioral, and social sciences in nineteenth- and twentieth-century Europe and the United States. Furthermore, in the early to mid-twentieth century, it was scientific practice that gave rise to new ideologies about race and racial differences. Ideology and practice, then, are coterminous, cofunctioning, and relational phenomena.

We also wish to emphasize that our treatment of race is distinctively *not* an examination of stable, fixed, and/or essentialized categories of subjectivity. Further, while in contemporary race scholarship it is common to consider race as a matter of identity, this is not our focus. In fact, James M. Thomas has provided a critique of this very treatment of race, arguing that the consideration of racial identities as concrete, albeit contextual, phenomena has had the unfortunate consequence of essentializing racial identity as a political category, even while many of the same observers simultaneously argue for its social and cultural contingency.[36] In this book, we are less concerned with how Jews and blacks define themselves, collectively, and more concerned with how those categories emerge over time, in particular contexts, and how they become aligned to particular constructions of mental diseases. We are also interested in how racism in the post–World War II era similarly becomes tethered to particular constructions of mental illnesses, while the concept of race is (re)considered by the medical, social, and behavioral sciences as an idea with no basis in biological reality. To summarize, then, our treatment of race defines it as:

1. unstable;
2. shaped by historical, material, and discursive forces;
3. without basis in human biology, anatomy, or physiology;
4. nevertheless, ontologically real, in the sense that the category has been, and remains, a fundamental organizer of political, social, and economic opportunities.

Some readers may inquire about where "ethnicity" fits into our discussion. It is increasingly common among scholars of race and racism to collapse any distinction between "race" and "ethnicity," and employ "race" when referring to categories of difference that have political, social, and economic consequences. Though there are arguments to be made for treating the categories "Jew," "black," and "white" as ethnic distinctions because of unique cultural histories or contemporary cultural practices by members within those categories, we believe our consideration of how these categories became markers of mental disease, and thus, difference, highlights the historical fact that "blacks," "whites," and "Jews" are, first and foremost, techniques of governance. That is, the discursive and material apparatuses responsible for the emergence of those categories have *always* been oriented toward managing populations defined by those terms. For example, the United States Census, as one technique of governance, included only two racial categories ("white" and "colored") in 1790, added the category of "mulatto" in 1850, "quadroon" and "octoroon," along with "Indian," "Chinese," and "Japanese" in 1890, and "Mexican" in 1930, which was then removed until 1970.

Importantly, the assignment of groups of people to these categories has never been consistent in American, or European, history. Yet what has been consistent is that the assignment to these groups, in any era, subsequently influenced the political, economic, and social chances for their members. To reduce these categories to ethnic dimensions, or to their cultural uniqueness, would deemphasize the significance of their political and historical formations. Thus, our consideration of Jews, blacks, and whites in this book is an examination of racial formations, articulations, and governmentalities—material and discursive—and not a consideration of ethnic practices. However, we do leave open the opportunity for other scholars interested in culture, identity, and interaction to interrogate these concepts as ethnic dimensions. Rather than ask "is this a matter of race, or ethnicity?" we appreciate the contextual fluidity of these concepts, and their utility to function as "both/and" depending upon the type of research questions asked.[37]

Finally, the attuned reader will notice we refrain from capitalizing the terms "black" and "white," while capitalizing "Jew" and countries of origin (e.g., German Jew, black Americans). We have chosen to use the spelling "antisemitism" rather than the older "anti-Semitism" as it removes the ideological and pseudoscientific origins of this term, which we shall discuss. These choices reflect our above discussion of race as a matter of historical and discursive sets of practices, or regimes. Though there are patterned similarities in the emergence of these regimes within Europe and the United States, they are not identical. To capitalize "black" or "white" would place too much emphasis on notions of crystallized subjectivity, rather than their contingencies. Concerning the category "Jew," we capitalize this term to reflect that, though it too emerges through particular formations over time, there are a set of practices among its members, particularly within the nineteenth and early twentieth centuries, that provide more stability to the category than has existed among blacks or whites. This, indeed, reflects the prismatic properties of the category "Jew"—across time, it has served as a marker of religious, ethnic, and *racial* difference, as the consistent referential Other to white, Christian society. Indeed the lower-case spelling of "jew" as a verb has only offensive force in English, as the *Oxford English Dictionary* notes.[38] For the purpose of consistency, then, unless we are quoting directly from an original source, we use "black," "white," and "Jew" throughout our book. In the case of other racial categories, we use "Latino/Latina," "Native Americans," and "Asian."

Psychopathology, Biopower, and Governmentality

Governmentality, in this study, refers to its broad definition, "the art of government," taken from Michel Foucault's lectures at the Collège de France from 1978 to 1979.[39] Importantly, "government" as Foucault defined it, referred not only to state politics, but to a wide range of techniques used to manage conduct, and, more specifically, the process of subjectification, or *governance*. Thus, our description of an emergent mental health governmentality refers to the range of techniques— discursive, symbolic, corporeal—that are increasingly used to manage our knowledge of self and society, and, subsequently, how we practice that knowledge upon our selves and society.

In addition to clarifying our use of "governmentality," we want readers to be clear in our use and analysis of *racism*. Here, racism designates something to be explained, rather than a framework for describing, or explaining, a set of observations. The latter usage is quite common among scholars who are of course right to identify the various forms of institutional and systemic racism that exist within contemporary society.[40] While this is certainly important for scholarship and anti-racist politics, we find it equally important to identify the historical, social, ideological, and material conditions that produce, or give rise to, contemporary racial projects. In this sense, then, our aim is to demonstrate the historical shifts whereby projects become rearticulated, to paraphrase Omi and Winant's racial formation theory discussed above. In order to account for the simultaneous expansion of medical and scientific governmentality in the post–World War II era, and its impact on the pathological construction of racism in the post–Civil Rights era, we find it useful to frame these phenomena in a revision of what Michel Foucault categorized as a dynamic encounter between *biopower* and *biopolitics*.[41] This encounter has produced, among other things, an expanding scope of scientific and medical governmentality.

To be clear, neither "governmentality" nor "biopower" are terms that originate with Foucault. Foucault's use of "governmentality" arose to fill a gap when in the late 1970s Foucault was lecturing at the Collège de France and needed a structure toward which to gesture in order to distance his own use of the concept of power from contemporaneous uses of it in sociological theory. Thus, "governmentality" became the means for depicting what Foucault recognized as underlying structures of administration that shaped both historical individuals and collectives. Yet the term has its origins at least as early as Roland Barthes, who used "governmentality" to describe the transfer of the image of the author to the state in his *Mythologies* in 1957.[42]

Meanwhile, "bicpower" grew out of Foucault's attempt to identify different paradigms and practices of power that, beginning in the seventeenth century, were focused toward "achieving the subjugation of bodies and the control of populations" for the purposes of dominating subjects through *life*.[43] The term, however, was coined in 1905 when Rudolph Kjellé introduced it in *Stormakterna*, one of the very first sociological works on "geopolitics" and was radically reworked in the critical literature of the 1930s, such as Morley Roberts's *Bio-Politics: An Essay in the Physiology, Pathology and Politics of the Social* (1938).[44] Foucault's use, albeit brief, came out of his attempt to write a history of these dynamic and often contradictory structures after the publication of his *Discipline and Punish: The Birth of the Prison* (*Surveiller et punir: Naissance de la Prison*) in 1975. In that work and later in *La volonté de savoir* (*The Will to Knowledge*) (1976)—volume 1 of *L'Histoire de la sexualité*—Foucault focused on the often invisible, shifting approaches, withdrawals, claims, and enforcement that shadow multiple institutions and forms of knowledge in human society, linking them in complex ways. For him biopower became "a political technology that brought life and its mechanism into the realm of explicit calculations and made knowledge/power an agent of transformation of human life," but it also had a history.[45]

Indeed, we must also add that our project is in line with Foucault's claim about the writing of a potential history of biopower:

> History has no "meaning," though this is not to say that it is absurd or incoherent. On the contrary, it is intelligible and should be susceptible of analysis down to the smallest detail—but this in accordance with the intelligibility of struggles, of strategies and tactics. Neither the dialectic, as logic of communication, nor semiotics, as the structure of communication, can account for the intrinsic intelligibility of conflicts. "Dialectic" is a way of evading the always open and hazardous reality of conflict by reducing it to a Hegelian skeleton, and "semiology" is a way of avoiding its violent, bloody and lethal character by reducing it to the calm Platonic form of language and dialogue.[46]

Roger Cooter has noted that "to be aware of one's historicity, and therefore deny the 'objectivity' of historical knowledge is, I believe, the precondition to making history-writing engaged and political."[47] Yet, as Cooter notes, Foucault is in a bind, for the writing of history relies on the archive and the library, two institutions that are also shaped by the structures of power in which they function. In real terms his "genealogical" method, with its emphasis on discontinuity and break, can not provide a true alternative to history but is rather another version of history (stressing discontinuity over continuity), a kind of alternative to "bourgeois" history.

Our project has been to stress both continuities and breaks, with each rereading the past as well as shaping the future of both strands. When we locate this increase in the number of institutions, agents, and regimes now centered on the medical model and the answers to the creation and appropriation of this model we are analyzing their discursive and material formations as historical manifestations with deep political implications.[48] Such implications may be the untended consequences of the strategic uses of arguments about vulnerability and prejudice that succeed in accomplishing specific goals, yet perpetuate arguments that stress universal responses to specific social actions.

Biopolitics, on the other hand, is only alluded to within Foucault's *History of Sexuality, Volume 1*, when he writes

> But a power whose task is to take charge of life needs continuous regulatory and corrective mechanisms. It is no longer a matter of bringing death into play in the field of sovereignty, but *distributing the living in the domain of value and utility.* Such a power has to qualify, measure, appraise, and hierarchize, rather than display itself in its murderous splendor; it does not have to draw the line that separates the enemies of the sovereign from his obedient subjects; *it effects distributions around the norm* [emphases ours].[49]

Since Foucault, there has been important debate regarding the specifics of both biopower and biopolitics. However, the anthropologist Paul Rabinow and the social theorist Nikolas Rose provide a compelling formulation we find useful for our own analysis. Biopower, for Rabinow and Rose, "entails one or more truth discourses about the 'vital' character of living human beings; an array of authorities considered competent to speak that truth; strategies for intervention upon collective existence in the name of life and health; and modes of subjectification, in which individuals work on themselves in the name of individual or collective life or health."[50] Biopower, then, as a truth discourse, emerges out of a particular cultural conjuncture, where the authority over life increasingly becomes concentrated in the hands of modern science, including the psychological sciences.

This is quite different from the purely negative claims of Giorgio Agamben in his focus on the juridical and political spaces for the exercise of power (in *Homo Sacer: Sovereign Power and Bare Life*, among other publications). For him the "first principle" of biopolitics is the politics of death, which leads to an odd post-Heideggerian focus on technology and an ahistorical reading of the Holocaust. This has been recently problematized in Alexander Weheliye's *Habeas Viscus* for, among other things, neglecting that concentration camps had their origins in both early-nineteenth-century "Indian removal" camps in the southeastern United States as well as in German Southwest Africa at the turn of the twentieth century.[51] As for the post-Marxists Michael Hardt and Antonio Negri's oft-cited approach to biopower, one can paraphrase Rabinow and Rose to the effect that they describe everything and analyze nothing.[52]

Biopolitics for Rabinow and Rose refers to the *political* struggle over the various problems with human life and death, "all the specific strategies and contestations over problematizations of collective human vitality, morbidity, and mortality; over the forms of knowledge, regimes of authority and practices of intervention that is desirable, legitimate, and efficacious."[53] The distinction drawn between biopower and biopolitics helps demonstrate how the challenge of scientific racism presented by some social and behavioral scientists in the pre- and inter-war years involved a fundamental clash over knowledge and authority. This clash resulted in the rejection of one version of biopower, or truth discourse, about the meaning of race. However, the rejection of this truth discourse occurred alongside the emergence of a new truth discourse on the role of genetics, biology, and psychopathology in mental and physical health outcomes. The conflict between a collapsing truth regime and an emergent one reflects the relational qualities of biopower and biopolitics: the emergence of biopower, in any given iteration, is always a product of biopolitics; and, the constitution of biopolitics is the consequence of biopower.

Yet it is clear that Rose's attempt, as Cooter describes, "to skirt morals and politics through his partial adoption of Foucault (i.e., Foucault without history), [means] he is left within the sociological lexicon. This is belied by his use of the normative categories of 'human rights,' 'individualism,' 'liberal democracies' and so on—old categories that . . . inappropriately 'continue to organize current political discourse.'"[54] What we have undertaken is to write a history of biopower in the more limited confines of a fragmentary account of race, health, genealogy, reproduction, and knowledge, that, through their interplay, function as dynamic and always shifting regimes of discursive power; as a power/knowledge apparatus that claims uniformity but which is inherently self-contradictory.[55] Throughout this book we have questioned exactly the terms and concepts that have constituted the rhetoric of science as well as race. But we have also been extremely self-conscious about our own positionalities—as a historian and a sociologist by training, respectively—in regard to these political and critical vocabularies. We recognize that within these regimes there is what Foucault refers to as an "interplay of shifts of position and modifications of function." Over time, these regimes combine, transforming one another *through* their encounters. Emergent knowledge of medical and psychological health, for example, influences ideological constructs of race. This is evident in the prevalent use of case-study and case-series methods within the medical and psychiatric communities in the nineteenth century, including the use of these methods to "prove" the physiological differences between races.[56] In addition, these new forms of knowledge, or "truth regimes" within health, medicine, and genealogy radically shape the politics of race and racism. This is evident in many social policies from the late nineteenth through the early twentieth centuries that invoked scientific racism in claiming the contamination of the dominant white society by racial and ethnic minorities could be prevented only through population control, including forced segregation and, in many instances, forced sterilization.

The psychiatrist and historian of science Horatio Fabrega argues that the evolution of modern psychological sciences depended upon three sets of interrelated developments during the nineteenth century.[57] First was the growth of the asylum as a place for treatment and confinement of victims of psychiatric disorders. The growth of the asylum highlighted the separate identity of emergent disorders from the more widely recognized class of social, behavior, political, economic, and medical problems. The second development was a growing emphasis on moral therapy, which entailed "a transformation of the early modern view that insanity and madness implied or rendered its victims as less than human and more like beasts."[58] The third development was the slow evolution of the discipline and medical specialty of psychiatry and, simultaneously, concerted efforts among medical authorities to better understand the social, biological, neurological, and psychological basis of mental illness. It is this latter development, part of a wide range of changes affecting science, medicine, and all of the medical professions, that, through the inter-war and post-war years, sought to sharpen and validate the medical basis of psychiatric disorders and of the profession of psychiatry itself.[59]

The continued examination of the historical culture of race as part of the ongoing development of the psychological sciences produced what

Fabrega refers to as a "biocultural dialectic," where the role of culture in affecting manifestations of disorders, aspects of diagnosis, and responses to treatment became a critical response occurring *within* psychiatry and psychology.[60] This concept of "biocultural dialectic" is important for our framework of biopower and biopolitics, in that it accounts for the emergence of psychiatry as an effect of a mental health governmentality *and* the subsuming of racism within this mental health governmentality. The production, manifestation, and meaning of disorders within the psychological sciences in the post-war years develops through the dialectic interplay between *bio-logic*—that is, the logic of biomedicine, including the evolution of psychiatry in response to the biological sciences—and cultural schemas. So, while the post-war years began with the collapse of the Third Reich, the resulting slow death of the eugenics movement, and the early successes of the modern-day Civil Rights Movement, this same period was marked by a rapid expansion of the mental health industry, including the growth of licensed clinical practitioners *and* the number of recognized clinical disorders.

Racism, understood as a social problem from at least the 1930s through the 1950s, became a site for therapy by the end of the 1960s. The intensity of this development derived from a major cultural challenge to psychiatry concerning the issue of cultural relativity. This challenge appeared, at first, to discredit psychiatry as a medical and scientific enterprise. Within this view, the diagnostic categories of mental illness were argued to be arbitrary, culture-bound, and, possibly, politically contrived and devoid of scientific legitimacy.[61] Mainstream psychiatry responded to these criticisms, according to Fabrega, by intensifying the momentum of scientific objectivity:

> Neurobiologic science gained ascendancy, while psychoanalysis was less able to anchor its categories in an empirical idiom and deal effectively with the problems posed by mental illness. All of this moved psychiatry in the direction of [biological] science and away from attention to culture, symbols, and social meanings, which historically had been pivotal to the psychiatric enterprise.[62]

Historically, these twentieth-century claims of the "second age of biology" are clearly prefigured in the "first age of biology," the rise of a clinical psychiatry bound to race science in the latter half of the nineteenth century.[63] What social scientific thought had begun to recognize as a social problem in the early twentieth century gradually became absorbed through this mental health governmentality, and, over time and like other social problems, became reclassified as an individual and pathological problem.

Such reclassification demanded a reordering of the basic assumptions of both group identity and group constitution. Indeed, considerations such as individual autonomy and resilience come also to be reconfigured in this debate. The study begins, therefore, in the mid-nineteenth century with the origin of biopower within the world of the science of race. As William Bynum noted decades ago, it was the world in which all of the human sciences from medicine to anthropology were informed by racial science.[64] Such disciplinary boundaries drew powerfully on the idea of pathological predispositions of the "inferior" races. The false assumption of the equivalence of all such races, however defined in whatever system invoked, created a symmetry among the pathologies ascribed to such groups. Thus the madness of the Jews, of the blacks, of the Irish, and of the Native Americans all bore similar markers and indeed followed parallel etiologies, even when multiple, conflicting etiologies were proposed to explain specific forms of group psychopathology. What is striking is that the members of those "inferior" races, admitted or tolerated within the confines of the disciplines constituting the human sciences in the nineteenth century, turned the tables, creating a race madness that defined the group that had categorized their own group and others as deviant and mad. It is here we begin our tale . . .

1

Psychopathology and Difference from the Nineteenth Century to the Present

Who Is Crazy?

The debates about outlawing slavery in Great Britain and the civil emancipation of European Jews beginning in the late eighteenth century were paralleled by the growth in the rhetoric of scientific racism throughout Western Europe. The nineteenth century was for European Jews, especially for Jews in the German-speaking lands, the best of times and the worst of times. Civil emancipation, increased economic and social mobility, and access to secular education were all slowly acquired by European Jews, and counterbalanced by the rise of a political antisemitism that sought to reverse civil emancipation, and the reappearance in altered form of older manifestations of antisemitism such as the "blood libel," the accusation that Jews used the blood of Christians in their religious rituals. Meanwhile, political realities within the Russian Empire led to massive pogroms and the flight of millions of Eastern and mainly unacculturated Jews to the cities of Western Europe and beyond. The range of Jewish responses to these political realities included assimilation and conversion, the rise of political and cultural Zionism, and the establishment of secular Jewish political parties (at least in the Austro-Hungarian Empire). This snapshot is, of course, reductive, but it is broadly accurate.

Throughout Western Europe the gradual integration of Jews into the body politic was seen both as the cause of Jewish psychopathology and a source of danger to the nation-state. Various theories were put forth to explain the nature of Jewish madness. All of these explanations functioned to produce a uniform biological category, "the Jews." Thus Georg Burgl's handbook of forensic medicine of 1912 states quite clearly, "[T]he Jewish race has a special predisposition for hysteria." For Burgl, this was a result of the degenerative nature of the Jew, marked by "physical signs of degeneration such as asymmetry and malocclusion of the skull, malocclusion of the teeth, etc."[1] The visibility of the Jew was identical to the visibility of the degenerate, with signs and symptoms pointing to Jews' susceptibility.

Nineteenth-century liberal views of Jews shared a similar notion of a Jewish predisposition to madness.[2] In Paris, the most important neurologist of the time, Jean Martin Charcot, lectured that there is the stated presumption that "nervous illnesses of all types are innumerably more frequent among Jews than among other groups." Charcot described Jews as "the best source of material for nervous illness."[3] He described the predisposition of Jews for specific forms of illness as the result of the biological consequences of their religious practice, rather than as a result of their racial makeup. Jews were mad because of their *consanguineous* marriage (read: endogamous marriage), which in terms of nineteenth-century thought was understood as a form of incest. Religious practice, to Charcot, a radical opponent of all organized religion, was as much a sign of the primitive nature of the Jewish psyche as it was of Catholic sophistication. Acculturation could ameliorate this tendency but never eliminate it.

The madness of the Jews was also seen as a racial predisposition *triggered* by acculturation. Wilhelm Erb, at a birthday celebration for the king of Baden, commented on the increased nervousness among the "Semites, who already are a neurotically predisposed race. Their untamed desire for profit and their nervousness, caused by centuries of imposed life style [*auferlegte Lebensweise*], as well as their inbreeding [*Inzucht*] and marriage within families [*Familienheiraten*], predisposes them to nervousness."[4] The emancipation of the Jews was also seen as one of the explanations of their predisposition for madness. The dean of fin-de-siècle German psychiatrists, Emil Kraepelin, professor of psychiatry at Munich and founder of the Institute for Psychiatry there, spoke with authority about the "domestication" of the Jews, their isolation from nature, and their exposure to the stresses of modern life.[5] As with Charcot, according to Kraepelin it is the inherent biological weakness of the Jew that determines this predisposition.

By the turn of the century the view that the Jew was inherently predisposed to specific forms of mental illness had become a commonplace, with multiple etiologies proposed. In his widely read and translated *General Psychopathology* (1913), Karl Jaspers, the Heidelberg psychiatrist and one of the major innovators of clinical psychiatry in his day as well as one of the creators of a systematic existentialist philosophy, argued for the close relationship of race and mental illness, citing in great detail the claims that the Jews as a race were disposed to mental illness.[6] Such views about the madness of the Jews were not limited to medical conservatives in the German-speaking world. Jaspers, as a member of the sociologist Max Weber's circle in Heidelberg, was certainly liberal, if nationalistic, in his politics.

Given that the biology of race stands at the center of nineteenth-century "sciences of man" (which would include biology, medicine, and anthropology), anyone who thought of himself as a "scientist" during this period could hardly have avoided confronting this aspect of science. Meaning, even those male scientists (such as Jews) who were labeled as different within this knowledge regime had to come to terms with the fact that the arena of endeavor that assigned to them the status of "scientist" also demanded they acknowledge (or refute) their inherent biological difference. Even acculturated Jewish doctors had to accept this type of predisposition, as it was part of what defined clinical medicine at the time. Jewish physicians were forced to deal with the potential of Jewish mental illness because the problem reflected on their own mental stability. The standard Jewish medical rationale for the higher incidence of psychopathology among the Jews came to be that of the Jewish brain's inability to compete after "a 2,000-year diaspora" and "a struggle for mere existence up to emancipation."[7]

The premise that immigrant Jews were more at risk from mental illness was actually debated before the New York Neurological Society on April 7, 1914. The presentation was by the Jewish psychiatrists A. A. Brill (who was also trained as a psychoanalyst) and Morris J. Karpas, who focused on newly arrived Eastern European Jews admitted to the public mental hospitals from which they gathered their samples.[8] Functional psychopathologies, such as hysteria, they said, were more evident among Jews even in New York City, where they supposedly were freed from the state oppression of the Russian Empire. They stressed that the differences among the statistics reflect the national status of the Jews, and that while "the Jewish race contributes a rather high percentage to the so-called functional form of insanity . . . the Jew is not disproportionately insane."[9]

The debate that followed Brill and Karpas's presentation was intense. George H. Kirby argued that it was important to understand the frequency among the diseases, such as dementia praecox, in order to better treat the various immigrant groups. Smith Ely Jelliffe, the president of the Society, threw up his hands and stated that statisticians could make what they wanted out of the figures and render the superficial important. The physician-anthropologist Maurice Fishberg, a New York City public health official, who was present by invitation, presented his argument of the contextual cause of the higher incidence of mental illness. Jews were urban dwellers, they were engaged in "financial and commercial pursuits" more than others, and their proclivity for mental illness seemed to change based on where they lived and what the local conditions were. Indeed, he argued earlier, the new Jewish immigrants from Eastern Europe who were the focus of the debate were actually of a different racial stock than the older German immigrants, who seemed to be less at risk and more at home in the world of American capitalism: "the Jews in Russia are not Semites at all . . . and actually belong to an entirely different race."[10] In sum, the Jews as a collective, a race, or a social group, could be defined by a higher risk for insanity—but was racism at the root of this madness? Could such madness be manifested as self-hatred? Is racism, itself, a form of madness?

Such views were not limited to the discussions of the racial biology of the Jews. In the United States parallel diagnoses of mental illness aided in constructing blacks as physically inferior or weak, and the categories of mental illness were employed from the early nineteenth century to depict the nature of the black character and will as part of a justification of slavery. Drapetomania, explained by Samuel A. Cartwright as the desire of the slave to escape their master, was well-known as a classification of mental illness. Writing in 1851, Cartwright posited that if a slave owner keeps a slave "in the position that we learn from the Scriptures he was intended to occupy, that is, the position of submission; and if his master or overseer be kind and gracious in his hearing towards him, without condescension, and at the same time ministers to his physical wants, and protects him from abuses, the negro is spell-bound, and cannot run away."[11] Cartwright's claim was founded, in part, in a belief in blacks' unruly nature as wild savages requiring structure and servitude.

Among American abolitionists, Cartwright's conclusion was viewed with a certain amusement. For example, the landscape architect Frederick Law Olmsted, in his *A Journey in the Seaboard Slave States* (1856), observed that white indentured servants had often been known to flee as well. Thus, Olmsted satirically hypothesized that the supposed disease was actually of white European origin, and had been introduced to Africa by traders.[12] Among abolitionists such as Frederick Douglass, the charge of the slave's madness came to be read as a sign of the mentality of slaves:

> A Kentucky master owns a negro child. He brings that child up in a state of moral and mental blindness—in consequence of that blindness, the child commits many blunders and is guilty of many crimes. Can the child be held accountable for the crimes, which resulted from the control which his master exerted over him? If a man could render his neighbor insane and could induce him, which in a state of insanity, to cut the throat of a third person, no one would hesitate to excuse the madman and to hold the man who caused the insanity and induced the murder responsible. Now, although the master who holds a slave may not be to that fatal extent accountable for the slave's transgressions, those vices and crimes perpetuated by the slave that are directly, clearly and only traceable to the power exerted over him by the master, must be charged to the master.[13]

The argument here is from analogy, but the image of a man driven mad by his destructive environment is one that sees all actions of an oppressed people that are labeled sociopathic or psychopathic as having their roots in slavery.

Among white Southerners, however—medical professionals and laypersons alike—Cartwright's diagnosis became central to the design and implementation of treatment protocols for black slaves, and later, following Emancipation, for black mental health patients.[14] Central to the lasting legacy of Cartwright's claim was the misinterpretation of rates of insanity among black Americans in the 1840 United States Census. The 1840 Census had mistakenly (or fraudulently, depending upon the interpretation) reported the incidence of insanity among blacks in Northern states as roughly seven times greater than among Northern whites, and almost eleven times greater than among Southern blacks.

Edward Jarvis, a black physician and statistician, had challenged the findings of the Census in his 1844 paper "Insanity among the Coloured Population of the Free States," published in *The American Journal of the Medical Sciences*. Jarvis had examined the summary reports of each state and found "the secret of error": many of the reported "coloured insane" supported as public charges were actually white patients. In fact, within many towns, the Census had reported the presence of black mental health patients, but no black inhabitants! Jarvis cut straight to the heart of the matter when he wrote, "The same carelessness, which gave insanity without subjects in some places, may have given none in others, where it actually existed."[15] Despite Jarvis's criticism, a letter from the American Statistical Association to Congress, and a letter from former president John Quincy Adams to Congress to revisit the report, no corrections were issued. The 1840 Census became an especially powerful tool following Emancipation, as white physicians and reformers heralded this report and others as evidence of Reconstruction's failure, and the need to recreate some semblance of slavery's structure for the sake of the South's now-freed black population.[16]

Among Southern hospitals and asylums for blacks, for example, a therapy known as "moral treatment" was advocated: highly structured, slow-pace daily routines, including labor, combined with nearly absolute authority of the medical staff over the everyday lives of the patients. These conditions were intended to mimic what many whites believed to be the actual conditions of slavery. Moral treatment, for them, represented a medical ideal of "freedom from" rather than the more dangerous "freedom to."[17] Consequently, hospitals throughout the South experienced a sharp increase over the next several decades in the admission of black patients. For example, the number of black patients increased from roughly 3 percent in 1865 to almost 16 percent by 1870. By the turn of the twentieth century, blacks were close to a quarter of the patients, and the state of Alabama, in response, opened a second mental hospital at Mount Vernon. By 1910, blacks were roughly one third of the patients between the two hospitals, an increase of nearly 1,000 percent in just fifty years.[18]

The response among black intellectuals and white abolitionists during this time to claims about blacks' inherent dispositions to madness was, surprisingly, mixed. Some held fast to the notion that the price of freedom was perhaps too great for the "undeveloped" faculties of blacks. In 1887, presenting his paper entitled "The Future of the American Negro," General Samuel C. Armstrong, a member of the Freedmen's Bureau and founder of the Hampton School in Virginia, an institution dedicated exclusively to the education of black and Native American students, claimed the "real loss" of Emancipation had been on the part of white owners.[19] Armstrong was echoing a conclusion drawn by the superintendent of the Alabama Insane Hospital, James T. Searcy, who had written two years earlier that while slavery had provided whites "high tone and manliness," Emancipation only produced among them broken homes and laziness.[20] Two years after Armstrong's address, while speaking at the National Conference for Charities and Corrections in 1899, John H. Smyth, then president of the Negro Reform Association of Virginia, explained to a predominantly white audience that "up to 1860 there could not have been a dozen insane negroes in our State. Today we have in Petersburg alone one thousand."[21] The ensuing discussion among those in attendance suggested insanity was the result of blacks' inherent inability to civilize. Smyth's seemingly unquestioned acceptance of blackness as a marker of susceptibility to madness is odd, given that he was one of the earliest pan-Africanists in the United States, and through his organization had established the Virginia Manual Labor School as an alternative to prison for black children convicted of petty crimes.[22]

Meanwhile, the few black medical professionals in the United States challenged claims about increasing rates of insanity and blacks' susceptibility to insanity on the grounds of insufficient evidence. For example, in a paper read before the Association of Medical Superintendents of American Institutions for the Insane in 1851, Edward Jarvis responded directly to the Bureau of the Census's claims of increasing rates of insanity among freed blacks, stating the report featured gross and "palpable" errors.[23] In that same paper, however, Jarvis did not necessarily disagree with conventional wisdom that claimed an introduction to advanced civilization would produce higher rates of insanity among a previously disenfranchised caste:

> [In] an uneducated community, or where people are overborne by despotic government or inflexible customers, where men are born in castes, and die without overstepping their native condition, where the child is

content with the pursuit and the fortune of his father, and has no hope
or expectation of any other, there these undue mental excitements and
struggles do not happen, and men's brains are not confused with new
plans, nor exhausted with struggles for a higher life, nor overborne with
the disappointment of failure. Of course, in such a state of society . . . insanity cannot operate. But in proportion as education prevails, and eman-
cipates the new generations from the trammels and condition of the old,
and the manifold ways of life are open to all, the danger of misapplication
of the cerebral forces and the mental powers increases, and men may
think and act indiscreetly, and become insane.[24]

In his concluding remarks, speaking more generally, Jarvis continued:
"Insanity is then a part of the price we pay for civilization. The causes
of the one increase with the developments and results of the other."[25]
Jarvis's contention, then, is that slavery cannot produce insanity because
it requires little mental expenditure of its constituents. However, as
slaves entered into free society, as they encountered the complexities
of free life, their rates of insanity should increase in proportion to their
incorporation. To the reader, of course, this logic flies in the face of contemporary evidence suggesting that the ill effects of American racism,
like massive disparities between whites and blacks in nearly every socioeconomic indicator, produce among the latter poorer health—including
mental health—outcomes. However, for Jarvis and his contemporaries,
mental illness was simply a byproduct of complex societies, an argument
that would be revisited by intellectuals in subsequent decades, including
Sigmund Freud.

In comparing the medicalized responses of Jews in Western and Central Europe to those of blacks in the United States in the nineteenth
century, the central difference is the gradual integration of Jewish males
into the world of science, where they were required to accept such arguments concerning race as part of their certification as physicians and
scientists. There was an inherent difference in the acceptance of such
language of biological race between groups that saw themselves as being
able to enter into the world of science and those who were seen as per-
petually marginalized.[26]

This assumption became part of the negative eugenics of the nineteenth century. Visual categories were literally seen as the markers of

racial pathology among European Jews, and the physical and biological inferiority of the Jews was equated with psychopathology in late-nineteenth- and early-twentieth-century Europe. No longer easily identified by external markers such as dress, occupation, or location, the Jew came to be identified by specific biological and, thus, physical markers. Further, perceived physical markers of degeneration (the Jewish nose, eyes, etc.) were linked to a prevalence of diagnoses of mental illness among the European Jewish population. Central to this development was that this paralleled, and was partly driven by, newer theories of race science, such as Francis Galton's notion of eugenics as the improvement of the race through selective breeding for what were seen as positive qualities and the elimination of those understood as defective, especially mental illness. In an interview with a British Jewish newspaper at the end of his life, he remarked:

> It is one part of eugenics to encourage the idea of parental responsibility: the other part is to see that the children born are well born. It is a praiseworthy feature of the Jewish religion that, as a religion, it enjoins the multiplication of the human species. But it is still more important to determine that the children shall be born from the fit and not the unfit.[27]

Social practice may encourage positive eugenics, but eliminating the unfit trumps all. At this point the unfit are the mentally ill; but the corollary is eventually the elimination of the unfit racist.

Thus by the late nineteenth century, there was a growing trend among academicians in Europe and the United States to locate the foundations of mental illness in social relations. Like their European counterparts, many medical authorities in the United States perceived mental illness as rooted in physiological dysfunction, or anatomical disorder, of the brain and nervous system. Blacks, they argued, possessed less advanced neurological functions, making them more susceptible to mental illness, which was viewed at the time as a physical disease. As we demonstrated above, this logic led to arguments that Emancipation had removed blacks from the sheltered confines of forced servitude to compete independently in a world for which they were simply "unfit."[28] Freedom for the African American as well as emancipation for the Jew provides the context for their increased rates of mental illness.

Epidemiological findings in Europe about the excessive numbers of mentally ill Jews, and in the United States of the equivalent problem among American freemen, came at the beginning of the expansion of statistical evidence in the mental health field. The new science of measurement became one of the tools of contemporary clinical psychiatry among public health figures such as Joshua Billings, the creator of the Surgeon-General's Library in Washington, D.C., and one of the most important epidemiologists of his day.[29] Madness became linked to notions of degeneracy in race science, and rates of mental illness among African Americans and Jews were frequently evoked as empirical evidence of their inability to deal with "modern life." This drove the development of new tools for the evaluation of mental status that later became linked to both restrictive immigration policies in the early twentieth century and, subsequently, the modern-day Civil Rights Movement.

By the close of the nineteenth century, certain ideas about the science of race became commonplace: there was always a fixed boundary, a bright line, between races; there was a hierarchy of the races based on observable phenomena; mixed races were inherently inferior to pure races; race was mapped in some inherent way on to geography; and less able races could trump superior races by sheer numbers. Now all of these claims were clothed in the newest sciences of the day, from epidemiology and its statistical apparatus, to eugenics and early genetics with its models of inheritance, to clinical medicine with its classification of diseases and its claims of a biological and often inherent etiology for such diseases. The techniques of governance were well established within the medical and biological sciences, and in the first three decades of the twentieth century would become essential for social policy intervention concerning the "Jewish problem" in Western Europe and the "Negro problem" in the United States.

Racism as Insanity

During the nineteenth century, more and more members of minorities entered into the public sphere (and, especially among Jews, into the world of academic medicine and biology), which led to a questioning of the mechanism of causation, but not the claim of predisposition. Thus major medical figures such as Cesare Lombroso, the Jewish founder of the

Italian school of positivist criminology and the most vocal proponent of the theory of degeneration, denied any inherent biological weakness in the Jewish psyche but rather saw the inheritance of such predispositions as the result of "2,000 years of oppression." After authoring a number of studies on the degeneracy of the prostitute and the criminal, Lombroso was confronted with the charge that Jews, too, were a degenerate sub-class of human being, a class determined by their biology. Lombroso's answer to this charge, *Antisemitism and the Jews in the Light of Modern Science* (1893), attempted to counter the use of medical or (in his estimation) pseudoscientific discourse to characterize the nature of the Jew. For Lombroso "antisemitism" is a faulty appropriation of what looks like a scientific term for a political purpose. Indeed, the term seems first to appear in 1860 in the Austrian Jewish scholar Moritz Steinschneider's use of the phrase "antisemitic prejudices" (*"antisemitische Vorurteile"*) in categorizing the French philosopher Ernest Renan's contrast between the "Semitic" and the "Aryan" soul.[30] The term, however, was popu-larized only in the 1880s by the journalist Wilhelm Marr in his widely read pamphlet attacking the "Jews," *The Way to Victory of the Germanic Spirit over the Jewish Spirit Der* (*Weg zum Siege des Germanenthums über das Judenthum*) (1880), in which the word first appeared to mean "Jew hatred."[31] That year Marr founded the League of Antisemites to combat Jewish influence in Europe. The term had a clearly political meaning thereafter, not as a pejorative label for a prejudice but as a call to arms.

Yet Lombroso and many of his Jewish contemporaries also accepted the basic view that the Jew was more highly prone to specific forms of mental illness. He quotes Charcot to this effect, but he sees the reason for this tendency not in the physical nature of the Jew but in the "resid-ual effect of persecution."[32] Lombroso assumes that there is an inherent plasticity to the psyche that can be so deformed by prejudice as to cause mental illness, but that (as in his case) acculturation would lead such forms of madness to become less frequent.[33]

Yet Lombroso does not define *why* such persecution occurs, only seeing it as an historical given. He accepted the view that some type of degenerative process, leading to the predominance of specific forms of mental illness, exists among all Jews. The only difference from non-Jewish savants was what he saw as the cause of this process. In rejecting the charge of inbreeding, Lombroso also rejected the implications that

Jews indulge in primitive sexual practices that violate a basic human taboo against incest. The confusion of endogamous marriage with incestuous inbreeding was a result of both the level of late-nineteenth-century science and the desire of this scientific discourse to have categories with which to label the explicit nature of Jewish character, as Charcot did.

Such views are echoed in Martin Engländer's essay on *The Evident Most Frequent Appearances of Illness in the Jewish Race* (1902).[34] Engländer was one of the early supporters of the Viennese intellectual and newspaperman Theodor Herzl and the early Zionist movement. He discussed the cultural predisposition of the Jews to neurasthenia as a result of the "over-exertion and exhaustion of the brain . . . among Jews as opposed to the non-Jewish population." He wrote, "the struggle, haste and drive, the hunt for happiness" have caused a "reaction in their central nervous system."[35] He echoed Lombroso in describing neurasthenia as the result of the Jewish brain's inability to compete after "a two-thousand year Diaspora" and "a struggle for mere existence up to emancipation." Engländer thus attempted to dismiss the etiology of neurasthenia as a result of inbreeding, citing the U.S. population as an example of a "race" in which neurasthenia predominates and in which Americans marry outside of their "racial" cohort. He pinned European Jews' illnesses on their confinement in the city, the source of all degeneracy, prescribing "land, air, light."[36] Engländer's views were not idiosyncratic. Theodor Herzl too had spoken of the potential plasticity of the urban Jew given his own land and his own ability to tend it. Herzl's views on adaption and maladaptation aligned with the evolutionary notion of regeneration: "Education can be achieved only through shock treatment. Darwin's theory of imitation [*Darwinsche Mimikry*] will be validated. The Jews will adapt. They are like seals that have been thrown back into the water by an accident of nature . . . if they return to dry land and manage to stay there for a few generations, their fins will change back into legs."[37] For Herzl and the Zionists the madness of the Jews is a direct result of the Jews' political and social position in the West, yet he never articulates *why* this is the case.

The question of *why* Jews in the Christian West were the targets of opprobrium had been easily answered for more than a thousand years: they had committed deicide.[38] It was the fault of the Jews alone that they were socially excluded and condemned. They were to be excoriated and damned because they were blind and would not see the revealed word of God as manifested in Jesus Christ. As Paul stated: "We preach Christ crucified: a stumbling block to Jews and foolishness to Gentiles" (1 Corinthians 1:23). In other words, Christian anti-Judaism was clearly the fault of the Jews' obduracy. As the age of belief morphed into the age of science during the course of the nineteenth century, this view of a Jewish intransigence that warranted such condemnation became part and parcel of secular anti-Jewish feelings. Even liberals such as Lombroso's equally famous contemporary, the Italian physician Paolo Mantegazza (1831–1910), condemned in 1885 what was seen as the Jewish separatism that was the cause of their social isolation:

> Circumcision is a shame and an infamy; and I, who am not in the least anti-Semitic, who indeed have much esteem for the Israelites, I who demand of no living soul a profession of religious faith, insisting only upon the brotherhood of soap and water and of honesty, I shout and shall continue to shout at the Hebrews, until my last breath: Cease mutilating yourselves: cease imprinting upon your flesh an odious brand to distinguish you from other men; until you do this, you cannot pretend to be our equal. As it is, you, of your own accord, with the branding iron, from the first days of your lives, proceed to proclaim yourselves a race apart, one that cannot, and does not care to, mix with ours.[39]

No question that those who disdained the Jews saw them as being at fault; the Jews were the sole cause of their own dilemma, even as Mantegazza says, to their friends and supporters. Yet in this new age of science, the idea that the Jews themselves were at fault for their own exclusion and condemnation seemed incoherent and aberrant, especially to Jewish scientists. The first documented explanation of the *why* that did not rest on blaming the Jews themselves could have been found in the subsequently important but, at the time, little recognized work of the proto-Zionist physician Leon Pinsker (1821–1891), *Auto-Emancipation* (*Mahnruf an seine Stammgenossen*) (1882). Pinsker was born in Polish Russia and educated at the University of Odessa, where he trained to be a physician. His training was "modern," which in the nineteenth century meant German and biologically oriented. Horrified by the series of pogroms against the Jews beginning in 1871 in Odessa, Pinsker, writing in

German, pleaded for a Jewish state on the basis of the inherent nature of Jew hatred (*Judenhass*) in Europe. As a physician he uses the category of mental illness to explain this hatred, calling it an obsession of the European Christian regarding Jews as "for the living . . . a dead man, for the natives an alien and a vagrant, for property-holders a beggar, for the poor an exploiter and a millionaire, for patriots a man without a country, for all classes a hated rival."[40] He undertakes the first systematic attempt at analyzing "Judeophobia" as a disease that can never be cured:

> Along with a number of other unconscious and superstitious ideas, instincts, and idiosyncrasies, Judeophobia also has become fully naturalized among all the peoples of the earth with whom the Jews have had intercourse. Judeophobia is a form of demonopathy, with the distinction that the Jewish ghost has become known to the whole race of mankind, not merely to certain races, and that it is not incorporeal, like other ghosts, but is a being of flesh and blood, and suffers the most excruciating pain from the wounds inflicted upon it by the timorous multitude who imagine themselves threatened by it. Judeophobia is a psychic disorder. As a psychic disorder it is hereditary, and as a disease transmitted for two thousand years it is incurable.[41]

For Pinsker it is in racism as an "inherited predisposition" that madness lies.[42] In this passage he may be employing a German version of the term Hebrewphobia, first used by the Irish reformer Richard Lalor Sheil in his speech "On the Disabilities of the Jews," delivered February 7, 1848, before the House of Commons on the occasion of the reelection of the British Jew Lionel de Rothschild to the House. Rothschild, a practicing Jew, would not take the oath that required he state, "I make this Declaration upon the true Faith of a Christian." The Whig leader, Lord John Russell, introduced the Jews Relief Act, also called the Jewish Disabilities Bill, following the election to allow him to take the oath without this caveat. The ninth speaker who arose to debate the measure was Sheil, who had sat in the Commons as a Whig representing constituencies in Ireland since 1831.[43] Educated at Trinity College, Dublin, he was one of the Irish stalwarts who had accompanied Daniel O'Connell ("The Emancipator") to London to protest against the suppression of the Catholic Association, of which he was a founding member, and continued to support O'Connell until Catholic emancipation was granted in 1829.[44] Unprepossessing in appearance to his contemporaries, as he was only five foot tall, he was acknowledged to be one of the greatest of the Irish orators of his day, even if, as a contemporary member of the House said of his "detestable" brogue, "he was not pleasant to listen to."[45] William Gladstone was somewhat more complimentary, comparing his voice to

> a tin kettle battered about from place to place, knocking first against one side and then against another. . . . There was a peculiar character, a sort of half-wildness in his aspect and delivery; his whole figure, and his delivery, and his voice and his matter, were all in such perfect keeping with one another that they formed a great Parliamentary picture.[46]

George W. E. Russell wrote in his memoir: "Sheil was very small, and of mean presence; with a singularly fidgety manner, a shrill voice, and a delivery unintelligibly rapid. But in sheer beauty of elaborated diction not O'Connell nor any one else could surpass him."[47] What is striking about all of these comments are the euphemisms ("half-wildness," "shrill") that branded Sheil as Irish. Nevertheless Sheil's oration came to be one of the classics of British parliamentary oratory addressing the question of the legal equality of the Jews.[48]

Sheil makes the most extraordinary claim concerning the beliefs in Jewish difference that underpinned the older objection to Jewish civic emancipation:

> What is it you fear? What is the origin of this Hebrewphobia? Do you tremble for the Church? The Church has something perhaps to fear from eight millions of Catholics, and from three millions of Methodists, and more than a million of Scotch seceders. The Church may have some thing to fear from the assault of sectaries from without, and still more to fear from a sort of spurious Popery and the machinations of mitred mutiny from within; but from the Synagogue—the neutral, impartial, apathetic, and unproselytising Synagogue—the Church has nothing to apprehend. But it is said that the House will be unchristianised. The Christianity of the Parliament depends on the Christianity of the country; and the Christianity of the country is fixed in the faith, and inseparably intertwined with the affections of the people. It is as stable as England her self; and as

long as Parliament shall endure, while the constitution shall stand, until the great mirror of the nation's mind shall have been shattered to pieces, the religious feelings of the country will be faithfully reflected here.[49]

Sheil had seen Parliament go from Anglican to Protestant (when the Quakers were allowed to affirm their oath) to Christian (with Catholic emancipation in 1829, which allowed him to enter the House of Commons). Why does Sheil evoke the phobic in his talk if he does not believe that prejudiced individuals were suffering a form of mental aberration?

In Sheil's day the notion of the "phobia" had reached beyond the merely medical. Indeed the most often cited "phobia" in the medical literature of his day was "hydrophobia," rabies, which even in the mid-nineteenth century before the work of Louis Pasteur was no longer to be associated with the run-of-the-mill various forms of mental illness, from aerophobia to photophobia, which are much less often cited.[50] Phobias were popularly understood at the time "to be a fear of an imaginary evil, or an undue fear of a real one."[51] While the metaphoric use of "phobias" proliferated in the early nineteenth century (Anne Seward in 1824 notes that one of her acquaintances "laboured under a perpetual dustophobia; and a comical disease it was"), it was only in the mid-nineteenth century that the French conceit of labeling dislike of nationalities as "phobias" (as in "Anglophobia") had appeared in English. Indeed, Sheil's use may be counted among its earliest appearances, as the *Times* first used "Anglophobe" in 1851.[52] Sheil uses it only to signify a chronic aversion to the Jews, and certainly framing his defense of the Jews against "Hebrewphobia" was a sense that "Irishphobia" was as endemic a disease in Great Britain.[53]

Leon Pinsker is the first to provide a clinical definition of the term "phobia" in the context of the Jews of Europe as well as a forensic label to answer the widely popular term "antisemitism," which had become the marker for the political attack on Jewish emancipation after the 1880s. Pinsker also isolates the etiology of the madness of the Jews from the inherent racism of "Judeophobes." For him it was the Enlightenment demand that the Jews become "like everyone else" in a national society— become Germans, French, English, while repressing their own Jewish national identity—that was the cause of their madness. He agrees with the notion that the Jews are predisposed to mental illness, but sees the endless torment from the pressure to acculturate, not from religious persecution, as the cause. The statelessness of the Jew in the age of nationalism condemns him to be an outlier. Judaism, he writes,

> The stigma attached to this people, which forces an unenviable isolation among the nations upon it, cannot be removed by any sort of legal emancipation, as long as this people produces in accordance with its nature vagrant nomads, as long as it cannot give a satisfactory account of whence it comes and whither it goes, as long as the Jews themselves prefer not to speak in Aryan society of their Semitic descent, and prefer not to be reminded of it, as long as they are persecuted, tolerated, protected, emancipated. . . . Intelligent and rich in experience . . . we have never asked whether this mad race . . . will ever come to an end.[54]

Pinsker's ideas seem to be a radical break from the claim of nineteenth-century biological psychiatry that madness lies in the predisposition of racial cohorts to madness. His attribution of Jewish madness to the loss of nation, and with it independence, and the resulting fall "into a decay which is not compatible with existence as a whole vital organism" responds to such constructions. As a result of this decay, according to Pinsker, Jews began to seem to others like ghosts—which is the root of Judeophobia, as "the fear of ghosts is something inborn." It is interesting how the metaphor of ghostliness is concrete enough for Pinsker to incorporate, as though literal, into a medicalizing statement. His claim that the madness of the Jews is the result of faulty acculturation was widely recognized in the critical literature about European Jewry of the time. Intellectuals of the late nineteenth century agreed that the Jews were mad, but some thought that their madness was a reflex of antisemitism internalized as self-hatred. Friedrich Nietzsche's poetic reading of Spinoza makes this quite clear. Christianity's claim of universal love was the Jew's vengeance for his treatment by Christianity:

> Unheimlich glimmernder Rachebrand:
> —am Judengott fraß Judenhaß!—
> —Einsiedler, hab ich dich erkannt?
> [an eerily shimmering fire of vengeance:

—The Jewish God devoured by Jewish hatred—
Hermit, have I recognized you?][55]

Ultimately, Pinsker's argument relies on the notion that "the misfortunes of the Jews are due, above all, to their lack of desire for national independence."[56] Nationalism will cure self-hatred, but nothing can cure the obsessive racism of the world in which the Jew is exiled. But is it the Christian alone who is racist? Is this the category that alone perpetuated Jew hatred or is it also the fault of the Jew who has lost any sense of national identity? And, if this is the case, what about other forms of race hatred that are not tied to the experience of Jews in the West?

The power of the argument rests on the image of psychopathology. Pinsker writes, "In a sick person the absence of desire for food and drink is a very serious symptom," and "we would hear nothing of taking our malady at the root, in order to effect a complete cure."[57] His essay uses pathological language for both Jews and antisemites, and acknowledges fault on the part of the oppressors, while placing the onus for change on the oppressed. Pinsker writes, "If the basis of our reasoning is sound, if the prejudice of the human race against us rests upon anthropological and social principles, innate and ineradicable, we must look no more to the slow progress of humanity"[58] Pinsker's views become part of the ideology and the vocabulary of Zionism. He is not alone in such a position.

If Pinsker sees himself in the role of physician as political commentator, then the earlier work of Martin Robison Delany may provide a moment of contrast to nineteenth-century *racialist* fears of black emancipation by a commentator situated similarly to Pinsker. Delany, like Pinsker, was trained as a physician, and was one of the first three black students admitted to Harvard Medical School (though they were soon dismissed at the request of a group of white students). Delany was also the first black American man to publish a novel.[59] Now recognized by contemporary black studies scholars as a pioneering expression of the nineteenth-century pan-Africanist emigration movement, Delany's 1852 *The Condition, Elevation, Emigration, and Destiny of the Colored People of the United States* was, at the time, a controversial book among both abolitionists and proponents of chattel slavery. In it, Delany sees the refusal of freed blacks to acknowledge their inherent marginality as a "folly to deny, insanity not to understand, blindness not to see, and surely now full time that our eyes were opened to these startling truths, which for ages have stared us full in the face."[60] Madness is the state of denial, not the position of the slave owner.

Both Pinsker and Delany evoke the other's collective in underscoring their own situations. Pinsker relates the Jewish plight to that of blacks, Delany compares the oppression of "Colored People" to that of the Jews. Pinsker, however, assuming black inferiority through the lens of contemporary racial science, writes that the Jews must be emancipated "like the negroes, like women, and unlike all free peoples, they must be *emancipated*. It is all the worse for them if, unlike the negroes, they belong to an advanced race, and if, unlike women, they can show not only women of distinction, but also men, even great men."[61] Delany, meanwhile, compares blacks to Jews when he writes of "the Jews, scattered throughout not only the length and breadth of Europe, but almost the habitable globe, maintaining their national characteristics, and looking forward in high hopes of seeing the day when they may return to their former national position of self-government and independence, let that be in whatever part of the habitable world it may."[62] Delany goes on to justify the necessity of black emigration by providing the Biblical example of the Hebrews escaping Egypt, arguing that "that there are circumstances under which emigration is absolutely necessary to their political elevation, cannot be disputed."[63] Here is the key difference between arguments such as Pinsker's, with the language and power of scientific medicine at their core, and Delany's argument. As one of the present authors, Sander L. Gilman, argued about Delany's use of Biblical models in his later *Principia of Ethnology* (1879):

> [H]is strategy made sense within the black tradition but it rendered his book a cultural and linguistic hybrid reflected in its very title, half English, half Latin. Religiously oriented ethnology survived as a form because it served the political and psychological needs of the African-American. Isolation from the norms of science meant that those norms were less internalized. The creation of a different narrative form resisted the conventions of science, but as a strategy of resistance, theological arguments had the disadvantage of seeming illegitimate or "unscientific" when measured by the canons of mainstream science.[64]

As an epistemic culture, the rhetoric of science is more powerful if it is presented unadulterated, even if its assumptions about racial science seem to a contemporary reader "unscientific."[65]

Both Pinsker and Delany offer emigration as a necessary solution to oppression, but emigration must be self-initiated. Human autonomy stands at the center of the political claims of both. Pinsker and Delany agree that the law of the oppressor is not to be trusted in such matters, as it is simply a façade for the continuation of social oppression. Legal statutes, they acknowledge, are an inadequate form of, as Pinsker calls it, emancipation—"legal emancipation is not social emancipation"—or freedom, as Delany, who references and reprints the Fugitive Slave Law of 1850, claims.[66] Understanding the Jew as a perpetual "stranger par excellence," Pinsker acknowledges that the Jew is "not a native in his own home country, but he is also not a foreigner."[67] The only way that Jews will be recognized as independent subjects, not subject to the reality of a foreign nation as home, is if they emancipate themselves and emigrate to a new, permanent land. But this sounds a lot like Delaney's definition of "freedom." For Pinsker's Jew, "the only thing known is that he has no home."[68]

Delany's struggle, meanwhile, is not *just* for freedom. He asks, "Where shall we go? We must not leave this continent; America is our destination and our home."[69] He continues: "We love our country, dearly love her, but she don't love us—she despises us, and bids us be gone, driving us from her embraces; but we shall not go where she desires us; but when we do go, whatever love we have for her, we shall love the country none the less that receives us as her adopted children."[70] Delany advocates for an emigration of "Colored People" to other newly free nations without slavery in the Western Hemisphere such as Canada, Mexico, and various countries in the Caribbean and South America, but not slaveholding Brazil, or Liberia, the creation of the oppressor as a means of exiling blacks rather than emancipating them, and located in Africa, a continent "benighted enough, even to an apparent hopeless degeneration."[71] For Delany, the rhetoric of racial science disqualifies Africa as a site for true emancipation. He does not imagine an ideal "homeland" but a safe harbor. It is in such safe harbors that Delany imagines a physical, mental, and moral recuperation of "Colored People."

Pinsker, too, sees a specific national state as the catalyst of the moral, mental, and physical regeneration of the surplus Jews (a version of the

Victorian notion of the deserving poor) who are saved by the actions of "our greatest and best forces—men of finance, of science, and of affairs, statesmen and publicists—must join hands with one accord in steering toward the common destination. This would succeed chiefly and especially in creating a secure and inviolable home for the *surplus* of those Jews who live as proletarians in the different countries and are a burden to the native citizens."[72] This claim is rooted in a science that has different valences in the claims of the European Jew and the American black.

The question of social, political, and *mental* emancipation for the Jew is at the center of the work of Max Nordau, the most important figure in early Zionism after Theodor Herzl. In his opening speech at the Second Zionist Congress in Basel on August 28, 1898, he invented one of Zionism's most famous, most fraught, and most challenging ideals: the "muscle Jew." For him the diasporic experience makes the Jews unhealthy physically, morally, and mentally. It is only with the new ideal of a self-conscious Jewish identity that such illnesses can be cured and the Jew become "deep chested, sturdy and sharp-eyed."[73] This claim becomes central to modern Zionism. Aaron David Gordon (1856–1922), the Labor Zionist, could write of the "parasitism of a fundamentally useless people" that "was broken and crushed . . . sick and diseased in body and soul."[74] Zionism would cure the ills of the body and those of the mind.

Zionism was a form of nineteenth-century European nationalism rooted in the notion that a national state was necessary to define a people and that a people was necessary to define a state. This was in tension with the Enlightenment notion that the Jews were themselves not a people in the sense of a nationality but rather a religious or ethnic community that could become integrated into a new national state no longer defined by religious or ethnic homogeneity but by the "rights of man." Jewish defenders of the Enlightenment ideal in the late nineteenth century became viewed, as Pinsker showed, as having a false consciousness as a German or Frenchman while all the time being seen as a Jew.

The debates about Zionism very early included the labeling of the defenders of the status quo of European Jewry as self-hating, as Pinsker had done; Theodor Herzl, for example, attacked his Jewish opponents in October 1897 as *Mauschel*, unhealthy ghetto Jews without the mental capacity to understand the need for an independent Jewish national identity. Such an understanding was defined by him and his supporters, including Max Nordau, as demonstrating a healthy, rather than pathological, psyche.[75] Herzl labels those who are opposed to Zionism as corrupt and see the proof of this in their attitude toward Zionism: "*Mauschel* was quick to put forward an insidious catchword against the Zionists: namely. That they are Jewish antisemites. We? We, who acknowledge before all the world, without consideration for our acquired positions and our advancement, that we are Semites; we who cherish the cultivation of our national heritage, who stand by our unfortunate brethren? But *Mauschel* figured out with lightening speed what we are: we are anti-*Mauschel*."[76] Being anti-assimilationist, Herzl argues, is seen in the eyes of acculturated European Jews as a form of self-hatred. The early Zionists also made the counterargument. Nordau, a neurologist and one of Herzl's earliest supporters, had argued in 1896, "It is the greatest triumph of antisemitism that it has brought the Jews to view themselves with antisemitic eyes."[77] For the early Zionists identification with the aggressor defined not only anti-Zionists but also acculturated Jews.

In the major *New Free Press* daily in Vienna, Herzl writes a feuilleton entitled "New Noses" in 1903:

> It is now a question of style . . . every province must have its own nose! Still others will let national interests rather than the lottery of birth determine the selection of the nose. Whatever the case, even in this matter we will certainly see the reappearance of the demand that those closest as well as most distant be converted to a specific nasal shape, instead of each being happy with the cut of his/her nose [*statt jeden nach seiner Façon sich schnäuzen zu lassen*].[78]

Theodor Herzl was mocking the claims of the new cosmetic surgery pioneered in the 1890s by the Berlin surgeon Jacques Joseph, who argued that making new German noses out of Jewish noses was not primarily a surgical intervention but rather a psychological one. For Joseph, "the psychological effect of the operation is of utmost importance. The depressed attitude of the patient subsided completely. He is happy to move around unnoticed."[79] Herzl sees this as a manifestation of false consciousness, for to imagine that you could be happy by living with someone else's nose is a sign of psychopathology.

The paraphrase that ends Herzl's comment is of a marginal note in 1740 by Friedrich II of Prussia commenting on the rights of Catholics in his state to practice their religion. It came to be shorthand for Jewish emancipation and acculturation by the nineteenth century, though it had nothing to do with this. By the 1920s Zionists such as Leo Strauss had accepted Herzl's and Nordau's views of self-hating Jews. Strauss, building on Herzl's essay on *Mauschel*, stated that the support of German national interests by German nationalist Jews has no basis in German law. Jews are not a national minority, according to him, but rather adherents of a religion, and thus should not oppose Zionism as "against nature" as their own civic position as German nationalists was at best tentative.[80] The journalist and critic Theodor Lessing, whose 1930 book *Jewish Self-Hatred* did more than any other work to publicize this category, saw it as an inherent quality of all Jews in the Diaspora: "There's no person of Jewish blood in whom we couldn't find at least signs of Jewish self-hatred."[81] The collective was seen as a totality under the pressure of antisemites, however defined.

Self-hatred was the model for a sense of the inauthenticity of a Jewish identity that was in opposition to that which the writer or speaker held as healthy. Indeed, as Paul Reitter has noted, radical assimilationists of the pre-war period took the label of "assimilationist" as signifying their healthy psyche, showing their competency within European culture in opposition to the Zionists.[82] Authenticity is a concept, Kernis and Goldman have written, "at the 'limits of language,' being loosely described in such diverse topics as ethics, well-being, consciousness, subjectivity, self-processes, and social or relational contexts, or characterized in terms of its opposite (i.e., inauthenticity), with references to inauthentic living, false self behaviors, or self deception."[83] One can add here psychopathology. For normality can be defined in these terms only by the existence of its antithesis, the pathological. Thus self-hatred came to define those whose sense of Jewishness was different in some way from the writer's.

From the beginning of the biological definition of race, in fields such as medicine in the course of the nineteenth century, it was the neutral medical observer who defined the nature of madness and its causes. Racial theory defined who was most at risk for madness. With the rise of the sciences of sociology and psychology in the course of the same period, race continued to play a substantial role in defining the objects of study. Later, the construction of the crowd as an alternative form of classifying human beings as a collective, analogous to the construction of race, provided a space where asocial activities, such as criminal acts, could be defined by analyzing this new collective. It is only with this theorizing of the crowd within the debates during and following World War I that the shift from seeing the racialized victim as mad to seeing the crowd as mad because of its racism begins to become clearly defined. While we pick up this movement in Chapter Three, we first must attend to the shift from pathological accounts of race to "racial attitudes" as pathological conditions—what we refer to as the long, slow burn in the social and behavioral sciences, from roughly 1890 to 1940. While the development of crowd theories to explain racism and group prejudice in many ways overlaps this period, we want our readers to understand that a "crowd" explanation for group prejudice cannot exist without a redefinition of the very concept of race itself—from a biological predisposition to a socially constructed phenomenon.

2

The Long, Slow Burn from Pathological Accounts of Race to Racial Attitudes as Pathological

Toward Explanations for Racism

Early-twentieth-century American race scholarship, both in the social and behavioral sciences, posited racial differences as innate, as cultural variations, or as linked to different evolutionary processes between "varieties of mankind." This scholarship was fairly similar to its nineteenth-century predecessors in both the United States and in Europe. Even the shift from biological accounts of racial differences to an account of cultural differences during the first two decades of the twentieth century held strongly to an evolutionary framework. Then the inter-war period (1918–1939) marked, within the American social sciences, the emergence of social-structural explanations for racial differences that, by the end of World War II, would become a dominant paradigm. These explanations, however, lacked the coherency and consensus *across* the social sciences that others have attributed to them. It was not until *after* World War II that social-structural explanations for racial differences were considered mainstream among behavioral and social scientists. Among behavioral and social scientists working within the United States, explanations for blacks' susceptibility to mental illness in the rapidly modernizing world were simply replaced by a "dysfunctional Negro" hypothesis in the inter-war period. It was this hypothesis, then, that would structure the production of race scholarship *and* racial policy through the 1960s.

In this chapter, we start by tracing the emergence of the aforementioned sociostructural explanation for racial differences at the very beginning of the twentieth century, with particular emphases on W.E.B. Du Bois and his contemporaries in the Chicago School. Du Bois, throughout his career, was explicit in rejecting biological and evolutionary explanations of racial differences. His Chicago School contemporaries, however, were not nearly as coherent or clear in their perspectives, despite much lip service to the contrary.[1] Furthermore, neither Du Bois nor his contemporaries in Chicago necessarily challenged the emergent view of cultural evolution as a significant factor in racial differences; in fact, they were some of the view's strongest adherents. Nevertheless, the fact of Du Bois's blackness made for a deep neglect of his empirically driven research by mainstream social scientists, especially other sociologists. As a result, the "cultural" explanation for racial differences crystallized within the Chicago School of sociology and anthropology, and by the end of World War II resulted in an adoption among sociologists, anthropologists, and even politicians of the "dysfunctional Negro" hypothesis that shaped how racial differences would be characterized within both the academy and popular American discourse.[2]

The Emergence of Structural Explanations for Race and Racism in the Social Sciences

The collapse of scientific racism, including its causes, catalysts, and consequences, has been well documented.[3] The historian Peggy Pascoe notes, however, that the range and richness of these studies often end during the period between World War I and World War II. Here, the narrative reads that the demise of scientific racism was the consequence of a rise of a vanguard of social scientists, trained by the Columbia University cultural anthropologist Franz Boas and his sociological contemporaries at the University of Chicago. The oft-mentioned narrative posits that when modern social science emerges, racism runs out of intellectual steam.[4] This supposed collapse of American racialism necessarily depends upon a discursive split between biology and culture.[5] That is, pre-modern social and behavioral sciences theorized race as a biological property, and any differences between the races were matters of evolutionary development. Modern social and behavioral science, meanwhile, is argued to have, by the very fact of being modern, shunned a biological explanation for racial differences in favor of a more social and cultural one. Racial differences in the modernist perspective are matters of unequal economic, political, and social access between whites and nonwhites.

We generally agree with Pascoe's claim that many scholars of twentieth-century race and racism have reduced the demise of scientific racism to a "trickle-down" theory in which University of Chicago social scientists ride into the debate like war heroes, dismantling scientific racism within the universities in the 1920s, in the courts in the 1940s and 1950s, and finally within government policy in the 1960s and 1970s. As Pascoe notes, this romantic notion eschews the fact that social and behavioral scientists never fully reached consensus on the matter of race's *physical* ontology, or its lack thereof.[6] For roughly sixty years, the "essential fact" of race was grounded first in anatomy and physiology, then later in susceptibility to disease, including madness, and finally in the inability to adapt to "modern" (read: white) society.

In addition to this, however, we would add one other problem to the romantic notion of the movement toward a "modern" scientific perspective on race: during the period between roughly 1890 and 1940, or what we term in this chapter the long, slow burn, race was an ever evolving concept among behavioral and social scientists. Its mutability became the driving force behind how scientists and policymakers came to approach their understanding of prejudice, ethnocentricity, and racism, as well as other overlapping concepts that were structured by and structured their understanding of race. In this way, the eradication of racism never depended upon the nonrecognition of race, as Pascoe suggests. Rather, the eradication of racism depended on a fundamental reorienting to the concept of race (and, as we show in the later chapters, a reorienting to the problem of racism).

To tell this part of the story, we begin with Fredrick Ludwig Hoffman (1865–1946). Hoffman was born in Germany, but relocated to the United States in 1884. Though several biographies identify him as a professional statistician, it is unclear where his training took place. Most likely, Hoffman was apprenticed by his father, an accountant, until his father's death when Hoffman was ten years old. In 1891, Hoffman accepted a position with Prudential Life Insurance Company in New Jersey. While there, he would establish himself as a "leading authority on public health issues," and develop an international reputation through the publication of over 1,300 articles and books, some of which were published on behalf of the U.S. Department of Labor and Bureau of Labor Statistics. In addition, Hoffman would serve as Prudential's spokesperson at many of the professional meetings for insurance companies, both national and international, while also serving as board member for the American Cancer Society and the American Tuberculosis Association.[7]

Hoffman's first book, *Race Traits and Tendencies of the American Negro*, is his most important for our purposes.[8] The book, published for the American Economic Association, was the final product of a collection of "vital and social statistics" describing U.S. blacks over roughly a decade of Census Bureau data. Prior to its publication, Hoffman had disseminated some of the results from his study in medical and professional journals between 1892 and 1895. In the preface to the book, Hoffman is clear in his purpose:

> During the course of my inquiry it became more and more apparent that there lie at the root of all social difficulties or problems, racial traits and tendencies which make for good or ill in the fate of nations as well as of individuals. It became more apparent as the work progressed, that, in the great attempts at world bettering, at the amelioration of the condition of the lower races by those of a higher degree of culture and economic well being, racial traits and tendencies have been almost entirely ignored.[9]

According to Hoffman, "The large body of facts accumulated has made a more elaborate treatment seem feasible, and the final result is the present work."[10]

It is unclear from the preface for whom this report was intended. At the time of its publication, many scientists and laypersons in Europe and the United States held fast to the dominant scientific perspective that racial differences were due to inherent properties of the "varieties of mankind." Though among the more explicitly racist subgroups of scientists and policymakers there existed a disengagement with "world bettering," among the more general racialists this does not appear to be the case. Nonetheless, Hoffman's analysis and conclusions demonstrate the dominant racialism of his time, reading as a sympathetic, albeit paternalistic, account of the condition of black Americans:

> If the work accomplishes its purpose and leads to a more searching investigation into the underlying causes of race progress or retrogression; if it leads to more scientific attention to the relations between the superior and inferior races, as contrasted with the dangerous method of guess work, it will not have been written in vain. For after all it is the question of *living beings* and not of theories; and no philanthropy or charity that in

all its missionary efforts has not been able to save the *living man*, has any claim to be called successful [emphases in the original].[11]

Hoffman's analysis, based primarily upon data from the 1890 Census, has been discussed at length by several other scholars.[12] Rather than revisit these discussions, we will draw readers' attention to the fact that there is overwhelming consensus now that the eleventh U.S. Census was fraught with inadequacies and misreporting, not unlike many of its predecessors. This fact was, of course, lost on Hoffman at the time, who wrote, "I am convinced that the eleventh census was as carefully taken as any one of the ten preceding enumerations."[13]

Hoffman examined a variety of Census data comparing ills and vices between whites and blacks, alcoholism and madness in particular. Quoting from the physician Norman Kerr's 1894 *Inebriety or Narcomania*, Hoffman writes:

> Alcoholism among Negroes differs materially from the same disease in the white and Indian races. The negroes, with their vivacity and enthusiasm, from their nervous sensitiveness, are easily excited. Their drunkenness is more demonstrative than profound, but the anesthetic influence is less lasting. They may be characterized as more readily intoxicated than the white men of western countries but less liable to the diseased condition which I designated narcomania, intoxicate mania or inebriety.[14]

Hoffman's own belief as to why blacks would be less susceptible to madness associated with alcoholism is grounded in an evolutionary framework similar to other scholars of his period. Quoting from the physician Robert Reyburn, Hoffman writes, "My own belief is that the true explanation of this exemption is to be sought for in the want of development of the cerebral hemispheres, which so often exist among the negroes."[15]

Hoffman did acknowledge that the counts for mental illness rates were not completely accurate, given that the Census only used "mere approximations" and complete statistics on the comparisons between white and blacks rates of mental illness "have never been collected."[16] To remedy this, Hoffman drew his analysis from U.S. Army rates of discharge during the Civil War. Hoffman found the reported rates of medical discharges on psychiatric grounds for blacks was half that of their white counterparts. According to Hoffman, the U.S. Army data demonstrated "the general opinion that insanity was not a common disease among the colored population before the war."[17] His examination of data from the Freedmen's Bureau, the Census, and the Washington, D.C., Government Hospital for the Insane, showed no significant increase in rates of insanity among blacks. Drawing attention to the number of insane treated, and their mortality rates, at the Colonial Hospital at Sierra Leone from 1843 to 1853, however, Hoffman notes, "insanity was not an uncommon disease among the natives." Therefore, he concludes, "The prevalence of the disease at the present time, may, therefore, be as much due to the consequences of heredity as to the effects of the struggle for life."[18] Echoing a proposition drawn by none other than Émile Durkheim in 1897, Hoffman writes of blacks' susceptibility to suicide:

> It is true that suicide is most frequent in those states where intellectual culture has advanced most, but it is not true that it is intellectual culture which has caused the increase, but rather the want of it or the maladjustment of the individual to the conditions of life. . . . The individual who attempts by some means or others to overcome by force obstacles that hinder him from reaching the level of others will often, in despair, end his own life, but more often because he violated the common law and lacks courage to face the result.[19]

Hoffman agrees with Phillip Bruce, whom Hoffman quotes from his *The Plantation Negro as a Free Man*: "As a corollary of their comparative immunity from insanity for moral reasons, it is found that blacks rarely commit suicide, a fact weary of explanation when a full knowledge of the character of the race has been obtained. In the first place no cause of anxiety presses long enough upon the mind of the individual negro to foster a desire to put an end to life."[20] Blacks were, to put it abruptly, too simple to be suicidal. Their predisposition was thought to lead more toward imbecility than mania.

In *Race Traits and Tendencies*, Hoffman also takes up the topic of miscegenation, or race mixing, a concern shared by many of his contemporaries, and a topic that would be revisited by the scientific and policymaking communities up through the 1930s. Hoffman, like many other racialists, believed the mixing of the races led to the production of a progeny who were "morally and physically inferiors of the pure black."[21] Citing almost a dozen other scholars within the medical professions, Hoffman reaffirmed the dominant position that the mixing of the races diluted the intelligence of whites, while also impairing the physical prowess of blacks: "On the basis of these observations, the conclusion is warranted, that the mixed race is physically the inferior of the white and pure black, and as a result of this inferior degree of vital power we meet with a lesser degree of resistance to disease and death among the mixed population, in contrast with the more favorable condition prevailing among whites and pure blacks."[22] One can add here that Hoffman saw equivalent problems in the intermarriage of Jews and non-Jews resulting from the "dissimilarity of the two contracting parties, the disappointment which follows such unions on account of the inability of the Christian to adopt the mode of living or sympathize with the inner life of the Jew and *vice versa.*"[23] Race mixing leads to psychopathology.

Hoffman's work was praised for what was described by one reviewer as great attention to detail and logical inferences. In a review published in the *Political Science Quarterly*, for example, Gary Calkins of Columbia University wrote, "His logic is convincing, and his data, collected with difficulty . . . point to the one conclusion that the race of negroes is on the downward grade."[24] Calkins, in fairness, was critical of Hoffman's thesis that the deterioration of blacks is indicative of their racial traits, given that many blacks were relatively recent arrivals to rapidly industrializing urban centers. Calkins wrote, "Any rural population suddenly transferred to such unfavorable conditions of city life must suffer. . . . Under such conditions no peculiar 'race traits or tendencies' are necessary to explain a sudden increase in infant mortality or physical degeneration."[25] Calkins's objections are of course still firmly entrenched within the dominant racialist perspective. He expressed sympathy for the conditions of blacks, yet grounded those conditions within a framework of biological inferiority. Meanwhile, a review in the *Publications of the American Statistical Association* found few problems with Hoffman's conclusions, applauding the volume for its "most thorough and painstaking compilation."[26] Among Hoffman's contemporaries, then, *Race Traits and Tendencies* was relatively well received.[27]

There was one social scientist, however, who not only issued a strong critique of Hoffman's work, but did so through a rigorous methodological attention to the study of a black America that defined his entire career. From the end of the nineteenth century through the first two decades of the twentieth century, the black sociologist W.E.B. Du Bois embarked on an unprecedented academic endeavor to chronicle the social ills of blacks living in the United States. His *The Philadelphia Negro* is, perhaps, the most widely known of these works, a five-hundred-page methodological masterpiece of sociological inquiry.

The Philadelphia Negro really began in 1896 while Du Bois was at the University of Pennsylvania, his first research position following his 1895 graduation from Harvard University, where he had become the first black man to earn a Ph.D. from that university. It was not until three years later that *The Philadelphia Negro* was published, however, and by that time Du Bois had moved to Atlanta University, where he would remain until 1910.[28] While in Atlanta, he established what would become the premier research incubator for studies of black American social life.[29] There, he and his graduate students produced the same type of empirically sound work on black communities that characterized his earlier research in Philadelphia. Du Bois and his students investigated a wide range of topics pertinent to blacks in the United States, with a focus on Southern blacks and blacks in cities, including mortality, social and physical conditions of city life, education, the black church, the health and wellbeing of blacks in America, black economics, and the black family.

A common thread throughout the Atlanta studies, and Du Bois's body of work more generally, was the unrelenting thesis that the ill conditions facing black Americans were not the result of physical or mental inferiority, but rather the product of deleterious social conditions. Upon the publication of Hoffman's aforementioned *Race Traits and Tendencies of the American Negro*, Du Bois penned a review, published in the *Annals of the American Academy of Political and Social Science*. In it, he took Hoffman to task for drawing the majority of his data from the eleventh Census, citing the emerging reservations concerning its accuracy. In addition, Hoffman had incorporated collected anthropological data from wartime soldiers, which, as Du Bois points out in his review, "relate to one sex only, and to the most healthful years." Finally, the data drawn from large cities in Hoffman's analysis "give little or no clue to conditions in the country where over three-fourths of the Negroes live."[30] In perhaps his most pointed criticism of Hoffman, Du Bois wrote:

> The proper interpretation of apparently contradictory social facts is a matter requiring careful study and deep insight. If, for instance, we find among American Negroes to-day, at the very same time, increasing intelligence and increasing crime, increasing wealth and disproportionate poverty, increasing religious and moral activity and high rate of illegitimacy in births, we can no more fasten upon the bad as typifying the general tendency than we can upon the good. Least of all can we subscribe to Mr. Hoffman's absurd conclusion, that "in the plain language of the facts brought together the colored race is shown to be on the downward grade." Such contradictory facts are not facts pertaining to "the race" but to its various classes, which development since emancipation has differentiated. As is natural with all races, material and mental development has, in the course of a single generation, progressed farther than the moral: to save a little money, to go to the mission schools, were paths of progress much easier of comprehension to the dazed freedman, than the rehabilitation of the family relationship which slavery so fatally destroyed. On the other hand, when the younger generation came on the stage with exaggerated but laudable hopes of "rising," and found that a dogged Anglo-Saxon prejudice had shut nearly every avenue of advancement in their faces, the energies of many undoubtedly found an outlet in crime.[31]

While Du Bois acknowledged Hoffman's study as interesting in its collection of data, he nevertheless put the last nail in the coffin when he wrote that most "of the conclusions drawn from these facts are, however, of doubtful value, on account of the character of the material, the extent of the field, and the unscientific use of the statistical method."[32] His final jab at Hoffman concerned formatting: "As a piece of book-making this work invites criticism for its absence of page headings or rubrics, and its unnecessary use of italics. Moreover, Mr. Hoffman has committed the unpardonable sin of publishing a book of 329 pages without an index."[33]

Du Bois's review would not be the last time he or his Atlanta University colleagues would reproach Hoffman for his *Race Traits and Tendencies* volume. Later that same year, the Second Annual Conference for the

Study of Negro Problems was held on the Atlanta University campus. Though Du Bois had not fully integrated into the Atlanta University community at this point, and would not be a primary contributor until the third annual conference the next year, the participants in the second conference specifically reference Hoffman's book in their proceedings. Taking a position virtually identical to that of Du Bois in his review, the conference proceedings called into question Hoffman's premise that racial differences were matters of biological and evolutionary developments. In highlighting the fact that, prior to the Civil War, consumption among slaves was "virtually unknown," while since 1865 it has been increasing steadily, the contributors posed the following rhetorical question: "Is [this change] because the Negro is inherently more susceptible . . . or is it because of his changed environment. . . . If his tendency to consumption is due to his inherent susceptibility, what was it that held it in check until after the war?"[34]

The Philadelphia Negro implicitly took on Hoffman in its characterization of the state of the black condition in the United States, debunking evidence against blackness as a pathological condition. In a central declaration, and one oft quoted by others, Du Bois wrote, "Broadly speaking, the Negroes as a class dwell in the most unhealthful parts of the city and in the worst houses of those parts; which is of course simply saying that the part of the population having a large degree of poverty, ignorance, and general social degradation is usually to be found in the worst portions of our great cities."[35] He drew his audience's attention toward the rates of poverty and crime within certain areas of Philadelphia in which blacks were concentrated, arguing that in areas where racial segregation runs parallel to class inequality a higher rate of crime and general social malaise should be expected:

> A study of statistics seems to show that [crime] follows in its rise and fall the fluctuations shown in the records of whites, i.e. if crime increases among the whites it increases among Negroes, and *vice versa*, with this peculiarity, that among the Negroes the change is always exaggerated— the increase greater, the decrease more marked in nearly all cases. This is what we would naturally expect . . . the condition of a lower class is by its very definition worse than that of a higher, so the situation of the Negroes is worse as respects crime and poverty than that of the mass of whites.

Moreover, any change in social conditions is bound to affect the poor and unfortunate more than the rich and prosperous.[36]

Following this line of logic, Du Bois concludes that the two greatest causes of the ill social, economic, political, and physical conditions of blacks living in Philadelphia, and by corollary, urban blacks throughout the United States, were

> [s]lavery and emancipation with their attendant phenomena of igno-
> rance, lack of discipline, and moral weakness; immigration with its in-
> creased competition and moral influence. To this must be added a third
> as great—possibly greater in influence than the other two, namely the
> environment in which a Negro finds himself—the world of custom and
> thought in which he must live and work, the physical surrounding of
> house and home and ward, the moral encouragements and discourage-
> ments which he encounters.[37]

This conclusion summarizes what would become Du Bois's legacy within the study of race relations: a structural argument centered on the external forces—economic, political, and social—that shape the opportunities and outcomes for black Americans within the United States.[38] Yet, while this conclusion would be foregone among Du Bois, his colleagues, and the graduate students he trained within the Atlanta University incubator, the massive volume of reports, manuscripts, and studies he and his colleagues produced between 1896 and 1914 were largely ignored by mainstream social scientists. In *The Philadelphia Negro*, for example, Du Bois had demonstrated strong empirical evidence in favor of the historical and social nature of social problems, including forms of maladaption that plagued the black community.[39] His early-twentieth-century Atlanta papers provided further grounds for rejecting pathological explanations of race and racism, but among his white academic contemporaries, Du Bois was simply not widely read.

While Du Bois countered contemporary theories of a damaged black psyche, such as Hoffman's *Race Traits and Tendencies*, his work was also informed by his exposure to and identification with the conflicting theories of racial science concerning the mental status of the Jews and the reasons for their psychopathology that he had absorbed during his education in the early 1890s at the Friedrich-Wilhelms-Universität zu Berlin, the home of the newly self-invented field of the social sciences (*Sozialwissenschaften*). Du Bois had received a traveling fellowship while at Harvard that had enabled him to study abroad and he chose Berlin as his destination. Berlin in the 1890s was also the hotbed of both political antisemitism as well as the site of an entrenched academic understanding of Jewish biological inferiority in the medical and social sciences. Not only was Du Bois exposed to antisemitism, but he reported that he was "several times mistaken for a Jew" in Hungary; "arriving one night in a town of north Slovenia, the driver of a rickety cab whispered in my ear, 'Unter die Juden?' [To the Jews?]. I stared and then said yes. I stayed in a little Jewish inn."[40] This experience brought with it a stigma that echoed the feelings he felt as a black student at Harvard.

Du Bois fully developed his theory of double consciousness and its role in the formation of black identity in his groundbreaking book of 1903, *The Souls of Black Folk*, with its caricatures of Southern Jews.[41] He described double consciousness as the tension that shapes the black psyche. It was "two souls, two thoughts, two unreconciled strivings; two warring ideals in one dark body, whose dogged strength alone keeps it from being torn asunder."[42] It was the cause of both psychological strengths and weaknesses. A term of art in the psychology of the nineteenth century, it was also the state of the German Jewish psyche as understood and described at the turn of the century.[43] As Anthony Appiah has argued in his recent study of Du Bois, its roots lie in his time in Berlin.[44] In 1893 Du Bois wrote:

It may surprise one at first to see a recrudescence of anti-Jewish feeling in a civilized state at this late day. One must learn however that the basis of the neo-anti-Semitism is economic and its end socialism. Only its present motive force is racial hatred. It must be ever remembered that the great capitalists of Germany, the great leaders of industry are Jews; moreover, banded together by oppression in the past, they work for each other, and aided by the vast power of their wealth, and their great natural abilities, they have forced citadel after citadel, until now they practically control the stock-market, own the press, fill the bar and bench, are crowding the professions—indeed there seems to be no limit to the increase of their power. This of course is a menace to the newly nationalized country. . . .[45]

Du Bois was quite aware of the double problem of a German nationalism that both enabled Jews to function in the society and charged them
with being unable to become real Germans. The reason for this lies in
the psychology of the Germans:

> The whole nation in spite of excellent qualities seems largely to lack that
> robust faith in itself which builds men and peoples. It is thus that the
> American comes to realize that this new federation of the old world is
> starting its history from premises dramatically opposite to those from
> which the old federation of the new world started. Instead of a bound-
> lessly optimistic state founded on individual freedom, we have a restlessly
> pessimistic state founded on obedience.[46]

Du Bois also see the economic presence of the Jews as a menace to
the untested nationalism of the new Germany. While there, he wrote,
Germans heaped "on the shoulders of the Jew all the evils ever attributed
to capitalism. All that [Karl] Marx, [Louis] Blanc, or [Edward] Bellamy
ever laid at the door of capitalism, is by the German anti-Semitic party,
charged upon the Jew because the Jew happens to be the great capitalist
of Germany."[47] But the Jew is also the antithesis of the "slow-going good-
natured German burger" who does not succeed in modernity because
of his "lack of capital and business sense, together with the irresistible
competition of sharp, and sometimes unscrupulous, Jews."[48] Du Bois
also thought that such racism was limited and could well be ameliorated
over time. He saw in the status of German Jews the economic, political,
and social factors that *The Philadelphia Negro* defines as central to the
status of blacks in the United States. The Jew strives in all of these areas
and still remains the focus of a collective German character that articulates this difference in the form of stigmatization.

Race in Chicago

While Du Bois was writing on the condition of black Americans, and
race relations more generally, from his Atlanta base, a somewhat parallel research agenda was advancing within the social sciences at the
University of Chicago. Here, under the leadership of Albion Small, and
later Robert E. Park, several important, and now classic, studies were

produced on the conditions of various groups of first- and second-generation immigrants who, due to the racial discourse at the time, were "not quite white," but would eventually become so. Treating Chicago like a living laboratory, Chicago School anthropologists and sociologists challenged the dominant thesis of the time that racial differences were best characterized by tensions between superior and inferior categories of humans. However, the Chicago School's first generation (1890–1925) illustrates the long, slow burn concerning scientific racism in two parts: (1) an epistemological shift from a predominantly racist to racialist account of group differences, including mental attributes, and (2) a shifting away from overtly bio-evolutionary accounts of racial differences to accounts through which bio-evolutionary language marked emergent cultural explanations of race relations. Consider, as an example, the early years of sociology's flagship journal, *The American Journal of Sociology*. Established in 1895 at the University of Chicago, many of its early issues were littered with articles that, as sociologist James McKee characterizes, "spoke of civilization and savagery, of advanced and backward races."[49] McKee's analysis of sociology's disciplinary history regarding the "race problem" focuses primarily on the second shift of the long, slow burn, with the former implied.

Often described as holding great sway over the development of the Chicago School's perspective on culture and its relationship to race as well as racial differences is the ethnologist Franz Boas. Boas had undertaken the task of representing "advanced" and "backwards" races as part of the Chicago World's Fair in 1892. After leaving Chicago's new Field Museum in 1896, where much of the fair's exhibits were then housed, to move to New York City and an eventual appointment at Columbia University, Boas exerted a crucial influence on the early Chicago School, but this influence was largely insular.

Boas's view was that the variety of cultures was not to be confused with a hierarchy of cultures. His work influenced the more critical approach that sociologists Lester Ward and W. I. Thomas held in the late nineteenth and early twentieth centuries. Yet Boas's claim that blacks were fully capable of learning "advanced culture" and fully assimilating into the United States was not nearly as influential on the disciplinary perspective as it has been made to appear, as few outside of Ward, Thomas, and the Chicago School were influenced directly by Boas in the first decade of the twentieth century. By the time his work was recognized as scientific, competing claims from geneticists and other medical and behavioral scientists would have an even stronger influence on the discourse.[50] In fact, the evolutionary perspective that dominated sociological theorizing about race and civilization processes did not begin to loosen its hold until roughly midway into the second decade of the twentieth century.[51]

We need to locate Boas as a self-consciously liberal "German of Jewish ancestry" who saw himself much more in the Enlightenment model of the European intellectual than as a Jew. Yet it was as a Jew (he never converted to Christianity) that his academic career in Germany had been blocked. When he arrived in the United States in 1887, however, he rarely stressed the role of antisemitism in shaping the very social sciences that he espoused as means of examining and combating racism. His *The Mind of Primitive Man*, published in 1911, stressed the universals of human perception based on fieldwork he had undertaken in the Arctic. Nonetheless, when Boas spoke in 1906 at an Atlanta University commencment at the invitation of Du Bois, his speech raised the question of antisemitism as a constant in the European (here French, not German) psyche: "Even now there lingers in the consciousness of the old, sharper divisions which the ages had not been able to efface, and which is strong enough to find—not only here and there—expression as antipathy to the Jewish type. In France, that let down the barriers more than a hundred years ago, the feeling of antipathy is still strong enough to sustain an anti-Jewish political party."[52] For Boas, the image of a national French psyche and of a "Jewish type," here real rather than imagined, defined the essence of racism. It is defined by cultural antipathies, not simply by the perceived reality of race. Du Bois's world was quite different from that of Boas. In 1906, as William Adams stated, Europe was "a world in which one could move comfortably between a German, a Jewish, and an American identity, or be simultaneously all three."[53] Franz Boas agreed, but thought that "a Negro will never become a European."[54]

Nevertheless, it was not until the latter part of the 1920s and into the 1930s that a perspective on race relations—one advanced by Robert Park and a new cohort of social scientists at Chicago—resembled anything remotely close to what Du Bois had produced nearly three decades prior. Yet the "race relations" model developed by Park was still deeply entangled within an evolutionary framework. Park and many of his students distinguished between "modern" and "primitive" societies, citing differences in commerce, markets, industrialization, urbanization, bureaucracy, rationality, and Western science. The civilizing process, for Park, was a matter of mass movement through trade, exploration, and conquest. These processes produced encounters among diverse populations, which led to the collapse of insular, traditional ways in favor of cosmopolitanism and "high culture."[55]

Though Park's model would remove blacks and other immigrant groups from the context of biological evolution within scientific discourse, it kept them firmly planted within a model of social evolution, where blacks and other nonwhite groups would be typified as less culturally and socially competent. This aspect of Park's research program is often overshadowed by attention sociologists place upon his "race relations cycle"—a model Park himself wrote about only twice: in a 1926 brief within the popular magazine *Survey Graphic*, and again in 1937 in the introduction to *Interracial Marriage in Hawaii*, written by his advisee, Romanzo Adams.[56]

One gets the strongest flavor of the social evolutionary model from Park when reading his writings on multiracials, or "mulattoes," including his widely cited "marginal man" thesis. In a 1928 article for *The American Journal of Sociology*, he outlined a social evolutionary model where race classifications were, on the one hand, separated from biological determinism, yet still haunted by a bio-evolutionary perspective. Races, for Park, are "the products of isolation and inbreeding," yet modern society is a "consequence of contact and communication."[57] Civilization, he writes, is a paradox: it creates conflict through the bringing together of "higher" and "lower" cultures; yet "the forces which have been decisive in the history of mankind are those which have brought men together in fruitful competition, conflict, and co-operation."[58] Contact with a new culture causes a breakdown of the traditional organization of society, including traditional customs and norms. The effect, according to Park, is that the "emancipated individual invariably becomes in a certain sense and to a certain degree a cosmopolitan."[59]

Park's thesis on the "marginal man" would be refined just a few years later in his 1931 article "Mentality of Racial Hybrids." In it, he writes that one important effect of human migration, and the coming together—

willingly or not—of two cultures, is the "racial hybrid," or multiracial. His two exemplary groups that engage in race mixing are the Jews and the blacks, even though most of the essay is devoted to race mixing among the latter. The "mulatto," for Park, "is the product of divergent racial stocks, but just because of that fact he is, at the same time, the cultural product of two distinct traditions. He is, so to speak, a cultural as well as a racial hybrid."[60] The collapse of race into culture is evident in Park's analysis, as is the evolutionary framework through which he views the development of racial hybrids:

> [There is] no question at all in regard to the actual superiority of the mu-
> latto in comparison to the Negro, provided superiority is measured by
> present achievements and by the relative status of each in the existing
> social order. . . . [The] mixed blood as a class has shown himself more
> enterprising, and his progress, accordingly, has been more rapid. Not only
> in the learned professions and in politics, but particularly in literature
> and the expressive arts, the mulatto has outdistanced the Negro. . . . The
> Negro, by contrast, is described by one who has known them on the plan-
> tations in the South as "docile, tractable and unambitious," and invariably
> contented and happy "when free from the influence of the mulatto and
> the white man." . . . If the mulatto displays intellectual characteristics and
> personality traits superior to and different from those of the black man,
> it is not because of his biological inheritance merely, but rather more, I
> am inclined to believe, because of his more intimate association with the
> superior cultural group.[61]

By the end of the 1930s, then, despite a broad rejection of a biological ontology of race, an evolutionary model of race relations was firmly entrenched among social scientists. This model employed bio-evolutionary language to describe "cultural development" as the difference between whites and nonwhites. Even among those who viewed Park's idea of race relations and conflict as problematic, the language of biology and evolution remained central to how they thought about the "race problem." For example, Frank Hankins, a sociologist at Smith College who would later become the twenty-eighth president of the American Sociological Association (ASA), wrote in 1926 that average "mulattoes are doubtless superior to average pure negroes in general intelligence, but inferior to whites."[62] Edward B. Reuter, a sociologist trained by both Park and Albion Small at the University of Chicago and later the twenty-second president of the ASA, claimed in his 1917 *American Journal of Sociology* article that multiracials were not inferior, but superior, to pure-blood blacks because they "stand nearer to the Caucasian than to the Negro parent."[63] Declaring that biological selection favored the mulatto group, Reuter concluded that races and cultures were independent issues: "[Neither] racial amalgamation nor racial purity is a causal factor in civilization."[64] Reuter would later write in his highly influential 1927 book, *The American Race Problem*, that slavery and Jim Crow had left blacks a "culturally backward people."[65] In addition to Hankins and Reuter, Charles Ellwood, fourteenth president of the ASA, adapted the cultural evolutionary framework of Park to conclude in 1924 that blacks' inability to adapt to city life and its complex demands demonstrated they were better suited for agricultural labor than industrial labor.[66] Nevertheless, while within sociology a biological account of racial differences was being replaced with a cultural account, albeit one aligned with an evolutionary perspective on the development of customs, habits, and norms, within the psychological and medical communities this was not the case. Instead, the major authorities of the time looked to keep their hold on a racialist account of black inferiority in a turn we'll call "the last gasp."

The Last Gasp: Race, Culture, and Pathology in Early-Twentieth-Century Behavioral and Medical Discourse

The turn of the twentieth century was a point of great tension within the scientific community. While emergent disciplines like sociology were slowly building toward structural accounts for a range of social problems, including the "race problem" in the United States, the authority of the medical and psychological sciences remained deeply resistant. The life cycle of viewing race itself as cause and effect of psychopathology was in its final stages; yet, much like the life cycle of a star, these final stages were not ones in which the "race as psychopathology" perspective would simply fade away. Instead, within the medical and psychological disciplines, the last gasp of racialism would be a powerful one, with unanticipated consequences.

Early-twentieth-century scientific racism was a widely popular perspective within specialty journals such as *The Eugenics Review* (1909–1968) and the *Annals of Eugenics* (1925–1954), outlets established as a consequence of nineteenth-century racialism. However, even the more mainstream scholarly outlets shared the view that race was a predictor of mental and physical outcomes.[67] For example, George Dawson, writing in *The American Journal of Psychology* in 1900, asserted that the "lower races," including Native Americans and blacks, demonstrate signs of arrested psychical development, including vagrancy and pauperism: "Many causes operate to produce such individuals, but incapacity to adapt themselves to social and economic conditions that oblige every man to work for a living is one of the most important."[68] Dawson continued:

> The native Africans are generally children of Nature, making very little effort to improve upon their methods of support. When they were imported to the United Sates and placed under white taskmasters they were obliged to work somewhat after the manner of the civilization surrounding them. But after they became their own masters and took their places as self-supporting members of a free society, the race instinct of carelessness and improvidence asserted itself.[69]

Gluttony and drunkenness, according to Dawson, were closely related, and represented the persistence of the undiscriminating food appetite found in animals, young children, and the "lesser races": "Wherever savages have been able to invent intoxicating drinks, they have used them in excess; and wherever they have secured the more intoxicating liquors of civilization, they have drunk themselves to extinction."[70] Dawson's view was not atypical among his contemporaries. In his review of Dawson's work, Sidney Mezes, an American philosopher who would later become the president of the University of Texas in 1908, and then of the College of the City of New York in 1914, described Dawson's discussion as "judicious," well supported with facts and accepted theories of the time, saying that as a result, it "strengthened [those theories] greatly as a basis for practical measures."[71]

Twentieth-century medical and psychological racialism continued to stress nineteenth-century prevailing wisdom that racial differences were indicated primarily through physical dissimilarities. At the same time, this brand of racialism also stressed that dissimilarities of mental attributes and capacities were so strongly correlated with physical differences that mental health was an important factor for making categorical distinctions among identified racial categories. In a paper delivered to the American Neurological Association's annual meeting in 1921, the physician Pearce Bailey asserted that "the negro exhibits a tendency toward mental defect and away from every other neuropsychiatric condition, while the native-born Scot shows a tendency away from mental defect and toward alcoholism and certain other neuropsychiatric conditions."[72] Citing statistics concerning mental diseases among the various races, Bailey claimed:

> [It] appears that [blacks and Native Americans] could not under any present circumstances attain the average intelligence of the cultured races . . . not because there is any detailed information as to the potentiality of the primitive mind, but because mental deficiency is so profusely distributed among [them] that their average intelligence must be inferior to that of average European intelligence. . . . [The] existence of a mental disease implies a developed intelligence, a kind of intelligence that would possess imagination, ideas, a certain quickness in mental processes.[73]

Thus, blacks and other "inferior races" were less susceptible to madness *because* they were racially inferior! In presenting his data, Bailey argued that of the nineteen states with higher mental deficiency rates than the national average, the insanity rate was below the national average among blacks, Native Americans, Italians, and Mexicans.[74]

Similarly, the psychiatrist and clinical director of the Georgia State Sanitarium, E. M. Green, would write in *The American Journal of Psychiatry* that the Southern plantation lifestyle was more fit for the natural tendencies of blacks than urban centers, and as a result, blacks were less prone to depression as fieldworkers than they were as industrial laborers. Their "natural tendencies"—active, boisterous, emotionally unstable, constantly looking for excitement—were more viable within their "normal environment," that is, poor, agrarian lifestyles: "In the southern states the average negro lives under conditions which are natural to him."[75] Though Green would also, in this same article, argue that blacks were more susceptible to manic-depressive psychoses and dementia, he admittedly was stumped as to the causes, though he speculated, "The fear of the supernatural, the suspicions of his fellows and the necessity of guarding at all times against bad luck and machinations of enemies, each of these factors may play a part in bringing about a psychosis."[76] George Ferguson drew similar conclusions in his 1916 "The Psychology of the Negro: An Experimental Study," writing, "Strong and changing emotions, an improvident character, and a tendency to immoral conduct are not unallied. They are all rooted in uncontrolled impulse. And a factor which may tend to produce all three is a deficient development of the more purely intellectual capacities."[77]

In his paper read before the Society for Nervous and Mental Diseases in Washington, D.C., on March 17, 1921, William M. Bevis, assistant physician at St. Elizabeth's Hospital in the nation's capital, verified Green's claim that manic depression was increasing among blacks, citing it as the second-highest diagnosis among admissions records in 1920: "In a people naturally care-free, fond of excitement and motion, it is expected that their mental unbalance would be colored by this mood swing and disposition and find expression in the manic type of the manic-depressive group."[78] Obtaining admissions information from state hospitals throughout the South in 1920, Bevis identified the most common diagnoses of insanity among blacks: "Dementia praecox easily stands at the top in frequency, representing more than one-fourth of the psychoses of those admitted, a considerably higher percentage than among whites. This is not surprising when their racial character make-up and the atmosphere of superstition in which they move are considered."[79] Bevis also regurgitated a claim made in J. W. Babcock's 1895 "The Colored Insane" that excesses and vices among blacks were "potent factors in the production of mental diseases" among them.[80] These excesses and vices were the product of a "slowing of mental development and a loss of interest in education as sexual matters and a 'good time' begin to dominate the life and have the first place in the thoughts of the negro."[81]

The nostalgia for "simpler times" as a means for addressing blacks' susceptibility to mental disease continued throughout the first three decades of the twentieth century, as clinical practitioner and scholar alike would assert that increases in certain mental illnesses, including general paresis (dementia related to syphilis), among blacks was the result of, as one put it, "increasing stresses of civilization, and the fact that the negro is being forced more and more to rely on his own efforts. [These have] have put a burden on the negro that he formerly did not have to bear."[82] It was not uncommon, for example, to suggest a return not only to the agrarian South, but even slavery, as a "cure" for a variety of mental and physical ailments among blacks. For example, Thomas Mays, in a 1904 article, suggests the "true and only rational path" to eliminate pulmonary consumption among blacks was a return to bondage.[83] Mays's argument, like those of many of his contemporaries, simply holds the truth of racial inferiority to be self-evident. Citing military records and census data from before the Civil War, Mays asserts consumption among slaves was comparatively unknown, and no more prevalent among urban blacks in the South than it was among Southern urban whites: "This fact was so obvious and is verified by so many lay and medical authorities that it does not call for any extended statistical support."[84] The susceptibility of early-twentieth-century blacks to consumption, he writes, resided in them being "brought into the most intense competition for existence with a people whose civilization is thousands of years ahead of their own development."[85] Comparing the condition of emancipated blacks to that of an animal faced with a new "geological epoch to which it must adjust itself or perish," Mays claims their brains and nervous systems, unable to cope with the new stresses of modernity, simply shut down. Mays quotes from Dr. T. O. Powell, superintendent of the Georgia Asylum for the Insane: "I am forced to believe that insanity and tuberculosis are first cousins, or at least closely allied. The sudden outburst of insanity with the colored race of the South came associated with tuberculosis, hand-in-hand, keeping pace with one another."[86]

As the above examples illustrate, the scientific perspective on racial inferiority that typified the mid- to late-nineteenth-century "sciences of man" still had a firm grip on the psychological and medical sciences up through the early 1930s, despite paradigmatic shifts taking place within the social sciences during that same period. This begs two important questions: Why were medicine and psychology more resistant than the social sciences? And what allowed psychology and medicine to shift their disciplinary perspective on racial differences by the end of World War II?

The psychologist and historian Franz Samelson has suggested that the passage of the Immigration Restriction Law of 1924, which shifted the problem of race from one of differential exclusion to conflict resolution; the influx of nonwhites into the "lily-white" psychological and medical professions; the leftward shift within the medical and psychological sciences following the Great Depression; and nationalistic fervor against the Third Reich were important contributing factors.[87] While Samelson's account is a strong one, we're hesitant to accept his conclusions as they stand.

First, it is unclear that conflict resolution was a position that united either scientists or policymakers. The quotas on particular immigrant populations from the 1924 Johnson-Reed Act remained in place, with minimal changes, until 1965. This suggests that, while conflict resolution may have become a part of the national agenda for the "race problem," there was not a clear transformation in the period immediately before and after World War II. Furthermore, the Great Depression produced a strong anti-immigration sentiment even as the social reforms that followed gave the impression of a more left-leaning public base. From 1929 to 1933, immigration was essentially blocked by the FDR administration. From 1925 to 1931, as many as two million people of Mexican descent living in the United States, many of them citizens, were coerced or forced to leave as part of Mexican Repatriation.[88] This expulsion of Mexican immigrants was a direct result of the Great Depression and the sharp increase in unemployment, particularly among native whites. During the 1920s, thousands of legal and undocumented workers of Mexican descent were being used as cheap labor throughout the Midwest and Southwest, on farms, ranches, mines, and in construction. Their presence during the economic downturn simply fueled anti-Mexican sentiments among a newly threatened white laboring class.

Samelson's account of a "united front" against a common enemy in the Third Reich is, to a degree, true. However, he neglects that, from 1942 to 1946, Japanese Americans were lumped into the category of "common enemy," rather than "common friend," and as many as 110,000 to 120,000 were forcefully interned due to fears their true loyalties lay with their ethnic lineage.[89] Finally, Samelson's point that, as more nonwhites became credentialed and took up positions within the medical and psychological professions, perspectives on racial differences began to shift perhaps places too much emphasis on the degree to which one's racial and ethnic identity determines one's position on race relations. This, we believe, is a point that deserves serious attention, given that we argue the relationship between race, racism, and psychopathological differences is one of knowledge production and cultural shifts.

It is true, of course, that during the 1930s within the psychological sciences a number of Jews became very active, especially within the developing field of social psychology. Samelson points to this trend as indicative of a developing interest in prejudice within social psychology, and while these two events are correlated, that the rise in Jews within psychology would lead to a new inquiry in prejudicial attitudes is too strong of a conclusion based on the available evidence. First, Samelson's account of Jews within the professions only accounts for those Jews *marked*, either by last name or known religious affiliation. It makes no mention of a potentially significant number of Jews who, through a change in last name, or veil of secrecy, kept their affiliations hidden from their contemporaries, particularly *prior* to the development of the field of social psychology, and later, consequently, attitudinal research. One can note that Jews who hide their Jewishness might be different from Jews who do not—this may be a selection issue, i.e., Jews willing to hide are different, or an effect, i.e., the experience of hiding changes you (not least that you don't want to call attention to your own experience of oppression by studying something related to it). More importantly, however, there exists within the annals of psychology and medicine a significant amount of racialist scholarship produced by *nonwhites*. This suggests that one's racial and ethnic identity does not preclude one from adopting the dominant epistemological perspective of a given period.

It is helpful here to distinguish between *racism* and *racialism*, the latter of which nonwhite scholars more frequently displayed. The sociologist Graham Richards makes this distinction in his 2011 *Race, Racism, and Psychology*. Racism, for Richards, refers to individual attitudes and expressions hostile and denigratory toward people categorized as a particular "race." Racialism, meanwhile, refers to a "theoretical or ideological belief in the reality of races and the scientific validity of analyzing human affairs and human diversity in terms of racial differences."[90] The positions of many racialists within late-nineteenth- and early-twentieth-century science were remarkably paternalistic concerning the fate of blacks and other nonwhite groups of people. It is true, of course, that one can be both a racialist and a racist, meaning one can subscribe to a theoretical belief in the reality of races and racial hierarchies, and be a complete bigot. However, they can occur independently, and racialism in the absence of bigotry more readily infiltrated nonwhite spaces.

Take, for example, the concerns expressed by the Temple University physician J. Madison Taylor in his 1915 "Remarks on the Health of Colored People." In it, Taylor writes that one of the great threats to the survival of American blacks was their being located in a climate too different from their native Africa: "Most of the Negroes or black people in the United States came form the lowlands of Equatorial Africa; hence, they cannot possibly be expected to do well in a country where it freezes hard during the winter."[91] In order for blacks to survive the United States, he recommends they "keep out of the big cities and live in the open country," in addition to seeking warmer regions and avoiding harsh winters. This leads to a condemnation of miscegenation: "The white and black races will not fuse; they are too totally unlike in racial characteristic and in conformation. Unless the colored people as a body realize these facts and adapt their forms of life in accord with them they will disappear. No denial, no protest, no prayer will change the laws of nature."[92]

Taylor's entrenchment in racialism, and his corollary opinion that both whites *and* blacks need racial segregation, appears to reflect an earnest desire to see the survival of blacks in America. This racialist perspective is quite different from that of the Third Reich, which not only held an ideological belief in the genetic superiority of Aryan stock, but also believed their survival as an "ideal type," to borrow a Weberian term, rested upon the physical extermination of Jews, the Romani and Sinti, and other "inferior" racial groups. Placing the perspectives of both Taylor and the Third Reich alongside one another highlights the importance of recognizing *racism* as historically, socially, and culturally contingent. This is a far cry from the contemporary perspective on racism within sociology, for instance, where racism is often articulated as a monolith.[93]

What makes Taylor's remarks so important for our point that racism and racial differences are matters of knowledge production, rather than identity configurations, is that his comments were published in the official journal of the National Medical Association, an organization of black physicians and medical practitioners founded as a result of their race-based exclusion from the American Medical Association. Neither

Taylor's being white, nor his arguments, prevented this perspective from making its way into the leading black medical journal of the time, because the perspective was dominant within the scientific communities.

The reader should consider the physician Alan P. Smith. The first black to be elected a member of the American Psychiatric Association, in 1930, Smith served at the Tuskegee Veteran's Bureau Hospital after having graduated from Iowa State University's College of Medicine in 1927. In a 1931 article for the National Medical Association's journal, however, Smith clearly articulates a racialist perspective: "In the psychological make-up one is forced to conclude that the Afro-American personality is in fact for the most part its prototype, African. Miscegenation and three hundred years of contact have not entirely eradicated the strong African traits, customs, superstitions, and traditions."[94] Smith describes an increasing stress and strain that makes blacks more susceptible to certain psychoses as they come into contact with whites in urban centers:

> In considering the reaction patterns of the large number of ignorant 'Negroes' in the United States thrust into close contact and keen competition educationally, economically, and politically with other groups "uninterested in and with unsympathetic understandings of their personalities, and ever cognizant of the desire of such groups to segregate them socially and economically, they merely absorb as much of the behavior patterns of these others as they deem sufficient for their needs."[95]

As the presentation of this statement in the journal suggests, many of his black professional peers shared this point of view.

Smith draws his conclusions from the records of over 1,077 blacks admitted to the U.S. Veterans Hospital's Neuropsychiatric Service in Tuskegee from 1923 to 1929, where he served as associate physician. Of these records, almost 70 percent of those admitted were due to the following diagnoses: schizophrenia (33 percent), "syphilo-psychoses" (13 percent), and psychoneuroses (32 percent). Blacks suffered from mental illnesses, according to Smith, because so many of them have left the "rustic, carefree, lackadaisical life" of the agrarian South for the emerging industrial urban cities of the North.[96] Here, the complexities of city life and "exacting" labor conditions, including ten-hour workdays, made blacks into automatons. Poorly educated in Southern schools, Smith writes, blacks became more aware of their inability to compete with better-educated whites and immigrants in the North. Quoting from William A. White's "Social Significance of Mental Disease," Smith writes, "Density of population and insanity goes hand in hand. Mental disease is a disorder of man as a social animal."[97] His claim about population density and insanity echoed an earlier one made by the chief officer of health for Savannah, Georgia, William Brunner, in 1915. Speaking before the American Public Health Association, Brunner argued blacks were an asset only if they were less than 40 percent of the population of a given area. Any higher than that, and "[the black's] progress is retarded and, in a community where he greatly outnumbers the white population, he goes ahead not at all and furnishes a low morality and a high mortality."[98]

It is rather counterintuitive, given contemporary understandings of race and race relations as familial, to think that one of the preeminent black physicians of the inter-war period would accept the cultural-biological paradigm of racial inferiority. Yet this view, as we have argued, is not a matter of the influx of staunch racists into the medical and psychological professions. Instead, it is reflective of science as a racialist enterprise. Smith actually advocates for measures to improve the condition of blacks, despite his belief that their plight is brought on by a culturally inferior condition, and exaggerated by segregation in Northern industrial cities. His treatment protocol, for example, states: "To better the situation it will be necessary to strengthen the individual and to lessen the stresses of city life. To accomplish this will require the united efforts of parents, teachers, physicians, and social and research workers on the one hand; and the employers, industrial leaders, city manager, and economists on the other."[99] A close read of Smith's argument makes it rather easy to draw an intellectual thread between his 1931 article and Hoffman's 1897 treatise on race and madness—both grounded in the dominant racialist perspective of their time, both "sound" in their theory and method so far as those theories and methods were acceptable by a scientific enterprise deeply committed to its racial ideology.

An important piece of evidence that situates the last gasp of early-twentieth-century racialism within the medical and psychological professions appears in a 1934 special issue of the *Journal of Negro Education*, entitled "The Physical and Mental Abilities of the American Negro." In their contribution, Charles S. Johnson and Horace Mann Bond, two blacks who had both studied under Robert Park, describe the "lay of the land" of scientific investigations of racial differences prior to 1910. They write that discussions of nineteenth-century racial differences often began with statements regarding the "well-known" psychological differences, and used anatomical and physiological data as a frame upon which to restretch the originally assumed mental differences.[100]

Yet few of the contributors to the special issue, most of whom were social and behavioral scientists or education specialists, made bold claims as to where the field of racial differences could move. In their critical summary of the field, Walter Dearborn and Howard Long write that, rather than critique the idea of race as a stable, unitary social phenomenon, "it is best for workers in the field of race differences to turn their full attention to technique and methodology."[101] In other words, there is little need to actually revisit conceptual or theoretical assumptions about the facticity of race; race is a given, we just haven't figured out how to properly objectify it through science. Factor analysis, more robust statistical models, or better sampling could all better prove or disprove the relationship of race to mental and physical abilities of blacks and whites.[102] As Solomon Rosenthal writes in his contribution to the special issue: "Racial differences in susceptibility to the mental diseases have been claimed by a number of writers. The statistics on which these conclusions have been based are not scientifically valid. . . . Until hospital statistics are corrected . . . we will not be justified in claiming racial differences in the mental diseases."[103]

Nevertheless, one article within this special issue stands out for its illustration of the distinct shifts in disciplinary perspectives taking place between the social sciences and the psychological disciplines. In the fall of 1929, Charles H. Thompson, professor of education at Howard University and founder and editor of The Journal of Negro Education, circulated a questionnaire to one hundred psychologists, selected largely from the membership of the Ninth International Congress of Psychology. In addition, Thompson sent the survey to thirty-nine education specialists, and to thirty sociologists and anthropologists with interests in the field of racial differences.[104] The point of the survey was to ascertain whether competent scholars in the field of race relations and racial differences held to one of three positions identified in Dale Yoder's previous and extensive literature review: that race superiority is a fact, and supported through evidence; that race inferiority is possible, but not adequately demonstrated; or a skeptical position that remains critical of the means used to demonstrate race inferiority, generally insisting upon racial equality.[105]

Within each discipline, how respondents selected what they considered the most valid of the viewpoints suggests the long, slow burn within psychological disciplines, while among sociologists and anthropologists, a rupture appears to have taken place. For example, in response to the question, "Do you conclude from recent investigations that blacks are inherently mentally inferior or equal to whites," 64 percent of psychologists indicated the data was inconclusive (second viewpoint); 25 percent of them indicated blacks were inferior, while only 11 percent indicated blacks were equal to whites in ability. Among sociologists and anthropologists, however, 57 percent indicated the data was inconclusive, while only 5 percent indicated blacks were inferior, and 38 percent indicated blacks were equal.

Concerning Thompson's question on whether existing literature and evidence supports the "mulatto hypothesis," that blacks of more white blood are by virtue mentally superior to blacks with less white blood (and, by corollary, blacks are inferior to whites), 68 percent of psychologists responded the evidence is inconclusive, while 23 percent claimed evidence supports the hypothesis, and 9 percent agreed that ample evidence rejects the hypothesis. Among sociologists and anthropologists, 76 percent responded the evidence is inconclusive, while 24 percent claimed the evidence rejects the hypothesis. Importantly, no sociologist or anthropologist responded that the evidence supports the hypothesis.

Taken as a whole, the survey itself is a fascinating illustration of just how far sociology and anthropology had come from their nineteenth-century paradigm concerning inherent racial differences, and how far psychology still had to go (though, to be fair, it too had come a long way). The 1930s, however, marked a significant turn in the disciplinary development of psychology, as "attitude research" began to carve out a massive area of scholarly interest. Many scholars have examined this shift in focus within psychology. As both Richards and McKee show, for example, John Dollard's 1937 *Class and Caste in a Southern Town* was an important part of the shift, though Richards's account is far less critical of Dollard's reification of whites' perceptions of blacks as sexually libidinous than McKee's.[106] For example, Richards sees the book as "brave and ambitious" in its attempt to address the sexual fear and envy of blacks among white men, while McKee asserts, "In arguing that blacks had sexual freedom and a freedom to be violent, though in both cases only with blacks, Dollard seemed unaware that the pattern he was analyzing psychologically had an ideological history in white myth-making about black people."[107]

Nevertheless, the intra- and post-war years were marked by the rise of attitude-focused research in social psychology, which quickly became part of the core of the discipline. As a result, racism became widely seen as a variety of individual psychopathology, a "psychological flaw arising from inappropriate conditioning, reliance upon stereotyping, or psychodynamic development."[108] This position was maintained within social psychology through the 1960s, and would set the groundwork for the major shift toward treating racism as a psychopathological property.

3

Hatred and the Crowd

World War I and the Rise of a Psychology of Racism

Crowds during the Great War and Beyond

It is only in the course of the early twentieth century that experts begin
to locate the cause of racism in the crowd or the mob. Created to define
a psychological state in the nineteenth century, this classification was
as troubling as race itself. If race is the defining category that creates
the bright lines for the classification of predisposition (or resistance)
to mental illness, then the question becomes *what type of category can
be generated to understand the source of racism?* As we will show, the
foundations for contemporary practices through which racism became
pathologized were firmly established within late-nineteenth- and early-
twentieth-century theories on crowds and collective behavior. Within
these theories, racism is not only constructed as a mental illness, but one
that expresses symptoms among crowds and crowd behaviors. Thus the
"crowd" became a real entity in late-nineteenth-century psychological
literature equivalent to "race."

The crowd as a forensic concept has its origin in Lombrosian criminal
psychiatry. The debate was begun in the early 1890s with Scipio Sighele's
study *La Folla Delinquente*, on the nature of individual culpability in the
case of criminal activity in the mob.[1] The underlying thesis was that in
such a collective a form of degeneration, a "morbid deviation from the
norm" (to use B. A. Morel's classic formulation from midcentury) occurs
that is primitive and atavistic.[2] Sighele's work was quickly translated into
French and then, in 1897, into German.[3] The sociologist Gabriel Tarde
answered him. Tarde's "Laws of Imitation" was based on a theory of unconscious actions as a form of hypnotic suggestion. In turn, this debate
inspired the German sociologist Georg Simmel's presentation of the

crowd in his 1908 introduction to sociology.[4] As early as 1903 Simmel was concerned with sociation (*Vergesellschaftung*), social forms, and the reciprocal effects (*Wechselwirkungen*) among individuals. The tension between a sociological and a psychological theory of the crowd set the agenda for much of the debates about racism as a social phenomenon or racism as a psychopathology until after the mid-twentieth century. Indeed, in many cases, as we show, there was a constant mixing of the two explanations.

It was with Gustave Le Bon's *La Psychologie des Foules* (1895; English translation, *The Crowd: A Study of the Popular Mind*, 1896) that the crowd as a concept came into its own in the public sphere. Le Bon's work comes out of this general late-nineteenth-century preoccupation with the role of the social as well as the psychological role of the individual in the mob, and was to no little degree inspired by the extraordinary explosion of public animus during the Dreyfus affair in 1894, when wave after wave of antisemitism swept through every social level in France.[5] For Le Bon the crowd is defined by three factors: anonymity, contagion ("a magnetic influence given out by the crowd or from some other cause of which we are ignorant"), and suggestibility ("an individual in a crowd is a grain of sand amid other grains of sand, which the wind stirs up at will").[6] Within the crowd, one can undertake acts anonymously that one would not do individually; such acts, the result of psychopathological forces in the new collective, become the acts *of* the collective. While one important focus of crowd theory was on the charismatic leader and his ability to whip up the crowd, for good or for ill, a focus that impacted on the political ideology of both Mussolini and Hitler, who read Le Bon with great interest, this aspect is of less interest in our context than the actual constitution of the crowd itself.[7]

Race appears as a variable in the construction of the crowd but in a manner clearly defined by the importance of the science of race in contemporary psychological and social theory. For Le Bon race is also one of the defining characteristics of the crowd:

> Whoever be the individuals that compose it, however like or unlike be their mode of life, their occupations, their character, or their intelligence, the fact that they have been transformed into a group puts them in possession of a sort of collective mind which makes them feel, think,

and act in a manner quite different from that in which each individual of them would feel, think, and act were he in a state of isolation. There are certain ideas and feelings, which do not come into being, or do not transform themselves into acts except in the case of individuals forming a group.[8]

For Le Bon, race stands in the "first rank" of those factors that help shape the underlying attitudes of the crowd. Racial character "possesses, as the result of the laws of heredity, such power that its beliefs, institutions, and arts—in a word, all the elements of its civilization—are merely outward expressions of its genius."[9] It shapes the crowd in its essence. Thus race theory and crowd theory become linked in what, to quote Le Bon, will be the "age [that] we are about to enter will in truth be the ERA OF CROWDS."[10] In more than one way he was quite correct. But it will take a major shift in crowd theory for race to become a psychopathological aspect of the mob rather than an attribute of the crowd.

While the impact of Gustave Le Bon's definition of the crowd was immediate and striking in all of the discussions of group action, it was with World War I that the question of racism was first raised.[11] What made the Germans or the French or the British hate the British or the French or the Germans? Part of the tone had been set by the discovery of Friedrich Nietzsche's work on the "herd" among the broadest audience in these three countries (as well as the United States).[12] For Nietzsche (and for Søren Kierkegaard before him) the "herd," the masses, function only as a mindless collective to be dominated by a strong (and charismatic) leader ("The ideas of the herd should rule in the herd," says Nietzsche, "and not reach out beyond it").[13] Slave morality (he takes the term from Hegel) is the morality of the herd and it is fine for the herd, but should not bind the higher man, the "superman."

Given Nietzsche's view that Judaism and Christianity encouraged such views, antisemitism was for him the classic case of herd mentality in his time. The herd mentality of Nietzsche's "aristocratic radicalism" was a central topic of Danish Jewish critic Georg Brandes's (1842–1927) lectures on Nietzsche in 1888. The lectures were the first exposition of Nietzsche's work and were widely translated (as was Nietzsche's work) at the beginning of the new century. Brandes writes of Nietzsche's view that the herd impulse is to be resisted:

On entering life, then, young people meet with various collective opinions, more or less narrow-minded. The more the individual has it in him to become a real personality, the more he will resist following a herd. But even if an inner voice says to him; "Become thyself! Be thyself!" he hears its appeal with despondency. Has he a self? He does not know; he is not yet aware of it. He therefore looks about for a teacher, an educator, one who will teach him, not something foreign, but how to become his own individual self.[14]

When Le Bon's crowd is polemically translated into the Nietzschean herd during World War I, it is the morality of the crowd that is placed in question, as the focus is on the psychology of the herd. The powerful association of Germans, German political action, and the image of the herd in Nietzsche's work colors the Allied psychological studies on the Germans as part of a destructive, amoral herd.

Certainly the most important of these works was by the British neurosurgeon Wilfred Trotter. Beginning in 1908, and then with the publication of his major work, *Instincts of the Herd in Peace and War*, at the beginning of the war in 1914, he examined the question of the psychology of German group consciousness in detail.[15] Historians, without any irony, have labeled this interest a form of "Germanophobia."[16] Trotter's analysis of the German mind asks why the Germans (he creates this category as the antithesis to the English) hate the way they do: "England and Germany face one another as perhaps the two most typical antagonists of the war. It may seem but a partial way of examining events if we limit our consideration to them. Nevertheless, it is in this duel that the material we are concerned with is chiefly to be found, and it may be added Germany herself has abundantly distinguished this country as her typical foe—an instinctive judgment not without value."[17] Yet it is only Germany that provides a case study of the herd mentality:

Germany affords a profoundly interesting study for the biological psychologist, and it is very important that we should not allow what clearness of representation we can get into our picture of her mind to be clouded by the heated atmosphere of national feeling in which our work must be done.... In making an attempt to estimate the relative moral resources of England and Germany at the present time it is necessary to consider them as biological entities or major units of the human species in the sense of that term we have already repeatedly used. We shall have to examine the evolutionary tendencies, which each of these units has shown, and if possible to decide how far they have followed the lines of development which psychological theory indicates to be those of healthy and progressive development for a gregarious animal.[18]

The fantasies of the healthy versus the ill, the moral versus the corrupt, the belligerent versus the pacifistic tendencies of Darwinian man are played out by Trotter in the contrast between the English and the German mindsets as seen by the neutral scientific observer.

It is solely Germany that functions as a herd: "It is one of the features of the present crisis that gives to it its biological significance, that one of the antagonists—Germany—has discovered the necessity and value of conscious direction of the social unit. This is in itself an epoch-making event. Like many other human discoveries of similar importance, it has been incomplete, and it has not been accompanied by the corresponding knowledge of man and his natural history, which alone could have given it full fertility and permanent value."[19] He describes the psychological makeup of the German herd thus:

The national arrogance of the German is at the same time peculiarly sensitive and peculiarly obtuse. It is readily moved by praise or blame, though that be the most perfunctory and this the most mild, but it has no sense of a public opinion outside the pack. It is easily aroused to rage by external criticism, and when it finds its paroxysms make it ridiculous to the spectator it cannot profit by the information but becomes, if possible, more angry. It is quite unable to understand that to be moved to rage by an enemy is as much a proof of slavish automatism as to be moved to fear by him. The really extraordinary hatred for England is, quite apart from the obvious association of its emotional basis with fear, a most interesting phenomenon. The fact that it was possible to organize so unanimous a howl shows very clearly, how fully the psychological mechanisms of the wolf were in action. It is most instructive to find eminent men of science and philosophers bristling and baring their teeth with the rest, and would be another proof, if such were needed, of the infinite insecurity of the hold of reason in the most carefully cultivated minds when it is opposed by strong herd feeling. It is important, however, not to judge the functional value of these phenomena of herd arrogance and herd irritability and convulsive rage from the point of view of nations of the socialized gregarious type such as ourselves. To us they would be disturbants of judgment, and have no corresponding emotional recompense. In the wolf pack, however, they are indigenous, and represent a normal mechanism for inciting national enthusiasm and unity.[20]

In what readers should note has a particular relevance for our subject, Trotter had perhaps the smartest of all the approaches to the study of the collective mind, and his work has a great impact after the war on thinkers in Britain about group dynamics such as Wilfred Bion. However, Trotter, and those who adapt crowd theory to explain the mindset of the enemy, is not speaking of racism. He is speaking of *character*, or what differentiates the Germans from "civilized" nations. The nature of the German mind is defined by its irrational hatred of, in this case, the British and all that they stand for. The German crowd is seen as an exaggeration of the normal:

> In her negotiations with other peoples, and her estimates of national character, Germany shows the characteristic features of her psychological type in a remarkable way. It appears to be a principal thesis of hers that altruism is, for the purposes of the statesman, non-existent, or if it exists is an evidence of degeneracy and a source of weakness. The motives upon which a nation acts are, according to her, self-interest and fear, and in no particular has her "strangeness" been more fully shown than in the frank way in which she appeals to both, either alternately or together.[21]

Trotter sees the German mind as defined by discipline and regards this as "infantile" as opposed to the more mature character of civilized nations. It is atavistic in nature, more the disposition of the wolf pack than the nation.

The reader should recognize that Trotter is interested in dominant and subservient nations. Thus he turns to the Jews as an example of what happens when powerful nations come to lose their superior role:

Thus we see society cleft by the instinctive qualities of its members into two great classes, each to a great extent possessing what the other lacks, and each falling below the possibilities of human personality. The effect of the gradual increase of the unstable in society can be seen to a certain extent in history. We can watch it through the careers of the Jews. . . . At first, when the bulk of the citizens were of the stable type, the nation was enterprising, energetic, indomitable, but hard, inelastic, and fanatically convinced of its Divine mission. The inevitable effect of the expansion of experience which followed success was that development of the unstable and skeptical which ultimately allowed the nation, no longer believing in itself or its gods, to become the almost passive prey of more stable peoples.[22]

Here Trotter postulates one of the reasons for the status of the Jews (he never speaks of their madness) as weaker than the other nations of the world. It accounts for Jewish submissiveness to the stronger and more aggressive nations such as the Germans.

Even more political is the approach in *The Group Mind* (1920) by William McDougall, one of the leading social psychologists of the day. For McDougall it is the question of the constitution of the collective unconscious that is central:

Do the Poles share in the "collective consciousness" of the German nation, or the Bavarians in that of Prussia? Or do the Irish or the Welsh contribute their share to that of the English nation? Coming now to close quarters with the doctrine, we may ask those who . . . regard the "collective consciousness" as a bond which unites the members of a society and makes of them one living individual,—Is this "collective consciousness" merely epiphenomenal in character?[23]

Thus he sees the Germans as an organism, functioning with a collective psyche as reflected in their state organizations:

As regards the mass of the people, the position of each individual in the organism of the German nation is officially determined by the written and codified law of the State; all personal status and relations are formally determined by official positions in this recently created system. Almost every individual carries about some badge or uniform indicating his position within the system. In England, the status and relations of individuals are determined by factors a thousand times more subtle and complex, involving many vaguely conceived and undefined traditions and sentiments. In Germany, it is almost true to say, if a man has no official position he has no position at all.[24]

It is clear that all these attempts to locate the German mind have a strong psychodynamic quality. Trotter was a strong supporter of the importation of Sigmund Freud's psychodynamic theory before 1914:

> The most remarkable attack upon the problems of psychology, which has been made from the purely human standpoint is that in which the rich genius of Sigmund Freud was and still is the pioneer. The school which his work has founded was concerned at first wholly with the study of abnormal mental states, and came into notice as a branch of medicine finding the verification of its principles in the success it laid claim to in the treatment of certain mental diseases.[25]

McDougall commented that his own work prior to the war was impacted,

> especially the development of psycho-pathology, stimulated so greatly by the esoteric dogmas of the Freudian school. . . . The only test and verification to which any scheme of human nature can be submitted is the application of it to practice in the elucidation of the concrete phenomena of human life and in the control and direction of conduct, especially in the two great fields of medicine and education.[26]

Freud turned to the question of mass psychology and the herd to no little degree because of Trotter's work and the animus he felt that it contained, which "does not entirely escape the antipathies that were set loose by the recent great war."[27]

A psychopathology of character that leads to hatred and violence forms the context for these debates. What is important is that the crowd provides a definition of the psychopathological context for a group definition of those who act not only immorally but also psychopathologically. Clinical psychiatry of the 1920s usually avoids this leap even in writings about mass psychosis. The British psychiatrist Theodore Hyslop in his 1925 study of mass hysteria begins by claiming:

> [The] history of the world is covered by shadows of beliefs germinated endemically and in ignorance. Social requirements and traditions have given rise to the most diverse religions, views and modes of life. Herein we have to consider how members of a society may combine to predispose to the genesis of a morbid mental condition, and how in the struggle for existence the stronger often seeks to carry off the prey from the weaker.[28]

Hyslop avoids any discussion of the war, the Germans, and the crowd, however, and instead focuses on outbreaks of mass hysteria such as the dancing mania of the early modern period. Only at the conclusion of the quoted chapter does Hyslop move to the political: "During the Russian revolution the transports of hysterical indecency indulged in by the women was somewhat analogous to the lust for blood shown by the women *tricoteuses* in the French revolution."[29] Here it is gender, not race, that defines mass hysteria. This is as close as any of the clinical psychiatrists of the 1920s get to describing the madness of the crowd. Indeed, even clinical psychiatrists whose work is informed by psychoanalysis, including Henry Dicks, who later becomes a major figure in attempting to provide a psychiatric evaluation for leading Nazis such as Rudolf Hess, fail to engage with this topic in clinical work of the era.[30]

The understanding that collectives possess a mass psychology that can become pathological is not limited to the post–Le Bon history of the crowd. The German Jewish scholars Moritz Lazarus and his brother-in-law Hermann Steinthal coined the term "*Völkerpsychologie*" (ethnic psychology) in the 1860s.[31] Rooted in linguist and explorer Wilhelm von Humboldt's work on language and thought, they developed a notion of a malleable ethnic psychology determined and expressed by language, where language was understood not as a biological quality of a human being as something that was learned and which changed both the mental set of the speaker as a member of a cohort and "the psychological nature" of that cohort.[32] Certainly the most important advocate of this at the close of the nineteenth century was the founder of experimental psychology Wilhelm Wundt, whose massive study of ethnic psychology took place between 1890 and 1920. Wundt defined ethnic psychology as the complement to individual psychology. By the close of the century this notion of a malleable collective psyche had been integrated into a racial psychology by popular thinkers such as Houston Stewart Chamberlain, who claimed that language and culture were both biological and immutable. By World War I such discussions had merged with notions of the crowd in German popular and scientific thought.[33]

By 1914 even Wundt had been captured by this notion of the collective mind as the source of psychopathological attitudes that lead to war (though, by the way, he strongly disavowed the war that erupted in Europe that year). In *The Nations and Their Philosophy—A Contribution to the World War* (1915) he attempted to describe "the war of minds, conducted silently but at times as bitterly as the war of arms."[34] He confessed that to him "the philosophy of German idealism has proven itself in the changing fates of individuals as well as of nations." But he found in the collective those qualities that lead to destruction: for the French "honor" and "glory" were the "values of life to be most highly appreciated." For the English it was "power and domination." The highest value of the Germans, on the other hand, was "duty." "It is the sense of duty which the German transfers from his peaceful occupation into the war where it becomes for him the noblest of all duties, the duty of sacrificing himself for the fatherland."[35] For Wundt, "England as a state is despotic, treacherous and underhanded" as is the individual Englishman and the Germans suffer "from false modesty."[36] The role of war provides insight into the healthy German mind:

> We shall learn three things [from this war]. The first derives from the unconditional trust which we may put in our much decried militarism. . . . No, we shall not follow the advice of our enemies to abandon our militarism. We shall be in need of it in the future, not only to be armed on land and on the sea in order to preserve the peace, but also because universal military training has become a means of education which provides physical training and an attitude of duty for our youth. German military service like German gymnastics is a genuinely democratic institution, other than sports through which the wealthy young people of England satisfy their need for physical exercise and for a stimulating pass-time.[37]

For Wundt in 1915 there are healthy and diseased minds. And the German collective is a healthy and productive one.

At the same moment the philosopher Max Scheler, whose refunctioning of Nietzsche's concept of *ressentiment* echoes through the early-twentieth-century understanding of the crowd, argues again for a healthy and diseased mass psychology. In his *The Genius of War and the German War* he called the war the "unique event in the moral world—the noblest of its kind since the French Revolution."[38] It is "folly and baseness to regard war as mass slaughter."[39] It is only the collective mind, the mind of the state (now a rational substitute for the crowd) that is engaged in war:

> Wars are conducted not against individuals but against states following a preceding declaration and a voluntary agreement. The principal goal of war is the disarming of the enemy state, or rather of its government, not the killing of men. . . . Such killing is a killing without hatred, a killing even with the attitude of respect. . . . Hatred of the enemy is an entirely alien element of true war.[40]

Scheler justifies World War I as "highly characteristic of the great principles of culture which have proven themselves in history [and] are standing behind the fighting powers."[41] For Scheler, the Germans are psychologically healthy, a "world folk," "a cosmopolitan folk, the national quality of which is this great world-gathering force, this great power of love and understanding of everything human, nay of everything living."[42]

Scheler published his *The Reasons for the Hatred against the Germans—A National-Pedagogical Discourse* in 1917.[43] In it, he distinguishes German militarism from its "enemy" counterparts: "Since our glorious victory of 1870 and 1871," there are "nations with predominantly utilitarian militarism"—Germany's enemies, of course—and the Germans with their "militarism from conviction."[44] Militarism from conviction "resembles a work of art more than a tool," and, ultimately, "militarism from conviction hence is the one which can go together with the greatest love of peace."[45] The conviction of the German people is, for Scheler, evidence they are advanced, and, importantly, healthy:

We Germans are the most democratic people of the world as far as social values and feelings are concerned . . . in which the principle of personality development [*Bildung*], democratic in its origin, unfolds the greatest force in the organization of society. . . . The German heart is tender and soft and hence only capable of that great and worldwide understanding which makes up the nation of Herder, Goethe, Leopold von Ranke, the folk of *"Geisteswissenschaften."* Under a rough shell the German heart is Greek, nay almost Indian in the noble capacity to open its soul in order to conceive the great image of the world in purity.[46]

The defense against being labeled psychopathological, epitomized by Scheler, is indeed a form of romantic reversal. All that is condemned is praised; all that is pathological is healthy.

For the Austrian Jew Sigmund Freud, at first a supporter of the war effort who became gradually disillusioned by it, group hatred cannot be nationally defined. Responding to the rise of crowd theory during World War I and the appropriation of psychodynamic models in it, Freud's work describes group hatred as resulting from the psychological conflicts arising from social proximity.[47] Most importantly it is in Freud's essay on "Group Psychology and the Analysis of the Ego," published in 1921, that he writes the clearest response to the anti-German use of group theory by his British followers during the war. There he comes to terms with the anti-German rhetoric of crowd theory on the part of psychoanalytically informed writers such as Trotter and MacDougall as well as acknowledges the "German" side of the argument. Freud notes:

Group psychology is therefore concerned with the individual man as a member of a race, of a nation, of a caste, of a profession, of an institution, or as a component part of a crowd of people who have been organized into a group at some particular time for some definite purpose. When once natural continuity has been severed in this way, if a breach is thus made between things which are by nature interconnected, it is easy to regard the phenomena that appear under these special conditions as being expressions of a special instinct that is not further reducible—the social instinct ("herd instinct," "group mind"), which does not come to light in any other situations. But we may perhaps venture to object that it seems difficult to attribute to the factor of number a significance so great as to make it capable by itself of arousing in our mental life a new instinct that is otherwise not brought into play. Our expectation is therefore directed towards two other possibilities: that the social instinct may not be a primitive one and insusceptible of dissection, and that it may be possible to discover the beginnings of its development in a narrower circle, such as that of the family.[48]

For Freud it is this web of associations that ties the individual to the crowd but that also provides any given individual with the ability to transcend this association:

> Each individual is a component part of numerous groups, he is bound by ties of identification in many directions, and he has built up his ego ideal upon the most various models. Each individual therefore has a share in numerous group minds—those of his race, of his class, of his creed, of his nationality, etc.—and he can also raise himself above them to the extent of having a scrap of independence and originality. Such stable and lasting group formations, with their uniform and constant effects, are less striking to an observer than the rapidly formed and transient groups from which Le Bon has made his brilliant psychological character sketch of the group mind. And it is just in these noisy ephemeral groups, which are as it were superimposed upon the others, that we are met by the prodigy of the complete, even though only temporary, disappearance of exactly what we have recognized as individual acquirements.[49]

Race, for Freud, following Le Bon, is a variable in constituting the crowd, but it is not pathological. Rather, it is one of the factors that define humanness. This is one of the rare moments when Freud, who objected to the very concept of a biological "race" as early as the marginal notes he made in his university textbooks, employs the category of race. It is clear that he is doing so because of his reading of Le Bon.[50]

Differences between groups, according to Freud, combined with close physical proximity, produces "insuperable repugnance":

> Every time two families become connected by a marriage, each of them thinks itself superior to or of better birth than the other. Of two neighbouring towns each is the other's most jealous rival; every little canton

looks down upon the others with contempt. Closely related races keep one another at arm's length; the South German cannot endure the North German, the Englishman casts every kind of aspersion upon the Scot, the Spaniard despises the Portuguese. We are no longer astonished that greater differences should lead to an almost insuperable repugnance, such as the Gallic people feel for the German, the Aryan for the Semite, and the white races for the coloured.[51]

Thus the image of racism here is a natural extension of social relationships. The term "repugnance" reflects the impact of the thinking of the Finnish philosopher and sociologist Edvard Westermarck and his understanding of the rejection of incest as a result of social proximity rather than any inherent anxiety about biological mutations. Ironically, such views are echoed in a number of quarters, among them the eugenics movement (as shown below), to explain the revulsion in response to "miscegenation" between the Aryan or white and "lesser" races. The consequences of close contact among Germans with Jews, and among whites with nonwhites in the United States during the early twentieth century, were viewed as potentially pathological.

Repugnance and Race in the United States and Germany

The rediscovery of Mendelian genetics in the early twentieth century partnered with the ongoing eugenics movement in both Europe and the United States to lend scientific merit to what at the time were widespread beliefs in racial differences (and racial superiority) among scientists and laypersons. As a result, within the United States there was a systematic attempt to formulate and implement a number of social policies aimed at controlling the prevalence of "inferior" races among the general population.[52] As Kenneth Ludmerer has argued, this rediscovery modified U.S. geneticists' approach to eugenics during the period 1905–1915. Their enthusiasm waned between 1915 and 1924, although, as Ludmerer notes, they did not "publically condemn eugenics."[53] The tension between the laboratory science, focusing on fruit flies, and the social claims of both positive and negative eugenics still echoes well into the twenty-first century.[54]

Perhaps no case better exemplifies the early-twentieth-century American taste for eugenic testing, policy development, and the "pathological" explanation of racial differences as that of Henry Goddard. Considered by some to be the primary catalyst behind the intelligence testing industry that arose in the mid-twentieth century, Goddard accepted a position with the New Jersey Training School for Feeble-Minded Girls and Boys in 1906.[55] Edward R. Johnstone, acting head of the school following the death of its founder, Stephen Garrison, had created the Psychological Research Laboratory that same year, and had sought out Goddard to be its first director. Though charged with conducting studies of feeble-minded children, Goddard admitted he had no expertise in this field.

Goddard sought to catch up quickly in the summer of 1908, when he went to Europe to study the methods of European researchers working with mentally challenged children. Here he became familiar with an instrument developed by Alfred Binet just a few years prior, and began implementing the test among the children at Vineland as well as New Jersey public schools upon his return.[56] By December 1908, five months removed from his trip to Europe, Goddard published his own version of Binet's instrument in two academic journal articles, "The Binet and Simon Tests of Intellectual Capacity," which outlined the instrument, and "The Grading of Backward Children," on its use within school settings.[57] The use of the test spread rapidly from this point forward. By 1911, it was being introduced among public schools throughout New Jersey, and by 1913 Goddard was administering the test among immigrants arriving at Ellis Island as part of government efforts to prevent the spread of feeblemindedness, imbecility, and other "diseases" associated with undesirable Southern and Eastern European (read: Jewish) populations.[58]

Goddard's use of his test at Ellis Island was a result of the enormous popularity of his 1912 book *The Kallikak Family*.[59] Here, Goddard wrote of a family whose origins in the United States dated to an American Revolutionary War veteran who married a "worthy" Quaker woman, but also was having an extramarital affair with a "feeble-minded tavern girl." According to Goddard, descendants of the marriage to the Quaker woman had produced normally functioning generations of adults, whereas the extramarital relations with the tavern woman had produced generations of imbeciles and criminals. The book's empirical foundation was shoddy at best, but it framed the harm that could come from intermingling with populations of lesser "stock" in a moral way. The book became quite popular among eugenicists of Goddard's era, including many with close or direct ties to the U.S. Congress, which helps explain how he was able to establish an intelligence-testing program at Ellis Island the following year.

In implementing the intelligence-testing program, Goddard instructed his assistants to bypass immigrants at Ellis Island who appeared "obviously normal," and instead choose individuals from the mass of "average immigrants" for testing purposes.[60] He and his research assistants selected thirty-five Jews, twenty-two Hungarians, fifty Italians, and forty-five Russians upon whom to administer his English-language test. Generalizing his findings to these immigrant populations as a whole, Goddard concluded that 80 percent of Hungarians, 79 percent of Italians, 87 percent of Russians, and 83 percent of Jews were "morons."[61] He ignored the fact that many of the immigrants being tested did not speak English, that many were unaware of the cultural norms that underlay his test, and that these immigrants were generally exhausted, confused, and to some extent fearful upon arriving at Ellis Island. Nevertheless, the results led Goddard to conclude that Southern and Eastern European countries were sending the United States "the poorest of each race." As a result, he began advocating strongly in both his scholarship and his public engagements for more restrictive immigration controls at the federal level.

By 1912, the debate over immigration restrictions had become so heated in New York that the state mental health authority blamed the rapid rise of inmates in the state asylums on "immigration [that] is chiefly responsible for the alarmingly large increase in the number of foreign born (Eastern and Southern European) insane in State hospitals." This in turn had led to "a tremendously heavy [economic] burden on the State." Morris Waldman, the manager of the United Hebrew Charities, responded that the increase was very much in line with the relative increase of the overall population and that native-born inmates had increased at a greater rate over the period, while "the foreign born have contributed a decreasing portion of the population." He noted the extraordinarily high rate of the insane in Washington, D.C., which "might lead superficial observers to the conclusion that Federal politics is conducive to insanity." But the increase "is probably due to the existence of a Federal hospital for insane soldiers."[62] In spite of such counterarguments refuting his claims, Goddard became one of the most vocal proponents of the 1924 Johnson-Reed Act, which was partly inspired by the fact that its congressional advocates invoked many of Goddard's papers, including *The Kallikak Family*.

The Johnson-Reed Act, composed by Congressman Albert Johnson (Washington) and Senator David Reed (Pennsylvania), was specifically designed to halt the immigration of Italians and Eastern European Jews, identified by Goddard and others as members of "lesser races," yet whose U.S. numbers had roughly tripled from 1900 to 1920.[63] The Johnson-Reed Act scaled back the number of immigrants allowable from each country to reflect their percentages of the U.S. population in the 1890 Census, when the dominant proportion of European immigrants came from Northern and Western Europe, that is, the "good whites." So, for example, under this new law, the quota for Southern and Eastern European immigrants was reduced from 45 percent to 15 percent of all immigrants. Signing the bill into law, President Calvin Coolidge made its intention clear: "America must be kept American."[64]

To be clear, the Johnson-Reed Act was only one in a long line of congressional bills intended to preserve the nativist racial and ethnic makeup of the United States.[65] In 1882, Congress passed the Chinese Exclusion Act, which suspended all immigration of Chinese laborers for a period of ten years, and disallowed any federal court to admit Chinese immigrants for citizenship; this act was not repealed until 1943. Fears about Asian immigrants on the grounds of their medical, moral, and racial fitness soon extended to others. By the early 1900s, the new theory of eugenics began to incorporate theories of racial superiority to augment the views that the criminal and "feebleminded" had become a drain on the American economy. Put forward most powerfully in Richard Louis Dugdale's 1877 study of a family in New York's Ulster County, *The Jukes: A Study in Crime, Pauperism, Disease and Heredity*, the eugenic claim was that such criminal and mentally defective families undermined American productivity through multiple generations of reproduction. The claim quickly transformed into the view that certain immigrant groups, like the Jukes, had higher rates of illness, criminality, and "feeblemindedness" that became exponentially more corrupting over generations. The American Eugenics Society disseminated their beliefs through provocative images, like the flashing light signs that appeared as part of "Fitter Family" contests at eugenics fairs across the country in the 1920s. These displays would feature several lights that flashed at different intervals, with provocative claims associated with each interval. For example, at one such contest in 1926, one part of a sign read, "This light flashes every 15 seconds. Every 15 seconds, $100 of your money goes for the care of persons with bad heredity such as the insane, feeble-minded, criminals, and other defectives."[66] Using these images and others, eugenicists attempted to convince a captive audience that selectivity in human breeding, including through immigration, would weed out those who burdened, rather than benefited, society. These ideas quickly gained traction, influencing new immigration restrictions, and culminating in the Immigration Act of 1924.

Three years prior to the passage of the Johnson-Reed Act, Congress had signed into law the Emergency Quota Act of 1921, establishing immigration quotas for several European and Asian nation-states based upon the number of foreign-born residents of each nationality living in the United States as of the 1910 U.S. Census.[67] The Johnson-Reed Act of 1924 was meant to replace the Emergency Quota Act with even more extreme immigration restrictions, in part by using the "scientific evidence" from American eugenicists about the threat of an "impure" American racial stock.

The question of racial intelligence, however, was certainly not limited to immigrants. From the passage of the Johnson-Reed Act to the 1952 Immigration and Nationality Act that revised quotas to reflect immigrant proportions from the 1920 Census, Congress produced numerous pieces of social policy centered on prohibiting potential threats to racial purity from *outside*. Simultaneously, during this same period, numerous states passed their own sets of laws meant to maintain racial separation *within* their territorial boundaries. A great number of these laws, broadly referred to as *anti-miscegenation laws*, focused on preventing both marriage and sexual contact between whites and "lesser races." The object was to prevent the reproduction of mixed ethnic and racial bloodlines, and reduce what was perceived to be the potential for various mental, physical, and social deformities that would follow.

While the prevention of sexual contact among whites and nonwhites was the concern of eugenicists and some public policy officials of this period, for legal purposes, marriage was often the focus of many of these laws.[68] This was due to the fact that marriage carried with it a degree of social respectability for the couple and their offspring as well as several economic benefits. Appeals courts adjudicated the legal issue of miscegenation as frequently in civil cases centered on marriage, divorce, paternity/maternity, and inheritance as in criminal cases concerning sexual misconduct.[69] Of the forty-one states and territories that prohibited interracial marriage at some point in their history prior to *Loving v. Virginia* in 1967, twenty-two states also had legal restrictions against interracial/interethnic sex. New York, though not prohibiting interracial marriage, legally prohibited interracial/interethnic sexual contact.[70]

The first laws criminalizing interracial sexual contact, including marriage, within what is now the United States were enacted among the colonies of Maryland and Virginia, in 1664 and 1691, respectively. By the 1930s, forty-one states employed eugenic categories and evidence in restricting interracial/interethnic sexual contact, not just among racial and ethnic groups, but also "lunatics," "imbeciles," "idiots," and the "feebleminded."[71] By the mid-twentieth century, in several of these states blood tests had become a standard legal prerequisite for marriage. In 1924, the same year that the Johnson-Reed Act was passed, Virginia passed one of the most restrictive anti-miscegenation laws in U.S. history, with a great deal of help from eugenicists. The Racial Integrity Act mandated it was unlawful for any white man or woman to marry a nonwhite man or woman, with "white" being defined as having "*no trace whatsoever of any blood other than Caucasian.*"[72] The single-drop-of-blood rule, in the absence of any realistic definition of "Caucasian" and given the social reality of "passing" in American society, meant that the law was simply a club aimed at visibly different minorities. It was ideology framed by the claims of the biological science of its day. One of the eugenic claims was that such marriages produced more insane offspring, which damaged the economic fabric of society. As early as 1909, for example, "the American Breeders Association [had created] subcommittees . . . for different human defects, such as insanity, feeblemindedness, criminality, hereditary pauperism and race mongrelization."[73] Such projects led directly to the creation of the Cold Spring Harbor eugenics laboratory on Long Island.

In addition to anti-miscegenation laws, states implemented forced sterilization practices as a method of population control, primarily targeting poor women and racialized immigrant groups. The justification was usually related to forms of mental illness (such as chronic depression) or developmental disorders or mental deficiency (feeblemindedness). In 1907, Indiana became the first state to pass laws allowing for forced sterilization of populations deemed "socially inadequate"; Connecticut followed suit in 1909.[74] This presaged the increased somatization of madness across the twentieth century. Medicine attributed more and more symptoms to specific neurological deficits such as dementia. Developmental disorders came to be sorted out from illnesses with complex neurological causes—reductively dividing environmental diseases from genetic ones, for example—and those diseases seen as purely illness of the spirit, the psyche, or the mind were still further separated out. Thus the idiot and the lunatic, often housed in the same state institution through the nineteenth century, were by the early twentieth century seen as manifesting quite different social and medical causes.[75]

Indeed, biological interventions such as sterilization dealt with such individuals not to aid them but to improve society by eliminating their ability to reproduce. In the 1927 *Buck v. Bell* ruling that upheld the constitutionality of such laws, U.S. Supreme Court justice Oliver Wendell Holmes, Jr., concluded in affirming the Commonwealth of Virginia's eugenic sterilization law: "It is better for all the world, if instead of waiting to execute degenerate offspring for crime, or to let them starve for their imbecility, society can prevent those who are manifestly unfit from continuing their kind. The principle that sustains compulsory vaccination is broad enough to cover cutting the Fallopian tubes. Three generations of imbeciles are enough."[76] Biological definitions of madness generated a wide range of biological interventions to limit and control madness. What was key to the ruling, and this was the state's purpose of using Carrie Bell, a white Virginia woman declared to be feebleminded, as the test case, was that this was not to be seen as part of American racial politics even though involuntary sterilization disproportionately affected black Americans.[77] Negative eugenics was presented as race blind; it never was.

The Supreme Court's *Buck v. Bell* ruling had an enormous impact on the subsequent passage of compulsory sterilization laws throughout the

United States. By 1935, twenty-nine states had passed bills allowing the forced sterilization of almost twenty-two thousand individuals, a disproportionate number of them nonwhite and poor. Most states discontinued compulsory sterilization practices by the mid-1960s, with one notable exception: Oregon, which conducted its last forcible sterilization in 1981![78]

In Germany, meanwhile, the link between the new genetics and eugenics of intermarriage was also powerful. German eugenics incorporated genetics into its racial argument as early as 1913 when Eugen Fischer, who was later to have a major role in Nazi eugenic politics as director of the Kaiser Wilhelm Institute for Anthropology, published his study *The Rehoboth Bastards and the Problem of Miscegenation among Humans*—an investigation of the biological effects of racial intermarriage between Dutch settlers and native Khoi Khoi (Hottentots) in German Southwest Africa (Namibia). His argument, that the product of such relationships suffered from greater rates of mental illness and developmental disorders, used American studies as part of its scientific basis. Fischer's study was subsequently billed as the first successful demonstration of Mendelism in a human population, although that claim has been recently and rightfully called into question.[79]

The scientific debates about "mixed race" individuals and their proclivity for or resistance to specific forms of illness that used the American models concerning intermarriage with blacks and claimed that the offspring of such relationships had higher incidences of mental illness have their parallel in the eugenic debates within Europe about the Jews as a race. While an assimilationist such as German chancellor Otto von Bismarck declared in 1892 that "the Jews bring to the mixture of the different German tribes a certain *mousseaux* [sparkle], which should not be underestimated," this was not as benign as it sounds.[80] He spoke quite openly about "putting a Jewish mare to a Christian stallion of German breed." The eugenic goal, as Bismarck notes, is "that to prevent mischief, the Jews will have to be rendered innocuous by cross breeding."[81] Stronger races trump weaker races.

Antisemitic writers of the late nineteenth century such as Max Brewer and Richard Wagner's widely read son-in-law Stewart Houston Chamberlain, on the other hand, saw the root of much of the weakness of the Jewish body and character as a result from the mixed-race status of the Jews.[82] For them the Jews could not be a pure race, like the Aryans, but were rather a "mongrel" mixture of the worst of all races. Jewish anthropologists at the turn of the century, such as Elias Auerbach, seem to echo these views about the weakness of the mixed race in regard to the offspring of Jewish intermarriages in Europe and the United States.[83] Expressing a view typical of German Zionists, the sociologist Arthur Ruppin argued in 1913 that "the descendants of a mixed marriage are not likely to have any remarkable gifts. . . . Intermarriage being clearly detrimental to the preservation of the high qualities of the race, it follows that it is necessary to try and prevent it and preserve Jewish separatism."[84] For Ruppin and other Zionists, agricultural work wasn't the lowest form of productivity as Samuel A. Cartwright had implied it was in relation to black Americans; the labor that would debase whites if they were forced to do it would improve the health of the Jews. Ruppin writes in his diary during 1898:

> Only a *Volk* engaged in agriculture can be healthy, only a state with the majority of its people engaged in agriculture comprises a firmly bound, organized whole. Agriculture is the well-spring of mankind. England and other states (whose agricultural populations are steadily declining) will always present only an aggregate of individual people who have been haphazardly thrown together.[85]

The debates about health and productivity were often placed within the tense arguments concerning the mutability of national identity and race.

In 1933, shortly after its seizure of power, Germany's Nazi government adopted the Law for Protection against Genetically Defective Offspring, providing the legal basis for sterilizations in Germany. Fischer had authored textbooks on eugenics in the 1920s and early 1930s and his coauthored 1936 handbook *Human Heredity Theory and Racial Hygiene* summarized the scientific basis for Nazi eugenic policies. Introduced at the very end of the Weimar Republic under Fischer's influence, the 1933 law echoed American eugenic policies toward the mentally ill and was supported by parties of the left, center, and right.[86] It was based on the California statute of sterilization inspired by Harry Laughlin's 1922 study of American sterilization policy, *Eugenical Sterilization in the*

United States. The scientists involved in drafting the law cited Goddard's work on the Kallikaks (well after he had withdrawn it) as well as the case of the Jukes as proof of the need to control the mentally ill and feebleminded.[87] It included as subjects for eugenic sterilization the feebleminded, the insane, criminals, epileptics, alcoholics, blind persons, deaf persons, deformed persons, and indigent persons. The Nazi law ordered the sterilization of "any person with a hereditary disease" and among those diseases were a wide range of forms of mental illnesses such as:

1. Congenital feeblemindedness
2. Schizophrenia
3. Circular (manic-depressive) insanity
4. Hereditary epilepsy
5. Hereditary Huntington's chorea[88]

In its first full year of operation, the Nazi program dramatically eclipsed activities in the United States, sterilizing about eighty thousand persons without their consent. Laughlin was given an honorary doctorate at Heidelberg in 1936 at the five hundredth anniversary of the university.

In 1935 the Nazis passed a series of eugenic laws inspired by their American models. The Law for the Protection of the Genetic Health of the German *Volk* (Healthy Marriage Law) forbade any marriage in which "either party, regardless of whether he has been declared legally incapacitated, suffers from mental illness which renders the marriage undesirable for the *Volk* community."[89] The American miscegenation laws were redrafted in September of that year in the Law for the Protection of German Blood and German Honor, which read:

> [C]ompelled by recognition of the fact that the purity of German blood
> is the prerequisite to the survival of the German *Volk*, and inspired by the
> unflinching will to secure the future of the German nation in perpetuity,
> the *Reichstag* has unanimously passed the following law, which is hereby
> promulgated that (1) Marriages between Jews and nationals of German or
> related blood are forbidden. Marriages concluded in defiance of this law
> shall be considered null and void even if, for the purpose of circumvent-
> ing this law, they have been concluded abroad.[90]

The Nazis accepted both the premises and the structures of the American laws.[91] The "anti-miscegenation laws" had as their goals the purification of the race and the elimination of weak and ill offspring. In 1941 the Weimar social reformer turned popular Nazi writer on human sexuality Hugo Hertwig stressed the importance of avoiding hybridization as it was a product of modernity and technology—"[t]hese utterly preposterous, inferior, and dangerous racial crossbreeds we often see today have been made possible only by a technology that [enables us to] transcend time and space." Modernity enables the production of eugenic monsters that are inferior either because of their weakness or their illness. Germany has not precluded

> absorbing the blood of inferior races into our lines and have, therefore, banned marriages with people who are alien to the species of the German *Volk* (for example, with Jews). Such laws for the protection of the blood have also existed in previous nations, in the United States of America, for example, or in the South African Union, etc. These laws are designed to prevent arbitrary crossbreeding that violates the natural order and that is made possible only by technological advances.[92]

The avoidance of such crossbreeding strengthens the nation by eliminating various illnesses, including forms of insanity.

The result of such eugenic laws first became evident in the fall of 1939 when Hitler signed a secret order that "broaden[ed] the powers of designated physicians to the extent that persons who are suffering from diseases which may be deemed incurable according to standards of human judgment based on a careful examination of their condition shall be guaranteed a mercy." Thus "life unworthy of life" or "useless eaters" were to be killed. Conservatively, five thousand institutionalized mentally ill patients were murdered in six gassing installations in asylums as part of the "euthanasia" action: Brandenburg, on the Havel River near Berlin; Grafeneck in southwestern Germany; Bernburg and Sonnenstein, both in Saxony; Hartheim, near Linz on the Danube in Austria, and Hadamar in Hesse. As Henry Friedlander has well illustrated, racial theory played a major role here also.[93] Jewish patients in these asylums were at much greater risk of being murdered than the general population. The assumption of a Jewish danger to the body politic through race mixing involved an anxiety about a greater risk based in the claims of a Jewish predisposition for mental illness. After the war, in an ironic twist, German racial scholars such as Eugen Fischer, who continued to publish well into the 1950s, attempted to rewrite their country's history by appropriating the terms "pseudoscience" and "pseudogenetics" to distinguish the work of Nazi ideologists from their own, putatively scientific, activities.[94]

By the end of World War I the original image of the predisposition of Jews and blacks for mental illness becomes circumscribed as self-hatred in the psychological as well as the popular literature. Such structural explanations dominated theories of the psychopathology of racism even following the rise of political antisemitism in the 1890s and then its instantiation in Austrian and German politics in the early twentieth century. Jew hatred evident at the time is like all other forms of group antipathy, debunking Pinsker's view of it as a specific formation triggered by the "rootlessness" of the Jew, which was in turn caused by the inherent Christian (Western) hatred of the Jew: Judeophobia.

The Rise of the Nazis and Racism as the Disease of the German Mind

It is the shift to the *Realpolitik* of race in the early twentieth century that changes the equation. While fringe parties in Germany and the Austro-Hungarian Empire used antisemitism as a plank in their party platforms (even getting candidates elected to important positions, such as mayor of Vienna) it was not until the mid-1930s, with the rise of the Nazis in Germany after 1933 and of clerico-fascism in Austria after 1934, that Sigmund Freud develops a specific theory of the origins of a specific German racial madness as defined by antisemitism. This shift is important to note because it moves the discussion from the impact of race or character on the crowd (using the model of Le Bon) to a psychopathological theory of racism:

> We must not forget that all those peoples who excel today in their hatred of Jews became Christians only in late historic times, often driven to it by bloody coercion. It might be said that they are all "mis-baptized." They have been left, under a thin veneer of Christianity, what their ances-

tors were, who worshipped a barbarous polytheism. They have not got over a grudge against the new religion, which was imposed on them; but they have displaced the grudge on to the source from which Christianity reached them. The fact that the Gospels tell a story, which is set among Jews, and in fact deals only with Jews, has made this displacement easy for them. Their hatred of Jews is at bottom a hatred of Christians, and we need not be surprised that in the German National-Socialist revolution this intimate relation between the two monotheist religions finds such a clear expression in the hostile treatment of both of them.[95]

This account of the specificity of a German neurotic impulse that leads to antisemitism (and, for Freud, more centrally, to anti-Christian self-hatred projected onto the Jews) is found in his late work, *Moses and Monotheism*, begun in Vienna in the mid-1930s and finished in London after his exile in 1938. It is framed, however, by a more general theory of antisemitism, which has its roots in Jewish belief and practice.

As stated in *Moses and Monotheism*, Freud's view of the cause of antisemitism in general, beyond the specific German case, was that it was the result of the straitjacket of monotheism, which the Jews created out of Egyptian practices and which they then bequeathed to the world.[96] According to Freud's account, it was the Jews who killed their leader, the Egyptian Moses, rebelling against him, and came only later to regret his death and build into their rigid, monotheistic faith the idea of the redemptive power of a returned Messiah. Jewish religious practices grew out of the repression of the memory of this original bloodletting and are at the root of antisemitism, as Freud noted already in his analytic case study of the five-year old child called "Little Hans" in 1909: "The castration complex is the deepest root of anti-Semitism; for even in the nursery little boys hear that a Jew has something cut off his penis—a piece of his penis, they think—and this gives them a right to despise Jews."[97] (We would remind the reader of Paolo Mantegazza's late-nineteenth-century comments on the same phenomenon in Chapter One.) Freud's creation of a special case for the "mis-baptized" Germans as self-hating Christians illuminates how complex the question of the nature of prejudice for Freud. The academic acceptance of theories of racial inferiority and degeneracy is the source of racism that self-hatred seems to internalize. Freud makes this turn only very late in the 1930s after a number of thinkers had already provided not only theories of race madness but also potential therapies for it.

From 1933 onward, in works by the Austrian psychoanalyst Wilhelm Reich and others, the image of the mentally ill racist absorbs much of the interest in the psychology of race. Wilhelm Reich's *The Mass Psychology of Fascism* (1933) was the first truly systematic attempt to define the etiology of a psychology of racism. Reich, like a wide range of German thinkers in the 1920s including Max Horkheimer, Erich Fromm, and Kurt Lewin, attempted to bridge the gap between Marx (economic explanations of human action) and Freud (deep psychological ones). His success at bridging this gap can be measured by the fact that he was expelled from the German Communist Party early in 1933 because of the unapproved publication of a short pamphlet called "The Sexual Struggle of Youth," which ironically had first been excerpted in the official Communist Party publication, *Die Warte (The Lookout)*.[98] The irony is that the publication of *The Mass Psychology of Fascism* prompted the Danish Communist Party to announce that Reich was being expelled from the group, but Reich had never joined the Danish branch. In general the Communists did not like how *The Mass Psychology of Fascism* began by noting the "failure of the workers' movement in a phase of modern history in which, as the Marxists contend, 'the capitalist mode of production had become economically ripe for explosion.'"[99] Anna Freud and Ernest Jones were behind Reich's expulsion for political militancy from the International Psychoanalytic Association in 1934 after a hearing held by a high-level subcommittee of the IPA.[100] According to a recent historian, Reich's expulsion was due to the fear that his writing endangered the existence of the German Psychoanalytic Society and was implemented in order to avoid a ban on psychoanalysis by the Nazis.[101]

Reich's argument rests on a development of Freud's view of the repressive qualities of society. This was best articulated in Freud's essay "Civilized Sexual Morality and Modern Nervousness" (1908), intended to be readable by the general public, as well as his more technical *Three Essays on Sexuality* (1905). Reich linked Freud's views to Engels's argument about capitalism and its crippling of the individual through its creation of a "false consciousness." Such psychological analysis was offered to explain the inability of members of capitalist society to understand their own repression. For Reich it was the authoritarian nature of the capitalist family that inhibited sexual curiosity and created a specific character type that was easily dominated and controlled. Using Freud's model of superego formation, Reich saw capitalism as promoting the creation of an individual that was easily manipulated in the family and therefore easily subsumed to the demands of the crowd.[102]

Thus the crowd, now defined as the fascist state, is the product of the sexually repressive family. The family is the

> central *reactionary germ cell*, the most important place of reproduction of the reactionary and conservative individual. Being itself caused by the authoritarian system, the family becomes the most important institution for its conservation. In this connection, the findings of [Lewis H.] Morgan and of [Friedrich] Engels are still entirely correct.[103]

The therapy is the development of "a social ideology [that] changes man's psychic structure, [in that] it has not only reproduced itself in man but, what is more significant, has become an active force, a material power in man, who in turn has become concretely changed, and, as a consequence thereof, acts in a different and contradictory fashion."[104] This view challenged Freud's statement in *Civilization and Its Discontents* (1930), where he wrote against the view of those psychoanalysts who tried to incorporate the view of the historical materialists such as Friedrich Engels. Freud writes,

> [A]ggressiveness was not created by property. It reigned almost without limit in primitive times, when property was still very scanty, and it already shows itself in the nursery almost before property has given up its primal, anal form. . . . If we were to remove this factor, too, by allowing complete freedom of sexual life and thus abolishing the family, the germ-cell of civilization, we cannot, it is true, easily foresee what new paths the development of civilization could take; but one thing we can expect, and that is that this indestructible feature of human nature will follow it there.[105]

Reich stated his opposition to such a dismissal of the role of capitalism in his defense against his expulsion from the IPA in 1933. He "stated that he understood his exclusion if opposition to the death instinct concept and Freud's theory of culture were incompatible with membership. At the same time, he considered himself the legitimate developer of natural-scientific psychoanalysis and, from that viewpoint, could not concur with the exclusion."[106] Reich's scientific theory of racism was rooted in his understanding of the relationship between psychological social structures exemplified by Nazi Germany.

Wilhelm Reich focuses on racism as a symptom of sexual repression in the mind of the authoritarian racist. He describes racism in terms that derive from Freud but which incorporate a direct critique of the Nazi rhetoric of race:

> There is a direct connection between the "dominion" over animals and racial "dominion" over the "black man, the Jew, the Frenchman, etc." It is clear that one prefers to be a gentleman than an animal. To disassociate himself from the animal kingdom, the human animal denied and finally ceased to perceive the sensations of his organs; in the process he became biologically rigid.[107]

Reich describes fascist race theory as following the model of sexual repression using the vocabulary of hygiene and eugenics:

> The race theory proceeds from the presupposition that the exclusive mating of every animal with its own species is an "iron law" in nature. The National Socialist went on to apply this supposed law in nature to peoples. Their line of reasoning was something as follows: Historical experience teaches that the "intermixing of Aryan blood" with "inferior" peoples always results in the degeneration of the founders of civilization. The level of the superior race is lowered, followed by physical and mental retrogression; this marks the beginning of a progressive "decline."[108]

Reich writes of such a predisposition for madness among the racists in a world in which the internalization of racism as a form of mental illness remains a commonplace. Thus the product of the authoritarian society is equivalent to the product of the racist society. However, this is not a German problem in Reich's view, unlike that of thinkers such as Trotter, but a modern one: "The race theory is not a creation of fascism. No: fascism is a creation of race hatred and its politically organized expression.

Correspondingly, there is a German, Italian, Spanish, Anglo-Saxon, Jewish and Arabian fascism. *The race ideology is a true biopathic character symptom of the orgastically impotent individual.*"[109] For Reich, race hatred defines the center of the authoritarian society.

Reich positions his intervention into the conversation about mass psychology by claiming his own medical authority. He raises the stakes for the analysis of group psychology by claiming that the rise of Nazism stems not from Hitler's power or some form of "mass psychosis" but rather from the qualities inherent in a group living in a sexually and economically authoritarian society. Similarly, by insisting that readers not think of fascism as a national (i.e., German or Japanese) quality, but one that has firm roots in international social and economic structures, he appropriates the entire world population as suitable for medical and psychological study. He situates the source of his knowledge as his medical profession: "[M]y medical experience with individuals from all kinds of social strata, races, nationalities and religions showed me that 'fascism' is only the politically organized expression of the average human character structure, a character structure which has nothing to do with this or that race, nation or party but which is general and international."[110] Here and elsewhere, Reich refers to himself as an objective doctor and a scientist, and in this way positions himself as more authoritative than a "mere" economist or sociologist.[111] His training as a psychiatrist becomes important as he clarifies, following the deadly riot on July 15, 1927, in Vienna (the violent culmination to that point of the political struggle between left and right in Austria) what is pathological about mass psychology, namely, that it does not simply arise from socioeconomic issues. He saw the spontaneity of the crowd in the circumstances and the mechanical responses of the state functionaries as well as the police. Thereafter he dismissed the widespread belief that the working class could not suffer from sexual repression or stasis and rethinks the meaning of mass psychopathology.[112] His training as a psychiatrist becomes important as he clarifies what is pathological about mass psychology, namely, that it does not simply arise from socioeconomic issues. The example Reich gives is that socioeconomic factors may account for why the poor would steal bread—but fail to account for the reality, which is that most poor people do not steal, and even provide political rationales for those whose policies ensure their continued poverty. In this way, he positions perversity and irrationality as a medical, rather than simply economic or social, issue.

Reich castigates Marxism for its unswerving privileging of material conditions over psychological factors, and positions Freud's new approach to psychoanalysis as a corrective. He uses the language of science—"brain" and "psychological structure"—to contest the ability of Marxism to answer its own questions: "The Marxist dictum that economic conditions transform themselves into ideology, and not vice versa, ignores two questions: First, *how* this takes place, what happens in the 'human brain' in this process; and second, what is the retroactive effect of this 'consciousness' (we shall speak of *psychological structure*) on the economic process?"[113] He does not wholly follow Freud, however, and critiques him for analyzing mass psychology as individual psychology, suggesting instead that mass psychology is related to the individual because it is made up of typical traits. He suggests, "political psychology alone—not social economics—can make us understand the human character structure of a given epoch, how the individual thinks and acts, how he reacts to the conflicts of his existence and how he tries to manage them."[114] Using the language of Freud's psychoanalysis allows him to integrate economic and psychological issues in his medicalization of group psychology as the sexual life and family structure become elements that can pathologically predispose those living in authoritarian societies toward fascist regimes. He uses the language of illness to great effect: "the fact should not be overlooked that fascism, ideologically, is the revolt of a deathly sick society, sick sexually as well as economically."[115] Ultimately, by combining economic approaches with what he sees as "medical" approaches, Reich positions himself as a scientific authority on social phenomena.

Reich does not directly examine the response of the victim to the worldview of racism as he is interested in the collective, the crowd, rather than the individual. The other side of the question about how the victim responds to the hatred of the crowd is articulated in a more limited fashion in Anna Freud's *The Ego and Mechanisms of Defense* (1936), where the varieties of ego defense mechanisms described by her father (repression, displacement, denial, projection, reaction formation, intellectualization, rationalization, undoing, sublimation) are augmented by a new category very much of the 1930s: identification with the aggressor. Much later she commented that this innovation, which she notes she borrowed from the child psychologist August Aichhorn, was not one "of the recognized defense mechanisms"; nonetheless, she says, "I felt modest about this new one. I didn't think it had a claim to be introduced yet."[116] Aichhorn, in his 1925 lectures on juvenile delinquency, stressed the role that the superego had in structuring our relationship to the world.[117] For him, it is "the father who represents to the child the demands of society, forces him to fulfill those demands through the child's identification with him."[118] Aichhorn stresses the normal identification of the child with the same sex parent. For him the ego retains the form into which it was structured by the demands of the father and by society. Thus we become ourselves through our own identification with the ideal represented by our parents. When this identification is faulty, delinquency results. Aichhorn notes that such a pattern leads to a "renunciation of these wishes through the laying bare of unconscious relationships."[119] This is "a matter of reeducation" rather than psychotherapy.[120] "Life forces him to conform to reality; education enables him to achieve culture."[121] Aichhorn provides case studies of such reeducation through riding the delinquent of his identification with the aggressive or destructive parent, where the child had "identified himself with his father and doing as he did, escaped his own unpleasant situation."[122] Aichhorn postulates that a youth counselor can overcome such identification with the negative aspects of the parent and therefore of the superego through focusing the transference of the youth with the counselor. Thus the destructive forces are reformed and the negative identification modified.

Anna Freud transforms this, arguing that the child identifies with the parent by "impersonating the aggressor, assuming his attributes or imitating his aggression, the child transforms himself from the person threatening into the person making the threat."[123] Her focus is not, as was Reich's, on the level of the constitution of superego formation, how and why capitalist society shapes the individual through its repressive rule making, but rather on the individual's resistance to all such forces, a resistance that, however, can become the source of mental illness.

The pattern is one that she sees as part of a normal course of human development, when the child mimics the adult in order to avoid punishment: in "'identification with the aggressor' we recognize a by no means uncommon stage in the normal development of the superego. Nevertheless, it can become pathological."[124] She continues, "It is possible that a number of people remain arrested at the intermediate stage in the development of the super-ego and never quite complete the internalization of the critical process. Although perceiving their own guilt, they continue to be peculiarly aggressive in their attitude to other people. In such cases the behavior of the superego toward others is as ruthless as that of the superego toward the patient's own ego in melancholia."[125] Thus psychopathology can result in harm to the ego: "If the child introjects [internalizes] both rebuke and punishment and then regularly projects this same punishment on another, 'then he is arrested at an intermediate stage in the development of the superego.'"[126] The key to what comes to be understood as projective identification is the image of "assimilation":

> The German word is *Angleichung*. The child becomes like the teacher. "Assimilating himself" is a rather clumsy translation. But, you know, the best example I now have of this process is one which I didn't possess at the time. It came later at the Hampstead Nurseries from the little girl who had a small brother who was so afraid of dogs that she said to him, "*You be doggie and no dog will bite you.*" That is a perfect expression of the whole thing.[127]

Anna Freud argues that it can also be at the core of racism, for "vehement indignation at someone else's wrongdoing is the precursor of and substitute for guilty feelings on its own account."[128] Intolerance of other people precedes intolerance toward the self.

This category had been exemplified much earlier in German Jewish writings about the internalization of racism and is a commonplace in early-twentieth-century popular psychology.[129] The German Jewish novelist Jakob Wassermann's widely read and translated *My Life as German and Jew* (1921) reflected such images:

> I have known many Jews who have languished with longing for the fair-haired and blue-eyed individual. They knelt before him, burned incense before him, believed his every word; every blink of his eye was heroic; and when he spoke of his native soil, when he beat his Aryan breast, they broke into a hysterical shriek of triumph. . . . I was once greatly diverted

by a young Viennese Jew, elegant, full of suppressed ambition, rather melancholy, something of an artist, and something of a charlatan. Providence
itself had given him fair hair and blue eyes; but lo, he had no confidence
in his fair hair and blue eyes: in his heart of hearts he felt that they were
spurious.[130]

But for Wassermann this was a form of superego deformation, which
Anna Freud transformed into a normal aspect of ego development. For
Wassermann it is "self-shame" that marks the relationship of the Jew to
his own sense of self as a human being.

> I was often overcome by discouragement, by a sense of shame at all those
> tumbling, stumbling selves among whom I too now was numbered, but
> who from far away had seemed to me superhuman creatures dwelling in
> an enchanted garden. At times I was moved to wonder whether the nar-
> row spitefulness, the pecuniary squabbling combined with the striving
> toward universal goals, the provincial dullness and brutal ambition, the
> mistrust and stubborn misunderstanding where achievement and perfec-
> tion, ideas and an exchange of impulses were at stake, where thoughts
> and images were concerned—whether all this was a peculiarly German
> disease or a by-product of the metier as such, its somber lining, the same
> with us as in other lands.[131]

Wassermann notes the inauthenticity of such forms of identification
and their concomitant rejection, evident to the outside observer, which
destabilizes Jewish identity. It neither enables the Jew to become part
of antisemitic culture nor does it provide a positive Jewish identity for
him. It transforms him into a psychopathological case, and such characters haunt the literature of the day in works by the non-Jewish Thomas
Mann ("Blood of the Walsung," 1905) and Arthur Schnitzler (*The Road
into the Open*, 1908), the Jewish friend and neighbor of Anna Freud's
father.

Indeed identification with the aggressor even becomes a theme in
Jewish American writing of the 1920s with Ludwig Lewisohn's novel *Island Within* (1928). In an essay written in 1938 Lewisohn labels all of the
"Jewish accusations against Jews today [as] pure and unadulterated bit-
ter escapist mechanisms, Masochistic mechanisms, mechanism of self-

hatred."[132] Identification with the aggressor becomes a means of labeling internal conflicts among the various groups that evolve in exile from Europe. As late as 1945 Zionist and educator William Chomsky (father of Noam) can provide a case study as telling as that recounted by Wassermann, but in the American context: "'Whenever the word 'Jew' or a Jewish person is mentioned when I am among gentiles, I immediately become tense to see if what is being said is complementary or otherwise. . . . When a name that is definitely Semitic is mentioned in class or among other gentiles I try to laugh along with the others, but fortunately I feel that anyone with such a name should change it immediately and not single himself out so."[133] Chomsky condemns such anxiety and sees it as a part of the pressure to conform to standards of American culture rather than to the goals of Jewish education.

What is important to remember is that Anna Freud postulates that this mode of ego defense, stemming as it does from the son's Oedipal conflict with the father and simultaneous identification with him, is part of normal superego development. By internalizing the power of the authority, the ego is in a position to project its repressed aim and thus criticize others as well as to learn what is to be condemned and protect itself against the pain of guilt through identification. This process can become pathological, but what she is arguing is that it is merely one of the mechanisms of defense used by the ego in a nonpathological manner. It does not take long, however, for Viennese psychoanalysis, under the pressure of Austro-fascism and the complexity of Jewish identity in such a politically and culturally charged environment, to see such a "normal" defense as clearly a pathology, not of the ego but of the superego, of the interaction between the ego and the world beyond. In 1937 the Viennese Jewish psychoanalyst Theodor Reik argues that such identification is inherently a form of psychopathology:

> In connection with this part of Anna Freud's theory, I do not think it is right to say that an ego of this kind is intolerant of other people before it is severe towards itself and that we have here an intermediate stage in the development of the super-ego which at the same time represents some kind of preliminary phase of morality. On the contrary I am of the opinion that the subject's perception of his own guilt has in these cases assumed such an exceptionally severe and acute form that he must drive

his aggressiveness outwards if his ego is to remain intact. I hold that we are here confronted not with a defective development of the super-ego, but with a hypertrophied activity on its part—with a development, which is excessive at any rate in relation to an ego that is still weak and unconfident of itself. If the ego, finding itself in this situation, were not to seek relief by such a method of unburdenment, the sense of guilt, now become too powerful to bear, would turn against the ego and the result would be, not a greater awareness of guilt (which indeed is often perceived consciously) but an attack of melancholia.[134]

For Reik this is not inherent to superego development, but rather an exaggerated form of superego development. What psychotherapy can provide in these cases is for the analysand to trust the self more, which such identification denied. At this moment, shortly before the *Anschluß*, the question of ego anxiety undergoes a transformation into a psychopathology. Identifying with the aggressor is a form of madness unless it becomes the object of therapy.

In exile in London Anna Freud found her understanding of the identification with the aggressor confronted in her own clinical practice. In her Hampstead Clinic for Children there were boys and girls who had escaped on the trains rescuing children from Germany, Austria, and Czechoslovakia, the *Kindertransport*, who were observed playing "Nazis and Jews": everyone wanted to be a Nazi! She slowly began to alter her view, and after the war she commented on the nature of this aggression:

> The mechanism of identification with the aggressor, as a means of achieving the turn of passive into active, by implication deals not with libido but with aggression (or rather, masochism as its counterpart). The mechanism of *displacement of object* from the animate to the inanimate, or from humans to animals, does play some role in the conflicts with infantile sexuality but holds a much more significant place in the child's or adult's struggle with his aggression. *Undoing*, as it is known from the obsessional neurosis, is directed against aggression only. *Delegation* . . . is another defensive measure, effective in curbing the individual's aggression and does so in two ways. One consists in attributing responsibility for the aggressive action or wish to another person or external influence; this happens normally in early childhood or, abnormally, in the paranoid

reactions. The other is the familiar social phenomenon that the individual denies himself the fulfillment of aggressive wishes but concedes permission for it to some higher agency such as the state, the police, the military or legal authorities. This latter instance resembles somewhat the working of *altruism* on the libidinal side; the "altruistic" individual "delegates" to others the libidinal wishes, which he denies to himself, i.e. he "externalizes" or "displaces" them, with the result that he can enjoy their fulfillment vicariously.[135]

Here there is a glimpse of her critique of the societal context of aggressive behavior and how the individual can abdicate his or her own anxiety about identification with the aggressor to greater societal forces such as the state. What is of interest it that while obsessional neurosis is evoked here the general idea that racism was a mass obsession is rare to this point.[136]

The Social Psychology of Race in the United States

The reader can only understand the renewed and revitalized interest in social psychology within the social and psychological sciences in the United States in the 1930s in historical context. As one of the standard histories of social psychology from the 1970s states:

> If I were required to name the one person who has had the greatest impact upon the field [of social psychology], it would have to be Adolf Hitler. There are several reasons why these events in the world at large were so important for social psychology: They came at a critical stage in its development; they were largely responsible for the spectacular increase in its rate of growth; they basically influenced the subsequent demographic composition of the field; and they exerted a fundamental influence upon its entire intellectual complexion right up to the present.[137]

Among other psychologists in exile the topic of identification with the aggressor lead to other approaches to this question of the predisposition to madness of the Jews. Kurt Lewin (1890–1947), trained in Berlin and long associated with the Institute of Social Research (better known as the Frankfurt School) that married psychoanalytic approaches to society with Marxist theory, was one of the most prominent pioneers of social and applied psychology in the modern era.[138] In 1933 Lewin immigrated to the United States, eventually ending up teaching and researching at the Massachusetts Institute of Technology, and then later heading the Center for Group Dynamics.

Lewin began to formulate his theory of group dynamics in 1937, looking at the *Gestalt* of such formations, in that an individual's psychology could be comprehended only in the context of the environment of the group, its members, and the situation in which all find themselves: $B = f(P, E)$, behavior (B) is a function of a person (P) in their environment (E). The whole is truly, as in the discussions of the crowd during World War I, greater than the sum of its parts but is also constituent of its parts. Lewin's emphasis on the importance of the present moment of lived experience rather than Freud's emphasis on the centrality of early child experiences paralleled other psychoanalytic thinkers in the Frankfurt School such as Erich Fromm (and others in the Berlin psychoanalytic association such as Karen Horney). In 1941 Lewin, who would later become involved in the rehabilitation of concentration camp inmates, turned to the question of the identification with the aggressor in the context of Nazi antisemitism in what becomes the classic psychological paper on "Jewish self-hatred."[139]

Lewin begins his study in the context of Nazi antisemitism, and by discounting the idea that all self-hatred stems simply from identification with the aggressor:

> There is an almost endless variety of forms which Jewish self-hatred may take. Most of them, and the most dangerous forms, are a kind of indirect, under-cover self-hatred. If I should count the instances where I have encountered open and straightforward contempt among Jews, I could name but a few. The most striking, for me, was the behavior of a well-educated Jewish refugee from Austria on the occasion of his meeting a couple of other Jewish refugees. In a tone of violent hatred, he burst out into a defense of Hitler on the ground of the undesirable characteristics of the German Jew.[140]

While Lewin seems to discount such moments of identification for a broader theory of what comes to be called group dynamics, he returns to this theme later in the essay: "the development of Palestine, the recent history of the European Jews, and the threat of Hitlerism have made the issues more clear. A few Jews, such as the infamous Captain Naumann in Germany, have become Fascistic themselves under the threat of Fascism."[141] Lewin's reference is to the ultranationalist Max Naumann, an Army officer and holder of the Iron Cross during World War I, who was the chairman of the *Verband Nationaldeutscher Juden* (League of Nationalist German Jews) in Weimar and a violent opponent of Eastern Jews, whom he accused of being the true target of German antisemites. In 1933, on the eve of Hitler's appointment as chancellor, Naumann supported one of the political parties allied with the Nazis, hoping that this might mitigate the Nazis' radical antsemitism. These are for Lewin "real" cases of self-hatred and not the typical manifestations of the phenomenon. While Lewin desires to limit his investigation to the field of social dynamics, the specter of the identification with the aggressor haunts this essay.[142]

Lewin claims that psychoanalytic explanations are incomplete because they fail to encompass

> what Freud calls the drive to self-destruction or the "death instinct." However, an explanation like that is of little value. Why does the Englishman not have the same amount of hatred against his countrymen, or the German against the German, as the Jew against the Jew? If the self-hatred were the result of a general instinct, we should expect its degree to depend only on the personality of the individual. But the amount of self-hatred the individual Jew shows seems to depend far more on his attitude toward Judaism than on his personality.[143]

By "Judaism" Lewin seems not simply to mean religious belief but the totality of the meanings ascribed to the symbolic Jew, positive as well as negative, religious as well as ethnic. Lewin does address the general charge that Jews are particularly susceptible to psychopathology, as he seems to admit that there are greater manifestations of pathological self-hatred among Jews, but that most cases are the result of the context of self-loathing.

> Self-hatred seems to be a psychopathological phenomenon, and its prevention may seem mainly a task for the psychiatrist. However, modern

psychology knows that many psychological phenomena are but an expression of a social situation in which the individual finds himself. In
a few cases, Jewish self-hatred may grow out of a neurotic or otherwise
abnormal personality, but in the great majority of cases it is a phenomenon in persons of normal mental health. In other words, it is a social-
psychological phenomenon, even though it usually influences deeply the
total personality. In fact, neurotic trends in Jews are frequently the result
of their lack of adjustment to just such group problems.[144]

There may be individuals who are psychopathological and their symptoms may be articulated as self-loathing. But it is the social environment
that generates self-hatred in a group, it is not intrinsic to the group itself.
It can, however, be a form of identification with the aggressor, as much
as he wishes to discount this. For Lewin's self-hating Jew "sees things
Jewish with the eyes of the unfriendly majority."[145]

Lewin does not deem this a problem of the Jews as a group alone.
Residing now in the United States, he sees the phenomenon in black
American identification with the aggressor as well as that of other im-
migrant groups as analogous to that of the Jews:

> One of the better-known and most extreme cases of self-hatred can be
> found among American Negroes. Negroes distinguish within their group
> four or five strata according to skin shade—the lighter the skin the higher
> the strata. This discrimination among themselves goes so far that a girl
> with a light skin may refuse to marry a man with a darker skin. An ele-
> ment of self-hatred which is less strong but still clearly distinguishable
> may also be found among the second generation of Greek, Italian, Polish,
> and other immigrants to this country.[146]

Lewin sees identification with the aggressor, which is clearly the phenomenon that he is addressing even though he never uses the phrase, as
the core problem. Its cure is to be found not in the therapeutic treatment
of Jews or black Americans but through amelioration of the racism of
the society in which they find themselves: "Jewish self-hatred will die
out only when actual equality of status with the non-Jew is achieved.
Only then will the enmity against one's own group decrease to the relatively insignificant proportions characteristic of the majority group's.

Sound self-criticism will replace it."[147] It is the race madness of the Nazis in Germany and American society that generates self-loathing in individuals as well as in collectives of oppressed minorities.

Such debates echoed among the various émigré therapists. In the 1950s, building on earlier studies, the Berlin-trained non-Jewish psychoanalyst Karen Horney's popular work codified the discussion about the unstable nature of identity formation where there is a constant need to reify one's self-image, which being "essentially false, is never really secure."[148] Such insecurity leads to self-hatred or the projection of such feelings toward others. Horney, a close collaborator of Erich Fromm, opens the field well beyond oppressed minorities to reappropriate Anna Freud's model free from specific social contexts. The question is not whether such phenomena exist but rather what are their parameters and limitations. These parameters and limitations shift over time and are shaped by the demands of the theorist.

Race Madness and the Nazis

In 1934 Adolf Hitler was convicted of "crimes against civilization" because of actions "against Jews, minorities, labor, democracy, women, religion, world peace, civil liberties, sciences, arts, education, liberals, free press and assembly." The trial was held at Madison Square Garden in New York City before an audience of twenty thousand. Sponsored by the American Jewish Congress and other anti-fascist organizations, the judge, Bainbridge Colby, a former U.S. secretary of state, heard testimony from a wide range of witnesses. Among them was Dr. Lewellys F. Barker, professor emeritus of medicine at Johns Hopkins University, who stated, "Hitler is an egocentric fanatic while Hitlerism is a 'psychic epidemic.' . . . It is an abnormal emotional mass movement that reminds us of the Dark Ages. . . . To understand Hitler and Hitlerism one is compelled to enter the domain of psychopathology—that is to say, of the mentally abnormal."[149] Hitler is an "egocentric fanatic" but "no imbecile." Racism is one of the symptoms, not merely of Hitlerism but of the Germans, at least of the German middle class: "The Jew was to be made the scapegoat, and hatred of the Jew was systematically cultivated. The depressed middle classes of Germany, undernourished and preternaturally susceptible to suggestion, welcome any message that promised to release them from the pinch of want, that would give relief from their intolerable hardships and limitations." In his testimony, Barker "confessed that he knew of no effective antitoxin for a psychic epidemic, which, he held, might have to run its course."[150] The image of the Nazi state as dominated by psychopathology represented by antisemitism resuscitates some of the World War I images of the Germans as victims of a racial mass psychology of destruction. Among the exiles who began to deal with this topic the focus was also on the role of identification in the part that Jews, too, played on the right.

In his recent account of the discussions of Hitler's mental state before and during the war the British historian Richard Evans summarized the claim that Hitler was mad in part by citing a number of academic studies arguing for his sanity. Books such as that by the Austrian émigré psychiatrist and dean of the Yale medical school Fritz Redlich, *Hitler: Diagnosis of a Destructive Prophet* (1998), refuted the claim that Hitler was psychopathological based on post facto analysis of the documents available on his mental state. But such retrospective diagnoses are generally useless except as ideological counterarguments. Thus the core of Evans's analysis is not that Hitler was sane but that "the idea that Hitler was insane was something that many Germans came to believe in during the later stages of the war, and for sometimes afterward, not least as a way of excusing themselves from responsibility for his actions. . . . The idea of Hitler's insanity was only one of an enormous range of speculations through which people tried, then and later, to explain the Nazi's leaders actions."[151] Madness of the leaders releases the Germans from culpability except within the general theory of the madness of crowds, now lead astray by a charismatic leader.

During the late 1930s, the obsession with the madness of the Nazi leadership as the force that shaped the individual German became a preoccupation of not only popular psychology but of state agencies. If racism was a symptom of the psychopathology of fascism, understanding the fascist mind had to be one of the operative undertakings of the war effort. Daniel Pick, in a brilliant study of British and American intelligence agencies' use of such analysis to get "inside the minds" of the enemy, shows how the needs of the war effort shaped the needs of analysts and psychologists examining the madness of the racist.[152] While Pick provides detailed accounts of a wide range of theoretical approaches to the psychology of the Nazis (from Wilhelm Reich in 1933 on), he focuses on the "real" case of the deputy führer, Rudolf Hess, whose flight to the United Kingdom in 1941 provided a live Nazi for the British psychiatrists to examine and analyze and Adolf Hitler, whose psyche was plumbed through a data base of a thousand pages of material culled from interviews with those who knew him (and had fled Germany), newspapers that printed accounts of his activities, as well as pure inventions, such as the "first-hand" account of Hitler's life by his (nonexistent) doctor Kurt Krueger, written by the American pornographer Samuel Roth.[153]

The players in this game of intelligence gathering ranged from Walter Langer and Herbert Marcuse in the United States to Henry Dicks and Anna Freud in the United Kingdom. Indeed, few of the major psychoanalytic thinkers of the time were not engaged in such activities. This is not a great surprise as psychiatrists and analysts were understood to be an essential part of the war effort given the success in dealing with forms of debilitating mental illness, such as "shell shock," among the troops during World War I. But their role was enhanced by 1939 because the very idea of examining the inner life through analytic models (often bowdlerized and flattened) had become part of the common coin of mass culture during the 1920s. But the social scientists too, especially the émigrés, felt that this was their task. Thus Jacques Barzun in his 1938 *Race: A Study in Modern Superstition* defined racialism as "an alternative to madness for intelligent educated men balked in what they consider their legitimate ambitions."[154] His examples were the Nazi ideologue and pseudointellectual Alfred Rosenberg and the Nazi minister of agriculture, Richard Darré.[155] That psychoanalysis was under attack from before World War I as a "Jewish science," and that many of the German-speaking analysts were Jews, also added to the pressure to provide answers about the nature of the "Nazi mind" and the role of antisemitism in shaping that worldview. But this was true even of psychoanalytically informed clinical psychiatrists such as Henry Dicks, who diagnosed Rudolf Hess as a paranoid schizophrenic.[156]

The difficulty with providing these types of answers was the simple fact that the construct of a "Nazi mind" could not exist even within Freudian psychoanalytic theory, which rejected the very idea of race. No exemplary "Nazi" was possible; even Hess had to be seen as an individual. In addition, the pragmatic fact that such knowledge provided little or no predictive advantage did not stop the Allies from generating it and attempting to make use of it. Indeed, multiple studies of the "Nazi mind" were commissioned by the intelligence services, including studies of mass movements from émigré psychologists and psychiatrists from occupied Europe.[157] Thus the psychoanalyst Erich Fromm's *Escape from Freedom* (1941) in complex ways recapitulated a Marxist-Freudian analysis of the fascist mind from the standpoint of the Frankfurt School, which we shall discuss later, in a more subtle and critical manner.[158] He sees the economic displacement of modern Germany as having loosed "the traditional binds" while exacerbating the "feeling of powerlessness and aloneness."[159] A "compulsive quest for certainty" and a "desperate escape from anxiety" allowed lower-middle-class Germans to submit to the power of a charismatic leader and focus their hate on those considered weaker than they. He writes, "The victory of freedom is possible only if democracy develops into a society . . . in which the individual is not subordinated to or manipulated by any power outside of himself, be it the State or the economic machine. . . . The irrational and planless character of society must be replaced by a planned economy that represents the planned and concerted effort of society as such."[160] This was at the core of what Fromm called the "authoritarian character" and could be overcome through social and psychological interventions.[161]

The émigré psychologist Erik H. Erikson's analysis of the German mind as that of an adolescent mind run amuck paralleled Fromm's understanding of the psychopathology of racism.[162] All such studies by émigré psychologists, psychiatrists, and psychoanalysts focused on the German manifestation of racism as antisemitism and provided for Anglo-American readers a rethinking of the implications of the relationship of madness and racism as a means of explaining the German mind in the 1930s as a manifestation of some greater source of psychopathology.

Certainly one of the most popular and controversial studies of racism and psychopathology during the war was Richard Brickner's *Is Germany Incurable?* (1943).[163] Brickner (1896–1959) was an American, rather than an émigré, a neuro-psychiatrist whose work was heavily impacted by Sigmund Freud (he writes that "Freud has contributed fundamentally to this book") but whose expression of this influence owes perhaps more to Le Bon.[164] Brickner built on the earlier claims of clinical psychiatrists such as Edward Strecker at the University of Pennsylvania, who sought to diagnosis the psychopathology of totalitarianism "beyond the clinic frontiers," building on the crowd theory of World War I. Active in the mental hygiene movement in the 1920s, Strecker, in his *Beyond the Clinical Frontiers* (1940), sought to define the mind of the modern masses in their retreat from reality, of the "emotionalized group with a 'mission'" into totalitarian fantasies such as racism.[165] Likewise the émigré psychoanalyst Franz Alexander, who had been recruited from Berlin before the Nazi takeover to create a short-lived psychoanalytic institute at the University of Chicago, sought in *Our Age of Unreason* (1941) to answer the growing power of the Nazis and their racist philosophy through having

> democracies finally recognize their historical vocation to assume leadership toward a new league of nations. This must be based at first both on justice and on armed force, the latter to be discarded only gradually at the same pace as the indispensable psychological ally in man's personality gains strength. This internal ally, a slowly growing product of education, is an advanced form of humanism which does not stop at economic, linguistic, or racial borders.[166]

This is moral reeducation as psychological therapy.

Such views were broadly popularized by Brickner, who diagnosed the German character as "paranoid" and prescribed "a vast educational program" for post-war Germany.[167] At the core of the reeducation he proposed must be the family, as for Brickner "the child is father to the man."[168] He picks up a thread from the work of individuals such as Trotter, looking at the German character as manifesting "aggression" throughout its history:

> Massive evidence summarized in this book shows that the national group we call Germany behaves and has long behaved startlingly like an individual involved in a dangerous mental trend. . . . Clinical experience can identify the specific condition that Germany's mental trend approaches. It is paranoia.[169]

Thus aggression is a symptom of an underlying mental illness, which is universal but which can be exacerbated, for these "tendencies may be stimulated and whipped into action."[170] It is the group that manifests these symptoms: "group means a number of individuals or objects that share certain identifiable characteristics: all the component elements have in common the possession of telephones or a belief in spiritualism or attach a special emotional significance to blond hair in females."[171] Once so activated the herd mentality is triggered: "A useful metaphor for this phenomenon, which has often been observed but never accurately described, is 'paranoid contagion.' The word contagion thus means no that paranoid thinking is a disease lime measles that can be caught from another person, but that it is an inflammable potentiality that can be easily ignited."[172] And "German culture has developed a set of densely paranoid values."[173]

Paranoia has a wide range of symptoms. Megalomania is one of them: "This trait arises from the paranoid's conviction of his own a priori world-shaking importance, of the supreme value and significance of his every act and thought."[174] This trait is manifest in Hitler's belief that the Nordic race has a right to dominate the world:

> The paranoid's feeling that God and Destiny attend his every move and are supporting any special mission upon which he feels impelled to embark, has often been expressed by Hitler: "I am certain that my name will never be forgotten as that of a great man of this country. I believe it was the will of God—the will of the Supreme Power was fulfilled through me."[175]

Control is also a symptom of the German form of paranoia: "the need to Dominate everybody with whom he comes in contact, to control every situation in which he finds himself, as a means towards putting into concrete terms this superiority he knows he possess, is part and parcel of the paranoid's megalomania."[176]

Brickner's final symptom is Anna Freud's identification with the aggressor and its projective form as a persecution complex. "Because he himself is so important, he is obviously destined to rule others who are less important. Because of his superiority and potential power are so unmistakable in his eyes, he feels nobody could miss them. All other people are naturally consumed with jealously of him and hostility toward the inevitable consummation of his supremacy."[177] It is the fear of others that spurs the racism of the Germans!

Brickner's example is an account, reported in the media, of a discussion that Hitler had following the "Night of the Long Knives," in June and July 1934, when Hitler ordered the mass murder of the leadership of the *Sturmabteilung* paramilitary wing under his longtime supporter Ernst Röhm:

> Hitler expressed this attitude magnificently in a statement after the blood-purge of 1934. Speaking of private meetings among his victims that his under cover men had reported, he said he would have such men shot, even if it should turn out that they had discussed "nothing but ancient coins or the weather." The very fact that something should go on without his knowledge is intolerable to the paranoid.[178]

The final symptom of the paranoid state is what Brickner labels "retrospective falsification." "Nearly every speech of Hitler's leads off with a long period of blustering instruction for the world in the past history of Germany. The general theme is that Germany has never been defeated in a war."[179] That includes World War I. The Nazi government, to prove that "all Jews are cowards," claimed that the many German Jews decorated for valor during World War I had actually purchased their awards from the needy widows of "Aryan" heroes for shamefully small sums and that all such certificates were forgeries.[180] For Brickner antisemitism is a reflection of such paranoid thinking and thus Nazi antisemitism is a reflex of the German mindset: "There are several good paranoid reasons for German hatred of Jews. The first is projection. . . . The second reason is that the numerically insignificant Jews—five hundred thousand among sixty million Germans at the time Hitler came to power [provided a convenient scapegoat for the projection of German anxieties]."[181] Brickner writes that "the systematic butchery of the Jews now in progress is merely the end-product of that kind of thinking."[182] The reduction of Auschwitz to a form of madness that can be cured is problematic even in the 1940s.

Brickner's text generated a heated debate in the noted literary magazine *The Saturday Review*. Thinkers such as Bertrand Russell and Erich

Fromm were asked to respond to his thesis. Russell simply ignored Brinkner's claims, writing instead about the need for post-war reeducation and reform of education institutions. As an émigré Jew Fromm did not have that luxury. He grappled with the idea that Germans were psychologically predisposed to paranoia and came to a rather startling conclusion given his own interest in the social construction of German racism:

> The increasing literature dealing with a psychiatric approach to the German national character suggests a twofold danger. On the one hand that psychiatric concepts are used as rationalizations for political slogans, thus depriving us of valid knowledge, which we need for the conduct of the war and for realistic and rational plans for peace. On the other hand, that they become a substitute for valid ethical concepts; that they tend to weaken the sense for moral values, by calling something by a psychiatric term when it should be called plainly evil.[183]

Fromm has raised the stakes here, as he had provided a psychological explanation for racism in his own work, and introduced a problem that will become more and more important after the end of the war: are we dealing with a form of madness for which there may be a therapy and which may have a specific etiology or are we dealing with a form of moral bankruptcy, evil not in the sense of the demonic but in the Enlightenment sense of moral choice. Evil seems to be tangential in modern philosophy and psychology dealing with racism and prejudice through the 1930s. Yet following 1945 it reappears in the debates about madness and racism with ever-greater force. Perhaps understandably so, for as the philosopher Susan Neiman states, evil "threatens the trust in the world that we need to orient ourselves within it."[184] And the 1930s was the era of a search, for good or for ill, for precisely that trust so badly lost after 1919, even though, as Neiman observes, this loss of trust seems to us today "both intelligible and contingent, the lethal fruit of old-fashion imperialism and modern technology."[185] It did not appear so then.

4

The Holocaust and Post-War Theories of Antisemitism and Racism

The Holocaust and the Results of Psychic Trauma

In 1960 the historian and psychoanalyst Bruno Bettelheim, then the director of the most prestigious center for the treatment of autistic children in the world, the University of Chicago's Sonia Shankman Orthogenic School, published his bestselling *The Informed Heart: Autonomy in a Mass Age*.[1] Trained in art history at the University of Vienna, the Jewish but secular Bettelheim had been arrested after the *Anschluß* because of his anti-fascist activities in Austria before 1938. In testimony for the Nuremburg Tribunal in 1946 he recounted:

> I was taken into custody and imprisoned. It was stated to me that my confinement was the result of orders issued by the Gestapo in Berlin. I spent three days in jail in Vienna after which I was transferred to the concentration camp at Dachau early in May 1938. I spent approximately four months in Dachau after which I was transferred to the concentration camp at Buchenwald. Meanwhile my wife had proceeded to the United States. I was released from Buchenwald in April 1939. My release was effected through the aid of some influential friends of mine in America who were able to enlist the assistance of the State Department of the United States.[2]

Bettelheim's account of his experiences was virtually word for word also his first major American scholarly paper on psychopathology, as he notes in his deposition to the Nuremberg Tribunal.

When he came to the United States in 1939 it was this experience that shaped Bettelheim's interest in psychology under duress. *The Informed Heart*, along with similar accounts, such as Viktor Frankl's 1962 bestseller *Man's Search for Meaning* and Ernest Becker's 1974 Pulitzer Prize–

winning *Denial of Death*, came to define the American concept of the psychopathology of the victims of Nazism as well as the perpetrators of Nazi crimes.[3] The portrayal of survival in extreme circumstances fit the Cold War anxieties of Americans as well as Europeans at the time.

The success of *The Informed Heart*, both within academic circles and beyond, led to Bettelheim's appointment as professor of psychology and child development at Chicago. His 1943 essay, "Individual and Mass Behavior in Extreme Situations," formed the core of his 1946 deposition, and became central to his 1960 book, which rocketed him to national prominence.[4] Written when he was still at Rockland College, in this essay Bettelheim asked the question, *why was it that some people (such as himself) survived the concentration camps and others succumbed?* The core of Bettelheim's thesis is that there is a pattern of adaption to traumatic circumstances that structure victims' responses to their experiences:

> The first of these stages centers around *the initial shock, of finding oneself unlawfully imprisoned.* The main event of the second stage is *the transportation into the camp and the first experiences in it.* The next stage is characterized by a slow process of changing the prisoner's life and personality. It occurs step by step, continuously. It is *the adaptation to the camp situation.* During this process it is difficult to recognize the impact of what is going on. One way to make it more obvious is to compare two groups of prisoners, one in whom the process has only started, namely, the "new" prisoners, with another one in whom the process is already far advanced. This other group will consist of the "old" prisoners. The final stage is reached when *the prisoner has adapted himself to the life in the camp.* This last stage seems to be characterized, among other features, by a definitely changed attitude to, and evaluation of, the Gestapo [emphases in the original].[5]

This is Anna Freud's identification with the aggressor writ large. Bettelheim sees the psychological response to the camp experience as uniformly leading to psychopathology. The question of survival guilt is thus likewise a problem of the identification with the aggressor.[6] Surviving itself becomes a cause of the psychopathology generated by the camp experience. Other commentators of the day, such as Viktor

Frankl, saw the potential for reciprocity within the camp experience as a balancing factor that provided an alternative to identification with the aggressor.[7] For Bettelheim, this is the primary symptom of the experience of the camp, of the individual now reduced to a member of the crowd: "The pattern of these behaviors was similar in nearly all prisoners with only slight deviations from the average, these deviations originating in the prisoners' particular background and personality. We call 'mass' behavior those phenomena which could be observed *only* in a group of prisoners when functioning as a more or less unified mass."[8] What is striking was that the longer the prisoners were in the camp the more they identified with the perpetrators:

> Old prisoners who seemed to have a tendency to identify themselves with the Gestapo did so not only in respect to aggressive behavior. They would try to arrogate to themselves old pieces of Gestapo uniforms. If that was not possible, they tried to sew and mend their uniforms so that they would resemble those of the guards. The length to which prisoners would go in these efforts seemed unbelievable, particularly since the Gestapo punished them for their efforts to copy Gestapo uniforms. When asked why they did it they admitted that they loved to look like one of the guards. The identification with the Gestapo did not stop with the copying of their outer appearance and behavior. Old prisoners accepted their goals and values, too, even when they seemed opposed to their own interests. It was appalling to see how far formerly even politically well-educated prisoners would go in this identification.[9]

Bettelheim examines the puzzlement of some of those incarcerated, whose "crime" was their support for political parties other than the Nazis. He notes that few of the prisoners in 1938–1939 were incarcerated because they were Jews; even the "Jewish" prisoners, who were clearly identified as such, were there primarily because of other activities:

> The great majority of the *nonpolitical middle-class prisoners*, who were a small minority among the prisoners of the concentration camps, were least able to withstand the initial shock. They found themselves utterly unable to comprehend what had happened to them. They seemed more than ever to cling to what up to now had given them self-esteem. Again

and again they assured the members of the Gestapo that they never opposed Nazism. In their behavior became apparent the dilemma of the politically uneducated German middle classes when confronted with the phenomenon of National Socialism.[10]

Within *The Informed Heart*, Bettelheim places much greater weight on the role of antisemitism in his experience and in the camp experience generally. Writing for an American audience in 1960, the role of antisemitism and the problematic of an acculturated German Jewish identity loomed as more important for him and for his audience than the overall response to the trauma experienced by the survivors. He writes much later, "My affirmative sense of Jewish identity became especially important to me, and possibly even life-preserving, in the face of the abuse and mistreatment I suffered in German concentration camps because I was a Jew."[11] For émigré social scientists and therapists their own direct or indirect exposure to fascist antisemitism shaped their interest in race and psychopathology.

In the 1940s this self-affirming quality, given the anxiety about Jewish identity among American Jewish social scientists, is missing.[12] Yet those Jewish researchers, such as Irving Sarnoff at the University of Michigan, had already proposed a model for American antisemitism that focused on identification with the aggressor as the cause of Jewish self-hatred. Sarnoff uses the classic Oedipal model to explain identification with the aggressor. For Sarnoff the situation in the 1950s in the United States is the perfect ground for self-hatred:

> In so far as Jews are concerned, the contemporary American scene appears to fulfill all three of the above prerequisite conditions. Firstly, there is widespread antisemitism among majority group members. This negative attitude wanes in intensity from the crudely destructive outcries of the "lunatic fringe" category of bigots to the discreet practice of "gentleman's agreement" housing restrictions. Secondly, Jews are, in every sphere of life, ultimately dependent upon the good will of majority group members who control our social institutions The granting or withholding of ratification of such needs as education, work, and living quarters is sometimes determined by the degree of prejudice motivating the particular educator, employer, or landlord whose approval the individual

Jew is obliged to obtain. Finally, no Jewish person, unless he renounces membership in the minority group into which he is born and succeeds in "passing" as a non-Jew, can avoid personal experience with the social fact of antisemitism.[13]

It is the social situation that exposes all who see themselves or are seen (visibly or invisibly) as Jews to psychopathology.

In his later extension of this model in his book, Bettelheim examines the most radical case, that of the "musselmann" (Bettelheim uses the lower-case "moslem"), a camp term referring to those who have completely lost the will to live and become so passive that they are the targets of the guards and other prisoners and often die as a result of this apathy:

> Once his own life and the environment were viewed as totally beyond his ability to influence them, the only logical conclusion was to pay no attention to them whatsoever. . . . Seeing them made every prisoner afraid he might become like them. . . . Fear of sinking into that subhuman stratum of prison society—the asocials, the "moslems"—was a powerful incentive to fighting a class war against them.[14]

For Bettelheim this is another form of identification. Here the victim's identity is so defined by his status in civil society, a German or Austrian society that now has stripped him of rank and identity, there seems to be no core of identity left. This was the extreme result of another form of identification: that with the society in which the victim dwelt. In a later book review he commented, "One was forced to do things one would not normally have done, but internally there were always limitations derived from previous behavior patterns."[15] This also meant, however, that, for Bettlelheim, it was possible to avoid becoming a victim:

> But to survive as a man not a walking corpse, as a debased and degraded but still human being, one had first and foremost to remain informed and aware of what made up one's personal point of no return, the point beyond which one would never, under any circumstances, give in to the oppressor, even if it meant risking and losing one's life. It meant being aware that if one survived at the price of overreaching this point one would be holding on to a life that had lost all its meaning.[16]

On the other side of the coin were the professional criminals (the "anti-socials") as well as those who were also incarcerated as "asocials" and were as such directly targets of Nazi eugenics. For the Nazis in a newspaper article from 1937,

> asocial is in the first instance considered a behavior that does not live up to or contradicts the dominant social order. . . . His transgressions exhibit the stamp of his weakness: malingering, begging, vagabondage, drunkenness, delinquency, prostitution, petty deceptions and thievery, primitive document falsification, and resistance. This is also the distinctive boundary with the "antisocial," the downright criminal. The character deficiencies of the "asocial" that are harmful to the community are also hereditary defects, even though this diagnosis obviously does not mean that the asocial who is unfit for the community is on the same level as the hereditarily ill comrade.[17]

Bettelheim observed these "degenerate" individuals acting out their "their glee openly at finding themselves on equal terms with political and business leaders, with attorneys and judges, some of whom had been instrumental earlier in sending them to prison. This spite, and the feeling of being equal to these men who up to now had been their superiors, helped their egos considerably."[18] The individuals with whom these "asocials" found themselves now equals (or indeed to whom they now felt superior) were Jews. These perpetrators' sense of superiority was generated by their sudden identification with *their* aggressors as opposed to the other victims in the camp.

Indeed, Bettelheim focused not only on the psychopathology of the victim but also on that of the perpetrator: *why were Nazis and their allies in the camps the way they were?* He found that their behavior was that of the crowd, one motivated by a simple belief system in the uniform danger posed by the inmates: "Occasional talks with these guards revealed that they really believed in a Jewish-capitalistic world conspiracy against the German people, and whoever opposed the Nazis participated in it and was therefore to be destroyed, independent of his role in the conspiracy. So it can be understood why their behavior to the prisoners was that normally reserved for dealing with one's vilest enemy."[19] Meanwhile, in his analysis of the survivors in the United States Bettelheim focused on the meanings attributed to the mental state of the victims and saw the perpetrators as victims themselves of a systematic conspiracy theory. Later, in reviewing Hannah Arendt's *Eichmann in Jerusalem*, he returned to the question of the normality of the perpetrators:

> When in 1939, fresh out of the concentration camp, I tried to tell Americans about my experiences, I was told by most, including psychiatrists, that my views were incorrect, or that I was suffering from a prisoner psychosis, because I warned that the SS were not demented sadists or (in the words of the Eichmann trial) monsters, but in the vast majority mediocre men—banal, to use Arendt's term—but nonetheless deadly effective. I was told to let the after-effects of my camp experience subside before I said anymore, because my theories were apt to mislead Americans. To believe that the SS acted according to purposeful plan ran so counter to what most people then wished to believe, that it was also unacceptable to them when I said that the camps had a crucial role in the master plan of the Reich.[20]

Bettelheim was not the only émigré social scientist who survived the concentration camps and commented on the psychopathology presented by the inmates. Curt Werner Bondy (1894–1972) was a German psychologist, until 1933 professor of social psychology at Hamburg, who worked at the College of William and Mary in the 1940s. Bondy, like Bettelheim, had been incarcerated at Buchenwald after *Kristallnacht*. Yet, unlike Bettelheim, Bondy had long experience with institutions of confinement as a superintendent of prisons and a specialist in the justice system. While his primary interest was in the psychology of internees, such as those in prisoner of war camps, Bondy begins his account of his experience with a description of the psychic collapse of the middle-class inmates:

> What were the effects of this treatment upon the prisoners? No one will be astonished that many internees completely broke down physically, psychologically, and morally. Such treatment would cause similar reactions in any large group of human beings. The urge of self-preservation, bestial fear, hunger, and thirst led to a complete transformation of the majority of the prisoners. Never before—not even during the last war—

had I witnessed such a loss of self-control. The ruthless struggle of "each against all" began. No one spoke in ordinary tones, every one screamed. Some even satisfied their physical needs on the spot. The main thing was to get something to eat and to drink. When food was brought in, an excitement ensued which one can otherwise observe only among animals.[21]

Bondy, like Bettelheim, notes that there were exceptions. Bettelheim describes himself and two medical colleagues who spend their time observing the other inmates, which enables them to maintain their sanity. The assumption is that the loss of external identity leads to psychic collapse and assuming the role of the social scientist observer makes it possible to avoid such collapse. Bondy finds an alternative mode of maintaining psychic balance:

I should like to describe a special group who did not fall victim to the influence of the mass. The reason why I am presenting this description lies in the fact that it may be taken as a proof of a very important pedagogical experience: Previous systematic character forming enables people better to withstand extremely difficult situations. . . . This group comprised twenty young boys who were arrested on a training farm, together with the director of this farm. . . . This group succeeded in maintaining conscious control and complete reason despite the situation. It did not fall a victim to the general mass-suggestion. It maintained order and obedience; there was no screaming, although the nerves of these boys were also strained to the utmost. . . . From the beginning they set themselves the goal of bringing their entire group out of the concentration camp without loss of life or breakdown of nerves. They succeeded. Every one from this special group came out alive, without having suffered serious illness or loss of sanity.[22]

Why this is of such interest in our search for models of race and psychopathology is that Bondy, and to a lesser extent Bettelheim, argues that there are means of maintaining sanity under such circumstances, *but that there will be long-term psychic effects that result*:

The manner in which an individual reacts to a difficult situation and the effects which it has upon him are to be seen not only by his behavior

at the time of stress, but to a large extent by his behavior in the following months and even years. There is no doubt that many people received
physical and spiritual injuries during this period in camp from which
they will recover only very slowly, if at all.[23]

The question of whether racism has long-term effects on the psychic
structure of the victim becomes an important an issue in the context
of the concentration camp victims, and later the survivors of the death
camps, in the post-war period. It is parallel to the question answered in
the affirmative by the Supreme Court in the *Brown v. Board of Education*
decision, which was based in part on the psychological studies of
Kenneth and Mamie Clark from the late 1930s through the 1940s (which
we turn to later).

At the University of Chicago Bettelheim was part of the cadre of so-
cial scientists sponsored by the American Jewish Committee after World
War II. It was the AJC that, in 1944, sponsored a conference on antisemi-
tism that resulted in the series of volumes entitled *Studies in Prejudice*.
The most notable volume in this series was its first, *The Authoritarian
Personality* (which we will comment on later), but it also included Bruno
Bettelheim and Morris Janowitz's important 1950 *Dynamics of Prejudice:
A Psychological and Sociological Study of Veterans*. Janowitz received his
Ph.D. in 1948 from the University of Chicago, and, in the 1960s, be-
come one of the leading Chicago School sociologists. In *Dynamics of
Prejudice*, Janowitz and Bettelheim examine anti-black prejudice as well
as antisemitism, paralleling the work of Theodor Adorno and his col-
leagues on the West Coast:

> It is common knowledge that the institutional patterns and the informal
> mores of the community differ sharply for the Negro and the Jew. Im-
> puted racial differences also affect the status and treatment of the Negro
> to a greater extent than they do those of the Jew. This was particularly
> true among members of the sample, as was indicated by many statements
> to the effect that the Jew was "white after all," or that there was "no racial
> difference" between Jew and Gentile. Social scientists may agree on the
> fallacy of thinking in racial terms. But a scientific study of inter-ethnic
> hostility cannot overlook present day thinking in terms of "race" because
> of its widespread influence on attitudes and behavior.[24]

The idea that the Jew was white seems to be a *topos* of the interviews Janowitz and Bettelheim conducted. Their research, however, took place at a moment when the popular culture response to American antisemitism stressed that Jews were quite visible in American consciousness as nonwhite. For example, American antisemitism was the material of Arthur Miller's 1945 novel *Focus* and Laura Z. Hobson's *Gentleman's Agreement*, both in its bestselling novel form (first serialized in *Cosmopolitan* in 1946) and in its widely praised movie version of 1947, with Gregory Peck as the undercover journalist who passed himself off as Jewish.[25]

Hobson's novel drew attention to the overt racism directed at Jews in American society, prefiguring journalistic exploits such as the 1961 exposé by John Howard Griffin, *Black Like Me*. The Jews became white in the course of the mid-twentieth century. They became white as they became exemplars of upward economic mobility and attained for a moment the status of the exemplary American minority.[26] What Bettelheim and Janowitz reveal in their volume is their own need to be seen as neutral observers, not as Jews, certainly a theme of Bettelheim's own work on the Holocaust.

Bettelheim and Janowitz find, in their interviews with veterans, clear differences between the European and American models of antisemitism. Yet what they do not take into consideration is whether the racial stereotypes held by the veterans they are interviewing may be in part a response to the American propaganda about Nazi ideology. While they are aware of this propaganda, they seem to discount any effect it might have had on their subjects, as the idea of a unique Nazi antisemitism haunts their work:

> German propagandists, in order to make the German people (or a sizable segment of it) accept genocide, had to employ the notion of racial differences, of the inferiority of the Jewish "race" and the danger that it might contaminate the "superior" German race. That genocide, where it was accepted, was approved of only on racial grounds is indicated by the fact that before the large-scale extermination of Polish and Russian people was launched, the idea of their racial difference and inferiority had first to be propagated with great vigor.[27]

Such a reading of the German image of antisemitism is, of course, correct, but Germans also had a radical image of black inferiority that rested on the notion of black hypersexuality. The debate in the 1920s about the "Rhineland Bastards," the offspring of "German" women and "black" French soldiers in the occupied Rhineland after World War I, centered on the hypersexuality of the sub-Saharan soldiers and the inherent eugenic inferiority of their offspring. A major theme in the eugenic literature of the time was that, under the Nazis, the offspring were secretly (and one might add, even by the Nazi laws in place, illegally) sterilized. Wilhelm Reich had already written in 1933:

> The irrational content of the race theory is explained by the misinterpretation of natural sexuality as "filthy sensuality." The Jew and the Negro mean the same thing to the Fascist, the German as well as the American. The race struggle against the Negro in America takes essentially the form of sexual defense: the Negro is thought of as the sensual brute who rapes white women. Hitler wrote concerning the occupation of the Rhineland by colored troops: "Only in France does there exist today more than ever an inner identity between the intentions of the Jew-controlled stock exchange and the desire of the chauvinist-minded national statesmen. But in this very identity there lies an immense danger for Germany. For this very reason, France is and remains by far the most terrible enemy. This people, which is basically *becoming more and more negrified*, constitutes in its tie with the aims of Jewish world domination an enduring danger for the existence of the white race in Europe. *For the contamination by Negro blood on the Rhine* in the heart of Europe is just as much in keeping with the perverted sadistic thirst for vengeance of this hereditary enemy of our people as is the ice-cold calculation of the Jew thus to begin bastardizing the European continent at its core to deprive the white race of the foundations for a sovereign existence through infection with lower humanity [emphases in the original].[28]

For the émigré social scientists, who certainly knew this debate in detail, this was an American variation, as it was necessary to differentiate American racial politics, especially anti-black racism, from antisemitism.

The double focus of racism in the United States on both blacks and Jews caused the veterans to split the stereotype on which their prejudice rested. They saw blacks as hypersexual, Jews as sources of malignant power. The cause of both images, Bettelheim and Janowitz argued, resulted from an oppressive superego.[29] The cause of both was identical; its expression was different and yet the context is important as it provides a space for a therapeutic intervention that is beyond individual therapy:

> The difference between anti-Jewish and anti-Negro attitudes, as it emerged in this study, also belies the assumption that ethnic intolerance is purely psychological in origin and hence beyond the reach of social reform. On the other hand, the association of intolerance with subjective rather than objective deprivation speaks against its purely social origin. Nor can the argument be accepted that ethnic intolerance cannot be dispensed with as an outlet for hostility. Hostility is continuously accumulating in the anxious and the insecure, and cannot be discharged in single or infrequent explosions. With rare exceptions it is not possible to discharge the accumulation of years of hostility, particularly if it did not originate in a particular person whose death or removal alone might yield a cathartic relief. Violent outbursts of ethnic intolerance are still so relatively rare, and provide so few of the intolerant men with direct or vicarious outlet, that the rationalization of the need for ethnic discrimination seems untenable. Moreover, it should be realized that while ethnic hostility only rarely provides full outlet for hostility, it frequently adds to already existing frustrations. Compared to the underlying hostility toward Jews and Negroes, which some of the subjects revealed, the outlets of verbal animosity and an occasional physical aggression of little consequence seemed quite insufficient. On the other hand, a mental preoccupation with the hated minority together with a felt inability to do anything about it seemed to add more to the frustration of the very intolerant than it gave outlet for hostility. For these reasons it does not seem true that ethnic hostility is incorrigible because it originates in the hostile personality and is needed as an outlet. Less hostility and less continuous frustration would accumulate if the intolerant person were forced to recognize once and for all that this outlet was no longer available. Some intolerant men would have to find other outlets, but many others would learn to integrate

those hostile tendencies, which they now try forever and in vain to discharge against ethnic minorities.[30]

For Bettelheim and Janowitz, "reeducation," the model applied to German racism, was the solution, but it was not *therapy*. Reeducation did not demand a social restructuring, but instead required only the use of propaganda as a vehicle for removing racism as a social phenomenon. The racist was to be rehabilitated, rather than cured.

Such views of a universal predisposition to prejudice haunt American Jewish researchers within human psychology during the 1950s and 1960s. The American Jewish psychologist Stanley Milgram published his *Obedience to Authority* in 1974 based on work he had done at Yale in the 1960s. He described in detail experiments he had conducted on authority and control using unwitting student volunteers delivering ever-greater "electric shocks" to other volunteers, who were in on the tests. He claimed to have shown that most students would deliver shocks up to, and even including, lethal doses of electricity based on the direction of the experimenter ordering the shocks. Milgram had developed his experiments based upon earlier sets of benign tests about obedience by Solomon Asch at Swarthmore College, but Milgram asked a new and pointed question: "Could a group, I asked myself, induce a person to act with severity against another person?"[31] As flawed as they turned out to be, Milgram's experiments came, in the 1970s, to be a standard by which the issues of authority and control were measured and debated.[32] The question that underpinned Milgram's experiments was not only a universal one about human behavior but also one that aimed to explicate what had occurred in the Holocaust: "Let us stop trying to kid ourselves; what we are trying to understand is obedience of the Nazi guards in the prison camps, and that any other thing we may understand about obedience is pretty much of a windfall, an accidental bonus."[33] Were the Germans unique or was their behavior an example a universal flaw in human character? His answer was clear:

I would say, on the basis of having observed a thousand people in the experiment and having my own intuition shaped and informed by these experiments, that if a system of death camps were set up in the United States of the sort we had seen in Nazi Germany, one would be able to find sufficient personnel for these camps in any medium-sized American town.[34]

The Milgram experiments thus were an attempt to deny any specific psychopathology to the Germans, to the Nazis, or indeed to the guards in the camps. Desensitization and obedience to authority could work hand in glove not as a sign of psychopathology but as a marker of normal human psychology. German racism and its attendant horrors were not a specifically German phenomenon but an intrinsic aspect of human behavior. The Germans were no more insane than anyone else under the circumstances.

Survivor Syndrome: German Reparations and the Madness of the Jews

The question then remained in the post–World War II era, *how crazy were the survivors*, who by the 1950s were seen in the United States as essentially Jewish. The 1963 case of a cancer research study in New York City that used infirm Jewish Holocaust survivors, among others, as guinea pigs was read in the public sphere as a replication of the experiments on Jews in the Nazi death camps.[35] Most of the patients in the study were Jewish, and many were mentally and physically impaired. While the claim was that the experimenters had obtained oral consent, many of the patients in question were deaf, spoke only Yiddish, or were senile. Equally important, the experiments were neither conducted for the benefit of the patients involved nor did the physicians experiment first on themselves.[36] Indeed, the case altered the very notion of informed consent in U.S. medical research that had been so strongly touted as a product of the 1946 Nuremberg Doctors' Trial.

Defined as Jews and as the subject of medical interest, concentration camp survivors became the focus of debates about the impact of trauma on victims, victims specifically defined as Jews. What about the survivors' mental status? Did they have psychic damage from their experience? Were they now chronically mentally ill?[37] These debates shadowed the discussion of reparations for the suffering experienced in the camps, and the mental status of the inmates and the survivors became a central question in West Germany (the Federal Republic of Germany) in the 1950s and 1960s.

The question of mental competence and the long-term impact of racism within the world of the Holocaust survivor (a term that has had elastic qualities over the decades since) was raised in a serious way immediately after the war, even as the Cold War was effacing interest in the survivors. The new state of Israel, speaking for all of the victims and the survivors, demanded reparations for looted property though a systematic indemnification law. The Federal Republic, after some negotiation, agreed to such indemnification in 1951. The funds were directed to the resettlement of Jewish survivors in Israel.

The question of individual indemnification for suffering and chronic illness was also raised. The West German authorities demanded proof of damage to an individual's health through medical certification done primarily by German physicians. In the German Democratic Republic (East Germany) indemnification of citizens was granted by a committee made up of former camp inmates, admittedly mostly Communist bureaucrats, but without a specific demand for medical proof.[38] Medical certification for physical disability seemed relatively clear-cut; that for mental illness, however, became hotly contested.

The West Germans rested their view of mental illness caused by trauma on the position of the Weimar Republic's Reich Insurance Office, which stated in 1926 that for "medical and legal significance of traumatic neurosis" no obligation existed in Germany to provide a pension for neurosis resulting from accident. According to that ruling, the organism's ability to compensate after psychological trauma is practically unlimited, so no lasting loss of earning capacity through accident-based neurosis may be claimed. This was based on research concerning shell shock in soldiers after World War I, which concluded that any subnormal psychological reaction to trauma was actually the manifestation of the "desire for a pension." The Berlin clinical psychiatrist, and vituperative opponent to Sigmund Freud, Karl Bonhoeffer, in 1926, wrote that *traumatic neurosis* as a social illness could only be cured by social remedies. Bonhoeffer had been one of the first to make a clear distinction between endogenous and exogamous psychosis. According to his findings, all of his cases had a preexisting hereditary predisposition that was endogenous. The trigger, however, was the availability of compensation: "The law is the cause of traumatic neuroses," that is, "the disorder was caused by secondary gain, a compensation neurosis."[39] The image of the Jews as defined by their desire for economic advantage was an ancient trope of Christian antisemitism, and it became a central quality defining the Jew in the racial antisemitism of the Nazis.[40]

Still, in 1960, Gustav Störring, who held the chair in psychiatry at the University of Kiel, stated that such neurotic reactions were "calculated, wishful reactions. . . . that cannot be viewed as consequences of harm."[41] Such views became translated in the psychoanalytic literature of the post-war period into a depth psychological impulse. Reparations were, in the words of the Viennese psychoanalyst F. R. Bienenfeld, "not created by the desire of the perpetrator of the faulty action to *make* restitution, but, on the contrary, by the desire of the victim to *receive* restitution—and this desire alone is really a fundamental psychological urge."[42] They are deeply rooted, more so than the feeling of owing reparations:

> If the urge to make reparation for damage caused constituted an essen-
> tial and effective force of the human mind at the earliest stage, and if its
> impetus were so conspicuous, it would have been bound to build up an
> essential part of all legal systems, as the aggressive urge did in forming
> criminal law or the impulse to support in creating social law. In fact, an
> impulse to make reparation is hardly apparent in any law.[43]

Even émigré jurists, such as public law theorist Hans Kelsen, argued this in the immediate post-war period.[44] The German psychoanalytic perspective reinforced this position in Germany, claiming that persistent psychopathology could result only from a neurosis in early childhood development and therefore any survivor suffering psychic reactions was already damaged before they entered the camps.

The immediate implications of this view were evident. Individuals who suffered physical disability in the camps were acknowledged as incapacitated and thus were granted financial relief. Individuals who experienced sever mental illness during or following their experiences in the camps were not. Goren Rosenberg recorded his father David's descent into severe mental illness in post-war Sweden after surviving the ghetto at Lodz and then Auschwitz-Birkenau. He quotes a Dr. Herbert Lindenbaum, a German psychiatrist based in Stockholm and chosen by the German government to evaluate his father's application for relief, who writes in 1956 that "[w]ithout a doubt the patient is exaggerating." Lindenbaum concludes that the elder Rosenberg "seems to have survived his internment in the concentration camps without suffering any persistent consequences to health. The symptoms of psychoneurosis that the patient alleges he has can no longer necessarily be linked to possible harm inflicted in the concentration camps." But more than this, the physician is convinced that the psychic damage Rosenberg evinces predates his internment: "He also gives the impression of doing all he can to prevent any investigation into his past."[45] He is insane now because he was already damaged before he entered the camps.

Yet it was clear by the 1950s that the camp experience had long-term effects. The Dutch Jewish psychoanalyst J. Tas, who had been held in the concentration camp at Westerbork and was transferred to the death camp at Bergen-Belsen in 1944, provided a detailed account of the psychic damage suffered by the inmates.[46] He diagnosed and treated patients, mainly children, in Bergen-Belsen:

> Among others, I remember a phobia in a five-year-old boy, who awakened from his sleep screaming, having dreamed that the Germans had opened the gates of the camp and let in all kinds of big animals, elephants, giraffes, etc. In these infantile animal phobias we know that the animals usually symbolize the parents. It is very understandable that in this case, two sources of anxiety, the parents and the Germans, were linked together. In a few interviews the little boy was cured, surely because the anxiety was neutralized by the positive father-transference which had developed.[47]

What is noticeable in such accounts is the assumption of an underlying universal psychic structure disturbed by day residue, the memories of immediately experienced events, but processing it through the "normal" psychic channels. Tas continued:

> In some instances, it was possible to follow up such a case after the war, thus obtaining more insight into these paradoxic abreactions. Groen, an Amsterdam internist and psychosomatologist, saw, after the war, a patient

whom he had treated before the war for ulcerative colitis, and who also had survived Bergen-Belsen. In the camp, where most everybody suffered extremely from dysentery, this patient merely had diarrhea from time to time, but never blood or mucus in his feces. He even asserted that he had less trouble from his intestines than the others. Back in Amsterdam, he relapsed into his ulcerative colitis. Further particulars may explain this phenomenon. The patient was strongly fixated on his mother, and was very unhappily married to a woman who was too masculine and robust for him. He missed, in her, all maternal feeling and love. However, the patient stated that, in the camp: "My wife was a regular angel to me; she was afraid that I would not survive the camp. She worked in the kitchen, saved some food for me, in a word our marital harmony had never been so good before."[48]

Again, the assumption is that underlying neurosis manifested themselves, here even corrected themselves, in the camps. But among most survivors, Tas observed

an immense accumulation and bottling up of sentiments of anxiety, rage and aggressiveness, which not only must have been the cause of many disturbances but which also defined the character of these disorders, at the same time retarding their coming to light and hampering their treatment. As these sentiments had to be suppressed and encapsulated from the very beginning, it was even more difficult than usual for the psychotherapist to liberate them. This factor of suppressed and encapsulated aggressiveness, and the frequent ensuing repression of every affect, certainly can often explain the phenomenon in which psychic disturbances arising from a stay in a camp frequently come to light only months or even years after the return home.[49]

Other Jewish psychoanalysts, such as renowned New York psychotherapist Kurt Eissler, found the possibility that there would be no psychic damage unimaginable. Eissler poses a question in the title of his 1963 essay "The murder of how many of his children can one bear without symptoms, in order to prove that one has a normal constitution?"[50] The assumption that camp experiences necessarily lead to psychopathologies was not a universal position even among émigré psychiatrists in New York, as can be seen in the debate between the clinical psychiatrist Lothar Kalinowsky and psychoanalysts such as William Niederland. Kalinowsky stressed that preexisting conditions account for inmates' traumatic reactions; Niederland, on the other hand, saw such responses as "concentration camp syndrome."[51] It was only in the years 1957–1958 that counter voices appeared in Germany that diagnosed "restitution neurosis" or "uprooting depression" or "complete rupture in the life line" resulting from the impact of the camp experience itself.[52] By the 1960s those diagnoses were recast as post–concentration camp syndrome. With the Vietnam War and the resultant reevaluation of the psychic damage done to the soldiers in the war (now, one must add, to the victims of the soldiers on all sides), the consensus was framed that traumatic neurosis was real and a new label, post-traumatic stress disorder, evolved out of the politics of the anti–Vietnam War movement.[53] Thus it is the politics of war from World War I Weimar to post-Vietnam America and Germany that defined the "madness" of the victims as neither mercenary (a common post-war charge against the Jews in West Germany) nor inherently mentally ill (as we have seen, a commonplace about the Jews in psychiatric discourse).

The pathologization of the survivor came to be a problem, as the claim seemed then to be that all survivors were permanently scarred and thus constantly presenting symptoms resulting from their experiences. Yet there could still be the basis for a successful adaptation in spite of or even because of the experiences of the camps. This comes to be a theme in a number of studies in the 1980s and 1990s. William Helmreich, a professor of sociology and Judaic studies at City University of New York, wrote in his *Against All Odds: Holocaust Survivors and the Successful Lives They Made in America* that camp survivors were not only successful, having more stable families and lives than other American Jews of comparable age, but that they seemed to present with fewer symptoms of mental illness as only 18 percent had seen a psychologist, social worker, or psychiatrist compared with 31 percent for other American Jews.[54] Helmreich's analysis relativized the conclusions of earlier studies of survivors with severe mental illnesses, which were based on those who had been seen in therapy or, as in the case of the oft-cited work of Dori Laub, in mental hospitals.[55] Earlier work by the sociologists Zev Harel and Eva Kahana and the psychologist Boaz Kahana stressed that camp trauma did not necessarily lead to debilitating mental illness; indeed it may well have engendered greater levels of resilience.[56] The discourse of successful surviving came to be interpreted in terms of Robert Jay Lifton's account of "psychic numbing" developed in his study of Japanese survivors of Hiroshima.[57] Such reactions were seen as ego defense mechanisms, following Anna Freud, and could clearly take both negative and positive form.

The debates about the impact of trauma were framed by the question of the inmates' predisposition to psychopathology, and, by the 1950s, this predisposition for specific forms of mental illness was defined as "Jewish." As a medical student, Freud had already rejected any definition of such a predisposition as racial, and indeed one can argue that the entire underlying model of traditional psychoanalysis moved to the universal qualities of psyche and development against the racial model.[58] It is clear that the structures that framed the debate about trauma and reparations after 1945 looked at the question of predisposition as a primary one. How this was to be understood mimicked the debates about racial predisposition to such a degree that even at the time the question was posed as to the motivations of the psychiatric theory. It was only with the posing of the question, not about the victim, but about the motivations of the perpetrators, that this became a focused debate.

Guilt or Neurosis?

In 1946 the question of what had motivated the Germans, the German government, or Hitler and his henchmen (depending how the question was asked) to murder six million Jews was a question of American policy. "Reeducation" was the mantra and it was based on the assumption that the bulk of Germans (at least in the American Zone) were not mentally ill, but merely misinformed by their leadership's ideology.[59] Not madness per se, for even at the first Nuremburg trial of the Nazi leadership in 1946 (the only international trial of the perpetrators) not one claim of mental incapacity was offered or heard. Even Rudolf Hess, whom his British captors had unambiguously diagnosed as mentally ill, was deemed competent to stand trial. He was sentenced to an Allied prison in Berlin, where he eventually committed suicide in 1987. But reeducation is clearly not therapy. Sigmund Freud had stressed this in his introduction to August Aichhorn's *Wayward Youth* in 1925:

[T]he effect that the work of education is something sui generis: it is not to be confused with psycho-analytic influence and cannot be replaced by it. Psychoanalysis can be called in by education as an auxiliary means of dealing with a child; but it is not a suitable substitute for education. Not only is such a substitution impossible on practical grounds but it is also to be disrecommended for theoretical reasons.[60]

Aichhorn was dealing with juvenile delinquents. The Allies were dealing with Germans whose ideology had made their nation into an international pariah. But with the Cold War looming, therapy was not demanded, only a new form of education.

In late July 1945, two young American sociologists in uniform, Major Donald V. McGranahan and 2nd Lt. Morris Janowitz (Bettelheim's co-author), examined the status of "German boys and girls" aged fourteen to eighteen through a series of questionnaires as representatives of the Intelligence Section Information Control Division.[61] Given that they were interviewing the young Germans at the very end of the war and that they were in uniform, they acknowledge:

There is no doubt that on a number of topics the youth answered with an eye cocked on the American eagle. The results, particularly on the more direct questions, must therefore be viewed with this fact in mind. However, it must also be remembered that the Allied occupation is a dominant and real fact in the psychological environment of every German.[62]

With this caveat they produced

a hypothetical picture of the "average" German civilian youth under American occupation. . . . This youth wants to continue living in Germany, and considers Russia the worst place in the world in which to live. He feels that the Germans as a people are superior to the Italians, Poles, Russians, and French but not to the Americans and English. The officers were justified in attempting the Putsch of 20 July, 1944, he feels, because it was clear that the war was lost at that time. It was lost primarily because of the material superiority of the Allies, especially in air power. He is ready to admit that Germany started the war, although he is apt to add that the Jews or Englishmen or Poles were also responsible. He agrees that the German Jew should be permitted to return to Germany, and that Hitler Youth and BDM leaders should be prevented from taking leading positions in any new youth movement. As for women, their place is still in the home, not in outside careers. This youth expresses the view that Germany should now become a democracy. At the same time, however, he says that the idea of National Socialism was good but it was not carried out right. He hesitates on the question as to whether Hitler himself was bad or whether it was just his advisers who were bad. In any case, he feels quite strongly that Germany now needs a strong Fuehrer in order to recover from her destruction and devastation.[63]

The sentiments expressed by the teenagers were viewed as the result of the authoritarian personality meeting American democracy, an experience of American occupation that McGranahan and Janowitz knew all too well. The underlying character of the Germans (writ large even though we are looking at a subset, the youth, which should be the most malleable, according to the principles of reeducation) was encapsulated:

In a sense, the very manner in which they quickly pick up and express democratic and pro-American views reveals their totalitarian attitude of implicit and uncritical submission to authority, ingrained by Nazi education and German tradition. There is little evidence from other sources that German youth, including those intellectuals who proclaim the necessity of "democratic" propaganda, understand what democracy means as a way of life in ordinary day-to-day community affairs. The danger exists that adherence to democracy will be used more as a formula to expect assistance and sympathy from American authorities than as a formula for self-help and community action. Untrained in democratic processes, German youth appear to presume that the American leaders will now solve their problems in an authoritarian fashion just as the Nazi leaders proposed to do, without the youth having to do anything more than obey orders and profess adherence to the official creed.[64]

They understand that this collective may well recognize the empirical necessity of seeming to act correctly, but there was a strong undercurrent of Nazi ideology: "Simple questions of fact also revealed Nazi residues. Although the youth, for example, in majority admitted that Germany started the war, a significant minority held other parties responsible. Half as many as those who mentioned Germany referred to other groups, the most common being the Jews."[65] Contrasted with POWs who were reeducated, the former soldiers seemed better equipped for transition. Yet the researchers' rationale for their findings, that POWs were more intensely exposed to Americans than most German soldiers who had not been incarcerated, was clearly incorrect given the political reality in the POW camps, where Nazi ideologies were often the dominant (if invisible) force.

> However, the extreme pro-American and anti-Nazi views of these "re-educated" youth should not necessarily be construed as evidence of fundamental conversion to democracy. Compared with the civilian youth, they revealed a greater susceptibility to the influence of their new masters and a greater identification with the American side; but this may be due to their greater exposure to the American point of view. The durability of these views when the prisoners return to their homes and occupations is, of course, open to question. In general, the young prisoners displayed little critical and independent thinking, but much servility.[66]

The question of the constitution of a mental collective, in terms now of collective guilt, but clearly building on the idea of the crowd or the masses, echoes in the background of their study. How much was the authoritarian character intrinsically German, and how much the result of indoctrination? How much, indeed, was ego identification with the aggressor? The very question of the collective itself is also debated. Karl Jaspers, while an anti-Nazi, was one of the most noted phenomenological psychiatrists during the Weimar Republic. He was, as a psychiatrist, fully aware and an advocate of the biological model of race, though he does makes a distinction between race and constitution. As we noted in Chapter One, Jaspers concludes his *General Psychopathology* with a summary of the literature on the general predisposition of the Jews for mental illness.[67] In Weimar he became, together with Martin Heidegger, one of the chief exponents of existential philosophy and psychology. Unlike Heidegger, however, who was an advocate of and spokesman for the Nazi regime, Jaspers was critical of the regime (as he had been of parliamentary democracy in Weimar). This may well have been because he remained married to a Jewish woman, which caused him to lose his chair in philosophy at the University of Heidelberg and be constantly at risk of being sent to the concentration camps. In 1946 he looks at the legacy of the Third Reich in his *The Question of German Guilt* after the Nuremburg trials:

> Morally one can judge the individual only, never a group. . . . This confusion, of the generic with the typological conception, marks the thinking in collective groups—*the* Germans, *the* British, *the* Norwegians, *the* Jews, and so forth. . . . Unfortunately natural to a majority of people, it has been most viciously applied and drilled into the heads with propaganda by the National-Socialists. It was as though there no longer were human beings, just those collective groups.[68]

Jaspers questioned the idea of any sort of collective guilt accruing to the Germans, yet at its conclusion the pamphlet argued that all Germans needed to accept moral, not legal, responsibility for the Holocaust in order to achieve some type of political and cultural renewal. "Full frankness and honesty harbors not only our dignity—possible even in impotence—but our own chance. . . . The answer is that this is the only way that can save our souls from a pariah existence." [69] He pointedly evoked Max Weber's (and Hannah Arendt's) notion of a "pariah people," always on the margins, isolated from the hosts, and always inferior to them, as his model of what the Germans must avoid. This model was first, and foremost, applied by Weber to the Jews, and Jasper certainly recognized this. But Weber's statement that, after 1919, "like the Jews we [Germans] have been turned into a people of pariahs" also influenced him.[70] Jaspers himself had had this experience after 1919 and anticipated it might repeat in 1945.

Hannah Arendt saw the post-war question of the very nature of antisemitism in a manner that clearly rejects her American colleagues' position. While she had been Jaspers's student, he later acknowledged that it was her insights into the nature of democracy and the nature of totalitarianism that influenced his own work. In her 1953 essay "On the Nature of Totalitarianism: An Essay in Understanding" Arendt disavows a psychological explanation, and notes her ongoing commitment to understand the empirical sociological and historical sources of the silence around prejudice: "The task of the social scientist is to find the historical and political background of antisemitism, but under no circumstances to conclude that Jews are only stand-ins for the petite bourgeoisie or that antisemitism is a surrogate for an Oedipus-complex, or whatnot."[71] A psychological explanation is, of course, exactly what some West Germans sought, an explanation that has a therapeutic dimension inherent in its very statement. While Jaspers clearly does not advocate for a psychological explanation for German actions, it is clear that he sees the moral gesture as itself recuperative for German society. Without it, they become a pariah people, as one of Hannah Arendt's groundbreaking essays of 1944 shows the Jews too had become, with positive as well as negative results.[72]

The debate about the collective nature of the German response to fascism puzzled and continues to puzzle historians. Perhaps the best of the émigré historians of the German Resistance, Klemens von Klemperer, wrote that the "consensual quality of Nazi control is one of its most vexing paradoxes. It made oppression all the more humiliating and rendered the task of resisting all the more difficult. In Germany, resistance had to be staged without the 'social support,' which was available, at least latently, to the Resistance in other countries." He stated that such a pattern of psychological submission meant that "there was, and could be, no popular resistance movement" in Germany.[73] Von Klemperer did not engage in any psychologizing, but when he imagined a German collective action he could see it only in terms of the "crowd."

The silence about the nature of the perpetrators after 1945, including the discussion of their psychopathology, was obscured as the Cold War and the economic rebuilding of West Germany, the *Wirtschaftswunder*, took precedence.[74] Stability meant the general acknowledgement of the victims, as in the 1951 decision of the Adenauer government to settle the reparations question with the young state of Israel, yet there was relatively little discussion in Germany about the question of collective acknowledgment or guilt beyond Jaspers's book, and its implication for a German psychopathy. The passage of time and the aging of the youngest generation born at the very end of the war or in its immediate aftermath, those who had no conscious awareness of the Nazi period and were shaped largely by the Cold War and the gradual Americanization, for good or ill, of West Germany, led to a sudden and rather startling confrontation with the past, producing what historians have called the generation of 1968. But the question had been first formulated in 1967 when two German psychoanalysts Margarete and Alexander Mitscherlich published their study entitled *The Inability to Mourn*.[75] An immediate bestseller in Germany, the text seemed to focus all of the anxiety about the past felt by the youngest generation on the to-that-point-unspoken question: What did you do in the war, Daddy? (And it really was "Daddy" who was asked.) This was not a new question for Alexander Mitscherlich, who had been engaged with the question of German guilt as early as Jaspers, and edited a volume on the Nuremburg Doctors' Trial in 1947.[76]

What the Mitscherlichs saw in West Germany was the total refusal to come to terms with recent history, marked by what they defined as the refusal to mourn the past and to understand the deep emotional bond that the Germans had had to Hitler and fascism.[77] It was the absence of any mourning for the loss of their emotional center that was crucial:

> To millions of Germans the loss of the "Führer" (for all the oblivion that covered his downfall and the rapidity with which he was renounced) was not the loss of something ordinary; identifications that had filled a central function in the lives of his followers were attached to his person. The loss of an object so highly cathected with libidinal energy . . . was indeed reason for melancholia. Through the catastrophe not only was the German ego-ideal robbed of the support of reality, but in addition the Führer himself was exposed by the victors as a criminal of truly monstrous proportions. With this sudden reversal of his qualities, the ego of every single German individual suffered a central devaluation and impoverishment. This creates at least the prerequisite for a melancholic reaction.[78]

And yet there was no such reaction. The vaunted stability of the *Wirtschaftswunder* and its silence about the Holocaust was seen by the Mitscherlichs as a simple refusal to come to terms with this emotional past. "Hard work and its success soon covered up the open wounds left by the past."[79] They claimed that the (West) Germans never were able to empathize with the victims of the Holocaust, who, by the 1960s, were more and more labeled the "Jews," and they would never be able to do so until there was a basic psychic working through of this lack of emotional connection (decathexis). No melancholy was seen in post-war Germany:

> We have argued that, had it not been counteracted by these defense mechanisms—by denial, isolation, transformation into the opposite, and, above all, by withdrawal of interest and affect, that is to say, by the de-realization of the whole period of the Third Reich—a condition of extreme melancholia would have been inevitable for a large number of people in postwar Germany, as a consequence of their narcissistic love of the Führer and of the ruthless crimes they committed in his service. In their narcissistic identification with him, the Führer's failure was a failure of their own ego. Though derealization and other defense mechanisms did prevent an outbreak of melancholia, they could only imperfectly ward off a "tremendous impoverishment of the ego." This seems to us the key to an understanding of German psychic immobilism and inability to tackle the problems of present-day society in a socially progressive fashion.[80]

Freud had defined "melancholy" as the normal response to the destruction of the sort of narcissistic emotional link (cathexis) that defined Nazi Germany. The Germans were defined by having chronically weak egos, which allowed them, no *demanded*, that they adhere to an identification with authority. The ego feels this submission "not as a burden but as a joy."[81] The perpetrators had suffered from a psychopathology, a weakness of the ego, which led them to lack any empathy with those they had murdered, and which in turn led to a refusal to deal with the emotional consequences of their actions after the war. Having been in a "symbiotic state" with Hitler, they could not mourn him, as "mourning can occur only when one individual is capable of empathy with another."[82]

The Mitscherlichs illustrate this lack of emotional connectedness through the reparations debate and the central question of the psychic impact of the Holocaust on the survivors:

> Germans have paid not ungenerous compensation to those remaining European Jews whom they persecuted but did not manage to kill. Yet Germans still have no emotional perception of the *real* people whom they were ready to sacrifice to their dream of being a master race: as people,

these have remained part of the de-realized reality. The medical evaluations, for instance, of physical and mental damage sustained by victims of Nazi persecution betray in many cases a terrifying lack of empathy. The evaluator is still thoroughly biased and unconsciously identifies with the persecutors. . . . Are such horrors supposed to leave no scars? Kurt R. Eissler has asked the shaming question: The murder of how many of his children must a man be able to bear without symptoms, for German medical experts to credit him with being normal? There is little difference in principle between the *form* of this administrated compensation to survivors and the forms of administrated slaughter of a whole ethnic group. At first Germans were prevented by their total self-dedication, and the dissolution of their own ego in the Führer's ideas and claims, from feeling any sympathy for the victims of persecution as human beings.[83]

They recognize the debate not as one concerning the psychiatric theory of trauma but as a very symptom of the repressed acknowledgement of the Holocaust in a world desiring only normality. How could the victims suffer from psychic wounds when the perpetrators have not acknowledged their own wounds?

The cause of the German genealogy of ego weakness was an unresolved Oedipal complex with submission to the parental authority and the sense of self-esteem that results from such subservience as the norm. Hitler was the focus of a national, unresolved Oedipal drama on the part of the members of the state. What seemed to be "normal" in Germany was in fact a pathological refusal to mourn the lost past. Its primary symptom was the Germans' insistence on getting back to normal and becoming a liberal democracy, something that was seen in the literature on the immediate post-war response to the Americans in their zone of authority. In order to make the case, the Mitscherlichs evoke the question of the treatment of the "Negro" and specifically American blacks to observe that racism is not limited to the Germans: "[W]hen human beings are deprived of basic rights or freedoms, intolerance must be at work. . . . The struggle between tolerance and intolerance is taking place before our eyes in the southern States of the United States, in relation to the abolition of racial segregation."[84] Yet they explain the status of the Southern black as the result of "the deformation of the weaker [that] turns out to be not a natural characteristic, as the oppressor pretends, but a product of the oppression itself."[85] Self-hatred is the natural result of oppression, and claimed by the oppressor as the essential character of the oppressed!

The Germans' predominant psychic abnormality, according to the Mitscherlichs, was their refusal after the Holocaust to confront their own culpability. What the Mitscherlichs do not question is the very nature of antisemitism itself. This is the central motivating factor for the Holocaust—this they articulate—but it is merely one more form of a universal disease, prejudice:

> Now as to the transmission of such unshakable prejudices, the way they spread, particularly in the political field, depends on the fact that *nuclei* of potentially delusional reactions, such as may be produced in all of us, can survive in our psyche in more or less isolated form for a very long time. In the wake of an exciting political development they can be powerfully kindled, nourished, and cultivated. They may then spread on a truly epidemic scale, only eventually to lapse once more into a sort of dormancy—after many horrors have been committed to satisfy the delusion. The drive energy that cathected the prejudice is then withdrawn from it. The genius of the demagogue lies in his ability to revive and re-intensify the cathexis—in the service of his own instinctual wishes. Like epidemics, prejudices that affect the consciousness of whole peoples can die down, leaving behind only an endemic remnant, the mistrust, for instance, that perpetually accompanies many disappointed people caught in neurotic misevaluation of reality. We all nurse some prejudices, perhaps against neighbors whom unconsciously we envy for some reason or other.[86]

The metaphor is one of an epidemic that affects entire populations, with residual consequences. Thus the Germans are like every other crowd in Le Bon's sense and it is not surprising that the Mitscherlichs positively cite Le Bon as a model for the analysis of a "logic of instinct."[87] The Germans are a crowd, responding to the infection of prejudice. Their continuing fault is not acknowledging and articulating this after it is revealed to be the cause of the Holocaust. Such an acknowledgement would have been therapeutic.

The Mitscherlichs' attack on Germans who were adults during the war resonated with the youth of the generation of 1968 in Germany. This was reinforced by the youth movements in France and the United States, which though stemming from very different causes radically reacted to the politics of their parents' generation. Anti-establishment feelings came to be defined as a "healthy" response to the perceived repression of the older generation. Whether "counterculture anti-establishment" was an accurate portrayal of the totality of the immediate post-war genera-tion's reaction to the past was rarely raised at the time. What was clear was that the argument about psychopathology was powerful and was heard.[88] That the Mitscherlichs evoked the very notion of masculinity in the Oedipal complex seemed to absolve the women of the Third Reich in an uncomfortable way. Indeed, even Klaus Theweleit's *Männerphan-tasien* (1977) (translated as *Male Fantasies*, 1987), a bestseller about the sexual repression that underpinned Nazi ideology among former sol-diers in the pre-fascist paramilitaries and then the *Sturmabteilung*, the Nazi party's paramilitary wing, stressed the damaged masculinity of the Nazi male.[89] This harked back to Wilhelm Reich and, to no one's sur-prise, one of the rediscoveries of the generation of 1968 was Reich's *Mass Psychology of Fascism*, which became an underground bestseller and impacted Theweleit and many other commentators of the time. When in 1983 Margarete Mitscherlich considered whether antisemitism was a male disorder, she claimed that the women of the Third Reich were in thrall to their male leaders, arguing rather obliquely that they identified with the aggressor.[90] Rooting it all in the Oedipal complex, whether in terms of anxiety about the male parent or the identification with the ag-gressor, makes the role of the female always contingent in these theories. Historians have recently argued quite differently about the post-war use of sexual psychology (especially on the left) as a means of explaining the actions and views of individuals in the Third Reich.[91]

But it is only decades later, in 1996, that the debate about the Nazi mind reappears on the bestseller lists and then not in a work from a psychologist or psychiatrist, but from an American Jewish political scientist and the son of a Holocaust survivor. Daniel Goldhagen's *Hit-ler's Willing Executioners: Ordinary Germans and the Holocaust* (1996) asks *why* the German soldiers were willing to undertake the Holocaust. He rejects out of hand the standard explanations: the idea of external compulsion—that they were in fear of their own lives, that they were in thrall to Hitler's charisma and blindly followed his orders, that they were under social pressure from their peers, that they were career-building technocrats, or that they could not understand their actions as part of a totality leading to the Holocaust:

> The explanations can be re-conceptualized in terms of their accounts of the actors' capacity for volition: The first explanation (namely coercion) says that the killers could not say "no." The second explanation (obedience) and the third (situational pressure) maintain that Germans were psychologically incapable of saying "no." The fourth explanation (self-interest) contends that Germans had sufficient personal incentives to kill in order not to want to say "no." The fifth explanation (bureaucratic myopia) claims that it never even occurred to the perpetrators that they were engaged in an activity that might make them responsible for saying "no."[92]

For Goldhagen there is a more compelling explanation—"that the perpetrators, . . . ordinary Germans," were animated

> by a particular *type* of antisemitism that led them to conclude that the Jews *ought to die*. The perpetrators' beliefs, their particular brand of anti-semitism, though obviously not the sole source, was, I maintain, a most significant and indispensable source of the perpetrators' actions and must be at the center of any explanation of them. Simply put, the perpetrators, having consulted their own convictions and morality and having judged the mass annihilation of Jews to be right, did not *want* to say "no."[93]

While Goldhagen seems to overtly reject a psychological explanation, his claim that the Germans of the Nazi era had a common historical consciousness, that they shared a form of "eliminationist antisemitism" that made it not only possible but morally justifiable to murder Jews, rests on the metaphor, if not the reality, of the psychopathology of the crowd.[94] The very term "eliminationist antisemitism" is coined by Goldhagen to evoke a German mindset that predisposed the Germans as a collective to genocide. This was analogous to the British views in World War I about the German psyche as a form of crowd psychosis. Both assumed that such patterns were rooted in social indoctrination and were malleable to reeducation after the war. The Germans showed a form of demonological antisemitism, of the virulent racial variety, [that] was the common structure of the perpetrators' cognition and of German society in general. The German perpetrators . . . were assenting mass execution-ers, men and women who, true to their own eliminationist anti-Semitic beliefs, faithful to their cultural anti-Semitic credo, considered the slaughter to be just.[95]

The source was cultural representations of the Jews, both in mass and high places. Goldhagen thus argues for a "cognitive explanation" for German behavior, what social scientists usually label attitude-behavior consistency.[96] That is, the beliefs held by the Germans had a very high correlation with their actions in killing Jews. This is a collective expla-nation as Goldhagen, as we have seen, seems to reject any individual psychological explanation such as obedience and the pressures for conformity.

For Goldhagen, antisemitism is not merely generalized racism aimed toward a symbolic Jew but unique in and of itself as "negative beliefs and emotions about Jews qua Jews."[97] While the German antisemites seemed to their victims to be "pathologically ill . . . struck with the illness of sa-dism . . . diseased . . . tyrannical, sadistic," indeed "psychopathic" (quot-ing a "keen diarist of the Warsaw Ghetto"), the truth was that "Hitler and the Nazis were firmly in the grip of a hallucinatory ideology, but they were not madmen."[98] As their "beliefs [would have] seemed to us to be so ridiculous, indeed worthy of the ravings of madmen, the truth that they were the common property of the German people has been and will likely continue to be hard to accept."[99] Germans of the Nazi era are here depicted as obsessed yet not legally incompetent, not madmen but the crowd in thrall to an idea.

For Goldhagen German antisemitism is a form of obsession as the

Germans' violent anger at the Jews is akin to the passion that drove Ahab to hunt Moby Dick. Melville's memorable description of Ahab's motives may serve as a fitting motto for the unrelenting, unspeakable, unsurpass-able cruelties that Germans visited upon Jews: "All that most maddens and torments; all that stirs up the lees of things; all the subtle demonism of life and thought; all evil to crazy Ahab were visibly personified and made practically assailable in Moby-Dick."[100]

They are psychopathic yet not insane in their innate focus on the Jews as the symbolic foe.

> That Germans were fundamentally anti-Semitic is . . . less astonishing than was the cultural and political centrality of Jews in their minds and emotions. Perhaps the most striking feature of the discussion of the Jews' place in Germany was the obsessive attention paid to the subject, the avalanche of words devoted to it, the passion expended on it.[101]

They are consumed by the rhetoric of antisemitism so that "these accusations were hurled with enormous frequency and obsessiveness throughout German society, and, so widespread were they that they were increasingly held to be true even by those in Germany who had once been the Jews' allies."[102] The tension between a sanity deformed by ideology and the incompetence of the madman shapes Goldhagen's understanding of German antisemitism. His answer was that the Germans must be sane in legal terms, but that their ideology pushed them to a level of obsession. Their attitudes toward the Jews "would have sounded and been received like the 'logic' of a madman to anyone who did not share the Nazi eliminationist anti-Semitic creed."[103] Madness lies simply in our perception of their views, not in their individual psychology.

In a debate at the United States Holocaust Museum in 1996 Goldhagen is quite explicit about his idea of the prevailing German mindset:

> [T]he vast majority of Germans shared the same antisemitism that moved the perpetrators and because the perpetrators were themselves representative of German society and therefore indicate what other Germans would have done in the same position, the only conclusion that we can draw, indeed the conclusion that we must draw, is that the vast majority—not all, but the vast majority—of ordinary Germans during the Nazi period were prepared to kill Jews.[104]

Yet Goldhagen is anxious about falling into the trap of speaking about a German constitutional mindset: "I am not talking about German national character or any kind of eternal unchanging German beliefs or qualities: merely that for peculiar historical reasons, a brand of virulent antisemitism became part of German culture."[105] For Goldhagen knows that any claim for a constitutional German mind simply echoes the antisemitic rhetoric about the Jews. Likewise, trying to explain German antisemitism as a form of mental illness leads to another trap:

> All social psychological explanations deny the humanity of the perpetrators and the victims. I maintain that any explanation that fails to acknowledge the actors' capacity to know and to judge, namely to understand and to have views about the significance and the morality of their actions, that fails to hold the actors' beliefs and values as central, that fails to emphasize the autonomous motivating force of Nazi ideology, particularly its central component of antisemitism, cannot possibly succeed in telling us much about why the perpetrators acted as they did.[106]

The anxiety that Goldhagen shows in claiming a psychological basis for the internalization of German antisemitic rhetoric as a mechanism to explain not why but how such beliefs become entrenched is evident. Yet his book did exactly that. As the Israeli historian Steven Aschheim wrote at the time:

> We have come full circle. Goldhagen has again inflamed and re-energized the debate by revalidating and recirculating (what was thought to be) the discredited *Sonderspecies* archetype, the notion of ordinary Germans as anti-Semitic murderers, impelled to kill exclusively in terms of this historically conditioned, fanatic belief. Scholars have criticized this (correctly, in my view) by arguing that individual genocidal acts can be better explained in terms of a complex cluster of motivational factors. These obviously include antisemitism as a central force but also take into account other ideological ingredients. Moreover, they recognize the weight of situational factors and take into account generalized psychological mechanisms, evidenced by the equally murderous activities of other national groups (both in the Shoah and elsewhere) that render more intelligible the qualitative leap from conventional every-day prejudice to radical genocidal action.[107]

"Generalized psychological mechanisms" are what underlies Goldhagen's argument. Discredited as history at the time, uncomfortable as social psychology, his book placed the last claim on the notion of a collective, if malleable, German psychopathology. Ahab can no longer be a model for real experience any more than Kurtz would be for Hannah Arendt's Africa. Representations do not provide psychological theory beyond the world of the fiction in which they are embedded as thought experiments.

The general acceptance of antisemitism's impact on the psychology of its Jewish victims would, in many ways, parallel arguments made among American psychiatrists, psychologists, sociologists, and policymakers concerning anti-black racism in the United States. However, whereas there was an almost universal rejection of a special German psychopathology in the post–World War II era, especially among Jewish émigrés and camp survivors, in the United States, particularly in the heat of the modern Civil Rights era and then in the decades following it, there was a growing sentiment among professionals, policymakers, and even laypersons that racism has psychopathological characteristics. In the next chapters, we detail this emergent reconstruction of racism, from that of a social phenomenon to a medical and psychological one.

5

Race and Madness in Mid-Twentieth-Century America and Beyond

Rethinking Madness and Race between Germany and the United States

The émigré writers and their native North American colleagues wrote about fascism and madness in a context in which race and madness had already come to be explored not in terms of antisemitism but in terms of post-Reconstruction politics toward black Americans. Influenced by the European debates between sociologists and psychologists, American scholars looking at racism in the United States focused primarily on the experiences of blacks and Native Americans. By the early twentieth century, there had emerged within American scholarship an explanation of race and racism centered on their social and structural cause, but this was largely marginalized. Clinical research trumped sociological work, even though much of it, such as that of W.E.B. Du Bois, had a psychological component. In Du Bois's construction of a "double consciousness," for example (discussed in Chapter Two), the model of European Jewry and their necessary yet contested identification with Enlightenment models of national identity served as a template for understanding the complex relationship between post-Reconstruction black Americans and the American version of that Enlightenment identity. *The Souls of Black Folk* was also *The Souls of Jews*.

For example, when Du Bois writes in 1931 to Albert Einstein soliciting a piece on racism for his journal *The Crisis* (and identifying himself to Einstein by naming his teachers in Berlin forty years earlier) he could not have expected that Einstein, writing about racism against blacks in an antisemitic world, would observe:

> The tragic part of such a fate, however, lies not only in the automatically realized disadvantage suffered by [black Americans] in economic and social relations, but also in the fact that those who meet such treatment

themselves for the most part acquiesce in the prejudiced estimate because of the suggestive influence of the majority, and come to regard people like themselves as inferior.[1]

Racism creates a double consciousness in the form of self-hatred *among Jews as well as among blacks*. For Einstein racism was indeed a form of mental illness. Speaking at the historically black Lincoln University in the 1940s he told the assembled students and faculty, "The separation of the races [segregation] is not a disease of colored people, but a disease of white people," adding, "I do not intend to be quiet about it."[2] It is only the impact of racism that creates the madness of the oppressed.

How this identification with Jews, and the anxiety surrounding their biological and social status, merged with views of social causation of black self-hatred is central to the story we tell here, as the focus of much of American scholarship centered on the response of the victim to racism, rather than the nature of the mind of the racist. However, during this same period a similar, yet less marginalized, development was occurring within the American academy.

The inter-war years at the University of Chicago further solidified its model of "clinical" sociology, which focused intently on describing the conditions of inter-group conflict in "natural" settings. By the 1930s, Chicago alums E. Franklin Frazier and Charles S. Johnson had already raised questions about the source of self-hatred within the "social pathology of African American culture."[3] However, these years were in many ways still haunted by the biological specters of nineteenth-century race science. There were, of course, exceptions, but even these proposed a psychological explanation for racism.

The first systematic study, the German-born Jewish sociologist and social worker Bruno Lasker's *Race Attitudes in Children* (1929), for example, argued that there were no inborn hostilities to the other race, only "acquired habits."[4] Lasker (1880–1965) came to the United States in 1914 and was active in New York City social work at the Henry Street Settlement. In 1930 he edited the classic *Jewish Experiences in America: Suggestions for the Study of Jewish Relations with Non-Jews*, sponsored by the Jewish Welfare Board. His contribution to that volume was an essay on Jewish self-hatred.[5]

Meanwhile, many anthropological accounts of race through the early twentieth century continued to posit racial differences as innate, theorizing cultural variations as linked to different evolutionary processes between "varieties of men." By the late 1930s, Chicago School anthropologists had framed this as a result of "caste and class," as in the work of black scholars such as Allison Davis, who understood theorized racial differences as a problem of psychological development within economic castes.[6]

Among social scientists of this period, as well as other intellectuals, policymakers, and the general public, multiple racial ideologies were effectively collapsed into a commonly held belief that the eradication of racism depended upon the *nonrecognition* of race. As we identified in Chapter Two, through the metaphor of the long, slow burn, with few exceptions scholars of race and racism have largely attributed the demise of scientific racism to a trickle-down theory in which social scientists dismantled scientific racism within the universities first in the 1920s, then in the courts in the 1940s and 1950s, and finally within government policy in the 1960s and 1970s. What we, and a handful of other scholars including James McKee and Stephen Steinberg, have shown, however, is that while some elements of the biological fallacy of race were contested during these decades through social scientific research, many more scholars across the disciplines held tightly to biological explanations, even couching emergent cultural accounts within evolutionary language.[7] Furthermore, and important to our focus in this chapter, during this same period a simultaneous need to redefine *racism* as a pathological condition emerged out of the same general "truth regime" of medical and scientific authority, including that of social scientists.

Race and the Jewish Scientist

In reviewing scholarship on race and racism from the inter- and postwar periods, what is striking is how many researchers working within this field during the 1920s and 1930s were American Jews, often second-generation immigrants, and equally often hyperaware of antisemitism. Yet most of their interest focused on prejudice against blacks rather than Jews. Young sociologists such as Eugene Horowitz saw race patterns as determined by external attitudes toward the group; his spouse, the social psychologist Ruth Horowitz, was interested in self-awareness. The tension between an American experience where racism was defined through the black experience, and the experience and examination of racism by American Jewish scholars, added to the impact of subsequent research on the very nature of racism. Empiricism ruled, as Ruth Horowitz (1910–1997) developed a series of research strategies to plumb the psyches of the victims of racism. Trained in the Department of Psychology at Columbia University and receiving her Ph.D. in 1944, at the age of thirty-four, she and her husband had changed their name to Hartley in 1935 to avoid overt discrimination. For her dissertation, Horowitz conducted an experiment that examined sociality in boys from ten to twelve years of age.[8]

Horowitz was explicitly focused on examining racial dynamics and oppression in her published work. This model was developed by both Horowitzs in a groundbreaking paper entitled "Development of Social Attitudes in Children."[9] Their studies, undertaken in a "border state" of white children's attitudes toward blacks people, postulate "that the attitude of white children toward Negroes is developed in individuals as a result of community influence."[10] "Community influence" became a surrogate for the crowd or the herd. They used a variation of the standard intelligence test developed by Henry Goddard, based on Alfred Binet's model and Lewis Terman's 1916 version of the Binet-Simon test (Stanford-Binet test), and then ever more refined during the 1930s. These texts used visual images as the bases for evaluation:

> Two tests were devised to serve as a point of departure for further study: one, a "categories" test; the other, a standardized interview. The categories test was an adaptation in pictorial form of an occasionally used subtest in standard batteries designed to test verbal intelligence. In its customary form, five words are presented and the individual taking the test is required to select one item of the five which "does not belong." A pattern must be seen running through four of the items and not through the fifth. As adapted, five pictures were mounted on a page and the children taking the test (individually) were required to respond by rejecting one picture as "not belonging." The task still required the child to respond to a pattern running through four of the pictures and not including the fifth. In

the pictorial form, however, the items were selected so that the responses shed light on the way in which the social world was structured for the child. A page might contain five pictures: three white boys, one white girl, and one Negro girl. In attempting to superimpose a pattern, if it was not directly seen as one, the choice essentially lay between race and sex. The three white boys and the white girl might be seen as a belonging together, and the child could respond by setting off the picture of the Negro boy.[11]

Of course, the difficulties inherent in using visual sources as the point of departure, especially staged photographs or drawings, is that they already have biases built into them. For example, the critiques of the Szondi test for psychopathology (1935), which used older images of the institutionalized mentally ill, show that even slight variations from expectations structure responses.[12] Nevertheless, the Horowitzs' findings stressed that social norms among children were reflected in their evaluation of the images, specifically their levels of identification with the figures portrayed.

A revision of the "Show Me" test used in an earlier study (4) was undertaken. On a large sheet of paper were mounted 16 photographic portraits, 3" x 3" Y2, in four rows, four pictures in a row. Scattered on the page were pictures of three white boys, three white girls, three colored boys, three colored girls, three Filipino boys, and an owl. The children were asked to indicate all those with whom they might care to do certain things or about whom they had certain judgments. In each case, the children could indicate as many of the portraits as they cared to, and on repeated questioning they might select the same or different pictures.

The questions were:

Show me all those that:

1. you'd like to sit next to at school 2. you'd want to play with 3. live in a dirty house 4. you want to sit next to at the show 5. you do not want in your school 6. you'd like to have for a cousin 7. look stupid 8. you want to live near you 9. you do not like 10. you want to come to your house for a long visit 11. your folks would not let you play with 12. you would like to take to town This revision includes opportunity for the children tested to make unfavorable selections (items 3, 5, 7, 9, 11) as well as favorable. Further, the stimulus pictures include girls' pictures, making the test valid

for girls as well as for boys, and also permitting comparison of race attitude with sex attitude within the one instrument. The- inclusion of the
Filipinos and the owl permitted further comparisons, not here presented,
of response to unfamiliar with familiar, as well as to serve as distractions
and outlets for unfavorable responses without any necessary social reper-
cussions in the community.[13]

From this idea of the image as a measurement of "community attitudes" Ruth Horowitz explored the internal life of her subjects. For her it
was the question of projection, measured through the analysis of images,
that provided the best clues as to the inner life of the children.[14]

> Promising among these are the various toy and picture methods for re-
> vealing conscious and unconscious layers of motivation and personality,
> attitudes and needs important for teachers to understand. Three major
> streams of influence have flowed together to produce this trend. The first
> is the use of pictures and toys in the measurement of intelligence: pictures
> have been used in the various revisions of the Binet tests for nearly thirty
> years, while form boards, picture completion tests, etc. have been used in
> well known "non-verbal" tests almost as long.[15]

For Horowitz, however, these images have an objective meaning and an
interpretative one. It is the disjuncture between the two, and the mis-
reading of the child, that provides insight into the inner life. Much like
Freud's understanding of jokes or slips of the tongue, such creative mis-
readings provide clues:

> Photographs of clear-cut definite situations where individual objects
> fit into a specific unequivocal interpretation are examples of the highly
> structured material in the picture area. Here again "projections" appear
> unequivocally only when the obvious interpretation is distorted.[16]

Distortion is, as always, in the eye of the beholder. Its evaluation, however, seems to be in the eye of the objective scientific observer.

In Ruth Horowitz's most influential study, which deals "with the beginnings of race consciousness as a function of ego-development," she
examined children in a WPA nursery school, aged two to five, of both

sexes, with several black children in the group. A choice test was used: a page with two pictures relevant to the test item was shown the child, and the question "Which one is you?" was asked. A portrait series was also used, where ten portrait pictures were exposed one at a time, and the child was asked, "Is this you?" The white boys were more confused than black boys about race identification, but among girls there was no clear difference. In the portrait series, more black boys identified themselves as white than in the first test.[17]

The use of images of white and black children as a litmus test to measure self-evaluation provided Horowitz with a highly differentiated set of responses in segregated and integrated settings that reflected gender distinctions as well as racial and geographic ones. Thus one particularly notable thing in her essay is the black child who claimed he was both boys. Horowitz described the participant's identification as a member of the group "boy," rather than with the group "colored boy," as an operation "more abstract and more difficult."[18] A contemporary view reveals that his claim was actually simpler and more accurate; Horowitz's interpretation suggests how naturalized the idea of racial difference was when these studies were written. Psychological insight based on images provided snapshots of the internal life of the children, an internal life shaped by the communal attitudes (the crowd), but a crowd that reflected both white as well as black communities.

One significant mark of the inter–and post–World War II period was that through the scientific authority of the social scientists, social factors of racism were increasingly analyzed. Certainly, anti-Nazi Swedish economist Gunnar Myrdal's study *An American Dilemma: The Negro Problem and Modern Democracy* (1944), written with the collaboration of R.M.E. Sterner and Arnold Rose and funded by the Carnegie Corporation in 1938, arises out of similar concerns. Looking at the juxtaposition between the idealized American notion of equality and the racism of Jim Crow America, Myrdal examined the complex contradiction between an America of high values and moral beliefs (exemplified by Roosevelt's Four Freedoms as articulated in Myrdal's *Contact with America* in 1941, jointly written with his wife, Alva) and the reality of African American life.[19]

Gunnar Myrdal's adamant belief was that racial differences were purely cultural. The very notion of a psychological predisposition to madness, for Myrdal, was an artifact of racism. Yet, at the same time, racism shaped the self-awareness of its targets: "The study of women's intelligence and personality has had broadly the same history as the one we record for Negroes. As in the case of the Negro, women themselves have often been brought to believe in their inferiority of endowment."[20] The remedy, for Myrdal, was social integration, accomplished primarily through education. He describes education as "an assimilation of white American culture . . . [that] decreases the dissimilarity of the Negroes from other Americans."[21] Trained as a social scientist, Myrdal came to believe that science could "solve" the problem of prejudice. He even writes that an "increased general knowledge about biology" among whites would eliminate claims about racial superiority or inferiority.[22] Science is not merely a tool for explaining and justifying behavior, but is unequivocally intended to produce social change and policy.

Often Myrdal describes the use of science as the explicit basis for social improvement as genuinely helpful. He talks about the "vicious cycle" that maintains white prejudice and black degradation, declaring, "It is, or should be developed into, a main theoretical tool in studying social change."[23] He explains the importance of careful investigation when he qualifies his support for social measures to improve society: "The directing and proportioning of the measures is the task of social engineering. This engineering should be based on a knowledge of how all the factors are actually interrelated."[24] Thus, scientific inquiry is linked to "social engineering" and advocating for greater political equality. The acceptance of the economic status quo was central to his argument, something the American left critic Herbert Aptheker stressed in his critique of Myrdal's work.[25] Nevertheless, Myrdal's careful support for social engineering to combat the negative impact of racism and group prejudice marked a significant shift in how social and behavioral science had previously been used to influence race-based policy within the United States. Prior to Myrdal, of course, social and behavioral scientific research had contributed to policy reforms aimed at minimizing interracial contact. In the extreme cases, these policies targeted the reproductive capacity of the "lesser races" through anti-miscegenation and compulsory sterilization laws, as noted in Chapter Two. Yet the tail end of the long, slow burn, combined with broad-based support for Myrdal's research and conclusions, produced a largely new effort to reconsider race policy through an examination of the social, psychological, and political consequences of intense, systematic racism.

One complicating factor to Myrdal's attempt to use a scientific approach to improve equality, however, is that he openly admits his approach was not particularly empirical. He bemoans the observational, as opposed to rigorously experimental, nature of his work, writing, "It is desirable that scientifically controlled, quantitative knowledge be substituted for impressionistic judgments as soon as possible."[26] Additionally, though Myrdal uses psychological and psychoanalytic language, he uses it in a casual way—terms like "defense reaction" and "inhibitions" sound more like vaguely scientific synonyms for commonsense observations than technical jargon. Still, Myrdal is able to make powerful claims about the "sexual and the social complexes" that drive prejudice against people of color in America. By validating the importance of a scientific approach he positions himself as part of the scientific community, and thus as a researcher with authority, while also maintaining the benefits of speaking his opinions observationally.

Myrdal is very clear that the notion that black men are sexual predators is unfounded in reality. However, his rational explanations for the overestimation of rape by black men include the premise that white women will accuse black men of rape if they regret having sex, or because "neurotic white women may hysterically interpret an innocent action as an 'attack' by a Negro."[27] While he is overly sensitive to gender implications, here Myrdal posits a mental illness (hysteria) as a cause of white anxiety. He continues, claiming that only "psychopathic" black men could possibly commit rape in the South. However, he accepts women's "hysteria" and "neuroticism" as a given—this is about as much of a diagnosis as is pinned on anyone in his text. Myrdal feels that one could argue for the innocence of one marginalized group only by accusing another. Blaming a social problem on a devalued group can certainly be rhetorically effective, and it is of little surprise that he falls back on images of psychopathology to accomplish this.

Further, Myrdal tracks the differences between races that exemplify the drawing of a caste line, one that has yet to be transcended or erased. Throughout his account of racial difference as a form of caste delineation, the division of Northern and Southern habits problematizes his demarcation between races and race practices. The nuanced distinction he makes between regional behavioral modes is notable in his chapter on "Mental Disorders and Suicide," one of the standard sociological indexes of instability ever since Emile Durkheim's *On Suicide* (1897).[28]

Myrdal begins the chapter by explaining that mental disease increased among whites and blacks in the period following Emancipation. The change in mental states within all of America's population can be traced to a rupture within American history that was the product of political discontent between the North and the South. Myrdal argues that the Emancipation Proclamation was given not out of Lincoln's abolitionist sentiments, but as a political move to weaken the rebellious South. This crass political move destabilized Americans of all races after the Civil War. Myrdal asserts that the excessive number of black mental disorders in the 1930s in New York were due to migration. When migration is filtered out, the rate of mental disorder among whites and blacks is almost even.[29] Migration exacerbates underlying mental instability created in the segregated South.

A similar divide manifests in the words of Booker T. Washington, whom Myrdal frequently cites in his book for autobiographic evidence of the impact of racism.[30] In *Up from Slavery*, it becomes apparent that, while the news of Emancipation prompted heavy rejoicing, shortly afterward slaves began to worry about their lives to come.[31] For Washington, while freedom was a cause for celebration, the difficulty of life after Emancipation could have easily contributed to the rise in mental disorders that Myrdal discusses, especially since Washington claimed a shift toward equality that was reflected in the ability of blacks and whites to be treated in the same mental hospital. This was rarely the case in actual practice and where it was the expenditure for black patients in segregated wards was substantially less than for whites.[32]

Throughout *The American Dilemma*, Myrdal notes the differences in lifestyle between the North and the South, and occasionally states that the behavioral patterns of the Southern blacks he describes also generally hold true of whites in the South—yet the North-South divide that he recognizes does not inform or redirect his argument about caste: the line remains sternly demarcated by race. Within the delusions he lists that are associated with blacks, as opposed to whites, some additional North-South distinctions can be noted. Delusions common to the black include "topics of religion, possession of great wealth (often to help other Negroes), attainment of superiority in the literary and educational fields, and outstanding assistance to the race."[33] Just before this statement, however, he clarifies that lack of wealth has led to worse conditions in Southern facilities. Elsewhere, he also elaborates on the stronger adherence to religion and poorer access to education in the South. In essence, many of the divides between races, and therefore much of the caste system, Myrdal identifies might disappear if he highlighted more clearly the importance of the North-South divide.

Although Myrdal's work on race was utilized in the court's decision in *Brown v. Board of Education* in a way that helped begin to diminish the harsh caste line, the path toward erasing it entirely could have been even more readily apparent had his text utilized the importance of the North-South divide to show that a majority of the characteristics used to marginalize blacks are not specific to a race; rather, they highlight the ongoing division between the former Union and Confederacy. As a result, his call to employ democracy as a means to eliminate the caste line rings louder than he initially intends to suggest: if all parts of the United States have equal say in the workings of public policy, a positive cycle could begin by recognizing that the derogatory traits ascribed to blacks are not specific to that race and by starting to erase the line drawn between the Northern and Southern parts of the United States.

Supporting Myrdal's claims about the utility of social integration for reducing prejudice and achieving positive societal change were the results from the U.S. Army intelligence tests. While there was general dismay at the extraordinary low rate of success in the application of intelligence tests to recruits of all classes and races, the U.S. Army's Alpha Tests during World War I proved to most social scientists' satisfaction that blacks benefited from environmental change: though blacks had scored lower than whites across the board on intelligence exams, Northern blacks scored higher than Southern blacks *and* Southern whites. These studies began a long series of investigations into the effects of the environment on group differences, and though instrumentalist sociology played an important role in the eventual rejection of ideologies of Anglo-Saxon superiority, "it was the new science of cultural anthropology which proved to be the reformer's ally par excellence."[34] The psychological explanation for racism and its effects, for that is what came to be central in these debates, even extended to other groups in North America, including Native Americans.

The Mind of the Native Americans

The debate about the unique status of the "mind of the primitives" was a topic of great importance before World War I among the scientific avant-garde. With the appearance of Franz Boas's anti-evolutionist *Mind of Primitive Man* in 1911 social science was confronted with the claim that mental status could not be deduced from culture. In 1909 in a talk at Clark University he stated, "It will be recognized that here again the anthropological phenomena, which are in outward appearance alike, are, psychologically speaking, entirely distinct, and that consequentially psychological laws covering all of them can not be deduced from them."[35] Sigmund Freud may well have been in the audience for Boas's talk, and Freud's revisionist work on psychic development and mental illness in *Totem and Taboo: Resemblances between the Mental Lives of Savages and Neurotics* (1912–1913), as well as C. G. Jung's *Transformations and Symbols of the Libido* (1911–1912), joined the debate about the basic structure and development of the human psyche across time and geography.[36] Were we just like the "primitives" (Boas), or did the "primitives" lurk deep within our unconscious shaping our mental lives (Freud, Jung)? By the 1930s such questions merged into an analysis of the potential for mental illness among specific cohorts of "primitive minds."

While the preoccupation with the mental status of blacks remained central to this debate, the status of Native Americans was the subject of the Indian Personality Project. Created in 1940 by John Collier, then head of the Bureau of Indian Affairs, the Indian Personality Project set up a multidisciplinary group to investigate the formation of Native American personalities on several reservations in the United States.[37] The project was cast as something that would help the Bureau of Indian Affairs better administer the reservations, but it was also intended as a means whereby Collier's supporters could devise ways of helping Native American groups maintain their languages and cultures in the face of institutionalized prejudice. In other words, the ideology of this scientific undertaking was to prove not only that the so-called "civilizing project" applied to the Native Americans was faulty, but that the Native Americans were actually not in need of any such undertaking, as their cultures were rich and their identity not weakened, but strengthened, by their experience of "dominant" culture.

A complicating factor throughout this period is that the threatening overtones of the scientific approach to "social engineering," are, of course, quite clear, especially in the 1940s. This is, after all, only a few decades removed from the peak of eugenics in the United States, where local, state, and federal attempts to improve the general social welfare easily slipped into bureaucratic machines of biopolitical manipulation. The desire of the Indian Affairs commissioner to use respected scientific methodologies in order to make a case for Native Americans' importance as a distinct cultural group became bound up in the internment of Japanese Americans after Pearl Harbor. The tension between respecting cultural differences and eliminating them was also clear in Myrdal's work, as he tried to work through issues of the color line, miscegenation, and assimilation.

Using visual test models created by social scientists, Robert James Havighurst at the University of Chicago's Committee on Human Development undertook in the early 1940s a study of the intelligence of Native Americans as part of the Indian Personality Project. He was especially interested in education as a means of psychological restructuring of a potentially damaged Native American psyche. What he, and the project, found was quite different from what the Horowitzs and Myrdal found in their examinations of blacks. In a paper published in 1944, Havighurst argued against the claim that Native American intelligence was less than "white intelligence," a claim affirmed by a study in "1914 when Rowe administered Stanford-Binet examinations to 268 Indians and found 94 per cent of them to be below the norm for whites on the basis of chronological age."[38]

What the new tests showed was that children from tribes that had the most contact with whites, such as the Pine Ridge (Sioux) and Shiprock (Navaho) groups, did the best on these visual tests. Children from tribes with the least amount of contact, such as the Hickiwan-GuVo and Ramah, had the worst results in the study. The conclusions were clear:

American Indian children from several different tribes do as well as white children on a performance test of intelligence and . . . differences in test intelligence may be found between Indian tribes and between groups within Indian tribes, just as they may be found between various groups in the white population. There is some evidence that the Indian groups which are least influenced by white culture do not do as well on the Arthur test as those who have had more white influence and more schooling. But this evidence was not conclusive.[39]

The notion of integration here, the contact under the dome of the "civilizing project," was detrimental to Native Americans.

The next year Havighurst applied a version of the image evaluation test to children from six tribes, Sioux, Navaho, Papago, Hopi, Zuni, and Zia. The Draw-a-Man Test was based on the following argument: "[In] young children a close relationship is apparent between concept development as shown in drawing, and general intelligence. . . . The order of development in drawing is remarkably constant, even among children of very different social antecedents." Here the test did not examine *responses* to images, as in the tests administered by Ruth Horowitz, but instead examined how children *generated* images. The results showed that the

> Indian children exceeded the norms for white children by a statistically significant amount in seven of the nine groups. They exceeded their own Arthur IQ's in seven of the nine groups. The white children scored lower on the Draw-a-Man Test than on the Cornell-Coxe. It appears that the Indian children gave a definitely superior performance to that of white children on the Draw-a-Man Test.[40]

Thus poverty and isolation seem to have little impact on intelligence and self-esteem in this context. The key difference between the work of Ruth Horowitz and that of Havighurst was that Horowitz wanted to document the damage done to the black psyche by white society, and Havighurst wanted to show that Native Americans were relatively unscathed by racism.

Out of the Indian Personality Project came the work of American Jewish anthropologist Oscar Lewis (born Lefkowitz) on personality structures and resilience in poverty, including his famed 1961 sketch of the *Children of Sanchez*.[41] Many of the ideas for the Collier administration's reconstruction of the Bureau of Indian Affairs during the New Deal came out of contact with Mexican educational specialists who were concurrently trying to refurbish Native American village life in that country. The Indian Personality Project was thus extended to Mexico with the approval of Manuel Gamio and Moises Saenz. The former, an anthropologist trained by Franz Boas at Columbia, and the latter, a Protestant educational specialist trained in the United States by John Dewey, very much fit the profile of the sort of early-twentieth-century American Jewish (in the larger sense) scholar that formulated many of these theories in the 1940s.

The Psychology of Race in the World of Segregation

The politics of a new psychology of race impacted Jewish as well as black researchers in the United States in the 1940s and 1950s. One of Gunnar Myrdal's research assistants was Kenneth Bancroft Clark, then a Columbia University graduate student who had trained under the social psychologist of race and antisemitism Otto Klineberg. Together with his wife, Mamie Phipps Clark, Kenneth Clark had begun, in 1939, extrapolating from the work of Ruth Horowitz, herself a Columbia graduate, on the etiology of black self-hatred.[42] The Canadian Jewish Klineberg had been a student of Franz Boas and was quite aware of his refusal to highlight antisemitism as a major social and psychological force. He, like other Jewish students of Boas, such as Melville Herskovits and Ashley Montague, focused not on antisemitism but on blacks and American racism.[43] Later Klineberg became one of the most articulate witnesses in the court cases against segregation based on his research into the impact of racism on the mental state of blacks.

The Clarks built on the Horowitzs' image study of the construction of race consciousness through children's responses to images of white and black people. The Clarks famously substituted dolls for portraits in their version. They used four plastic, diaper-clad dolls, identical except for color. Almost all of the black children, ages three through seven, readily identified the race of the dolls. However, when asked which they preferred, the majority selected the white doll and attributed positive characteristics to it. Some qualities ascribed to the dolls were aesthetic: the children said they chose the white doll "'cause he's pretty" or "'cause he's white," and rejected the black doll "'cause he's ugly" or "'cause it don't look pretty."[44] But these categories were also seen by the children as having moral value: black dolls were "bad" and "mean," while white dolls were "nice" and "good." The Clarks argued that the children were "aware of the fact that to be colored in contemporary American society is a mark of inferior status."[45]

The Clarks also gave the children outline drawings of a boy and girl and asked them to color the figures the same color as themselves. Many of the children with dark complexions colored the figures with a white or yellow crayon. The Clarks concluded that "prejudice, discrimination, and segregation" caused black children to develop a sense of inferiority and self-hatred:

> Skin color differentials also seem to break down with a change in the environment of the subjects. In the segregated group racial identifications were made for the most part upon the basis of the skin color of the subjects. This same trend was found to be operative in the semi-segregated group. However, there was no tendency whatsoever toward this trend in the mixed group. This suggests the possibility that the racial identifications of children in the mixed group were to a large extent determined by the physical characteristics of those in their immediate environment. It is a question, to be settled by further work, whether this social factor has not gained priority over the factor of their own skin color as a determinant of the racial identifications of these Negro children.[46]

The focus solely on the response of the black children rather than on the comparative question of how other children responded in other environments led to the general assumption that self-hatred among blacks within a racially segregated society was ubiquitous and uniform in its origin.[47] What about the white kids in this study? Was their preference for white dolls a sign of psychopathology or health? The conclusion that there could not be any ambiguity, the failure to consider that cross-racial identification could lead to sublimation rather than repression of identity, echoes Anna Freud's findings in the Hampstead Clinic during the 1940s. Indeed, as a more recent sociological study has suggested, perhaps all the children, knowing the relative value of such toys in their culture, were "agential experts in children's culture" rather than "psychological dupes."[48]

The Clarks do address the social, writing that further work should investigate whether the "social factor has not gained priority over the factor of their own skin color as a determinant of the racial identification of these Negro children."[49] Still, they present their data without overtly explaining the political implications, even though it was built into the project, as it was supported by the NAACP's Legal Defense Fund. In one study, for instance, they write that "[t]he choices of mixed children at the four year level are rather confused as compared with the clean cut dropping off of irrelevant responses by the segregated and semi-segregated children," and state that there is a "retardation" of the development of ego and race consciousness in black students in mixed-race environments. Is race consciousness in young children coded "good" or "bad" psychologically? It was almost as if black children in segregated schools were seen as having "healthier," less delayed self-consciousness. This would be analogous to the readings of the Indian Personality Project, where the integrity of tribal culture provided a healthier mental environment for children.

The Clarks' study also claimed that black students in mixed environments, as in the claims about the exposure of Native Americans to white culture on and off the reservation, were more exposed to prejudicial treatment, whereas those in solely black preschools were on more "equal footing." Does desegregation, far from "reducing racism overall," actually *exacerbate* the effects of racism? The Clarks' argument clearly was the contrary: that the greater exposure to racism impacted children's self-consciousness negatively. Racial segregation, by definition a form of institutionalized racism, increased self-hatred. Desegregation becomes a strategy for reducing institutionalized racism, and would potentially increase black self-awareness, *even though it comes at the expense of initial prejudicial treatment*. The pitfall here was clear and the alternative to this argument was present in the form of the black power movement as well as earlier views of pan-Africanism.

The studies also reverse, again, the placement of the pathology—in these studies, it is those who are subject to racism that have psychological problems with ego and race consciousness, unlike in Myrdal, where it was the oppressor's psychological state that was being questioned. One is struck by the focus on black students' *ability* to identify the appropriate doll as opposed to their *desire* to identify with the privileged, white doll, since the number of students choosing the black doll actually seemed quite low—often scarcely better than chance. The Clarks concluded from these experiments that prejudice and segregation cause black children to develop a universal sense of inferiority and self-hatred.

The doll studies are problematic in a number of respects, yet the important point about this line of psychological research is that it moved the political discussion in the United States from looking at the *politics* of prejudice to the *psychology* of prejudice—to the *medicalization of prejudice* as the means for making a change in the existing political system, while not confronting the racist mentality of the "herd" inherent in shaping it. The movement initiated by the Clarks had several important ramifications. On the one hand, the movement played a positive role in the push to end segregation. On the other hand, the NAACP and other Civil Rights organizations invariably made legal arguments using the doll studies by invoking the universal psychological damage caused by segregation and racism, as the Clarks testified as expert witnesses in *Briggs v. Elliot*—part of *Brown v. Board of Education* in 1954. The Clarks' work contributed to the ruling in which the Supreme Court determined that de jure racial segregation in public education was unconstitutional.

The Clarks were not the only specialists in the study of the impact of racism on the black psyche to present their findings to the courts, though they were certainly the best known in the day. Among the others was the German Jewish psychiatrist Fredric Wertham. Wertham trained at Würzburg where he received his M.D. before moving to Munich to work in the major German center for clinical psychiatry run by Emil Kraepelin, the most important biological psychiatrist of the day and, as we noted in Chapter One, a scientist convinced of the predisposition of the Jews to madness. In 1922 Wertham was invited by Alfred Meyer to work at Worcester State Hospital in Massachusetts and soon moved to the Phipps Psychiatric Clinic at Johns Hopkins University in Baltimore with Meyer. A strong supporter of liberal causes and friend of Clarence Darrow, Wertham, along with the author Richard Wright and the Rev. Shelton Hale Bishop, in 1946 founded the Lafargue Mental Hygiene Clinic in Harlem, the first private outpatient psychiatric clinic established in and for a black community in the United States.[50] Laf-argue was a practical response to the need for low-cost psychotherapy and counseling for blacks trying to survive in a segregated American society. Wright's presence is telling. The character Bigger Thomas in his novel *Native Son* (1940) is the classic (and contested) account of the in-ternalization of the societal norms of racist America and consequent destruction of the psyche of American blacks. As James Baldwin says about Bigger Thomas in a radical critique of Wright's work, "The Amer-ican image of the Negro lives also in the Negro's heart; and when he has surrendered to this image life has no other possible reality."[51] The core image is that of identification with the aggressor's image of the black.

Employing the principles of social psychiatry, Wertham and his cli-nicians stressed the relationship between the psychological symptoms experienced by his patients and their daily lives. He saw the social pres-sures on them as the prime cause of any psychology difficulty; as he observed in an interview in 1946, "Of course, one can find dreams by Negroes in which there is an anxiety due to social pressures, but exactly the same thing exists frequently in white people who in our society are also exposed to many social pressures."[52] Such a view was distinctly dif-ferent, as contemporary commentators noted, from the attitudes at the major public hospital whose psychiatric ward was open to blacks, Bel-levue, where "at that time, [the] staff did contain racialist clinicians who still believed that African Americans possessed a racially unique and inferior psyche."[53] Were they mad because they were black and predis-posed to madness or did oppressive social forces make them mad? At the clinic Wertham saw proof that systematic school segregation was psychologically harmful to his patients. He testified in a school desegre-gation case in Delaware in 1951 that "the fact of segregation in public and high school creates in the mind of the child an unsolvable conflict, an unsolvable emotional conflict, and I would say an inevitable conflict."[54] The court's finding, which cited Wertham extensively, was that racial separation "creates a mental health problem in many Negro children with a resulting impediment to their educational process."[55] These stud-ies, along with his testimony for the NAACP, were cited in 1954 in the *Brown v. Board of Education* ruling.[56]

In the 1950s Wertham launched an attack on comic books as one of the most pervasive forces that deformed the psychic experience of children in the United States, including white children's attitudes toward their black fellow students. Here Wertham was following the Frankfurt School critique of American (capitalist) mass culture articulated by Theodor Adorno, whose work on American racism came to dominate American social science research at the time (as we shall discuss shortly). What is certainly clear is that Wertham's best-known work on the impact of social forces on children was very much in line with his work in Harlem.[57] Social improvement meant the elimination of those factors that posed universal risks to a healthy psyche.[58]

Brown v. Board of Education set a new standard for legitimatizing psychological evidence in a forensic setting. For the first time in a court case not concerned with questions of competence, an American court recognized the centrality of psychological evidence of the impact of racism on blacks, while not commenting at all on the question of whether the racism that produced damaged psyches was itself a form of mental illness: "Whatever may have been the extent of psychological knowledge at the time of *Plessy v. Ferguson*, this finding is amply supported by modern authority. Any language in *Plessy v. Ferguson*, 163 U.S. 537 (1896), contrary to this finding is rejected."[59] This claim rested on the objective nature of science, and the fundamental belief that the scientific enterprise was a developing one that had changed since the court case that legalized segregation in the United States. Given that *Plessy* had been about public accommodation and the Court under Chief Justice Melville Fuller was not at all interested in "science" but in the public policy of racial difference (indeed it rejected the argument that the practice of segregation in public accommodations was based on claims of racial inferiority), the court's new findings that science now proved a psychological harm unknown to Justice Fuller and his colleagues (even for Justice John Marshall Harlan, whose lone dissent was rooted in his reading of the Fourteenth Amendment) is an odd turn, but indicative of the new biopolitics of the time.

Justice Henry Billings Brown's majority opinion in *Plessy* supporting the doctrine of "separate but equal" had no recourse to science; it cited only convention. The Court's rejection of convention in *Brown v. Board of Education* was in turn based on the claims of an objective notion of science. As was later observed:

> Applying social science to active controversies is . . . playing with fire.
> Most justices lack strong backgrounds in economics, psychology, or soci-
> ology; they are not familiar with the current state of the art; they can but
> poorly distinguish what is reputable methodology from what is sham. . . .
> The force of the Court's views may blunted, as in Brown, by a collateral
> debate on the veracity of its sources. . . . As a member of the NAACP's
> legal defense team, Clark brought the concept of inferiority complex into
> the litigation.[60]

It was indeed the question of the psychological damage of the victim,
not the mental state of the racist, that came into focus in this case.[61]

Only in an amicus curiae brief dated September 22, 1952, appended
to the *Brown v. Board of Education of Topeka, Kansas, Briggs v. Elliott*,
and *Davis v. Prince Edward County, Virginia* cases did the question of
the origin of white racism appear.[62] The Clarks were the first signatories of the letter, which was signed as well as by their teacher Otto
Klineberg and two co-authors of *The Authoritarian Personality*, Else
Frenkel-Brunswik and R. Nevitt Sanford, in addition to more than
thirty other prominent social scientists. The Clarks begin by arguing
as expected for the impact of segregation: the "minority group child
is thrown into a conflict with regard to his feelings about himself and
his group. He wonders whether his group and he himself are worthy of
no more respect than they receive. This conflict and confusion leads
to self-hatred and rejection of his own group."[63] But, citing *The Authoritarian Personality*, they quickly shift, to examining the impact of
segregation on the majority child where "the effects are somewhat more
obscure. Those children who learn the prejudices of our society are also
being taught to gain personal status in an unrealistic and non-adaptive
way."[64] For such children "confusion, conflict, moral cynicism, and dis-
respect for authority may arise . . . as a consequence of being taught
the moral, religious and democratic principles of the brotherhood of
man and the importance of justice and fair play by the same persons
and institutions who, in their support of racial segregation and related
practices, seem to be acting in a prejudiced and discriminatory manner."[65] The question of the source of such feelings in the idea of innate
biological inferiority is not evoked, as it is over and over again in the

writings defending segregation and as it was in arguing for a biological antisemitism in Germany, which *The Authoritarian Personality* certainly discusses. The question is raised tangentially, as the Clarks note
"in passing that the argument regarding the intellectual inferiority of
one group as compared to another is, as applied to schools, essentially
an argument for homogeneous groupings of children by intelligence
rather than by race."[66] They come out as also opposed to such strategies of sorting by ability. For the signatories it is segregation as a social
strategy rather than any theory of racism that deforms minority and
majority children uniformly. Thus they argue against the institutions
that embody racism rather than racism per se.

Chief Justice Earl Warren wrote in the *Brown v. Board of Education*
opinion that to separate black pupils

> from others of similar age and qualifications solely because of their race
> generates a feeling of inferiority as to their status in the community that
> may affect their hearts and minds in a way unlikely ever to be undone.
>
> Segregation of white and colored children in public schools has a det-
> rimental effect upon the colored children. The impact is greater when it
> has the sanction of the law, for the policy of separating the races is usually
> interpreted as denoting the inferiority of the negro group. A sense of infe-
> riority affects the motivation of a child to learn. Segregation with the
> sanction of law, therefore, has a tendency to [retard] the educational and
> mental development of negro children and to deprive them of some of
> the benefits they would receive in a racial[ly] integrated school
> system.[67]

The vocabulary Warren uses here reflects the deep influence of Adlerian
psychology (inferiority complex), but the core of the statement reflects
Anna Freud's view in the 1950s that society must always ask what is in
the "best interest of the child," not what causes societal deformation.[68]
Kenneth Clark had used these terms in his presentation to the Mid-
Century White House Conference on Children and Youth in 1950 at
the very moment that the "best interest of the child" came to be introduced into American legal thinking.[69] It is of little surprise that Warren
cited Clark's 1950 paper on the "Effects of Prejudice on Personality
Development" along with Gunner Myrdal's study *An American Dilemma*

in footnote 11 of his decision. Though the focus was on recuperating the child, not ridding society of the psychopathology of the racist "mob," the embedding of psychological science into the judicial realm of American politics set a precedent for medicalizing the effects of racism on its victims. It would take only a slight shift to focus the attention of psychologists and psychiatrists on the assumed psychological conditions that give rise to racism and other forms of bigotry.

A year after the landmark ruling of *Brown v. Board of Education*, Kenneth Clark published the first edition of his monograph *Prejudice and Your Child*, which included and expanded upon some of the work done by himself and his wife and a number of other researchers across the country over the previous thirty years on racial attitudes and developmental psychology.[70] In *Prejudice and Your Child*, Clark argues that the racial attitudes of the parents and the home life of the child are essential in the development of a child's racial identity and connected attitudes. This implies that black children are taught not so much that they are black, but that they are not white, and that white is a positive quality. So when a child is asked to self-identify, they can only successfully do so when placed side by side with a white child.[71] But when they must self-identify without the benefit of another physical body present to which they can compare, the black child no longer has white as a point of reference. These children then develop self-loathing as they continue to see themselves through a white gaze, and once they realize they are not and can never be the ideal white, they may feel an incurable sense of inferiority, denial, and self-hate. Clark argues that identification with the aggressor is "an attempt to resolve this profound conflict either through wishful thinking or by seeking some form of escape from a situation that focuses this conflict for them." He mentions a young black boy who claims that he is actually white but that "he had a sun tan."[72] This boy, he says, desires to escape the trap of inferiority by denying identification with his own race. This is 1955.

In 1970 the future Nobel laureate Toni Morrison, teaching English at Howard University, published *The Bluest Eye*. This account of a nine-year-old black girl growing up in the American Midwest chronicles how she learns to hate her "ugly" black body and desire white skin and blue eyes. "Now she was asking for something that was just awful—she wanted to have blue eyes and she wanted to be Shirley Temple, I mean, she wanted to do that white trip because of the society in which she lived and, very importantly, because of the black people who helped her want to be that," Toni Morrison later stated.[73] The novel ends with the central character, Pecola Breedlove, going insane, fleeing into her fantasy world of racial transformation. Psychopathology, at least in the American public sphere, is caused by oppressive social structures, furthered by the minority that identifies with the aggressor, and takes the form of self-hatred.

Antisemitism and the Legacy of Fascism

The debates about the baleful impact of racism on the psyche of blacks in the inter- and immediate post-war years seemed to avoid much discussion about the nature of the collective that carries the force of racism. The "community" or the "crowd" or the "herd" was rarely seen in these debates. Yet in many of the studies of the crowd undertaken by Jewish refugee researchers, scholars as radically diverse as the Frankfurt School Marxist sociologist Theodor Adorno and the conservative Austrian novelist and philosopher Hermann Broch saw only pathology in their treatment of Nazi racism, and what they theorized as its American parallel in attitudes toward blacks.[74] In Great Britain the future Nobelist Elias Canetti was devoting himself in a parallel project to answering Freud's theory of mass psychology, which appeared in 1960 as *Crowds and Power*.[75] Much of these works were funded through philanthropies such as the Rockefeller and Rosenwald Foundations, organizations that had their own research agendas concerning racism and its impact. Ultimately, however, combatting prejudice through the employment of psychological theories of racism dominates the early 1940s. And perhaps no other academic collective influenced developing psychological theories of racism as much as the Frankfurt School.

Founded in the early 1920s, the Institute for Social Research at the University of Frankfurt brought together thinkers on the left, including Georg Lukacs and Karl Korsch, who wanted to transcend left party politics and make social research their mantra. In the early 1930s, Max Horkheimer became the director, and increasingly a synthesis of Marx and Freud shaped the work of Frankfurt affiliates, including Erich Fromm, Theodor Adorno, and Herbert Marcuse, all of whom fled to the

United States (some via Mexico) in the mid-1930s. That these scholars were Jews (secular, indeed, often anti-religious and anti-Zionist) played an enormous role in their understanding of their work once they were exiled.[76] Indicative of this is how Horkheimer shifts from considering antisemitism as a secondary effect of capitalism while in Germany, to seeing it as a primary aspect of fascism and, indeed, as a psychological state by 1939, exemplified in his essay "The Jews and Europe." The Institute for Social Research was reestablished in exile at Columbia University with Horkheimer as its director. Remarkable in its breadth, it hosted members of the Frankfurt School in exile as well as other émigré scholars.

In June 1944 the Berlin trained psychoanalyst Ernst Simmel, whose work on trauma during World War I had revolutionized Freudian psychoanalysis's understanding of adult responses to stress, chaired a workshop sponsored by the San Francisco Psychoanalytic Society on antisemitism.[77] Simmel's work during World War I had greatly impacted Freud's own thinking about the psychology of the crowd, specifically in his *Mass Psychology and the Analysis of the Ego* (1921). The publication in 1946 of the papers from the San Francisco meeting Simmel ironically entitled *Anti-Semitism: A Social Disease*. Social diseases, meaning sexually transmitted infections, were a major concern during wartime because of the model of infection and risk to the body of the soldier. Indeed, catching such a disease was, in many countries, a violation of the military codes.[78] Antisemitism was framed as a "social disease" because of its pernicious pathological nature and its "social" transmission, weakening the war effort against the Nazis.

The Simmel workshop spawned a volume that was quite revealing in its constitution of the idea of race and madness.[79] Simmel begins his contribution, an essay on "Anti-Semitism and Mass Psychopathology," by explaining that antisemitism is not a mass neurosis, but a "mass psychosis," because neurotics could not form a group and because it involves "unrestricted aggressive destructiveness under the spell of a delusion," which is driven by a desire to devour all that is frustrating to the individual.[80] To clarify the difference between individual and mass psychosis, Simmel emphasizes that mass psychosis allows the individual to remain tied to reality, while still overcoming his "infantile impotence towards reality."[81] Simmel stresses that the flight from mass psychosis is a flight not only from reality but also from individual psychopathology. Images of reality, for the individual, usually begin with the introjection of the image of the parent. The ego, he argues, breaks down during conflict with the parent or with later imaginary substitutes for them. It is the underlying problem of "loving or hating the parent" that is not resolved.[82] Drawing on Gustave LeBon and crowd theory specifically, Simmel claims that once the individual becomes integrated into the mass psychosis (antisemitism), "he becomes a child of that period in which the only fear he had was that of the external power of his parents. This external parent can no longer punish him because, together with his mass he has become as powerful as the parent."[83] In other words, the individual still fears the authority of the parents but since they are no longer present to punish him, he is left unchecked. The role of the parent falls to the authoritarian structure personified in the charismatic leader, who has the power to punish, an argument made earlier by the unmentioned Wilhelm Reich. By this point in his American career Reich had moved in radically different directions from his 1933 work with a new focus on sexual energy (that he called the "orgone") and had come to be considered a quack by most psychoanalysts.[84]

In his contribution to the workshop volume, Horkheimer begins to see the racist as *a specie* almost as clearly defined as the stereotypical Jew:

> The [anti-Semitic] attacks have been so stereotyped, they have always followed the same pattern so closely that one is tempted to say that though the Jews, who have changed much in the course of history, are certainly no race, the anti-Semites in a way *are* a race, because they always use the same slogans, display the same attitudes, indeed almost look alike.[85]

Neither national identity nor historical situation matters, even though Horkheimer stresses that antisemitism is "not merely a psychological problem." Yet, as Horkheimer puts it, "[t]he basic features of destructive hatred are identical everywhere."[86] Antisemitism is a universal hatred with a strongly psychological component that is evident even in the physiognomy of the oppressor. In the workshop volume, the Freudian psychiatrist Else Frenkel-Brunswik and her colleague, the Berkeley psychologist R. Nevitt Sanford, write, "The typical anti-Semitic girl differs in her appearance very markedly from those who are against anti-Semitism."[87] By refocusing the pathologizing gaze on the aggressor, a stereotyped antisemite is created. This reversal is clear but generates yet more "types" in need of exploration.

Psychoanalysis, at the time, was positioned as a discipline valuable on a societal rather than an individual level. It almost seems to become a method of public health following the pattern of the Berlin Psychoanalytic Society in the 1920s. Its aim is social reform rather than clinical therapy. Society-level psychoanalysis has its roots with Reich, but it is clear that by the 1940s even psychoanalysts were more open about suggesting that the remedy to prejudice would be education about psychoanalytic principles of the unconscious—not education or counter-propaganda about the logical problems with prejudice. The idea that psychoanalysis could actively liaise with other professions to make progress was interesting, as it suggests a move beyond theorizing toward social action. Horkheimer recognizes this when he writes, "It remains for sociologists and, more particularly, for statesmen to include concepts of psychoanalytic dynamic group psychology in their deliberations on the reconstruction of the post-war world."[88] Horkheimer also suggests working with educators in a number of capacities, proclaiming the need to find ways to make work meaningful, and to give people films they "need" instead of ones they "want," namely those with tragic endings. Such a politicization of psychoanalytic principles is part of the natural development of a field once it has become as well seated as psychoanalysis had at this point, and is more of a reaction to the political turmoil of a post-war world. Frenkel-Brunswik's quantitative approach certainly suggests that the disciplinarity of psychology and psychoanalysis in the university system is an important part of this move—her text suggests a move away from common language with literary allusions toward the specialized language of a science.

There is an ominous undertone in Horkheimer's essay—he talks about the need for "mental sanitation," a "planned program of *international* mental hygiene*," education in "psychological slums," and also, as earlier mentioned, the type of films people "need" to see. Such projects seem to echo the pathologies associated with authoritarianism and repression, rather than attempt to eliminate them. Though the ideals he sets forth are clearly less violent and repressive than those of a fascist state, they do seem to suggest rigid rules about how people ought to be educated.

Some of the essays in Simmel's volume are rough drafts of work that would appear in *The Authoritarian Personality* (1950), for which Theodor W. Adorno had collaborated with Frenkel-Brunswik, Sanford, and Frenkel-Brunswik's student Daniel J. Levinson at the University of California at Berkeley. In May 1944 a small conference funded by the American Jewish Committee had brought researchers from the Frankfurt School interested in pursuing a study of antisemitism together with researchers from the Department of Psychology at Berkeley, with the intent to begin systematic work on analyzing the nature and sources of antisemitism. Published as the first volume in the *Studies in Prejudice* series, and proclaimed as a study of the sources of antisemitism, *The Authoritarian Personality* defined racist personality traits and then ranked these traits and their intensity in any given person on what Adorno et al. referred to as the "F scale" (F for fascist). The personality type identified was defined by nine traits believed to cluster together as the result of childhood experiences. These traits include conventionalism, authoritarian submission, authoritarian aggression, anti-intellectualism, anti-intraception, superstition and stereotypy, power and "toughness," destructiveness and cynicism, projectivity, and exaggerated concerns over sex. These categories mirror those in the 1933 study by Wilhelm Reich, who is mentioned in passing, but in this case the questions of statistical measurement trumped an analytic concern with the social etiology of an antisemitic psychosis.

The Authoritarian Personality begins with case studies of two men, Mack and Larry, in an attempt to understand the socioeconomic factors that make the individual personality more or less susceptible to fascism, authoritarianism, racism, or antisemitism.[89] By his responses to interview questions about his biography, Larry is painted as somewhat of a poster child for nonsusceptibility, while Mack, on the other end of the scale, seems highly susceptible to the authoritarian agenda. Larry sees the image of the black and the Jew as shaped by the real social circumstances in which he believes they find themselves:

> The discrimination toward Negroes is because they aren't understood and because they are physically different. Towards Jews it's because of their

business ability—the fear that they'll take over business control of the country. There should be education in Negro history, for instance, the part Negroes have played in the development of the country; and education in the history of other minorities, too. How the Jews came to be persecuted, and why some of them are successful.[90]

Mack, on the other hand is, according to the analysis, clearly antisemitic and provides the counter to Larry's view. He sees that the sources of his hatred of Jews "may be grouped under three main headings: (a) violations of conventional values, (b) ingroup characteristics (clannish and power-seeking), and (c) burdens and misfits. The Jews are said to violate conventional values in that they are 'not courteous or interested in humanity' but, instead, are materialistic and money-minded. As businessmen they have 'second-class stuff' and are given to cheating."[91] Through his comments about his parents (his father on politics and work; his mother on religion) the authors deduce that Mack has an aggressive respect for authority that "comes into conflict with his explicit desire for independence."[92] In other words, he both wants to be "masculine" and independent, and also has an underlying need to be dependent. The authors suggest that this internal conflict could manifest in a willful submissiveness to a powerful authority. Thus the case studies delineate those who are predetermined by their upbringing to be racist or antisemitic and those who are not. The analysis juxtaposes Larry, who "spent most of his time talking about 'what's wrong with non-Jews' and 'what non-Jews should do about it,'" with Mack, who went on about "'what's wrong with the Jews' and 'what the Jews should do about it.'"[93] Each focuses on a stereotypical cohort (of antisemites or Jews) as homogenous and the constitution of a psychology of prejudice or its avoidance.

In *The Authoritarian Personality* the antisocial traits exhibited by Larry were measured on the F scale, with good correlations between F scores and measures of antisemitism and anti-black prejudice. Mack scored low on these underlying measures. It is family dynamics that explains the intra-psychic conflict that leads to surface personality traits as well as social beliefs and behavior. Now it is clear that much of the data was collected by the use of projective tests (also employing psychoanalytic ego defense categories), such as the Thematic Apperception Test (TAT), that have low reliability.[94]

But another serious criticism is that, because it looks at the individual level of analysis rather than collective social factors, the F scale fails to explain prejudice in societies where prejudice is the norm (e.g., South Africa, the American South). One can note that class, in spite of Myrdal's refusal to use this as a marker for racism in the United States, also played a major role:

> Even in *The Authoritarian Personality*, frequent reference is made to the presumed relationship between aspects of social status and prejudice. Thus Frenkel-Brunswik, in her summary of the interview results of the California studies, describes the high scorer on the F scale as tending to use status as the primary criterion in appraising people and to evaluate others according as they appear to be a threat to his own standing.[95]

For Adorno and the Frankfurt School, class and status always haunt racism.

The Authoritarian Personality's attempt to explain extreme bigotry and racist behavior as a psychopathological condition gained widespread notice among both academic and general audiences. An "enormous flood of research resulted from the stimulus [it provided]."[96] Aside from C. Wright Mills's *The Power Elite* and the Kinsey Report, few academic publications of its day could boast the level of public awareness it garnered. The central claim of the book is that acceptance of fascism depends on whether its ideology can be absorbed by specific personality types in ways that project the subject's own needs. According to Adorno et al., antisemitism, as an ideological construct, entails more than just simply negative attitudes toward Jews. Rather, antisemitism (and other prejudicial ideological systems, like anti-black racism or fascism):

> suggests that for each individual there are certain "nuclear ideas" . . . once the central or nuclear ideas are formed, they tend to "pull in" numerous other opinions and attitudes and thus form a broad ideological spectrum.[97]

By the time this volume appears the émigré writers had adapted the model put forth by the psychologists of the era that "race prejudice [and specifically, anti-black prejudice] is commonly assumed to overlap

extensively with the broader concept, ethnocentrism."[98] But was ethnocentrism psychopathological? Or merely a normal sign of the anxiety
generated by difference?

One of the other studies funded by the American Jewish Committee
was by the psychoanalysts Nathan Ackerman and Marie Jahoda, *Anti-
Semitism and Emotional Disorder: A Psychoanalytic Interpretation*. Here
their question was the very nature of the pathology of race. These psychoanalysts found that there was a much lower rate of depression and a
higher rate of anxiety tolerance among their diverse subjects, who were
from both traditional urban middle-class psychoanalytic practices as well
as from New York City social services. Ackerman and Jahoda, unlike the
scholars who worked on *The Authoritarian Personality*, approached the
question from traditional Freudian perspectives, using detailed, long-
term interviews rather than surveys as the basis of their work. They distinguished in their analysis of their cases not mere stereotyping but true
prejudice rooted in irrational hostility toward Jews. Their desire was to
identify a psychological rather than a social component that underpinned
this specific form of prejudice. Their subjects seemed not only to suffer
from low self-esteem, but perceived themselves as damaged and crippled,
and unable to tolerate different others. Where in other circumstances
such individuals would suffer from depression, these subjects projected
their internal sense of anxiety on to the Jews and did not manifest clinical
signs of depression. Antisemitism seemed to function as a prophylactic
against other forms of psychopathology such as depression. Ackerman
and Jahoda stated, "Every evidence of individuality in another person
becomes a painful reminder of the sacrifice the prejudiced person has
made in disowning parts of his self."[99] Prejudice in this case was a defense
mechanism of the ego against self-hatred.

Locating racial and ethnic intolerance, including antisemitism, within
an ideological spectrum theorized to be psychical in nature proved quite
powerful for the developing political discourse surrounding the emergent American Civil Rights Movement. Among Civil Rights activists like
Stokely Carmichael, Bobby Seale, and Huey Newton, and even anti-war
protest groups such as Youth against War and Fascism, there appeared
a common strand of anti-fascist discourse made possible by the widespread public recognition of *The Authoritarian Personality*. This paralleled the arguments used by the NAACP to examine the psychological

damage to the African American psyche caused by racism. Those who identified as more radical appeared much more interested in the forces that shaped the psyche of racists and in the wellspring of such forces, which many identified as the latent fascism of American society. Likewise, the reduction of antisemitism to a psychological problem of the antisemite drew relatively few objections.[100] It is ironic that this shift meant that the post-war fascist states such as Portugal, Spain, and Argentina, all of which had incorporated models of race into their political systems, vanished from Americans' attention as social conservatives fixated on the Cold War (and Soviet antisemitism), and social radicals fixated on the Vietnam War as a sign of an American fascism.[101]

French Race Madness

The diagnosing of *racism* as a psychopathological illness was not limited to the psychoanalytically informed émigrés in the United States during and immediately after World War II. With the general post-war acceptance of psychoanalysis (in all of its many variants) as a (if not the) primary model of the psyche, the assumption that racism makes you crazy because it is itself a form of madness became widespread. This viewpoint was typified by academic arguments aimed at specifying the specific mental, physical, and emotional disorders associated with *being* racist, or *having* racism.[102] Thus in his medical dissertation *Black Skin, White Masks (Peau noire, masques blancs)* (1952) the Martinique-born Algerian and French psychiatrist and philosopher Frantz Fanon uses psychoanalytical theory to explain the feelings of dependency and inadequacy that Martiniquan (read: black) people experience in a French (read: white) world. Fanon rejects the Enlightenment thesis that all people could become French by simply accepting French cultural norms in the name of anti-colonialism (but also in the time of a rising *Négritude* movement, launched in the 1930s, that stressed a black identity within the French cultural model).[103] He speaks of the divided self-perception of the black subject who has lost his native cultural originality and embraced the culture of the white mother country.

For Fanon it is the juxtaposition of cultures that creates self-loathing in the colonial subject: "a normal Negro child, having grown up in a normal Negro family, will become abnormal on the slightest contact of the white world." His model, and he cites it positively, is Jean-Paul Sartre's image of the Jew as elaborated in his *Thoughts on the Jewish Question* (1946), where Sartre expounds on the inauthentic Jew who is a creature that responds to the stereotype of the Jew in the dominant (read: German) culture.[104] Fanon does describe the experience of the Negro as inherently different than that of the Jew. He evokes the parallel source of antisemitism in Freud's depiction of the Jew killing his father in *Moses and Monotheism*; however, while they have both killed their fathers, the black man, according to the colonialist account, has engaged in cannibalism. The image of the black internalized by the colonial subject is exponentially more primitive and barbaric than of the Jew. Sartre and Fanon both provide images of the identification with the aggressor as developed by Anna Freud in Vienna in the 1930s. The racist world generates the inauthentic subject through the claims of culture and language. The means of such subjugation is language: "To speak . . . means above all to assume a culture, to support the weight of a civilization."[105] As a result the black subject will try to appropriate and imitate the cultural code of the colonizer as the inauthentic Jew mimics the antisemite's image of the Jew. This behavior, Fanon argues, is especially evident in upwardly mobile and educated black people who can afford to acquire status symbols. The result in all cases is identification with the aggressor:

> I recommend the following experiment to those who are unconvinced: Attend showings of a Tarzan film in the Antilles and in Europe. In the Antilles, the young Negro identifies himself *de facto* with Tarzan against the Negroes. This is much more difficult for him in a European theater, for the rest of the audience, which is white, automatically identifies him with the savages on the screen. . . .
>
> I will go farther and say that Bushmen and Zulus arouse even more laughter among the young Antilleans. It would be interesting to show how in this instance the reactional exaggeration betrays a hint of recognition. In France a Negro who sees this documentary is virtually petrified. There he has no more hope of flight: He is at once Antillean, Bushman, and Zulu.[106]

Fanon only tangentially is concerned with the origin of racism in white society:

The Negro is a phobogenic object, a stimulus to anxiety. . . . One dis-
covers all the stages of what I shall call the Negro-phobogenesis. There
has been much talk of psychoanalysis in connection with the Negro.
Distrusting the ways in which it might be applied, I have preferred
to call this chapter "The Negro and Psychopathology," well aware that
Freud and Adler and even the cosmic Jung did not think of the Negro
in all their investigations. And they were quite right not to have. It
is too often forgotten that neurosis is not a basic element of human
reality.[107]

Fanon's argument mirrors that of Freud in the 1920s, denying any historical specificity to the French situation but rather seeing it as part
of a universal anti-black feeling on the part of white, colonial society.
However, Fanon also believes that black women are much more sug-
gestible than black men and therefore, using the older model of female
psychological susceptibility, are at greater risk for psychopathology.[108]
French and indeed Western society is inherently racist in its attitudes
toward blacks, no matter what its professions of equality and the claims
of French culture to admit all. "Negro-phobogenesis" is Fanon's parallel to Pinsker's Judeophobia and indeed both stem from a perception of
the inauthenticity of the subject that proves the claims of the dominant
society about the inferiority of the subject.

Fanon cites the Detroit psychoanalyst Richard Sterba, one of the few
non-Jewish émigré psychoanalysts then writing on race in the United
States, concerning the June 1943 Detroit race riot.[109] Sterba describes
in detail the responses of his white analysands to the anti-black riots,
depicting white racism as a result of sibling rivalry:

We know of a specific infantile reaction that shows this characteristic
of intense hostility and this tendency to keep out or to drive out, which
is re-enacted with Negroes as substitute objects. It is the reaction to
the arrival of a newcomer into the family, an infant brother or sister.
The older child develops extreme jealousy of the younger sibling, often
openly shows his disapproval, or his hatred and disgust, and has only
one desire: to do away with the newcomer, or to shut him out from acceptance by the family. . . . In this respect the Negroes signify *younger
siblings*.[110]

One of his patients has a dream during the riots about his own sibling rivalry:

> The patient is in his parents' house. A group of Negroes are attacking the house, and are ready to set it on fire. This danger is all of a sudden removed by a magical procedure: The Negroes are all transformed into small balls of protoplasm which are contained in a bottle, so that they can easily be disposed of by emptying the bottle into the sink.[111]

The interchangeability of the black object of hatred with the hated sibling points to a competitive sense of identification with the sibling over the love of the mother, but also of Oedipal competition.

> The race riots in Detroit in June, 1943 provided an excellent opportunity for studying the unconscious motives of white patients in analysis. The findings were surprisingly consistent with some of Freud's theoretical ideas in connection with the primitive group and its development. . . . The male Negro as he appeared in dreams of white people even before the race riots often had to be recognized as representative of the dreamer's father, particularly the father at night or in his nocturnal activities. Many dreams of being threatened by a Negro were understood as the expression and repetition of the dreamer's infantile fears of his father. After having recognized this deep-seated equation of Negro with father one is able to understand much better the emotional reactions during the race riots with regard to their unconscious significance.[112]

Importantly, the riot was actually sparked by widespread rumors that a woman and her baby had been thrown off the Belle Isle bridge. The particulars of the victims and perpetrators, however, were altered within Detroit's white and black communities. The story told among whites featured a white woman and white baby thrown off of the bridge by blacks, while blacks shared stories of a black woman and her black baby thrown off the bridge by whites. In either case, there was no evidence to support the story; it was, apparently, imaginary.[113] Nevertheless, at the time Sterba suggested that proof of the Oedipal was to be found in the narrative—imagined or not—of a white woman being accosted by a group of blacks, a narrative constantly evoked in white racism.

What Sterba saw in Detroit was not an attack on black stores or institutions but white gangs murdering black individuals. This he defined in terms of mob (or crowd) formation:

> The mass psychological phenomena of the race riots in Detroit are those described as characteristic of short-lived groups by Le Bon and Freud. The Detroit race riots showed all the ear-marks of regression from individual to most primitive group psychology. Temporary and fleeting leadership was exercised by individuals. In the short-lived groups that were formed during the race riots in Detroit it was noteworthy that they lacked strong leadership, which is otherwise so characteristic of group formations, even of a temporary kind. It may be that the innermost emotional motives for the group formation, namely collective father murder, influenced the structure and character of the groups. It was precisely this fleeting character that contributed to the nervousness and excitement in the city during the riots.[114]

Sterba provides Fanon with a model that is not only sibling or Oedipal (an individual response) but also mass (crowd) in its understanding of the psychopathology of racism. Sterba also assumes an unspoken symmetry in this essay. While he does not have black analysands, he assumes that anti-white hatred would take on the same forms as anti-black racism. This assumption of symmetry of hatred of the Other is quite unusual in the literature, which almost always parallels perpetrator psychopathology with victim's internalization of that hatred, not with the projection of that hatred on to the group generating the racism. One wonders whether Sterba's anomalous position, as neither Jewish nor black, allowed him a perspective that was unique in the 1940s.

In 1961, well after Fanon had become the icon of Algerian resistance in France, Jean-Paul Sartre, in the preface to Fanon's *The Wretched of the Earth* (*Les Damnés de la Terre*), argued that everyone who lived within the system of colonial oppression was guilty of participating in it. Such participation is a form of dehumanization. Sartre, picking up on the psychiatric underpinnings of Fanon's critique of the impact of racism on the individual psyches of both the oppressed and the oppressor, used the insanity label to make his case for an understanding of violence as a symptom of oppression:

In psychiatric terms, they are "traumatized," for life. But these constantly renewed aggressions, far from bringing them to submission, thrust them into an unbearable contradiction which the European will pay for sooner or later. . . . Fanon reminds us that not so very long ago, a congress of psychiatrists was distressed by the criminal propensities of the native population. "Those people kill each other," they said, "that isn't normal. The Algerian's cortex must be under-developed." In central Africa, others have established that "the African makes very little use of his frontal lobes." These learned men would do well today to follow up their investigations in Europe, and particularly with regard to the French. For we, too, during the last few years, must be victims of "frontal sluggishness" since our patriots do quite a bit of assassinating of their fellow-countrymen and if they're not at home, they blow up their house and their concierge. . . . These learnt men would do well today to follow up their investigations in Europe, and particularly with regard to the French . . . since our patriots do quite a bit of assassinating of their fellow-countrymen. . . . In other days France was the name of a country. We should take care that in 1961 it does not become the name of a nervous disease.[115]

Sartre is following a very French thread of thought inspired by Alexandre Kojève's reading Hegel's "master-slave dialectic" as propounded by thinkers in the 1930s such as Georges Bataille, who transformed this into his image of madness as liberatory.[116] Here Sartre also understands the implications of madness as a pathology of the racist, for "Negrophobogenesis" had already been designated by Fanon as the disease of the oppressor, not a tool of liberation.

The Tunisian Jewish thinker Albert Memmi's *Portrait du colonisé, précédé du portrait du colonisateur* (*The Colonizer and the Colonized*, 1957) continued this argument.[117] He saw self-hatred as the key to understanding the Algerian situation:

The longer the oppression lasts, the more profoundly it affects him (the oppressed). It ends by becoming so familiar to him that he believes it is part of his own constitution, that he accepts it and could not imagine his recovery from it. This acceptance is the crowning point of oppression.[118]

For Memmi the politically oppressed risk becoming, in their struggle to gain status, just as or even more oppressive than their oppressors. In their effort to gain power, the oppressed "internalize" the values of the powerful. In fact, they may internalize the values of the dominant group so well that they, in turn, may become staunch defenders of the values of the dominant group that once oppressed them. Tanya Luhrmann has pointed out the problems in both Memmi's and Fanon's perspectives, given that both spoke from the position of a colonial elite, as the colonized, even after a successful revolution, "remains still tortured, still living in a psyche defined by the colonizer, defined by what he is not."[119] By the late 1950s Fanon's attention has also shifted to Algeria and he has abandoned a psychoanalytic for a revolutionary Marxist approach and yet he remains, as Luhrmann points out, in thrall to a colonial model that must be completely expunged, and yet could never be.

Civil Rights in the United States: After The Authoritarian Personality

The commissioning of the *Studies in Prejudice* series by the American Jewish Committee in the late 1940s clarifies what role, and to what degree, the scientific perspective exemplified by *The Authoritarian Personality* played in the "rising tide" of post-war scholarship on both the pathological conditions of prejudice and racism, and their psychopathological consequences on the targets of prejudice and racism. Addressing television reporters following the murder of Emmett Till in 1955, for example, then NAACP executive secretary Roy Wilkins characterized Till's murderers as *inherently* psychopathological:

> It was because it was a boy that they went there. They had to prove that they were superior. They had to prove it by taking away a fourteen year old boy. *You know it is in the virus, it is in the blood of the Mississippian. He can't help it* [emphasis ours].[120]

A few years later, in September 1958, Alfred J. Marrow, then chairman of the New York City Commission on Intergroup Relations, addressed the Annual Conference of the National Urban League, in Omaha, Nebraska. His paper, "Psychology of Racial Prejudice: An Aspect of

Mental Health," argued that the psychological consequences of extreme hatred were evident simply from scanning the daily newspapers. In his opening remarks, Marrow stated:

> Today we are not civil . . . a majority of the population is considered inferior by a minority. . . . As a result, emotional havoc has been created for both the oppressor and the oppressed. Therefore, *parallel to exploring the mental health effects of segregation on its victims, we must also consider the health impact on the segregators as well.* From the viewpoint of sound mental health, we must concern ourselves with the welfare of all citizens, even those with whom we disagree. *Since the problem is, primarily psychological in nature, we must turn for guidance and help to the behavioral scientists* [emphases ours].[121]

The link between Alfred J. Marrow and *The Authoritarian Personality* is an interesting one. Marrow had studied under the German American psychologist Kurt Lewin (highlighted in Chapter Three), for whom Marrow penned the definitive biography in 1977.[122] As mentioned, Lewin's views on Jewish self-hatred were part of the debates in the 1930s and 1940s about Jewish predisposition to mental illness. Recall that Lewin worked in Germany prior to the rise of the Third Reich, and while there he often collaborated with members of the Frankfurt School, including Adorno.[123] When Hitler rose to power, Lewin fled Germany and took a director position with the Commission on Community Interrelations, a research group under the American Jewish Congress, a global advocacy organization. A concurrent enterprise to the American Jewish Congress during the 1940s and 1950s was the American Jewish Committee, and Lewin's research group often collaborated with members of the American Jewish Committee.

At the same time the *Studies in Prejudice* series was under commission, Lewin was also working with the state of Connecticut's Interracial Commission to set up "change experiment" workshops meant to combat religious and racial prejudices. These "change experiments" are considered the building blocks of what is now known as "sensitivity training."[124] All this is to say that when Marrow delivered his address, his statement regarding racism—"As a result, emotional havoc has been created for both the oppressor and the oppressed"—derives from a paradigm that had been in development for over two decades. His recommendation that "parallel to exploring the mental health effects of the segregation on its victims, we must also consider the health impact on the segregators as well," becomes a touchstone throughout the remainder of the Civil Rights Movement, as more and more mental health researchers and practitioners concern themselves with the treatment of racism's victims as well as its perpetrators.

The political scientist David Rochefort argues that groundbreaking work in the field of psychiatric epidemiology from the mid-1950s through the early 1960s significantly contributed to the racism-as-disease model.[125] Though at the time many epidemiologists suggested the importance of socioeconomic factors in the origins and treatment of mental illness, several were also publishing important work that located racial and ethnic tensions within a "sick society" epidemiological framework.[126] Many mental health workers, particularly those serving the communities of the working poor and racial and ethnic minorities, adopted the "sick society" framework to claim that racism was responsible for the creation and sustainment of a "sick society." Charles Hersch summarized this shift, writing:

> The mental health worker legitimated his involvement in social reform by simply declaring that such issues as poverty, racism, and oppression were indeed matters of mental health and that he could appropriately engage them within the framework of his professional functioning.[127]

Hersch continues:

> But the context of social reform [in the 1960s] did more than provide a background that helped to shape the mental health field. It penetrated the mental health field. . . . As the mental health professional became concerned with populations and with problems of retention, there was an inexorable move into arenas of social change and political action. The mental health movement found itself drawn to problems and activities beyond the traditional framework of mental health. And at that point, the issues of social reform became fused with and confused with the issues of mental health practice.[128]

Based on an ideology of "social action," interventions by mental health practitioners aimed at "changing the social and economic arrangements of society, the institutions that carry them out, and the value systems that underlie them."[129] A significant factor in the crystallization of this social action strategy was the development, passage, and implementation of the Community Mental Health Centers Act (CMHCA) of 1963. Historically, the portrayal of mental illness has determined how the public is willing to treat it. From the nineteenth century up through the war years of the twentieth century, mental illnesses had been portrayed as matters of innate differences in human populations, as evidence of racial inferiority, and as diseases for which the only real "cure" was isolation or selective breeding. By the beginning of the modern Civil Rights Movement, however, scientific understandings of race had shifted to matters of cultural differences, if not outright social constructions. The result was a series of shifts that moved mental health practitioners beyond their traditional framework: the shift from mental health practice to social and community mental health action; the shift from the prevention of clinical illnesses to a concern with enhancing the overall quality of life of a community; the shift from conceptualizing everything through the dynamics of the family to conceptualizing everything through the dynamics of politics; the shift from service delivery to political power; and, finally, the shift from professional service to the construction of the professional as a public servant.[130]

As these shifts were taking place, Civil Rights activists escalated demands for increases in the funding, scale, and scope of community-based mental health centers in urban areas with high concentrations of racial and ethnic minorities in response, in no small part, to the higher rates of mental illnesses within these urban centers. A joint statement released by the American Hospital Association and the American Psychiatric Association in 1963, for example, referred to mental illness as the biggest health problem in America, potentially afflicting as many as 10 percent of urban dwellers.[131] Policymakers and activists alike drew upon decades of sociological and social-psychological theorizing on the negative impact of urbanization on social cohesion to make the case for why community health centers were crucial to preventing the spread of mental illnesses, particularly among already disadvantaged groups. The representative for the National Association of Mental Health, Charles H. Frazier, for example, explained to a subcommittee of the U.S. House of Representatives' Committee on Interstate and Foreign Commerce dealing with three bills on community mental health provisions:

> Separation and isolation of the patient from his relatives and friends, from his place of worship, from his normal human contacts in the community actually serve to intensify his illness and to make chronic patients out of patients who might be treated and discharged in a matter of days in a community setting.[132]

On October 31, 1963, President Kennedy signed the CMHCA into law, with a total funding of $150 million. Kennedy's hope for the act was clear in his press statement:

> Under this legislation, custodial mental institutions will be replaced by therapeutic centers. It should be possible, within a decade or two, to reduce the number of patients in mental institutions by 50 per cent or more. The new law provides the tools with which we can accomplish this.[133]

Among Civil Rights activists and the public alike, the passage of the CMHCA reflected the position that mental illness was both a cause *and* effect of racism. The passage of the CMHCA, in many ways then, legitimated the demands of mental health and Civil Rights activists, both of whom employed a psychopathological model of racism to advocate an increase in support for community mental health centers intended to treat the consequences of this "social illness." Less than a year later, during the Freedom Summer of 1964, over one hundred physicians, nurses, and psychiatrists—both black and white—formed the Medical Committee for Human Rights (MCHR). In addition to marching side by side with protestors, MCHR members provided emergency care, including counseling, to African Americans throughout Mississippi, arguing that both the conditions of Jim Crow and the stresses associated with combating it through Civil Rights Movement activities increased the likelihood of psychological trauma among blacks.

Racism and Race Theory: From Berlin to Johannesburg

While the American South served as the caldron for the politics of analyzing racism as a psychopathology in the late 1950s through the 1960s, developments in what was the Union (and then in 1960 the Republic) of South Africa prove equally important to our undertaking. While racial segregation had existed since the times of Dutch and British colonial settlement, it was only in 1948 that an official Afrikaner government policy dividing the races into "black, white, coloured and Indian" was formulated. Thus at the moment when scientific racism became state policy under the first apartheid prime minister, the Protestant cleric Daniel Malan, the world was becoming aware of the murderous policies that lead to the destruction of European Jewry in the Holocaust.

In 1937 the South African psychoanalyst Wulf Sachs had published *Black Hamlet: The Mind of an African Negro Revealed by Psychoanalysis.*[134] A sort of psychoanalytic parallel to Franz Boas's *Mind of the Primitive*, the overt intent of Sachs's book was to show that the unconscious processes in the African were universal using a rather strict Freudian model.[135] Sachs was a Lithuanian Jew who had trained at the Psychoneurological Institute in St. Petersburg (under Pavlov and Bechterev), at the University of Cologne, and at London University, where he took a degree in medicine. In 1922 he emigrated to South Africa with his family and began to practice as a general practitioner in Johannesburg. His interest in psychology was intensified by the experience of working with black schizophrenic patients at the Pretoria Mental Hospital beginning in 1928. In 1929–1930 Sachs underwent analysis at the Berlin Psychoanalytic Society with Theodor Reik, through whom he came into personal contact with Freud. As a psychoanalytic pioneer and authoritative expositor, he also published a book, to which Freud gave a stamp of approval, entitled *Psychoanalysis: Its Meaning and Practical Applications* (1934).

Black Hamlet presents the formal and informal analysis of a *Manyika nganga* (indigenous healer) who moved from his home in rural Zimbabwe to Johannesburg. Sachs gives him the pseudonym John Chavafambira. While it is clear that he views the "native" practices as ineffective, Sachs stages the analysis as a dialogue between alternative (African) medical approaches to mental illness and normative (Western) allopathic medicine and psychoanalytic practice. He identifies John Chavafambira as the "black Hamlet," using rather strict psychoanalytic approaches, echoing Ernest Jones's *Hamlet and Oedipus* of 1927. Sachs seeks to illustrate the universal applicability of psychoanalysis, grounded in the Oedipus complex. Hamlet, like Oedipus, becomes one of the literary touchstones for masculine neurosis. The play, according to Sachs, is "common to all humanity" and therefore "appeals to men of all races and nations."[136] In this case John Chavafambira is the son and heir of a famous *ganga* (native healer), who dies under questionable circumstances. He suspects that his uncle has poisoned him. He is also, according to Sachs, pathologically devoted to his mother. This is confirmed for Sachs by a dream related by John in which he sleeps with her. His pathology, like that of Hamlet and Ophelia, is that he is unable to form a successful relationship with a woman.

One needs to note that Sachs is in no way unique in his attempts to analyze the South African racial scene in terms of the universals of the human psyche. In the same year that he published his extended case study, the South African psychologist Ian Douglas MacCrone argued that the fundamental problems in South Africa resulted from the fact that

> the extra-individual conflicts between the two racial groups are but the intra-individual conflicts within the mind writ large, and until the latter are removed, reduced, or modified, they must continue to exercise their baneful influence upon the race relations and the race contacts of white and black.[137]

Change the underlying psychic structures, change the politics of racial oppression.

And yet the subtext of Sachs's study is the impact of informal but highly structured racism on his subject, which often defines his relationship with the women in his life. For Sachs, his own Jewish experience of antisemitism in Russia and Western Europe is the counterpoint to John's internalization of South African "scientific" racial attitudes. Yet Sachs sees the "primitive" African and his religious practices as analogous to the "primitive" Eastern European Jew with his built-in hypocrisy:

When I asked what he would do if his wife had no children, he told me: "Then I would take another wife." I suppose the orthodox Jew must be guided by the same notion when he regards barrenness as a legal ground for divorce. I knew a respectable old Rabbi who, on the grounds of childlessness, got rid of his wife, who happened to be old and ugly, and married a young and pretty girl. John would have had no need for such heartless proceedings: he would simply have taken a second wife.[138]

Secular Jews, even Zionists, saw the ultrareligious Jews of Eastern Europe, even those who had immigrated to South Africa, as somehow less civilized than their enlightened compatriots.

One needs to note that the status of Jews in South Africa was also highly contested. By World War I most European (read: British and German) Jews had integrated themselves in the South African white middle class of the large cities. They were a far cry from the Eastern European (read: Russian and Lithuanian) immigrant peddlers of the late nineteenth century who were labeled "Peruvians," as they were seen as an unassimilable, nonwhite minority.[139] Sachs thus entered into South African society as a professional and as white, but with the legacy of his marginality always at hand.

Sachs's liberal attitude toward race seemed to set him apart. Yet the reality was that he was white and John Chavafambira was black. John is constantly aware of "the cruel oppression of the white people."[140] He, indeed, sees the root of his problem in the racism that he experiences: "All of us were born good; but the white people made us bad with their cruelty and oppression, and also through our sorcerers and poisoners."[141] This combination of white and black oppression is a prominent theme in the book, and the Johannesburg it depicts is characterized by a mix of not only the various "races" but also of individuals from a wide range of indigenous groups (tribes) attracted to the urban environment. The conflicts among them, and John's struggle for status as a healer, is central to his account. While Sachs often comments on the inarticulateness of John's response to his treatment, it is clear that John at least is constantly aware of the racism he is internalizing in his anxieties about his status, both as a healer in his own community and as a black in the new cosmopolitan, segregated urban environment in which he finds himself.

Sachs was constantly reminded of his own status by his analysand. John Chavafambira saw that "[t]he liberal Englishman is no better than the Dutchman . . . and the Jew is just as bad as either. They all want to squeeze the last penny out of us and give us as little in return as possible."[142] He is employed in a hotel owned and run by a Jew, Mr. Kaplan, and he sees Kaplan as exploiting him:

> This man, a simple Russian Jew, seemed to John to be very rich—did he not own an hotel, a big house, a motor-car? Actually, the poor soul, whom I happened to know, was on the verge of bankruptcy, his house was *in* the hands of the bondholder. Worried out of his senses over money, he was rabid on little economies, small meannesses enforced by abrupt irritable orders. To John, this mean economy was quite incomprehensible, senseless, and annoying.[143]

It is at this hotel that a confrontation that marginalizes John takes place. One of the inhabitants believes that John has assaulted her; this forces Kaplan to fire him even though both Sachs and Kaplan know that the attack was imagined:

> The woman, I told him, had no life of her own; she dwelt in a world of romantic fantasies, but in real life had to remain chaste and good. So therefore, while she longed for love, she was terrified of everything connected with it and sex; and as a result of this she was in continuous fear (or desire?) of being attacked by men. (In Africa, all white women are brought up with the fear of being raped by a native.) And indeed when I had the opportunity of discussing the whole affair with the proprietor of the hotel, he confirmed the fact that her fear of being raped by natives made her a continual nuisance. She complained so much and so frequently of the most trifling matters that he often told his wife that he intended celebrating the return to prosperity, should that ever happen, by asking the woman to leave.[144]

John goes from a situation where he feels himself exploited to one where his economic viability has vanished and he is very much on the margins of society. Sachs too sees himself suddenly as someone on the margins of society and he cries out to the reader, "Didn't I myself, a Jew, belong to a people ceaselessly driven from pillar to post?"[145]

With the rise of the Nazis and the strong identification of the Boers with European fascism, Sachs, in a letter to Freud written in 1939, referred to himself as a "Zionist not for sentimental reasons or prompted by national-chauvinistic or religious ideals of returning to Zion," but rather because the tragic predicament in which Jews found themselves necessitated the transformation of Jewry "into a national group in the full sense of the word."[146] At least in 1939, Sachs does not see any analogy between this desire and the aspirations of his black analysand to be rid of racism.

Ralph Bunche, the African American political scientist from Howard University (and later UN diplomat) comes to South Africa and, together with Sachs, visits John Chavafambira and observes his marginality. Bunche is not at all convinced by John's claims to be a healer, rejecting out of hand any such designation based in indigenous medicine. Bunche dismisses him as a "a beady-eyed, sly and cunning-looking fellow, with pouting lips and a head pointed on top. Medium stature. Shows a very good memory. Probably not at his best in English because of a limited vocabulary. Very temperamental and addicted to Kaffir beer."[147] But Bunche is not much more impressed by Sachs, whose interpretations of all his patients' symptoms, as with John's, tend to be universal rather than specific. Thus Bunche reports that two women patients who have been domestic workers spend all their days washing floors. Overriding the obvious connection Bunche makes between the patients' madness and their former employment, Sachs draws an analogy between this compulsive floor washing and Lady Macbeth's compulsive hand washing, canonically discussed by Freud.[148] But by the post-war period and the beginnings of formal state apartheid, John Chavafambira's life and psyche is read very differently by Sachs.

In Sachs's updated version of Black Hamlet, published under the title of Black Anger in 1947, Chavafambira emerges as a politicized "New African."[149] He goes from suffering from the universal Oedipal struggle to suffering the ravages of race. Sachs's conclusion in Black Hamlet saw his analysand ready "to reconcile the past with the future, life in the kraal with that in the town." John understood at last "that the black and the white people must work together."[150] In *Black Anger* the conclusion is radically different. John has been arrested for carrying a "lethal weapon," a bicycle chain legitimately given to him by Sachs. He is released when Sachs pays his fine. Sachs later finds him living in poverty in Soweto, no longer practicing healing and regularly drunk. Sachs attempts to recuperate John by providing him with simple medications such as aspirin for his practice, and encouraging him to no longer prostitute his healing skills by pandering to whatever his patients think they desire but rather to serve as a true healer. By the end of the book, which takes John's story up to 1945, John Chavafambira has become a "New African," able to take control of his life once again. Again a healing has taken place for which Sachs claims credit.

One may note that John's transformation into a "New African" takes place under a fascist government overtly unfriendly to Jews, as Hannah Arendt writes:

> In other words, no matter how well they thought they were adjusted to the mob conditions of the country and its race attitude, Jews had broken its most important pattern by introducing into South African economy a factor of normalcy and productivity, with the result that when Mr. Malan introduced into Parliament a bill to expel all Jews from the Union he had the enthusiastic support of all poor whites and of the whole Afrikaaner population.[151]

The 1937 Aliens Act had already radically limited Jewish immigration to South Africa from Nazi Germany. Malan's Nationalist Party subsequently but unsuccessfully moved to ban Jewish immigration, limit Jewish naturalization, and prohibit Jews from practicing certain professions. Sachs's rethinking of the psychological reintegration of John Chavafambira into his world is paralleled by a potential decay in the status of the Jews in a fascist South Africa.

Decades later, one Rian Malan, a descendent of the first apartheid prime minister, writes a critical volume on life under apartheid, *My Traitor's Heart*, which provides a case study of South African madness in the 1980s. He recounts the tale of Simon, a Zulu who becomes a serial murderer known as the Hammerman (after the way he dispatches his sleeping white victims). His trial exposes life under apartheid and he is revealed as both "a victim and martyr, a potentially good man made monster by apartheid." For "in many ways, the story Simon told his judge was the tale of a black Everyman. Simon was a Zulu. His tribe was broken by whites in 1879 and striped of its best land. The Zulus were ground down by the British and ground down still further by D. F. Malan, who came to power the year of Simon's birth. Subjugation was his birthright, and further oppression awaited his people."[152] But as in Sachs's account there are greater forces also at work. For the Hammerman is "a dog, an outcast, a man who 'didn't fit in anywhere' and 'would never be like the others.' He told a psychiatrist that he had had only one friend and only one lover in his entire life."[153] Moreover, he claimed he had "a secret problem." Not an orphan, as he had claimed when asking for mitigation, he was the product of an incestuous union, the offspring of first cousins. Thus his own Zulu culture abhorred him because such an act destroys the relationship of the community to the spirit world.[154] The trial revealed little of the Hammerman's multiple stories as reconstructed by Malan. The judges are not part of his world at all. "It is not just their skin that's white; their minds are white, too." The entire "ritual of justice," he concludes, "has nothing to do with Africa."[155] Madness is not merely the misperception of the Afrikaners of the meanings associated with psychopathology among the Zulu, but the result of the inherent incapacity of each to understand the world of the other. "The psychiatrist who ultimately testified in the Hammerman's defense was also 'black,' also a victim of apartheid—but he was an Indian, not African, and as culturally alien from Simon as I was. . . . He reduced Simon's resonant dreams to pathological hallucinations and saw his life long loneliness as evidence of psychopathic disorder."[156] Here is where madness lies. What seems initially to be a story of paranoia and violence in South Africa becomes, like Sachs's *Black Hamlet*, a study of the impact of apartheid on the indigenous communities and the psychological makeup of their members in the greater context of their own belief systems.[157]

Sexual fear comes up at several points in Sachs's work, most especially when John Chavafambira is accused of attempting to rape a white woman and must flee, although his boss knows "all white women had a mania about being raped by blacks."[158] Social and economic fear also come up, and Sachs writes, "Patiently, laboriously, I endeavored to explain that the root cause of oppression was not color, but fear"—fear not only of Africans, but of their progress and the loss of racial exploitation.[159] It is striking that though the books were written so far apart, the racial tensions mentioned in Sachs's books—leading to protests and strikes—are still "building to a thunderhead" in 1983, according to Malan.[160] Fear is the crucial affect in *My Traitor's Heart*, as expressed both in Malan's analysis that in the wake of the "Hammerman" murders, "fear mounts toward hysteria, fed by increasing turbulence in the political sphere", but also in the narrative's use of second-person address, which asks "you" to feel the fear of white South Africans.[161]

Central to both presentations of the psychopathology of race and racism is the way that the "white" subject is figured in ways that echo the idea of identification with the aggressor. Sachs often parenthetically inserts the "correct" medical interpretation of something from John's narrative, and he writes that "civilization had penetrated into [John's] innermost being."[162] Though Sachs's liberal standpoint and opposition to racist systems is clear, he very much positions European civilization as the more developed, and his regard for John increases as John accepts Western ideas about medicine, education, and race relations. He ascribes to the idea that psychoanalysis with an African man can give him insights into the subconscious of all Africans, and thus uses his training to diagnose John Chavafambira's issues and draw inferences from them to "every African." He draws particularly universal views about the "retarding" effect of late breastfeeding, but is progressive in his claim that "this important psychological factor counts little compared with the poverty and starvation, the economic exploitation, and the sever racial discrimination to which black people are subjected in South Africa."[163]

Decades later, Malan initially follows this thread, framing Simon's crime as one almost forced by "white oppression." Ultimately, though, he concludes that Simon was seen as a violent and troublesome outcast within the context of his family and community, and that the interference or abuse of whites was incidental, in many ways, to the story of his violence. He writes, seemingly to himself, "In my time, in my country, white men assumed that they were the center of the black universe—that they had subjugated the dreams and psyches of Africans, along with their bodies. It simply wasn't true. That is what Simon taught me."[164] Malan complicates the notion of "cultural differences," pointing out that it is a phrase that can carry either liberal cachet or subtle justification for apartheid, and he takes the reader through the process through which he decentered the white subject in his own mind. He walks an oft-contradictory line—between documenting the injustice at the center of apartheid and refusing white oppressors the central position.

Malan's own racial and social identity is prominent as he wrestles with these questions, and in the very project of the book, but of greater interest to us are Sachs's subtler interjections. He only rarely mentions that he is Jewish, such as at a key moment where he is being asked to protect his analysand, and he feels as though he is being asked as a Jew to change the entirety of race relations in South Africa. He faces, in this scene, his inability to do so, calling on his own membership in an oppressed group to emphasize his powerlessness. Significantly, this is the scene where Sachs claims to begin seeing John Chavafambira not as an experiment, but as a person.

Yet Sachs is also aware that that John is parroting his own liberal view of race relations, which echo Shylock's most famous lines from *The Merchant of Venice*. John says that white people believe of a black child "if you starve it, it will not die; that if you freeze it, it will not sicken."[165] In this moment, then, a Victorian sentiment about the humanity of Jews read into Shakespeare's monologue is presented by John Chavafambira in Sachs's voice as an intermediary. The echo of Shylock is particularly telling given Sachs's universal diagnosis of "Hamletism" as the core neurosis exhibited by John.

Race and Madness from Germany via South Africa to the United States

From the late 1940s forward, alternatives to theories of racism and victimhood as psychological processes emerge. In Hannah Arendt's *The Origins of Totalitarianism* (1951) racism in nineteenth-century South Africa as well as antisemitism were not only linked but shown to be reflections of "colonial imperialism" on the part of Great Britain as well as the "continental imperialism" of Germany, not individual or mass psychopathology. Her initial focus is on antisemitism and the move from a quasi-national antisemitism to a biological antisemitism in the course of the late nineteenth century and its appearance as an "ideological weapon of imperialism" with the colonization of Africa. Indeed, the quote in the prior paragraph about the Jews of South Africa in the 1940s comes from her work.

Arendt's general position is to reject any psychologizing about the theories of race for "it is impossible ever to know beyond doubt another man's heart—torture in this context is only the desperate and eternally futile attempt to achieve what cannot be achieved—suspicion can no longer be allayed if neither a community of values nor the predictabilities of self-interest exist as social (as distinguished from merely psychological) realities."[166] For Arendt, "merely psychological realities" may well include the theories of mass action as well as of individual psychopathology as explained by contemporary psychology. She argued in a 1944 essay that a form of "race thinking" antedates "racism" and that it is through totalizing force of political persuasion that racism comes to be internalized as an ideology.[167] In *The Origins of Totalitarianism* she notes that "an ideology differs from a simple opinion in that it claims to possess either the key to history, or the solution for all the 'riddles of the universe,' or the intimate knowledge of the hidden universal laws which are supposed to rule nature and man."[168] In other words ideological power is rooted now in its internalized form, which has infiltrated into every nook and cranny of a society, as it becomes part of the collective unconscious. It is not a deviant force but the standard baseline, not madness but normality. Once racism is accepted as an ideology and becomes unquestioned, it is implicit in all of the ideas, institutions, and practices of a culture.

Even given Arendt's complex rhetoric about the nature of the African subject, it is clear that colonial racism thus comes to be a "fathomable response by Europeans toward Africans, who (in her estimation) lacked civilization, reason, culture, history, and political institutions."[169] Race as an ideology in South Africa comes to be "the emergency explanation of human beings whom no European or civilized man could understand and whose humanity so frightened and humiliated the immigrants that they no longer cared to belong to the same human species."[170] But it is a racism that comes to define the indigenous peoples of South Africa from the perspective of even Jewish and Indian immigrants (think of Gandhi in the 1890s) labeled as "inferior."

Such psychologizing views do however become part of her rhetoric. Arendt did not deny that the underlying assumptions of racism are the force of the "mob," and can take the form of irrationality and therefore psychopathology. Yet when she speaks of the Afrikaners and their racial policies toward the indigenous peoples of South Africa, she can imagine that "race was the Boers' answer to the overwhelming monstrosity of Africa—a whole continent populated and overpopulated by savages—an explanation of the madness which grasped and illuminated them like 'a flash of lightening in a serene sky: "Exterminate all the brutes.""[171] She is quoting here Joseph Conrad's problematic account of the mental collapse of the European in Africa into the madness reflected in the image of the African in *Heart of Darkness* (1902). Indeed the reader will notice that Arendt's image of the colonial explorers in Africa and their madness echoes Conrad:

> Many of these adventurers had gone mad in the silent wilderness of an overpopulated continent where the presence of human beings only underlined utter solitude, and where an untouched, overwhelmingly hostile nature that nobody had ever taken the trouble to change into human landscape seemed to wait in sublime patience "for the passing away of the fantastic invasion" of man. But their madness had remained a matter of individual experience and without consequences.[172]

But this gives way to the world of imperial colonial bureaucracy where madness is rationalized as part of the system of white control in Africa. Here it is the new elite, not the madness of the individual, that seeks control through racial oppression.

How does the victim of racism respond to such a bureaucracy of race theory? Arendt begins her analysis of the response of the victim to racism with her view that Jewish theories of collective identity ("race") are a psychological response of Jews in an acculturating moment. Here the analogy to Pinsker's critique of acculturation is clear but the result for her is very different. It is not Germany but Britain that provides her with her case study:

> Judaism, and belonging to the Jewish people, degenerated into a simple fact of birth only among assimilated Jewry. Originally it had meant a specific religion, a specific nationality, the sharing of specific memories and specific hopes, and, even among the privileged Jews, it meant at least

still sharing specific economic advantages. Secularization and assimilation of the Jewish intelligentsia had changed self-consciousness and self-
interpretation in such a way that nothing was left of the old memories and
hopes but the awareness of belonging to a chosen people. Disraeli, though
certainly not the only "exception Jew" to believe in his own chosenness
without believing in Him who chooses and rejects, was the only one who
produced a full-blown race doctrine out of this empty concept of a historic
mission. He was ready to assert that the Semitic principle "represents all
that is spiritual in our nature," that "the vicissitudes of history find their
main solution—all is race," which is "the key to history" regardless of "language and religion," for "there is only one thing which makes a race and
that is blood" and there is only one aristocracy, the "aristocracy of nature"
which consists of "an unmixed race of a first-rate organization."

The close relationship of this to more modern race ideologies need not
to be stressed, and Disraeli's discovery is one more proof of how well they
serve to combat feelings of social inferiority. For if race doctrines finally
served much more sinister and immediately political purposes, it is still
true that much of their plausibility and persuasiveness lay in the fact that
they helped anybody feel himself an aristocrat who had been selected by
birth on the strength of "racial" qualification. That these new selected
ones did not belong to an elite, to a selected few—which, after all, had
been inherent in the pride of a nobleman—but had to share chosenness
with an ever-growing mob, did no essential harm to the doctrine, for
those who did not belong to the chosen race grew numerically in the
same proportion.[173]

Thus Disraeli's renewed awareness of Jewish identity as a race is what
one of the authors has termed a form of "romantic reversal."[174] If the Jew
in Georgian and Victorian England is in fact impaired by his religious
practice and race to the extent that he is mad, then the reversal of this is
to claim superiority for the Jewish race. Arendt provides a psychological, indeed an Adlerian, reading of this as a means "to combat feelings of
social inferiority." And this is generated by "an ever-growing mob." This
is a form of psychological race theory—seen by her as mirroring British
notions of class difference, as that involved in the denigration of the
Jew—but which now places the "mob" as the new collective, the healthy
and the productive. Yet, of course, this is not an appropriate model for

a post-racial modernity in spite of the claims of a political Zionism that had discovered Pinsker and was reading him, shortly before the creation of the state of Israel in 1948, as a proto-Zionist.

All of Arendt's comments are, of course, in the light of the rise of the Nazis, of antisemitism and the resultant Holocaust. She writes during the unfolding of the Cold War following those horrors:

> Never has our future been more unpredictable, never have we depended so much on political forces that cannot be trusted to follow the rules of common sense and self-interest—forces that look like sheer insanity, if judged by the standards of other centuries. It is as though mankind had divided itself between those who believe in human omnipotence (who think that everything is possible if one knows how to organize masses for it) and those for whom powerlessness has become the major experience of their lives.[175]

"Common sense and self-interest" are the antithesis of madness and they are sadly lacking. Here she sees the claim that the perpetrators of the Holocaust were driven by a form of madness as also a potential rationale for explaining such horrors in other contexts:

> The "Germanic world empire," as Himmler said, or the "Aryan" world empire, as Hitler would have put it, was in any event still centuries off. For the "movement" it was more important to demonstrate that it was possible to fabricate a race by annihilating other "races" than to win a war with limited aims. What strikes the outside observer as a "piece of prodigious insanity" is nothing but the consequence of the absolute primacy of the movement not only over the state, but also over the nation, the people and the positions of power held by the rulers themselves.[176]

Here she is quoting Isaac Deutscher from his 1949 biography of Stalin. Both Arendt and Deutscher, a Galician Jew who escaped to Great Britain in 1939, see such claims through the eyes of those who had suffered through the "madness" of the Nazi genocide:

> The incredibility of the horrors is closely bound up with their economic uselessness. The Nazis carried this uselessness to the point of open anti-

utility when in the midst of the war, despite the shortage of building material and rolling stock, they set up enormous, costly extermination factories and transported millions of people back and forth. In the eyes of a strictly utilitarian world the obvious contradiction between these acts and military expediency gave the whole enterprise an air of mad unreality. This atmosphere of madness and unreality, created by an apparent lack of purpose, is the real iron curtain, which hides all forms of concentration camps from the eyes of the world.[177]

Thus Arendt uses the madness of the monstrous as an explanation or at least as a description of the difference between a rational model of understanding the function of the state and a racist one, in which utilitarianism is sacrificed to the ends of racism.

Yet Arendt's rhetoric may be at odds with her ideology. For at the core of totalitarianism of all stripes she sees "the truly radical nature of Evil":

The trouble is that our period has so strangely intertwined the good with the bad that without the imperialists' "expansion for expansion's sake," the world might never have become one; without the bourgeoisie's political device of "power for power's sake," the extent of human strength might never have been discovered; without the fictitious world of totalitarian movements, in which with unparalleled clarity the essential uncertainties of our time have been spelled out, we might have been driven to our doom without ever becoming aware of what has been happening.

And if it is true that in the final stages of totalitarianism an absolute evil appears (absolute because it can no longer be deduced from humanly comprehensible motives), it is also true that without it we might never have known the truly radical nature of Evil.

Antisemitism (not merely the hatred of Jews), imperialism (not merely conquest), totalitarianism (not merely dictatorship)—one after the other, one more brutally than the other, have demonstrated that human dignity needs a new guarantee which can be found only in a new political principle, in a new law on earth, whose validity this time must comprehend the whole of humanity while its power must remain strictly limited, rooted in and controlled by newly defined territorial entities.

We can no longer afford to take that which was good in the past and simply call it our heritage, to discard the bad and simply think of it as a dead load which by itself time will bury in oblivion. The subterranean stream of Western history has finally come to the surface and usurped the dignity of our tradition. This is the reality in which we live. And this is why all efforts to escape from the grimness of the present into nostalgia for a still intact past, or into the anticipated oblivion of a better future, are vain.[178]

Evil, in Arendt's view, is not merely as defined by Claudia Card— "foreseeable intolerable harms produced by culpable wrong doings."[179] Nor is it moral evil in any theological sense with which she is concerned, but rather the problem of evil most broadly understood as the problem of how to make sense of the world when that world is ineradicably a place of suffering.[180]

Arendt insists that morality demands that we make evil intelligible rather than, as Voltaire and much of the Enlightenment argued, incomprehensible and unintelligible. In 1963 she published her *Eichmann in Jerusalem: A Report on the Banality of Evil*, which argues that normality, not psychopathology, lie at the core of racism, thus rebutting many of the studies of the Nazis that saw them either as mad and/or infecting their populace with racist madness.[181] Eichmann's banality is not that he is normal in the sense that he is typical but that he is in no way mad, not in any way impelled to "explain" his actions beyond those of a competent (in legal terms) actor.[182] Eichmann was sane, according to Arendt and to the psychiatrists who gave testimony at his trail:

> Half a dozen psychiatrists had certified him as "normal"—"More normal, at any rate, than I am after having examined him," one of them was said to have exclaimed, while another found that his whole psychological outlook, his attitude toward his wife and children, mother and father, brothers, sisters, and friends, was "not only normal but most desirable"— and finally the minister who paid regular visits to him in prison . . . reassured everybody by declaring Eichmann to be "a man with very positive ideas."[183]

Until *Brown v. Board of Education*, remember, this is the sole space in criminal law (both Napoleonic and common) in which the question of mental competency is a mitigation of guilt.[184] As Arendt writes about Eichmann's complicity:

> [In] such an enormous and complicated crime as the one we are now con-
> sidering, wherein many people participated, on various levels and in vari-
> ous modes of activity—the planners, the organizers, and those executing
> the deeds, according to their various ranks—there is not much point in us-
> ing ordinary concepts of counseling and soliciting to commit a crime. For
> these crimes were committed en masse, not only in regard to the number
> of victims, but also in regard to the numbers of those who perpetuated the
> crime, and the extent to which any one of the many criminals was close
> or remote from the actual killer of the victim means nothing, as far as the
> measure of responsibility is concerned. On the contrary, in general the de-
> gree of responsibility increases as we draw further away from the man who
> uses the fatal instrument *with his own hands* [emphasis in the original].[185]

Whether or not Eichmann was complicit remains a contested question,
which relies on his consciousness of his actions as a crime. But there is
no question for Arendt or indeed for the court in Israel about his sanity.
Susan Neiman, well before the recent spate of critical books on Arendt's
study, sees her work as the most important rejection of a worldview that
wishes to provide psychological explanations for evil:

> Auschwitz embodied evil that confuted two centuries of modem assump-
> tions about intention. Those assumptions identify evil and evil intention
> so thoroughly that denying the latter is normally viewed as a way of de-
> nying the former. Where evil intention is absent, we may hold agents
> liable for the wrongs they inflict, but we view them as matters of criminal
> negligence. Alternatively, anyone who denies criminal intention is pres-
> ent in a particular action is thought to exonerate the criminal. This is
> the source of the furor that still surrounds Arendt's *Eichmann in Jeru-
> salem* . . . . The conviction that guilt requires malice and forethought led
> most readers to conclude that Arendt denied guilt because she denied
> malice and forethought—though she often repeated that Eichmann was
> guilty, and was convinced that he ought to hang.[186]

But in no case could the claim of a lack of competency (madness) mitigate guilt.

6

The Modern Pathologization of Racism

Racism and/as Pathology

To this point in our study, we have discussed in great detail the *pathologization of race* from the nineteenth century through the first three decades of twentieth-century medical and psychological sciences. Though the historical formation of race, including the role the sciences have played in its ongoing construction, is not a new story, few scholars have attended to the coterminous formations of race and madness across "racial" boundaries during this period. In the last chapter, we showed the paradigmatic shift that took place within the medical and psychological sciences between the inter-war years and immediately following World War II, whereby race increasingly was framed as a social problem while, at the same time, *racism* became pathologized. This pathologization of racism coincided with two related phenomena: the collapse of the Nazi regime following World War II and the rise of the modern American Civil Rights Movement beginning in the 1950s.

The reader may recall from the last chapter that during the 1950s and 1960s two branches of concern regarding racism emerged among policymakers and professionals. The first branch concerned itself with pathological *consequences* of racism. This concern was typified by academic analyses of the mental, physical, and emotional illnesses caused by structural and systemic racism, as well as remarks by elected officials and Civil Rights activists advocating on behalf of black communities. The second branch concerned itself with diagnosing racism as a pathological *illness*. Though largely typified by academic arguments aimed at specifying the specific mental, physical, and emotional disorders associated with *being* racist, or *having* racism, this discourse would make its way into the language of Civil Rights scholars and activists, as physicians, psychologists, and psychiatrists played an increasingly important part in the Civil Rights era from the 1950s through the 1970s.

As a result, the post–Civil Rights period of the United States has been marked by significant claims about mental health consequences for minority communities from the effects of long exposure to structural racism, as well as claims about the mental health status of individual and identifiable racists and bigots. The rise of the mental health explanation of racism in the 1950s and 1960s, much of which we documented in the last chapter, is best understood as the achievement of a specific *governmentality* centered on illuminating the negative consequences of racism for its victims, while simultaneously subsuming racist practices under an emergent pathological explanation. New developments in cognitive neuroscience provide further legitimacy to pathological explanations of racism that increasingly locate racism's origins in the cognitive functions of the individual racist. It is to this issue—the shifting meaning of racism's *interiority*—that we turn our attention in this chapter. Let's first consider several examples, all contemporary.

In January 2010, the John Hopkins University School of Medicine hosted a series of workshops for health care professionals, including faculty, students, and community advocates. Centered on the documentary *The Deadliest Disease in America*, participants were encouraged to consider the numerous racial inequities in medical treatment the film highlights. The film does not claim that racism itself is a medical condition, though the metaphor of a disease to describe racism was shown to be quite powerful for the workshop participants. Participants, for example, praised the workshops for illuminating the difficulty in communicating effectively with health care providers who do not understand the contours of racial inequity within the health care system.[1] Since 2008, the film and its workshops have been presented at over a dozen major medical schools, including Yale, the University of Pennsylvania, Vanderbilt, Case Western, the University of Mississippi, and the University of Tennessee. In addition, the film and its associated workshops have been presented at the U.S. Capitol Visitor Center in Washington, D.C.

The film's director, Crystal Renee Emery, runs an online blog as part of the educational toolkit associated with the film's website. Emery's entry from November 19, 2010, reads:

> The disease of racism affects everyone, *but we can eradicate it like any other deadly illness* [emphasis ours]. Smallpox, for example, killed mil-

lions of people just like racism is killing millions of people everyday through poor housing, education, economics and health. Smallpox was eradicated through wide-reaching and concentrated vaccination campaigns, which required both vigilant reporting of the disease and the collaboration of all stakeholders involved. Much of the early campaigning was primarily educational, discussing the vaccination with various populations to improve their willingness to participate. The same type of educational campaign can empower us to deal with racism and will require the same reporting of, and response to, incidents of racism.[2]

In Emery's blog, racism is an indicator of a "sick society," affecting (read: infecting) everyone. Emery's use of "disease" to describe racism reflects one version of its pathological construction: the *consequences* of racism upon its victims. Emery, in the above passage, likens racism to smallpox, in that racism can potentially affect *everyone* if left untreated. Further, like smallpox, racism disproportionately influences those from lower socioeconomic backgrounds, who remain less insulated from its harmful effects due to their lack of resources. Finally, like smallpox, Emery believes racism can be eliminated through comprehensive educational and policy reform.

Though Emery's use of racism here is largely a rhetorical strategy, the metaphor of "disease" to describe racism has been gaining currency within the medical and psychological sciences and within popular culture. Increasingly, the descriptor of "disease" is turning up in scholarly articles, treatment protocols, academic conference presentations, and in more general "shoptalk" among behavioral *and* social scientists. Behavioral scientists have asserted, for example, that racism produces among its victims a variety of clinical syndromes; while social scientists have argued that racist practices might actually produce psychological stress among whites who participate in, or benefit from, overt forms of racism.[3]

In a recent experiment conducted by psychologists at Purdue University, whites were asked to rate their frequency of aversive, appetitive, and neutral experiences with racial and ethnic minorities.[4] Included in this rating were participants' degree of fear, anxiety, and anger they felt when engaged in interactions with racial minorities. The results indicate that aversive contacts were associated with more fear, anxiety, and anger. However, direct avoidance was *predicted* by fear and anxiety. In other words, the degree of fear or anxiety among whites toward racial minorities manifests itself in their choice of whether to avoid interracial contact or not, indicating that there may indeed be a psychological effect to even minimal practices of racism, such as limiting one's contact with racial and ethnic minorities. While these examples illustrate the ever more frequent link between racism and psychopathological consequences, there exists a concurrent development in which racism is situated as a psychopathological *condition*. This framing of racism as a medical problem, whereby individuals suffering from it need to seek "professional help" or treatment, has inserted itself within mainstream press and popular discourse.

In June 2013, Riley Cooper, a wide receiver for the NFL's Philadelphia Eagles, was caught on video at a Kenny Chesney concert shouting, "I will jump that fence and fight every nigger in here, bro!" The video soon went viral across social media platforms, creating tension between the Eagles and their fans, many of whom are black.[5] As a result, both the Eagles and Cooper, who is white, issued public statements responding to the incident and to public reaction to the video footage. In his August 2, 2013, statement, Cooper declared:

> During this time, I'm going to be speaking with a variety of professionals to help me better understand how I could have done something that was so offensive, and how I can start the healing process for everyone.

That same day the team released its own statement on the incident:

> As we have said, Riley Cooper will be seeking counseling and we have excused him from all team activities. . . . He will meet with professionals provided by the Eagles during this period of time to better help him understand how his words have hurt so many.

Cooper's incident was hardly the first time a high-profile figure, following an overt act of racism, vowed to seek professional treatment. While performing at the West Hollywood comedy club The Laugh Factory in 2006, comedian Michael Richards lashed out at hecklers by referring to them as "niggers." Popular among audiences for his portrayal of

Kramer on the hit television series *Seinfeld*, Richards was subjected to an almost immediate public backlash following the release of hidden-video footage from the incident. Over the next several weeks, Richards began what is best described as an apology tour that included interviews with mainstream press and appearances on radio and late-night talk shows. On the Reverend Jesse Jackson's nationally syndicated radio show, *Keep Hope Alive*, Richards explained he was "shattered by [the incident]," and, as a result, "was in a place of humiliation." As part of Richards's self-professed healing from this incident, his publicist soon informed the media that Richards had begun psychiatric counseling.[6]

In August of that same year, following a drunken antisemitic tirade stemming from a DUI arrest, actor and Academy Award–winning director Mel Gibson issued a formal apology. In this apology, he claimed:

> I'm not just asking for forgiveness. I would like to take it one step further, and meet with leaders in the Jewish community, with whom I can have a one-on-one discussion to discern the appropriate path for healing. I have begun an ongoing program of recovery and what I am now realizing is that I cannot do it alone. I am in the process of understanding where those vicious words came from during that drunken display, and I am asking the Jewish community, whom I have personally offended, to help me on my journey through recovery.[7]

Note that Gibson describes his racism as more than just a moral failing. His actions require "healing," including an "ongoing program of recovery." Also worth noting is just how closely the language Gibson uses to describe his racism parallels the language used to describe an addiction to alcohol, another social problem medicalized in the post–World War II era.[8]

Several years prior to this, in a feature for the December 1999 issue of *Sports Illustrated*, then star relief pitcher for the Atlanta Braves John Rocker made racist and homophobic remarks concerning whether he would ever consider playing for the New York Yankees or the New York Mets:

> I'd retire first. . . . Imagine having to take the 7 train to the ballpark looking like you're riding through Beirut next to some kid with purple hair,

next to some queer with AIDS. . . . The biggest thing I don't like about New York are the foreigners. You can walk an entire block in Times Square and not hear anybody speaking English. Asians and Koreans and Vietnamese and Indians and Russians and Spanish people and everything up there. How the hell did they get in this country?

In this same interview, Rocker also referred to a black teammate as a "fat monkey" and mocked Asian women. Condemning his remarks as offending "practically every element of society," the commissioner of Major League Baseball, Bud Selig, ordered mandatory counseling and therapy for Rocker in 2000.

Selig's mandate for counseling and therapy drew both praise and criticism from experts and laypersons alike. In a letter to the editor of the *New York Times*, the psychiatrist Milton Sirota, wrote:

> I applaud the effort by Major League Baseball to become more informed about the judgment of John Rocker, the Atlanta Braves pitcher who made racist comments in an interview, and to determine whether Mr. Rocker shows signs of psychological damage. However, only an exhaustive clinical evaluation not limited to testing can give us clues about the nature and extent of significant psychiatric disturbance. We now have an opportunity to better understand a person who is outspoken in his racism. Such an evaluation may also help to define the breeding grounds for this social malignancy.[9]

However, in another letter to the editor of the *Times* published the following day, the psychiatrist Hugh Polk opined:

> As a psychiatrist who has practiced professionally for more than 20 years, I am alarmed by the decision by Bud Selig, the baseball commissioner, to order John Rocker, a pitcher for the Atlanta Braves, to undergo psychiatric counseling before deciding whether to discipline him for racist and homophobic remarks he made to *Sports Illustrated* last month. Many of my colleagues in the field share this concern. In a society in which seeking professional help for one's emotional problems is still viewed with suspicion and stigma, this punitive and coercive misuse of psychiatry does little to contribute to creating an environment in which everyone

(including Rocker and other sports figures) can get the help they need to develop more healthy emotional lives.[10]

Note that Polk does not necessarily object to the idea that Rocker needs psychiatric care, only that this care should not be framed as a punitive measure. Rather, Rocker should be encouraged to seek the (professional) help he needs.

That the psychological sciences, including psychology, medicine, and psychiatry are taking a professional interest in the nature and consequences of racism should be evident. To this point, our focus has largely centered on documenting the historical turn within the behavioral and social sciences whereby, from roughly 1880 to 1940, race became disjointed from its pseudobiological and psychopathological foundations and repositioned as a social construction. Yet, beyond World War II, with the general acceptance of race's social constructedness among social and behavioral scientists, scientific and public understandings of racism *also* shifted from a social and cultural effect to a pathological condition. What produced this second shift? And what are its potential reverberations?

One claim we believe worth considering is that the willingness among the scientific and medical communities to treat racism as a psychopathological problem, and the public's increasing acceptance of the disease metaphor to describe racism, is the product of a *specific conjunctural crisis* between politics, science, and ideology. In a 2010 interview with *Soundings* magazine, the late cultural theorist Stuart Hall defined a conjuncture as "a period during which the different social, political, economic, and ideological contradictions that are at work in a society come together to give it a specific shape."[11] Conjunctures, for Hall, are ways of understanding how history moves between and through crises, rather than the more common "history as evolution" model. Conjunctural crises are when what are perceived to be relatively autonomous sites—the economy, politics, ideology, science, public opinion, all sites with "different origins, driven by different contradictions, and developed according to their own temporalities—are nevertheless 'convened' or condensed in the same moment."[12] This is, of course, distinct from how Omi and Winant define "racial projects" (see our Introduction), in that racial projects for them overdetermine the contestation between the state and social movements in the production of racial meaning. Hall, meanwhile, acknowledges that ideological production is not exclusive to the domain of the state, but is itself a dynamic encounter between various institutions and their discourses. Hall's emphasis on the rupture in one particular hegemonizing discourse, and the ideological and structural necessity to resolve that crisis through a new articulation, provide the grounds from which to consider the role of epistemic culture in not only what *causes* the conjectural crisis, but also how actors and institutions respond. We also find Hall's formulation useful because it allows us to reject the *ontic* description of the state, and the politics that give it shape, in favor of a more relational description whereby changes in epistemic culture result in a rearticulation of the state's relationship to science, and vice versa. In the case of race and racism, changes in epistemic culture give rise to specific ideas of racism that direct scientific inquiry toward its causes and consequences.

In reflecting upon the period immediately following World War II, in the aftermath of the Jewish Holocaust and the collapse of the Nazi regime, there was a crisis that took place between the sites of medicine, which had helped shape the ideologies necessary to drive the political will of the German body politic in such a targeted manner toward the extermination of its Jewish population. The product of this crisis, then, to follow Hall's thesis, is that since that period we can identify a steady increase in the medicalization of social problems, including racism. This trend has had, however, the perhaps unintended effect of transforming larger social forces into matters of an individual's own mental constitution.[13] As a consequence, protocols for treating conditions previously under the purview of larger social institutions, like government, family, and education, have become increasingly individualized and absorbed within our contemporary health care system.[14]

Anti-Racism, the Psychological Sciences, and Public Policy after World War II

Since World War II the gradual expansion of the political claims about the role of state power in shaping the scientific debates about citizenship has allowed for the dismissal of biological explanations of race, thanks in large part to the role that social sciences have played in producing scientific knowledge and public policy centered on race as a social construction. Du Bois's sociological program at Atlanta University, and the first and second generation of the Chicago School in sociology, for example, produced a number of monographs, journal articles, and policy reports demonstrating the social constructedness of race and the problems with the biological model of racial hierarchy that dominated late-nineteenth and early-twentieth-century scientific and public knowledge.[15] Of course the latter was more widely read and well received, in large part due to the general dismissal of Du Bois's scholarship on account of his blackness.

On the other hand, the post–World War II expansion and acceptance of scientific and medical superiority in defining deviancy has also produced new, psychopathological accounts of racism, some of which employ social scientific research and arguments, while a host of others simply employ the language of the medical and biological sciences. One result of this has been that racism is increasingly depicted as a clinical disorder, a psychopathological phenomenon, and a target for treatment vis-à-vis drug therapy and behavioral modification.[16] As the sociologist Peter Conrad has shown, the past several decades have borne witness to several aspects of the human condition becoming subsumed under medical authority and reconstructed as treatable diseases.[17] Furthermore, over the past century, medical categories have expanded dramatically in order to account for a variety of human expressions and personal troubles.

We will not overdramatize our claim: the shift from seeing *race* through the lens of medical science to seeing *racism* through the lens of medical science was and remains a contested one. Yet we are today in a second "age of biology," the first having taken place in the latter half of the nineteenth century, the moment of the birth of scientific racism and the pathologization of race and racism. Today's "age of biology" includes but is not limited to the rise of the Human Genome Project, the growth of medical and pharmacological industries, and the increasing concentration of explanatory power within medical and psychological discourse. Our willingness to even *consider* prejudices as psychopathological phenomena, whether within scientific communities or within public discourse, is a foregone conclusion as it was in the nineteenth century. Meaning, it is already happening *again*!

The expansion of scientific and medical claims from the mid-twentieth century to the present is both cause and effect of the medical and psychological disciplines as legitimate regimes of authority. While the social sciences have predominantly turned their attention toward a social constructionist paradigm through which to understand race in the post-war era, the emergent authority of the medical and psychological sciences has produced a growing belief among laypersons *and* academics that *racism* is (1) an individual action and (2) a negative position to hold. Within the psychological disciplines, this sentiment was fueled, in part, by the growth of "attitude research," some of which has resulted in the promotion and promulgation of educational resources, social activism, and even social policy that aimed to make individuals *less racist* by raising their awareness of their own prejudicial beliefs. Despite conflicting evidence concerning the degree to which the public trusts the psychological sciences, public discourse on racism, prejudice, and antisemitism suggests that the psychological disciplines are best suited to treat these now "newly recognized" personal troubles.

Recall from Chapter Two that, by the late 1930s, within social psychology an emphasis on attitude research was taking place, with particular focus on prejudicial attitudes, including racial ones. From this period through the end of World War II and the beginning of the modern Civil Rights Movement, prejudice and racism were increasingly examined through the lens of individual psychopathology, as flaws "arising from inappropriate conditioning, reliance upon stereotyping, or psychodynamic development."[18] Though discussed previously, the work of Eugene and Ruth Horowitz on prejudicial attitudes among children stands as an exemplar of this trend within social psychology, and is worth revisiting.

Importantly, the Horowitzs refined the dominant understanding of attitudes that was grounded in the work of Gordon Allport. Recall that Allport had previously defined an attitude, generally, as a mental state of readiness organized through experiences, and, as a result, exerting influence upon a person's response to social interactions with which the attitude is related.[19] Extrapolating to prejudicial attitudes, however, the Horowitzs had started with the assumption that our national culture is normatively *intolerant*. Those who are racially tolerant are deviant, or rebellious. This suggests that, unless there is a psychological reason to rebel, the individual will be intolerant simply by being a member of the society.[20] Racial attitudes are, in Eugene Horowitz's words, "the interiorizations of prevalent social norms."[21] As a social norm in the United States, prejudice represents the "standard or accepted form of behavior."[22]

Almost ten years prior to this, using pictorial techniques with a sample of school-aged children, Eugene Horowitz had found that "children's attitudes toward Negroes are now chiefly determined not by contact with Negroes, but by contact with the prevalent attitude toward Negroes."[23] Though the pictorial tests used pictures of blacks with differing skin tones, there was no significant difference in the responses of the white children according to the lightness or darkness of the faces of blacks. Thus, Horowitz concludes, this "confirms the existence of the dynamic equivalent in young children of the southern attitude 'one drop of negro blood makes a man a nigger.'"[24] As Horowitz writes: "In the course of the general development of the child, the various phases of the attitudes representing the different societal organizations and emphases and different aspects of personal development become better integrated and more closely related to other aspects of the total personality of the individual."[25]

By the time Horowitz's paper was published in Otto Klineberg's 1944 volume, *Characteristics of the American Negro*, the psychosocial development of "race attitudes," or at least the psychological sciences approach to them, could be summarized as "part of the general culture pattern which includes racial, national, and religious affiliations as significant attributes relevant to the consideration and description of an individual."[26] In other words, a growing body of research suggested that sociostructural forces could account for the development of attitudes towards members of different racial and ethnic groups. Horowitz notes that within this general approach:

> Race prejudice is the result of four dynamics: race prejudice being part of the general culture, therefore prejudicial attitudes are simply attempts at conformity; the frustration-aggression sequence, meaning, wherever we find aggression, if we look we can find some underlying frustration even though it is not always directly related to the aggression (displacement of aggression); the role of personal experience (though, broadly, this is an unimportant factor); and the way in which race prejudice frequently

functions in terms of unconscious personal meanings. . . . These four [dynamics] have figured most prominently in analyses of [race prejudice and race attitudes].[27]

Horowitz's outline of the general approach to the study of prejudice in the post–World War II era would hold true up through the 1950s, though with some important modifications. One of those, already mentioned, was the influence of the *Studies in Prejudice* series, including the publication of its first volume, *The Authoritarian Personality* (*TAP*), in 1950.

We have noted the impact *TAP* and other works from the *Studies in Prejudice* series had on how behavioral scientists, Civil Rights activists, and policymakers understood the causes and consequences of racism in the post–World War II period. Recall, for example, how the antifascist discourse among antiwar protestors as well as Black Power revolutionaries including Stokely Carmichael, Bobby Seale, and Huey P. Newton was deeply influenced by the widespread public recognition of *TAP*.[28] It is also important, however, to note that one of the authors of the study, Nevitt Sanford, in reflections upon the history of *TAP*'s development, contested the oft-misread notion that an "authoritarian personality" was a relatively abnormal, or highly unusual, condition.

While "a very strict and punitive superego" is a part of the foundation for individuals identified as having the F-syndrome, Sanford notes that the authoritarian personality is "more or less normally distributed" within modern Western society. Furthermore, "anyone is capable of having his authoritarianism evoked by sufficiently strong stimuli." That is to say, the ability to express an authoritarian personality, while to some degree dependent upon the upbringing of the individual, is also *always* possible within advanced society, which creates the structures necessary to produce within the development of the child a strict and punitive superego.[29] Anyone can be an authoritarian, and within any advanced society, the potential for authoritarianism is always present.

The notion that a sick society produces sick individuals would be a recurrent theme within mental health discourse through the 1950s, and, consequently, would appear within the claims of public officials and activists who drew upon the authority of medical and psychological science to make claims about the nature, and consequences, of extreme racism. For example, the psychiatrist David Wilson identified racial prejudice as part of the "neuroses of everyday living," in that, though racial prejudice was *normal* in American society, its exaggeration in the form of extreme bigotry causes distortions that have injurious effects on normal individuals.[30] Several years later, in examining rates of hospitalization among blacks and whites in Virginia, Wilson found that, between 1914 and 1954, the ratio per 100,000 of blacks more than doubled over the forty-year period, with a rate of over 600 per 100,000 in 1954.[31] What caused this rapid increase of hospitalization among black mental health patients? Over the previous fifty years, Wilson wrote, the South had undergone rapid cultural change, including a steady migration from farm to city, from agriculture to industry; the transition from a slave culture to a more democratic one; and the transition of blacks from predominantly poor, illiterate people working as servants, to owners of homes and cars whose children "can go to high school, to college or university." The catch: "In spite of all this, [blacks are] more segregated now than 40 years ago and while then [their] status was fixed, now [they have] no status as [they move] from a culture of [their] own into a white culture."[32]

Wilson's conclusion was not his own, but instead was derived in part from several of his contemporaries, including noted anthropologist Margaret Mead and psychiatrist Richard L. Jenkins, but also Civil Rights attorney Jack Greenberg and longtime NAACP labor director Herbert Hill. Mead, in 1955, had expressed similar arguments about the instability of changing cultures, writing, "[Under] situations of stress and strain, of rapid changes and consequent disorientation, there is likely to be an increase in manifest mental ill health."[33] Meanwhile, Greenberg and Hill, in their 1955 book *Citizen's Guide to Desegregation*, had written broadly about the difficult transition blacks would make into white culture following the movement toward desegregation initiated by the 1954 *Brown v. Board of Education* Supreme Court decision. Finally, Jenkins, in his 1954 *Breaking Patterns of Defeat*, wrote that higher incidences of schizophrenia, which Wilson identified in his 1957 *American Journal of Psychiatry* article, were likely due to "a social or a culture situation which gives rise to insoluble problems and much frustration."[34] Interestingly, Jenkins had compared blacks' and Jews' ability to withstand segregation in his own work. Drawing inspiration from Jenkins, Wilson wrote, "The Negro has a very loosely constructed family organization, and worships strength. The Jew has a very closely knit family and can admit weakness. The former culture under stress yields psychoses and aggressive crimes, while the latter develops psychoneuroses and the ability to stand suffering without retaliating."[35] High crime rates in black communities, according to Wilson, were indicators of a frustrated community. That frustration, following his and Jenkins's logic, was the result from crossing over into "white culture," that is, moving from the rural South to the industrialized North, from an ostensibly "closed society" to a more "open" one.

Also influential in the emergent discourse on the deleterious effects of racism on the mental health of blacks in the United States was historian Stanley Elkins's widely cited *Slavery: A Problem in American Institutional and Intellectual Life*. In it, Elkins draws an analogy between the closed system of the plantation and the concentration camps of Nazi Germany, in terms of the effects on the personality development of members of the captive population. Independent reports from psychologists and psychiatrists who survived the concentration camps of Nazi Germany wrote of the changing behaviors of prisoners over time toward their guards. These reports described prisoners as behaving childishly in front of their captors, many expressing complete acceptance of guards as father figures. Drawing theoretical inspiration from Bruno Bettelheim, Elkins argued that any totalitarian environment would prohibit the ability of its population to resist, plan, or form positive relationships with one another. Furthermore, Elkins theorized that, over time, without massive upheaval in the totalitarian system, this personality pattern would persist across generations. Despite the fact that Elkins's thesis was controversial, it mirrored much of the research published in the major psychological and psychiatric journals. Kardiner and Ovesey's 1951 *The Mark of Oppression* had already theorized a relationship between the systems of chattel slavery and Jim Crow, and their effects on the personality development of black Americans, and prior to that the Clarks' now famous "doll studies," as well as the Horowitzs' aforementioned pictorial studies, identified the role of prejudicial attitudes in children's early development, theorizing how this then affected their transitions into adulthood. What became more commonplace among mental health researchers and practitioners, however, was their focus on the effects of systemic racism on the black family, identifying the family unit as the site of psychopathological formation.

Though at the time few studies had been conducted on black Americans specifically, how the absence of the father shapes personality had received relatively considerable research attention from the mid-1940s through the early 1960s. Findings from this body of research suggested father-absent boys were markedly more submissive and dependent, and had strong primary identifications with their usually overprotective mothers. Consequently, father-absent boys, within what researchers identified as the patriarchal structure of American culture, develop conflicting and secondary identification with men. In the few studies focused on black Americans, researchers claimed that pseudomasculine defenses were prevalent among neurotic black male patients, and that black male children from broken homes tended to become adults with unusually high needs for power and dominance.[36] Foreshadowing Daniel Patrick Moynihan's 1965 thesis that the disorganization of the black family is to blame for black pathology (to which we will turn shortly), these researchers and others would posit that how blacks bear the severe emotional stress caused by racial discrimination is largely a function of the degree of ego-strength they have developed in their early, family-centered years—"[the] 'psychologically vulnerable' Negro, crippled by weak ego development from earlier family disorganization, is more likely to fall prey to mental illness, drug addiction, or crime, depending on his particular life history"—and that segregation had its most fundamental influence on black personality development in the manner in which it affected black family functioning.[37]

Such arguments about the black family structure and its role in the promotion of mental illness within black communities, before Moynihan, had already crystallized as a foregone conclusion within some of the most influential and prominent circles of the academy. Thomas Pettigrew, the Harvard social psychologist, wrote in 1964 that the prevalence of schizophrenia and criminal behaviors among poor and working-class black communities "[may] have part of their personality roots in the matriarchal situation; for the strong-mother, weak-father family pattern seems to be related to schizophrenia, and patriarchal societies which separate young boys from their fathers tend to have higher rates of crime against persons."[38] The focus on the black family structure as the locus of blacks' psychopathology, though acknowledging that many of the social ills plaguing black communities were caused by legacies of racial rule, nevertheless constructed the black family as the target of intervention. This construction of the family as the target of intervention would reach a fever pitch with the leaking of the Moynihan Report in 1965, and its rapid circulation within American public discourse.

In his deeply critical reflection on the history of Moynihan's special report, the historian Kevin Mumford writes that it "outlined in broad strokes the dangers to society of uncontrolled black pathology: the loss of social control over the ghetto, leading to 'collective unrest' and the products of broken families and broken societies' filling the prison system, as well as deviance in 'sex life.'"[39] Moynihan, in his research and theorizing, had drawn heavily from a number of scholars already mentioned: of course, E. Franklin Frazier, who had been a student of Robert Park, but also Harvard psychiatrist Robert Coles, famed psychologist and psychoanalyst Erik Erickson, and historian Stanley Elkins, whose aforementioned thesis on the impact of slavery on the personality structure of blacks would inspire Moynihan's use of the term "tangle of pathology" in his description of the black matriarchal family structure.[40] As Mumford notes, however, of greater influence than these scholars was the work of Kenneth Clark, whom Moynihan met during the writing of the report. At the time, Clark's *The Dark Ghetto* had just been published. In it, Clark discussed at length the negative impact violent behavior and sexual promiscuity where having on Harlem's black residents. In characterizing his observations of black life in Harlem, Clark had used the term "pathology," arguing that the ghetto itself was what fueled pathology among blacks, signaled by their lack of sexual repressions.[41] Despite Clark's damning criticism of black social life, and his use of the term "pathology," it would be Moynihan's use of "tangle of pathology" that would generate far more criticism *and* gain far more currency after its publication.

In addition to Clark, Moynihan also drew from the collective works of Thomas Pettigrew, including his aforementioned conclusions that the personality structure of black Americans had its roots in the matriarchal family structure of black urban communities, where segregation had produced patterns of absentee fathers. In consulting Moynihan's personal digest and papers, Mumford finds that Moynihan noted Pettigrew's observation that "the effects of father absent families are to be seen in homicide, schizophrenia, and homosexuality." Citing Pettigrew, Moynihan would write of the personality development of blacks, "The inability to delay gratification is a critical factor in immature, criminal, and neurotic behavior."[42]

Without question, Moynihan's report, once made public, deeply influenced policymakers and Civil Rights activists concerned about the "Negro problem" in America. Yet even before it was leaked to the press, President Lyndon B. Johnson, in his now famous 1965 commencement speech in front of the graduating class of the historically black Howard University, referenced the Moynihan Report when mentioning the family as one of the number of problems that the government must address if the nation was to move beyond the Civil Rights Movement.[43] At the time, in response to the address, Martin Luther King, Jr., told Johnson, "Never before has a president articulated the depths and dimensions of the problem of racial injustice more eloquently and profoundly."[44] It was also in August of that year that, while the Moynihan Report was leaked to the press, riots broke out in the Watts section of Los Angeles. *Newsweek* ran articles on the rioting and the report with the headline "New Crisis: The Negro Family." In *The New Republic*, another discussion of the report framed the black family in similar fashion. In those cases and others, the press "accepted the basic tenets of the report, referring to the black community as 'broken humanity,' recapitulating the tenets of matriarchy, emasculation, and pathology."[45]

Though controversy would surround the report over the several months after its release to the press, this controversy was countered by affirmation among the mainstream media. Despite criticism from more progressive outlets like *The Nation* and *The Christian Century*, Moynihan maintained headline attention and was able to promote his policy recommendations through more wide-reaching vehicles like the *New York Times*. For example, Harvard psychologist William Ryan penned a scathing criticism for *The Nation* that declared the report

> draws dangerously inexact conclusions from weak and insufficient data; encourages (no doubt unintentionally) a new form of subtle racism that might be termed "Savage Discovery," and seduces the reader into believ-

ing it is not racism and discrimination but the weaknesses and defects of the Negro himself that account for the present status of inequality between Negro and white.[46]

Nevertheless, even over a year after the report was leaked, *Newsweek* revisited it through the headline "A Mother Can't Do a Man's Job." And a 1966 *New York Times* piece observed that "children, especially boys, who grow up in fatherless homes tend not to adjust to this country's essentially patriarchal society, particularly when their problems are complicated by poverty and racial prejudice," and that these young men failed to have "any stable relationship to male authority."[47]

Among Civil Rights activists, the report reverberated in similar fashions. For example, Bayard Rustin, considered by many as the architect of the modern U.S. Civil Rights Movement, was somewhat critical of the report in a 1966 article reflecting on the Watts riots. Comparing the Moynihan Report to the newly published McCone Report that framed the riots within the context of eroding social conditions, Rustin declared of the Moynihan Report that, "by emphasizing the breakdown of the Negro family, [it] also steers clear of confronting the thorny issue of Negro unemployment as such."[48] Yet Rustin at least partially accepted Moynihan's thesis when he opined in a separate outlet, "[The] Negro family can be reconstructed only when the Negro male is permitted to be the economic and psychological head of the family."[49] Rustin's comments were not unlike those of other Civil Rights leaders who echoed Moynihan's claim that a "tangled pathology" produced among black youth a condition of psychosocial alienation. For example, in his 1967 speech at the annual meeting of the American Psychiatric Association, Martin Luther King, Jr., declared that psychosocial alienation among blacks was responsible for the recent wave of urban riots.

> Urban riots are a special form of violence. They are not insurrections. . . . Often the Negro does not even want what he takes. . . . [A]lienated from society and knowing that this society cherishes property above people, he is shocking it by abusing property rights. *There are thus elements of emotional catharsis in the violent act* [emphasis ours].[50]

By the end of the 1960s, then, the "sick society" model, popular among scholars and activists alike, had laid the foundation for a psychopathological framework within which to situate "new racism."

In 1968, in the aftermath of Dr. King's assassination, two black clinical psychiatrists, William H. Grier and Price M. Cobbs, who were running a psychiatric clinic in San Francisco with many minority patients, published *Black Rage: Two Black Psychiatrists Reveal the Full Dimensions of the Inner Conflicts and the Desperation of Black Life in the United States.*[51] This case-based work emphasized that blacks' psyches were inherently unstable as "the psychological consequences of white oppression of blacks."[52] Dismissing traditional psychoanalytic as well as social psychological approaches to race, they sketched a portrait of the psychic life of American blacks as shaped solely by the social context in which they live. One symptom was repressed violence, the result of a "cultural paranoia in which every white man is a potential enemy unless proved otherwise."[53] Marginality was defined by racism and no black American was spared such repressed feelings no matter what their social status. Under pressure this could veer toward "paranoid psychosis no matter what [their] racial experience."[54] The outward demeanor of black Americans could seem to be one of ingratiating deference, but that only covered their inherent anger. "As a sapling bent low stores energy for a violent backswing," they wrote, "blacks bent double by oppression have stored energy which will be released in the form of rage—black rage, apocalyptic and final."[55] Thus the very psychic makeup of the American black was shaped by racism and, if anger did not result, psychopathologies did: "a certain quality of depression and hopelessness[,] these are the most common feelings tasted by black people in America."[56] Racism resulted in the internalization of a sense of "[their] own hatefulness and inferiority."[57] The numerous case studies presented a sense of pervasive and unmediated psychic trauma.[58]

Black Rage, as might be expected, was met with resistance upon its publication. Kenneth Clark, by 1968 clearly the most authoritative voice on the sequelae of racism, dismissed Grier and Cobbs's work in the *New York Times* as nonscientific, relying on "generalizations, no matter how obvious, as if they were brilliant new truths, which had not been previously seen or understood by others."[59] That is, they ignored his scientific

work on this question ("basic lack of scholarship") and relied on "anonymous case histories." "The authors of *Black Rage* have joined the present
fashionable cult of literate black and white flagellants who now believe
that America's racial problem can be clarified and racial justice obtained
through a sadomasochistic orgy of black rage and white guilt." The politics of the NAACP's strategic use of psychological evidence here meets
the psycho-politics of black rage. Clark's model had come to include a
therapeutic approach by this period. As a treatment for racism he had
prescribed "empathy" as early as the mid-1960s.[60] This was an aesthetic
term from German philosophy ("Einfühlung") that had been absorbed
into social psychology by experimental psychologists Edward Titchener
and James Ward around 1908–1909 and had come by the 1960s to represent a gold standard for the therapeutic situation across a wide range
of fields as well as popular culture. In the late 1940s the Canadian psychologist Rosalind Dymond Cartwright, then at Cornell, together with
Leonard Cottrell, a sociologist, presented experimental data concerning empathy as a collective trait. Empathy was evoked as a predictor of
another groups' preferences.[61] Thus Clark could use it both to define as
well as to alter racism.

Grier and Cobbs were taken aback, writing to the editor that they
were perturbed that "after 62 highly favorable reviews, the 63rd and first
critical comment came from a black brother. . . . We wrote a book designed to involve the reader." Equally importantly they wanted to avoid
"the petty rivalry between disciplines, where psychologist and psychiatrist array themselves as natural antagonists. The issues are too grave,"
they wrote. "We deliberately did not footnote our book, knowing that
no social revolution is brought about by footnotes. 'Black Rage' is an
expression of advocacy psychiatry designed to stir the reader to change."
They signed the letter "yours in the bondage of brotherhood."[62] But from
their perspective it was also a bondage of internalized racism. As with
the Clarks, the simple fact that they could isolate themselves sufficiently
from self-hatred and anger to be able to write *Black Rage* did not present
sufficient proof of the possibility of critical approaches beyond those of
psychic damage.

The framework of the new psychopathology of racism, well established within policy debates by the publication of the Moynihan
Report in 1965 and buttressed by the publication of *Black Rage* and

subsequent debates it engendered, would soon become an important repertoire from which the general American public would draw lay understandings of American racism, its origins, and its consequences. In the American context, perhaps no other psychiatrist had as profound an influence on the interpenetration of psychopathological understandings of racism in public consciousness as the black psychiatrist Alvin Poussaint.

Black Psychiatry, White Psychopathology, and Public Discourse

Born in East Harlem, in 1934, Alvin Poussaint was encouraged by his junior high school teacher to take the admissions test for Stuyvesant High School, one of New York's most prestigious prep schools. Upon passing, he enrolled as one of only a handful of minorities. It was there Poussaint experienced overt racism, including being verbally accosted by a police officer while walking a friend home from school through a nearby park. In 1956, he graduated with a B.S. in pharmacology from Columbia University, and subsequently enrolled at Cornell University's medical school as the only black student in his eighty-six-person cohort. In 1962, he pursued his residency at UCLA's Neuropsychiatric Institute, serving as chief resident in psychiatry. However, in 1965, at the request of his friend and Civil Rights activist Robert Parris (Bob) Moses, Poussaint left UCLA for Jackson, Mississippi, where he served the next two years as the Southern field director for the Medical Committee for Human Rights (MCHR).

As their field director, Poussaint took on the dual role of providing treatment for Civil Rights workers (black and white), as well as treatment for the black communities in which the MCHR network was located. While in Mississippi, he helped establish the first rural community health clinics in the Delta region. In an oral history interview with his niece, the journalist Renee Poussaint, he describes his role:

> I saw a lot of people psychiatrically . . . and I was rescuing people, and sometimes the way we rescued them, you know, a worker would have a breakdown, and we had a network of chapters . . . and sometimes we would send a nurse or we would get the office and tell them to bring "so and so" down.[63]

The success of the rural health clinics caught the attention of Tufts University School of Medicine, which recruited Poussaint to work with its first neighborhood health center in the Boston metro area.[64]

Though Poussaint left the South, his experiences there shaped his professional and personal perspectives on the issues of race, racism, and mental health moving forward. While in Mississippi in 1966, he found himself at ground zero of the beginning of the Black Power/Black Consciousness movement, when Stokely Carmichael, responding to a reporter who asked him how he felt about the tear gassing of Civil Rights workers in Denton just a few days prior, put his fist in the air and repeated, "Black Power!" multiple times. Poussaint describes the shift among many Civil Rights activists to Black Power as revealing a growing recognition that black people were so used to seeing white people as powerful, that down in Mississippi, if a white Civil Rights worker went to call for a rally or a march, black people would show up, whereas if a black Civil Rights worker made that same call, few if any would show up. Black people had "the opposite image of black people, of black leadership . . . as not powerful."[65] As a result, members of the movement felt there needed to be a change in its culture if they were to curb what Poussaint and others (most notably, Fanon, whose work Poussaint and many others in the black radical tradition had absorbed by this point) described among blacks as a form of internalized oppression, or self-hatred, the result of a legacy of institutionalized racism.[66]

Having built up some public recognition for his work in Mississippi, Poussaint's role *outside* of academia would be as much, if not more, influential in shifting public opinion on the nature and function of prejudice and racism than his work within his trained profession. When the Black Power movement began to resonate beyond Mississippi, Poussaint was contacted by *Ebony* magazine to write about the movement and its importance.

Founded by black entrepreneur John H. Johnson, *Ebony* by the 1960s had become the single most popular and widely circulated magazine, black or white, among black Americans. Prior to covering the Black Power movement, *Ebony* had already developed a reputation among both its readership and its competition for high-quality coverage of the Civil Rights Movement. Johnson reflects on the magazine's position in the 1960s in an oral history interview with Renee Poussaint:

JOHNSON: I think we played an important role, because, in the beginning Martin Luther King, Jr., was leading marches from city to city and the white press were ignoring the marches. So he called up Bob Johnson and said, "Bob, they're ignoring us down here. Tell your boss I want him to send you and the best photographer down to cover such and such event, and it would be helpful if you covered all of the events." So we covered that event, and we covered all of the events. We even, when it was very hostile in Mississippi, we would hire a white photographer to go down and take the pictures of the white people, and a black photographer to go down and take pictures of the black people. And the white photographer and the black photographer would meet at night and exchange views and things. And so it was very important, and we prided ourselves on going wherever he called us and told us to send someone.

POUSSAINT: Fantastic, and you have a big archive of that whole period.

JOHNSON: Oh yes, we have the whole thing.

POUSSAINT: Yes, of course.

JOHNSON: We have the only pictures of Emmett Till in the casket. I remember years ago the *Jackson Daily News* called me and wanted to buy a bundle of photographs and I said, "No, you should have taken them when it happened."

POUSSAINT: Yes!

JOHNSON: No, I can't do that.

POUSSAINT: Yes.

JOHNSON: I said, "You can't, don't even offer me any money because there is no amount of money you could give me that would make me do it. Because you should have done it when it happened."

POUSSAINT: Good for you.

JOHNSON: So we covered wherever it was.[67]

Discussing his role at *Ebony*, which was to give voice to and a perspective on the movement, Alvin Poussaint tells his niece:

I kind of got this role as like explaining, and writing, and I put out articles in the *Negro Digest*, which became the *Black Digest*, and I decided to do pop writing. And I wrote an article for the *New York Times Magazine* on the experience with that police officer to explain why black people were angry.[68]

The 1967 *New York Times* piece Poussaint refers to in this interview was titled "A Negro Psychiatrist Explains the Negro Psyche." In it, he had argued that the riots that plagued the cities of Los Angeles, Newark, Detroit, Rochester, Chicago, and Cleveland over the previous several years were "pathological manifestations of the consequences of racism."[69] Less than a year later, writing in the *Boston Globe*, Poussaint would reiterate this claim, writing, "White racism has made black folks feel inferior, dependent and beholden to the good will and paternalism of the white man."[70]

In explaining his position more than forty years after first publicizing it, Poussaint tells his interviewer:

> I felt it was important as part of the movement and the mission. I felt that as a psychiatrist that a lot of the things that I'm talking about deals with mental health issues. And if I wanted to take mental health issues to the people, to help explain, help them understand, help them get insight, whatever it was, that that was a very important mission. That that was a very important public health mission . . . who is supposed to talk to the people if you're only publishing in journals, which a hundred people read? . . . Fortunately, with the evolution of medicine, prevention has become more and more important, so you see more doctors and everybody jumping into media stuff, writing articles for the *New York Times* section, all kinds of other things. So it has become more acceptable and, actually, when people started giving me awards here and there for doing that . . . it, like, legitimated it.

In 1969, still reeling from Dr. King's murder just one year prior, Poussaint and other black psychiatrists, several of whom had previously worked with the Medical Commission of Human Rights and had been on the ground in the Civil Rights Movement in Mississippi and elsewhere in the mid-1960s, petitioned the American Psychiatric Association to include extreme bigotry as a mental disorder within its *Diagnostic and Statistical Manual of Mental Disorders*.

The importance of the DSM to the definition of mental illness at midcentury was as powerful as it is today. However, the manual reflects anxiety among psychiatrists and social scientists about the classification of mental illness that dates to the Enlightenment, when the rise of a medical science of madness provided a basis for the medical treatment of mental states as illnesses after the model of somatic illnesses. The criminologist Jacques Bertillon began the work on what would shape the DSM as a positivistic description of illness based on observable symptoms and analogous to his work in criminology; this approach soon became a global phenomenon. The analogy was to Robert Koch's "postulates," the rules laid down by the German bacteriologist in 1884 for the proof of the causal relationship between the etiology of infectious diseases and particular bacteria. Bertillon's classification seemed equally scientific. Revised in 1898 by the American Public Health Association as the *International Statistical Classification of Diseases, Injuries and Causes of Death* (*ICD*), the *ICD* appeared after 1948 under the auspices of the World Health Organization, as the *International Statistical Classification of Diseases and Related Health Problems* appeared. It became the gold standard for international psychiatric classification, gaining widest acceptance after its eighth edition of 1968. In 1973, the *Diagnostic and Statistical Manual of the American Psychiatric Association*, which had first appeared in 1952, assumed a global role in unifying the terminology for psychiatric classification. *DSM-5* was published in 2013 and continued to reflect the politics of diagnosis, but racism remains absent.[71]

In the mid-1960s, the APA's public response to the request that racism be included was to express gratitude for the presentation by the group of black psychiatrists, endorsing its "general spirit of reform and redress of racial inequities in American psychiatry." However, in a move that would repeat itself over the course of the next several decades and decisions on what was to be included in later editions of the *DSM*, the APA rejected their motion on the grounds that in order for extreme bigotry, including racism, to be included as a mental illness, it must be shown that extreme bigotry deviates from normative behavior.[72] In their rejection, the APA cited a series of studies conducted by Harvard social psychologist Thomas Pettigrew.

Interviewing residents of eight small towns in the North and South in the late 1950s, Pettigrew had tested, among other things, whether Southerners exhibited a stronger authoritarian personality than Northerners. Pettigrew concluded that, while Southerners exhibited a higher level of prejudice toward blacks than their Northern counterparts, the level of authoritarianism among Northerners and Southerners was virtually identical. In sum, racism was *normal* behavior, and thus could not constitute a mental illness. The APA's ruling highlighted the incongruence between psychological theories of racism and group-based prejudice: rather than existing among the fringe of society, racism is a trait characteristic of modern society. Normative behavior and attitudes *include* racism.

Despite the APA's rejection, many clinical workers had already begun researching and testing treatment models for the effects of racism, and for individual racists. One of the more infamous examples occurred in the aftermath of the 1967 deadly shootout between Houston police officers and students at the all-black Texas Southern University. Mayor Louie Welch called upon Dr. Blair Justice, a Rice University psychologist, to initiate a program to alleviate tensions between Houston police officers and the city's black community. Justice's program drew inspiration, both theoretical and methodological, from Kurt Lewin's "change experiments" in Connecticut. By 1969, large group sessions led by teams of psychologists were encouraging heated exchanges between police officers and community members as a means of getting deeply held prejudices out in the open. Based upon pre- and post-tests of police attitudes demonstrating a small decrease in identifiable prejudices, Welch declared the program a great success in 1970, less than one year after its initiation.

Meanwhile, the American Psychiatric Association's position on racism remained highly contentious within its own ranks. In 1971, the vice president of the Association, Charles Prudhomme, wrote an editorial for *The American Journal of Psychiatry* claiming racism "parallels and is an analog of psychosocial development." At the APA's 1978 annual meeting, Carl Bell presented a hotly debated paper, later published in the *Journal of the National Medical Association*, entitled "Racism: A Symptom of the Narcissistic Personality Disorder." Linking his diagnosis to *The Authoritarian Personality*, Bell claimed "covert racism is a psychological attitude and as such it should fall under the scrutiny of psychiatry, as a psychopathological symptom of a type of personality disturbance."[73] Racists, Bell argued, suffered from "a psychopathological defect of developmental processes involving narcissism, which precludes the subsequent development of such qualities as creativity, empathy, wisdom, and integrity"—or *narcissistic personality disorder.*[74]

Victims, Bell wrote, sought constant praise from authority figures as a means of sustaining their self-esteem, and would go to extreme lengths to achieve this praise. Finally, in his presidential address at the 1980 annual meeting, Alan Stone spoke about the APA's internal debate over whether to recognize racism as a psychiatric problem, a social problem, or both. Stone proclaimed it was the APA's professional obligation "to confront this conflict openly." While Stone's remarks did little to end the debate, many mental health practitioners, most of them black, including Poussaint and Bell, remained publicly critical toward the APA as racism was denied admission into *DSM-III* in 1974, its revision in 1987, and *DSM-IV* in 1994.

In reflecting upon the apprehension and unwillingness of the American Psychiatric Association to consider the addition of extreme forms of bigotry, including racism, into its *Diagnostics and Statistics Manual*, Poussaint opined:

> Sometimes you have to go to the opposite end, to the extreme, to make people pay attention to a point because they don't want to consider it anyway. So that piece I wrote, that op-ed piece I wrote for the *New York Times* where psychiatrists went bananas, when I said extreme racism is a mental illness. Now, the point of that was, nowhere in psychiatry, in the diagnostic manual or anything, is racism mentioned, race mentioned, prejudice mentioned, bigotry mentioned, nothing like that, like it doesn't exist, right? When we know that patients out there who get psychotic and think they should kill all black people, and all Jews, and all kinds of other people. So I was saying these extreme forms, if someone thinks they have to kill all blacks because blacks are going to get them, isn't that a delusion? Isn't it paranoia? And then the fact that they are not functioning, that is, they are impaired people because they got all of this crazy stuff, I said shouldn't that be a mental disorder? Why are you not calling it a mental disorder? And the reason you are not calling it a mental disorder is because you accept it as normative. And who decides what's normative? Well, they raised hell and wrote all kinds of nasty letters to the *Times*, and everything, I mean really, they were just outrageous. But you know what happened? In the inner circles, you know what they did? They have now made a call, a year ago, for research projects looking into the nature and function of racism in the psyche of people.[75]

In this last quote, Poussaint is referencing a 1999 editorial he wrote for the *New York Times*, entitled, "They Hate. They Kill. Are They Insane?" In it, he argues:

> People may be reluctant to consider racially motivated attacks to be symptoms of a mental illness because they don't truly understand what mental illness is. Human behavior occurs on a continuum; "insanity" is not always immediately obvious. Often, psychotic people with delusional disorder can function well enough that they aren't seen as seriously disturbed, even by some experts who may see them for evaluation. . . . [E]xtreme racists do not think rationally. Instead, they create fantastical theories about who is responsible for their problems.

Poussaint concludes his editorial:

> It's time for the American Psychiatric Association to designate extreme racism as a mental health problem. Clinicians need guidelines for recognizing delusional racism in all its stages so that they can provide treatment. Otherwise, racists will continue to fall through the cracks of the mental health system, and we can expect more of them to act out their deadly delusions.[76]

Poussaint's editorial touched off a heated debate among clinical practitioners and academics. In the *New York Times*, for example, several psychiatrists wrote letters to the editor expressing their disagreement. The variation in their disagreements was telling at the time. Some challenged Poussaint for omitting the essential factors in determining mental illnesses, and reducing the diagnostic instrument to simply a matter of irrational behavior or beliefs. For example, the physician Robert Spitzer wrote:

> Racism is not the only example of shared irrationality. Others include an uncritical belief in telepathy, alien abduction and reincarnation, to name a few. The last thing that psychiatry or society in general needs is to confuse the distinction between the sometimes overlapping concepts of evil, crackpot and mental illness.[77]

Others pushed the criticism further, claiming that Poussaint was actually excusing socially unacceptable behaviors by diagnosing them as personal problems. David Spiegel, professor of psychiatry at Stanford University, wrote:

> False, hate-filled beliefs are not psychotic delusions, and the willingness to act on them is anything but "readily classifiable as a mental disorder." Moreover, there is no evidence that violent racists are interested in psychiatric treatment or would respond to it. Calling bad people mad only provides an excuse for their criminal activities and stigmatizes those with genuine mental illness, who deserve our compassion and care.[78]

Even the president-elect of the American Psychiatric Association, Daniel B. Borenstein, chimed in, attempting to make transparent the process for how conditions become mental disorders:

> Alvin F. Poussaint's charge to the American Psychiatric Association to designate extreme racism as a mental disorder is compelling ("They Hate. They Kill. Are They Insane?" Op-Ed, Aug. 26), but fails to recognize the process of such designations. These designations are not developed through social or political demands but through deliberate scientific research. The five-year process by more than 1,000 psychiatrists that yielded the Diagnostic and Statistical Manual of Mental Disorders, Fourth Edition, included reviews of scientific literature, field trials of diagnostic criteria and the analysis of, or additional data from, clinical work.[79]

Nevertheless, Poussaint followed up his first editorial in August 1999 with a second one in January 2000, this time focused on the imposition of psychological testing and counseling on John Rocker following his racist and homophobic remarks about New York and his own teammates. Poussaint's position, perhaps counterintuitively given his previous writings, was that Rocker was not in need of counseling because his emotional outburst did not signal *extreme* racism: "My own view is that extreme racism, when it leads to violent attacks on specific groups, is a delusional disorder. Rocker does not appear to fall into this extreme category."[80] This position is further clarified in Poussaint's oral history interview, in which he poses the question:

> What happens along the spectrum? You can be a little bit prejudiced, and you can be extreme[ly] prejudiced. Is extreme prejudice a mental illness? Because you can be a little bit depressed, but if you get way over here, and you're a lot depressed, they say you have a mental disorder. You have a little bit of anxiety, but you get way over here, and you're anxious all the time, you have an anxiety disorder. So when does racism become a disorder? That's a legitimate question.[81]

Despite the lack of official recognition as a diagnosis, many clinical workers began to develop treatment protocols for addressing racism through the 1990s and 2000s. Judith Skillings and James Dobbins, for example, claim that racism can be diagnosed through identifying four manifest symptoms: a belief that one's heritage is superior to another; an infectious quality that exists without any conscious sense of antipathy by the person who is the host; distortion or confusion of one's perceptions; and when it acts as a "silent" mechanism that robs its hosts and targets of their mental and emotional well-being.[82] Dobbins and Skillings go so far as to suggest that individual racists, through the habitual access to power that racism affords, become psychologically dependent upon that source of power. Racism is *addictive*! Consequently, Dobbins and Skillings warn us of this addiction's signs: rationalization ("I know we need to increase diversity, in general, but why do *I* have to play a part?"), selective comparison ("I can't be racist, because I've never used explicitly racist language"), protecting the source of addiction ("Okay, maybe I have white privilege, but it's not like I can give it up"), and minimization ("I'm not being racist, I'm just being truthful").[83]

Others, like the African studies scholar Molefi Asante, have pointed to the harmful effects of internalized racism among communities of color. When internalized, racism impacts the health of these communities' members, including their physical health, their mental health, and their identity development.[84] Whether addicted to or internalizing racism, in these cases, all people are greatly influenced by racism, mentally and physically. Likewise, psychologist Mary Guindon and her colleagues claim that not only is racism a psychopathological disorder, but that it manifests itself in ways similar to sexism and homophobia.[85] They offer the diagnosis of *intolerant personality disorder* as a way to account for the rigid beliefs and attitudes people hold that then lead them to suppress the quality of life of another person or group, inflicting pain and suffering upon them. It should be noted that in this instance the medicalizing of intolerance is not the intent, nor is the intent to contribute to an intervention for racism that constructs it as a disease. Rather, Guindon et. al. argue that naming extreme intolerance as a psychopathological disorder will direct researchers toward developing treatment protocols. *Intolerance personality disorder*, here, functions more as an intervention in the psychiatric knowledge regime than an intervention in individual or group pathos.

The intervention suggested by Guindon et. al. had actually began at least a decade prior to the 2003 publication of their article in *The American Journal of Orthopsychiatry*, the flagship journal of the American Orthopsychiatric Association. In the mid-1990s, Edward Dunbar, a psychologist at UCLA, began developing a "prejudice scale" for measuring what he termed "prejudiced personality." Individuals with high scores on Dunbar's scale included those who distrusted financial advice from racial and ethnic minorities, experienced job loss due to inappropriate interactions with customers of color, and one who expressed support for the Oklahoma City bombing. By the early 2000s, among psychiatrists and psychologists racism already had several clinical names (though no *DSM* recognition): prejudice personality, intolerant personality disorder, and pathological bias. The latter was most recently considered for admission in the 2013 *DSM-5* under a rubric that would have included racism, sexism, and heterosexism. Though it was ultimately not included, an entire chapter of the 2012 *Oxford Handbook of Personality Disorders*, penned by the aforementioned Edward Dunbar and Carl Bell, was devoted to the assessment of pathological bias.[86]

American Exceptionalism, Self-Hatred, and Antisemitism

The idea of racism as a form of collective mental illness that, in turn, generates forms of mental illness in its targets is by the 1960s so well established that it seems to be a commonplace. As we have seen, it is also during this period that the classification of mental illness becomes regularized (if not uniformly accepted) within American psychiatry. What was remarkable about these widely accepted means of describing mental illness is that they codified the contemporary views and attitudes toward madness globally rather than locally. The claims were not that the *DSM*, or indeed the *ICD*, employed a national approach but that they had universal application to the diseases of the mind. And by doing so these classificatory manuals claimed a scientific uniformity that existed only within their own closed systems.

Racism and antisemitism, as we have seen, come to play little role whatsoever in this system of psychiatric classification yet haunt it at every step. Indeed, as late as the 1990s psychoanalysts such as Theodore Isaac Rubin can offer a simple definition:

> Jew-hating or antisemitism is a nonorganic disease of the mind. I believe that it cannot be understood or eradicated unless it is viewed as the grievous psychodynamic disorder that it is. Though there are, as in all emotional illness, sociopolitical, economic factors, and effects, this is primarily a psychiatric problem. Unfortunately, it is not contained as such in the various compendiums of psychiatric syndromes. It does not appear in the *Statistical Manual of Mental Disorders*, Third Edition.[87]

But, he notes, it should as it is a form of "symbol sickness."[88] Here he echoes Poussaint's idea that racism must be categorized as a mental illness.

The pressure to see antisemitism or anti-black racism or ethnocentrism or xenophobia as mental illnesses does cause them to constantly reappear in various forms within the classifications of mental illness. Yet it is in the political realm that this is used as a metaphor for the pernicious impact of collective hatred and fear of definable, if imagined, difference. Thus "xenophobia" becomes a political category when it is condemned in 1993 by the World Conference on Human Rights in what is called the "Vienna Declaration and Programme of Action" and comes to be the United Nation's label for group hatred. In the 1950s, one of the leading psychiatrists of the day, Jules Masserman, president of the American Psychiatric Association in 1978 and also president of the American Society for Group Therapy, the American Association for Social Psychiatry, the American Society for Biological Psychiatry, and the American Academy of Psychoanalysis, does include a chapter on racism in his textbook of psychiatry. A professor of psychiatry at Northwestern, Masserman, in this chapter, looks at "biodynamics and social issues."[89] It includes antisemitism under "Projection, Displacement and Grandiosity" and defines "mass phobias" as a form of projection—the attribution to others of one's own repressed motives, ideas, and conduct, following rather standard theories of projective identification of the time. Indeed, he uses the Nazis as a case, but to "balance" his argument he observes that inherent to such manifestations of racism is "grandiosity—a fantasy-formation implicit in many delusional states." And his example from the 1950s is that "Zionists continue to regard themselves as representing the rights and hopes of all the persecuted Jews everywhere."[90] Masserman, as a publically Jewish figure, evidently needed to balance the very idea of antisemitism with a rejection of Zionism as an equally delusional system.

The apparent effect of the founding of the state of Israel on American-born Jewish clinicians and the resulting shift in the viewpoint of émigré Jewish psychologists, such as Kurt Lewin in the 1940s, is notable. Lewin sees Zionism as the one possible force to eliminate self-hatred and therefore antisemitism:

> Today, a Jewish youth who has watched Palestine grow is in an infinitely better situation. Whatever one's opinion about Zionism as a political program may be, no one who has observed closely the German Jews during the fateful first weeks after Hitler's rise to power will deny that thousands of German Jews were saved from suicide only by the famous article of the *Jüdische Rundschau*, with its headline "*Jasagen zum Judentum*" ("Saying Yes to Being a Jew"). The ideas expressed there were the rallying point and the source of strength for Zionist and non-Zionist alike.[91]

The reference here is to a 1933 essay by the German Zionist journalist and editor of the *Jüdische Rundschau* (*Jewish Review*) Robert Weltsch, "Wear the Yellow Badge with Pride!" His widely cited editorial articulated the strongly Zionist position after Hitler's appointment as chancellor and the beginning of state antisemitism in Germany. This was marked initially by a boycott of Jewish businesses, which were defaced with yellow

Jewish stars. In this call for Jewish pride in the light of Nazi antisemitism, Weltsch decried those German nationalists as Jews who bear

> a great burden of complicity because [they] failed to heed Theodor Herzl's
> call and even mocked it in some instances. The Jews refused to acknowl
> edge that the "Jewish question still exists." . . . At a time of bourgeois self-
> righteousness, one might expect these elements to be applauded by Jewish
> audiences if they lampooned and made light of Jews and Judaism.[92]

Herzl's 1897 attack on self-hating Jews, discussed in Chapter One, reappears in 1933 as part of a response to fascism, but also as a specifically Zionist answer to the psychopathology of self-deception and the identification with the aggressor that he saw as marking German Jewry. Lewin's support of Zionism was also an affirmation that viewing Jewish self-hatred as a psychopathology was inherent to social integration into German (read: Western) societies, for, as Weltsch wrote, "The events of that day have not only political and economic aspects, but moral and psychological ones as well." Self-awareness of Jewish difference through Nazi antisemitism is a cure for Jewish identification with the aggressor. Such a view is clearly present in Gershom Scholem's condemnation of Hannah Arendt's *Eichmann in Jerusalem* as showing an inherent self-hatred: "There is something in the Jewish language that is completely indefinable, yet fully concrete—what the Jews call *ahavath Israel*, or love for the Jewish people. With you, my dear Hannah, as with so many intellectuals coming from the German left, there is no trace of it."[93] She replied in a manner that is striking given the discussion of the constitution of the "crowd" in the debates about racism and indeed self-hatred: "How right you are that I have no such love, and for two reasons: first, I have never in my life 'loved' some nation or collective—not the German, French or American nation, or the working class, or whatever else might exist. The fact is that I love only my friends and am quite incapable of any other sort of love."[94] To speak of self-hatred in such contexts does mean defining (or accepting the definition of) the collective that is being postulated as that which is rejected.

　　Lewin's model for extirpating racism and self-hatred becomes a cornerstone of American social psychology. Jules Masserman's textbook is an exception in clinical psychiatry in its advocacy of the inclusion of racism as a psychopathological category. As we have discussed, the American Psychiatric Association debates these questions in the 1950s and 1960s, systematically refusing to included racism as a diagnostic category even with the dominance of psychoanalytic models. After this dominance wanes by the establishment of *DSM-III* in 1973, this issue seems remote to the general movement of clinical psychiatry, even with the efforts of black psychiatrists like Alvin Poussaint and Carl Bell.

The tension between social psychology represented by Lewin and clinical psychiatry as articulated by Masserman also reflects a post-war fascination with the psychopathology of self-hatred and the continued discussion of a damaged or a healthy Jewish (or indeed, black) psyche. In a survey of the meanings attached to "Jewish self-hatred" during this period, Susan Glenn observed "the 1940s and 1950s might well be described as the age of self-hatred. When the term 'Jewish self-hatred' came into critical vogue in the aftermath of World War II, it dramatically transformed the public discourse on Jewish identity."[95] At least, one must add, in the public sphere in the United States. It had been, as we have seen, present from the late nineteenth century in Germany and the Austro-Hungarian Empire. She goes on to note that "during and after the war, individuals and groups across the intellectual, social, cultural, religious and political spectrum deployed the term variously, inconsistently, and with conflicting social and political agendas."[96] What this contentious account of a Jewish psychopathology centered on was "a contentious public debate revolving around the question of Jewish group loyalty, Jewish group 'survival,' and Jewish nationalism. This debate—a struggle between advocates of Jewish particularism and nationalism and defenders of liberal universalism and cosmopolitanism—was the latest in a succession of longstanding disagreements about the relationship of Jews to the wider non-Jewish society."[97] While this was certainly true, it was the Holocaust and the question of a stable and healthy Jewish identity in the light of this horror that made the politicization of self-hatred a factor.

Early on, as one could see in the positions of Lewin and Masserman from the 1940s and 1950s, it was the question of Zionism, and then the new Jewish state of Israel, that triggered a charge of psychopathology. It was not merely "identity politics" but very specifically the question of what had been labeled as "dual loyalty" or a Jewish commitment to a

Jewish national identity as defining being Jewish in the post-Holocaust world that became or continued to be the litmus test of a healthy or a deranged identity. Indeed Masserman's parallel between fascism and Zionism was not unique. The literary critic Harold Rosenberg suggested, "Isn't it the presence of the same modern impulse to be one who is one-hundred-percent-something that makes Jews so uncomfortable when they debate whether one can be both an American and a Jew." It was the psychopathology of the Zionist that needed to resolve such a seeming contradiction. Indeed, he continued, "the basic attraction in our time of orthodoxy and totalitarian philosophies, including nationalism was the relief they offered from anonymity and multiple identity."[98] Such views, as we noted in Chapter One, were also those of the Zionists who saw identification with the antisemite as a key to understanding the fragile position of the Jew in the post-Enlightenment world.

For the immediate post–World War II period the question that defined identification with the aggressor was clear: Was the creation of the state of Israel necessary to the creation of a healthy Jewish identity and as such as cure for diasporic neuroses? Or was the state of Israel itself a form of neurotic compensation? In the United States the historian Edward Shapiro claimed that support for Israel became a marker for a healthy American Jewish identity after the Six Days War in 1963 and then again after the Yom Kippur War in 1973, indeed part of "the existential definition of American Jewishness."[99] The search for the litmus test for a healthy or pathological American Jewish identity after the Holocaust was one of the themes of American Jewish historians at midcentury. The earlier debates within American Reform Judaism during the pre-Nazi period had pitted a national Jewish identity against that of an American religious one. By the post-Holocaust moment this was no longer an acceptable dichotomy. It was the Holocaust that had changed the definition of a "healthy" Jewish psyche. As early as 1948, David Bernstein argued in an article in *Commentary* that American Jews were in a state of psychological turmoil:

It may be oversimplification to describe this as mental flight from America. Yet there is in the phrase something strongly suggestive of the truth. Psychologically, many American Jews are uncomfortable here, though they cannot define the causes or the implications of their discomfort, and though they show themselves to be good and patriotic citizens. Their problem is not one of loyalty or subversion. It is one of adjustment; of discovering who they are, and working out their lives in terms of the realities of the world they live in—not the imaginary "realities," but the actual realities.[100]

Germany and the Holocaust represented to many American Jews "a hypocritical flight from Jewishness, generally including conversion to Christianity, changing one's name, denying or at least hiding the fact that one is Jewish. And the Jews of Germany are recalled as the most shameful example of this kind of 'assimilation' with the ironic recollection of what happened to them when Hitler achieved power."[101] Even if Germany's Jews "did seek to escape" their 'Jewish past,'" Bernstein argued, "The catastrophe that befell German Jews was not the result of their assimilationism. It was the result of Hitlerism. This means that the lesson that Jews have to learn from the German experience is not so simple as the current Jewish nationalist cliché would have us believe."[102] Here he references Gunner Myrdal's study of American blacks:

> Gunnar Myrdal, studying the Negro problem in America, concluded that there was an American faith in democratic, libertarian, equalitarian principles, which was not always carried into American practice; and the conflict between faith and practice he called the "American dilemma." In Germany, for a few years under the Weimar Republic, an attempt was made to superimpose democratic, libertarian, equalitarian practices on the generations-old German faith in force and authoritarianism. This was the German dilemma; it was resolved by Hitler in 1933, to the satisfaction of too many Germans.[103]

But writers such as Bernstein were reacting to the charge that German Jews had overly identified with the aggressor, becoming almost willing victims of the Nazis as they had integrated or assimilated into European culture after the Enlightenment. No such fate could befall American Jewry if they identified with the Jewish state.

Such debates about self-hatred as a form of identification with the aggressor in the United States soon were paralleled by discussions of a healthy or an unhealthy coming to terms with the Holocaust and the immediate historical past. This was coupled with a debate about the very function of the Holocaust in the construction of a post-war American Jewish identity. Hasia Diner, in her *We Remember with Reverence and Love: American Jews and the Myth of Silence after the Holocaust, 1945–1962*, claimed that immediately after 1945 one could speak about the Holocaust as the ultimate Jewish experience of victimization, at least within the confines of the Jewish community.[104] Her work was an answer in part to Peter Novick's 1999 claim in *The Holocaust in American Life* that the Holocaust had become the new "civil religion" of American Jews only after the 1970s, with a "perverse sacralization" that valorized Holocaust survival over all other ethnic and religious identities.[105] In other words, focus on the Holocaust was a form of neurosis. For Diner speaking about the Holocaust in America was a sign of mental health; for Novick, a sign of psychopathology. The assumption is that by some point (Diner after 1945; Novick in the 1970s) a generation of American Jews felt themselves to be a secure and successful minority that accepted or needed a "victim identity." Their sense of security enabled them to speak about the past, even if such articulations of memories of the past had radically different readings. This is very different from the questions raised by writers such as Bernstein immediately after the Holocaust where the anxiety recorded had to do with the identification with the aggressor and the potential loss of a fragile American Jewish identity. Indeed, if there is a writer who consistently asks these questions after the fragility of the American Jewish psyche in the second half of the twentieth century, it is the novelist Philip Roth.

In Israel, Yad Vashem, the national monument to the victims of the Holocaust, had been founded in 1953, while the U.S. Holocaust Memorial Museum opened only in 1993. However it was only when the state of Israel was felt by the majority of its citizens, most of whom had never experienced the Holocaust, to be a successful and permanent part of a stable global order that it become possible for individual Holocaust survivors, such as Otto Dov Kulka, the Israeli historian, to remember their experiences publically.[106] Yet there were at the same time voices such as that of Yehuda Elkana, the late historian of science at the Hebrew University, who called for a systematic forgetting of the past as part of a healing of the Israeli psyche. A critic of the "Holocaust industry" and

Israel's occupation of the Palestinian territories, in an article published in *Ha'aretz* on March 2, 1988, Elkana wrote:

> For our part, we must learn to forget! Today I see no more important po-
> litical and educational task for the leaders of this nation than to take their
> stand on the side of life, to dedicate themselves to creating our future, and
> not to be preoccupied from morning to night, with symbols, ceremonies,
> and lessons of the Holocaust. They must uproot the domination of that
> historical "remember!" over our lives.

For him "Never again" is for everyone, not just the Jews: "The past is not and must not be allowed to become the dominant element determin-ing the future of society and the destiny of the people." He urged Israeli Jews to be freed from "the deep existential 'Angst' fed by a particular interpretation of the lessons of the Shoah" and "[t]o stand for life, to divert ourselves for building our future and not to deal over and over in symbols, ceremonies and lessons drawn from the Holocaust."[107] For him, as for Novick, this focus on the Holocaust was a form of neurosis.

Such systematic coming to terms with the basic question of an au-thentic Jewish identity for Jews both in Israel and in the United States still was read as defined by its inauthentic *Doppelgänger*, the self-hating Jew and his forms of mental aberration. This is the central theme paro-died in Philip Roth's 1993 novel *Operation Shylock*.[108] Thus the clinical psychiatrist Kenneth Levin of the Harvard Medical School published in 2006 an essay through the Jerusalem Center for Public Affairs that tried to explain in terms of identification with the aggressor the self-deception of those Israelis who believed in the peace process begun be-tween the Palestinians and the Israelis at Oslo:

> But within the Jewish Diaspora, there was a notable weakening of com-
> munal institutions as a result of political changes that marked the emer-
> gence of the modern world and modern nation-states. This weakening
> left Jews even more vulnerable than they had previously been to the psy-
> chological corrosiveness of chronic attack. . . . There is a profound truth to
> this on the level of Jews' sense of themselves as individuals. For example,
> the Jewish child subjected to constant taunts, even physical attacks, and

social exclusion in the schoolyard will very often respond by questioning what is wrong with him and how he can change to win acceptance. This response is comparable to that of the child abused at home. If the Jewish child's parents and community fail to convey a strong-enough counter-message, such a response becomes virtually inevitable and will likely be carried by the child into adulthood, with the child as adult feeling himself tainted and flawed by virtue of his Jewish identity.[109]

W.M.L. Finlay has observed the charge of being self-hating was an attempt to muster the politics of the healthy psyche in support of a specific notion of a healthy Jewish identity and to dismiss all other positions (he focuses on those politically to the right) as neurotic and therefore inauthentic.[110] For Finlay such critiques assume that being Jewish "is or should be a primary identity" and therefore engaging or rejecting an assumed definition of "Jewishness" as a political, religious, or ethnic identity, is psychopathological.

The psychology of self-hatred becomes the stuff of American popular culture. American playwright David Mamet attacked self-hating Jews in his book *The Wicked Son: Anti-Semitism, Self-Hatred, and the Jews* as neurotic apostates: "For the unspoken, the resistance, *is* the neurosis, and the neurosis is: self-loathing. All the apostate's information eventuates in self-loathing, which, because it is too painful to feel, is directed outward. 'I dare not blame This World, I cannot blame myself—I will blame the Jews.'"[111] He likens such Jews to alcoholics who can only be cured by a desire to change.[112] They may be redeemable but only through some type of acknowledgement or therapy, as he claims about the alcoholic. One of his (and most of the other critics on the right who evoke self-hatred as a model's) bête noirs is the MIT linguist and political critic Noam Chomsky.[113] Indeed, Chomsky has been labeled as "America's most prominent self-hating Jew."[114] Given that Chomsky's father (as we noted in Chapter Three) had been one of the first post-war critics to evoke self-hatred as a model to explain secular American Jewry, the irony is rather sharp.

One can expand this to include positions taken by those on the left who see their opponents as neurotically dependent on the authoritarianism of Zionist politics. The British liberal Jewish critic Antony Lerman took such views of the self-hating critic of Israeli politics to task as being in essence unanswerable: "it is deployed as the 'killer fact': to be called a self-hating Jew explains everything. No more need be said. Self-hatred means being a traitor to your race, an Uncle Tom, siding with the enemy, willing the destruction of your own people."[115] It is more than a label. It becomes a charge about the mental status of your enemy. Yet when the British sociologist Jacqueline Rose, another bête noir of those who seek out critics of Israeli politics to label as "self-hating Jews," attempts to answer her critics, she too sees them as neurotics:

> Rather than attacking Jews who criticize Israel for self-hatred, we should therefore be asking ourselves what love—a love that is creative rather than self-deceiving and suffocating—can and should bear to tolerate in itself. To demand only love is autocratic. At the very least such autocracy—the demand for one line only—goes against the spirit of Judaism which is endlessly open to the different meanings and interpretations invited by the Bible. . . . Traditionally, self-hatred refers to the internalization of anti-Semitic stereotypes by the Jew. In fact we can see this process taking place in one of the founding myths of the Israeli nation: in its hostility to the diaspora Jew as weak and abject, and its glorification of the new, strong, Israeli Jew.[116]

Not "we" but "they" are psychopathological because of their view as to what must define a healthy Jewish psyche.

The debates come to be framed not as specifically historically determined but as universal truths about identity formation and psychopathology. Jewish self-hatred comes to be seen as a universal psychopathological response to the diasporic situation of the Jews having its roots in being

> rejected, attacked, punished, abused, rebuked, scolded, or made to feel that it is bad [to be Jewish, which], tends to develop a bad sense of itself and to hate itself. This self hatred then becomes part of oneself and may lead to sadism and masochism, self-destructive acts, even suicide. . . . Individual and collective Jewish self-hatred has occurred ever since the ancient Jews were besieged by the Assyrians, Babylonians, and Romans, defeated, massacred, exiled from their land, dispersed and persecuted.[117]

Thus the Israeli psychoanalyst Avner Falk talks about the universal experience of self-hatred among Jews from their earliest history. Not merely a poor or damaged self-image but the very roots of psychopathology and self-destruction.

The Israeli historian Shulamit Volkov sees such charges as not exclusively Jewish, and not particularly American either. Given the parallels in the arguments about the mental health of black Americans, she is, of course, correct. But she also sees this as a reflex of nationalism:

> Accusations of self-hatred have a long tradition of being applied by one Jew to another, often as part of some political dispute. Present-day Israelis encounter the term all too often in public discourse, where it is used indistinctly and often demagogically, mainly to avoid coping with criticism from within. It is, in fact, no less commonly applied in contemporary Germany and has often been heard in discussions concerning the legitimation of nationalism in that country. There, too, self-hatred is often confused with self-criticism. . . . From its inception, indeed, the discussion of modern antisemitism in Germany has been intertwined with the issue of Jewish "self-hatred."[118]

And, we can add, the discussion of a damaged Jewish psyche has remained a constant to the ongoing discussions of the damaged black, as well as the unhealthy German, psyche.

While the debate about self-hatred as a reflex of racism persisted as a powerful tool in the debate about an appropriately healthy Jewish psyche in the public sphere, psychoanalysis too remained focused on racism and antisemitism and their impact. Yet its classification was hotly debated. Was antisemitism *sui generis*? Given the complex interweaving of the research into anti-black and antisemitic expression during the immediate post-war period, this question is not only contested among Jewish and non-Jewish researchers, but causes some to question the very classification of racism (and its responses) within the system of mental illness even though it was clear that "common traumatic experiences produced highly individual effects."[119] That it is mental illness is rarely queried (the psychoanalyst becomes like the carpenter who sees everything as a nail).

The question of uniting or splitting definitions of ethnocentrism, racism, antisemitism, or xenophobia becomes one of the contested questions of the latter half of the twentieth century.[120] Let us take three commentators on the question from the last three decades of the twentieth century and see how they deal with what is essentially a question of classification. In 1970 the Jewish psychiatrist and psychoanalyst Joel Kovel, then at the Einstein School of Medicine in New York City, published his study of *White Racism*.[121] The study stresses the universal roots of anti-black prejudice and reflects his (and America's) preoccupation with this specific form of racism during the Civil Rights era. Kovel recognizes three models of race: dominative, aversive, and meta. Each is embedded in psychoanalytic models, with the dominative reflecting power, sex, aggression, following Richard Sterba's reading of the Detroit riots and reflecting the Oedipal, and the aversive symbolized by contamination and avoidance of contamination reflecting even earlier models of fixation at the stage of anality and Fanon's thesis about blackness. Kovel sees this specifically as an American variant:

> We have observed that the general direction of American reform has been to paint over an older symptom with a newer one in order to protect the underlying disease. Thus did slavery yield to late-nineteenth-century racism. In terms of the ideal types we have been employing, dominative racism was succeeded by aversive racism as the principal mode employed by our culture to utilize and defend against the darkness within it. Now in modern times, racial distinctions themselves are anachronistic, and culture must choose a different structure to preserve its inner plague. Once again an erotic, life-giving, trending assault upon racism—has become infiltrated with the forces of destruction.[122]

What is new about his analysis of American racism is the category of metaracism:

> Racism, which began with the random oppression of another person, and moved from directly dominative, systematic control of his being, into abstracted averted use of his degradation, now passes beyond consciousness, holding only to its inner connections with the symbolic ma-

trix. Metaracism is a distinct and very peculiar modern phenomenon. Racial degradation continues on a different plane, and through a different agency; those who participate in it are not racists—that is, they are not racially prejudiced—but metaracists, because they acquiesce in the larger cultural order which continues the work of racism.[123]

Racism has become so entrenched in American society that it is the very social structures of American society that perpetuate it. Indeed he argues that the very concept of "race" is generated by racism. It exists only to provide a concrete reality for racism, which has now become the base line for American society.[124] This argument has some parallels to those of many contemporary sociologists, especially within the critical race studies tradition. For example, sociologists have increasingly focused on how racial discourse in the post–Civil Rights era is marked by a normative "colorblindness," or racial nonrecognition, that perpetuates race-based inequalities by denying its role in the shaping of race-based outcomes. Through the entrenched denial that race even matters, metaracists, to use Kovel's term, acquiesce to the larger cultural order that facilitates racism.

Yet, where Kovel and the critical race paradigm depart is that Kovel sees the problem of racism as self-hatred now projected on to the Other, onto blacks by white society. Here Kovel evokes what Freud, too, in *Totem and Taboo* as well as *Moses and Monotheism*, sees as the origin of the Western projection, and that is the totemistic killing of the Father, specifically in terms of Western society, the killing of Moses. It is the Jews who provide the model for such projective identification:

> [T]he most important element was the tendency to internalize aggression in the interests of group cohesion and intellectual activity. The West owed this boon to the Jewish people, and the guilty pains associated with the change became forever after the justification for the scapegoating and persecution of the Jews. Pain aside, what this creative development ensured was the appearance of coherent superego systems, both in culture and in the individual. Internalization has occurred before, of course, and occurs in all forms of culture; it must exist wherever mentality does. The Western style had a coherence and extension, however, which the others lacked. Here was the nuclear synthesis of man and his world that

could become extended into infinity. A price had to be paid, however. The unique father-God—who had overthrown the pre-existing melange of polytheistic and matriarchal deities and who had by his uniqueness thereby certified to the Jews their chosenness—this one God had to receive all the mixed feelings hitherto deployed throughout a pantheon. But hatred and love could not be at the same time directed toward a deity without destroying his synthetic unity. Hatred—the inevitable consequence of the eternal ambivalence of the human situation—had to be kept out of awareness; and, since aggression could not he kept out of human life, hate had to be turned inward.[125]

Thus Kovel (like other commentators on the curse of monotheism such as the German Egyptologist Jan Assmann) sees the origin of antisemitism as the claims of Jewish chosenness and sees the legacy of monotheism in the projection of such anxieties (now about the chosenness of whiteness) onto other groups, such as blacks.[126] Thus antisemitism and anti-black racism (white racism in Kovel's terms) have similar but not identical causes. It is striking that Kovel's later work *Overcoming Zionism* (2007) focuses on denouncing the political form of Jewish chosenness, Zionism and the state of Israel, as embodying precisely these qualities and the Palestinians are seen by him as the new Jews. He positions himself as a "non-Jewish Jew" in order to claim a distance from the model he had evoked in *White Racism*.[127]

In the 1980s the turn moved from racism to difference. One of the present authors, Sander L. Gilman, in his *Difference and Pathology*, evoked another model, which looked at the universal ability of infants to make distinctions between positive and negative objects as the core of racism.[128] Looking at the negative stereotypes of blacks, Jews, women, and the mad, he traced their core to the infantile narcissism that divides the world into objects that can be controlled and those that cannot be. The core of negative stereotypes is the projection of the infant's inability to control the world onto the "bad" (uncontrollable) actor. "Stereotypes arise when self-integration is threatened. . . . We project that anxiety onto the Other, externalizing our loss of control. The Other is thus stereotyped, labeled with a set of signs paralleling (or mirroring) our loss of control."[129] In contrast to the "good" Other that is "which we fear we cannot achieve," the "bad" Other that assumes the negative stereotype is the one that "we fear to become."[130] Thus stereotypes, positive or negative, are never arbitrary. The qualities of the Other are rooted not only in "real-life experience (as filtered through the models of perception)." They are also essentially historical as they are shaped by the needs of a specific time and place: "Every social group has a set vocabulary of images for this externalized Other."[131] Yet what is argued in this context is that any such explanation must examine the historical context of the construction and function of the image as actually used to see how such psychological universals are shaped by the historical moment. Thus antisemitism or misogyny or racism all need to be seen both as psychological underpinnings but simultaneously as employed in the historical moment. The very idea of "the pathological is a central marker for difference."[132] Thus other categories, including race, gender, and mental status, when used to define difference evoke specific moments of defining the difference between the normal and the pathological.

Many noted psychoanalysts were not sure of the autonomy of racism or the claims of difference in the American context. The Kleinian psychoanalyst Otto Kernberg at Cornell, himself a Jewish child refugee from Vienna to Chile and then in the 1960s to the United States, uses the emotion of hatred to subsume all forms of racism. Kernberg looks at emotional responses on a broader scale, as

> a spectrum of severity of hatred in the transference, ranging from the need to destroy the object (or to destroy oneself in identifying with that object) at one extreme, through an intermediate zone in which what predominates is the need to make the object suffer physically or mentally while preserving it, to milder forms of hatred expressed in the need to exercise power over a submissive object.[133]

When he begins to examine the social contexts, however, it is the most severe forms of mental illness that define group interaction: "On the broader political scene, massive historical trauma, such as economic crisis, a lost war, or political struggles among religions, and ethnic or racial groups provide fertile ground for paranoid developments, while conditions fostering regressive group processes proliferate and may be captured by corresponding paranoid leadership."[134] Social explanations are always partial for Kernberg, as "the massive killing of civilians, the social sanction of torture and persecution, and of open disregard for standards of decency in the treatment of minorities, require a psycho-dynamic, in addition to sociological and historical explanations of that sudden shift in human behaviour from ordinary civilized interaction and respect for human life to massively expressed and sanctioned social violence."[135] His reading of such a psychodynamic explanation of groups such as the Nazis focuses on the primitive emotional forces at work. Returning us to Le Bon, racism for Kernberg is located in the crowd: "Mass psychology as a major individual disposition, stimulated by mass media, focused upon paranoid ideology formation that rationalizes and stimulates aggression, may rapidly escalate into social violence against a social subgroup onto whom primitive aggression has been projected and is now seen as having to be controlled by the exercise of omnipotent and destructive hatred."[136]

Totalitarianism accompanied by a leader with "severely paranoid and antisocial features" can generate the "consolidation of sharp divisions between social groups." Such leaders are marked "by malignant narcis-sism [that] fosters narcissistic and paranoid regressions in this social body." Such racism may, however, be accompanied by "ordinary family and social systems [that] may nonetheless permit the construction of a normal superego system."[137] Psychopathic racism does not demand psychopathic responses.

Other models of racism present in the 1960s and beyond also stress the unity of all forms of prejudice. The Menninger-trained psychoana-lyst Harold Searles, in his detailed studies of schizophrenia in 1960, sees all forms of prejudice as forms of projection of the internalized weak-nesses of the individual onto specific aspects of the external world. Sear-les's work is viewed at the time as not belonging to any given school, and yet his interests, like that of Kernberg, focused on borderline as well as schizophrenic patients. Unlike Kernberg, Searles's focus was on the relationship of individuals to the world around them. Yet for Searles the schizophrenic asks the question that all humans asked: Should I relate to others in the world? The schizophrenic, for Searles's (and here he is in good company in the 1960s, as this is the view of R. D. Laing, among others) is the normal mindset reflecting upon itself:

The schizophrenic person's relatively healthy fellows tend to reject him not merely on account of their often-mentioned unenlightened prejudice against mental illness, but also on account of their sensing quite accurately, when they come into his proximity, how intensely scornful he is toward them and all that they represent to him. Several years ago, in the course of my work with a deeply paranoid woman, it occurred to me that her seemingly limitless scorn, cynicism, and distrust were the qualities one would expect to find in a person who was fixed in a state of unresolved—that is, incomplete complete—*disillusionment*. Crudely put, the complete disillusionment-process involves one's seeing the other person as wholly good, then—with the appearance of an unlovable side of him—as wholly bad, followed by one's integrating both "good" and "bad" percepts of him into a realistic appraisal of him. By contrast, this woman was, I saw, as if fixed in the second stage of this process: she apparently saw the world about her, and all persons in it, as almost unrelievedly bad.[138]

Searles's schizophrenic thus is in the stage of complete rejection, the mirror for Searles of racism and psychopathological prejudice. It is a stage of normal development before the melding of the positive and negative images of the neonate into the more nuanced manner of seeing the world as an adult:

> The first [of two aspects of man's anxiety about not being human] is the great proclivity on the part of human beings, even adult human beings, for the development of prejudicial attitudes toward groups of other human beings, prejudicial attitudes, which include the conviction that these groups of their fellow men are really subhuman, really more animal than human. Such prejudicial attitudes, to which I believe we all are in some degree drawn, betray our own unconscious lack of sureness that we ourselves are fully and unmistakably human. We all have some tendency, great or small, to project onto fellow men who are members of other racial or religious groups, or who are hospitalized with psychiatric illness, or who in some other respect can be looked upon as alien to ourselves, the less-than-human creature which we unconsciously believe to reside in us.[139]

The "less-than-human-creature" within is projected onto others in the world we inhabit. Here racism is but one form of projection and is a core form of transference. It is the animal within us that we see in the world beyond us: "As for animal nature, we reduce our enemies and the racially degraded to non-human status. We diabolize them, call them monsters, rape, lynch and gut them. We make animals, mummies, zombies, werewolves and vampires the subjects of horror stories and films. On the other hand, many love animals more than people and a few will kill humans in the name of animal rights. We routinely anthropomorphise all over the place—the sun and moon and living and dead nature. Transference feelings, projections and identifications abound."[140] (Think about how Wilhelm Reich utilizes this argument in 1933.) For Searles such forms of projection are our means of denial of our inherent relationship with the greater world that we inhabit, our ecology. They also represent an incomplete integration of the self, a psychopathology that is even greater than racism; it is an alienation from the totality of lived experience.

Central to the undertaking in the United States was the documentation of the impact of slavery and "Jim Crow" on the black experience. As Eli Zaretsky has recently noted, "political Freudianism aimed less at a theory of racism (though attempts at this were made) than at uncovering the memory of the slave experience and its aftermath."[141] When black psychoanalysts such as the pioneer Washington, D.C., psychoanalyst Dorothy Evans Holmes and others began to engage the basic problems of racism, it was from the perspective of the victim. Holmes focused on the black analysand in the therapeutic situation, as when "race comes up between a black patient and a black therapist or analyst, as in the case of Mr. C who tried to get me not to interpret the projection of his intrapsychic problems on to 'whitey.' Understandably, it may be difficult for therapists generally to maintain curiosity and therapeutic neutrality when the patient, of whatever race, uses racial trigger words (e.g. 'whitey,' 'honky' or 'nigger'), or presents other evidences of prejudice or racism."[142] Holmes felt it is necessary to bracket racism as a social phenomenon as the cause for such attitudes: "It is my impression that this bias in our approaches results from the fact that our culture generally, and behavioral scientists particularly, still have a significant investment in emphasizing one vantage point on race, i.e. race as racism. This 'preference' reinforces our collective tendency to use race as a focal point for projections of all that we find most unacceptable. As such, working on the problems of race 'from the outside,' as in the community, is favored over the engagement of these issues on the *inside* of the consultation room between therapist and patient."[143]

But what motivates the racist as well as the psychological response of the victim is also clear to her. It is when "ego functions are distorted and mobilized to support the hating of others, including disidentification with the hated others, substitution of indiscriminate misperception of—rather than differentiated thought about—others, and suspension of judgment and control in the service of hateful acts. It is my proposition that those employing such defenses have de facto serious ego disturbances. Likewise, those on the receiving end of such defenses also develop ego disturbances."[144] For Holmes the problem of pathological ego defense mechanisms trumps the social context as the source of racism.

Parallel to such debates about racism as a form of neurotic adaption is the perspective on racism within contemporary American society that sees it more and more as a problem of caste privilege. "Whiteness" thus becomes problematized within psychoanalytic theory over time as it becomes a category of growing importance within race theory. Yet this perspective's focus is not on the psychopathological as it originates in theories of the social construction of race.[145] American "whiteness" itself seems from the beginning an unstable category within psychoanalysis— the question is raised by Neil Altman, "a Jewish, white man," according to his own account, drawing on the work of one of the authors of this volume, Sander L. Gilman, in exploring how American and British Jews acquired white privilege in the recent past.[146] Altman sees "whiteness" as resulting from the Enlightenment dichotomy between rationality (which is defined as white) and irrationality (which come to define all other groups labeled as "primitive"). In his account of his analyses with a black client he recounts how he became hyperaware of his own anxiety about being seen as white yet imagined through the lens of antisemitic stereotypes of Jews. Being "Jewish" and privileged comes to be part of the analyst's conflict in the countertransference to the analysand.

The white American psychoanalyst Melanie Suchet, "born and raised in South Africa and now a U.S. citizen, yearning for a different way to be inhabited by race," sees examining her own "white privilege" as her means to do so.[147] She too draws on the work of Gilman to show how race actually stands at the heart of the psychoanalytic project.[148] Defining racism in 2004, she writes that to become "American is to be initiated into American whiteness."[149] She evokes "white privilege" as an inherent aspect of a psychoanalytically informed race theory, seeing it always in contrast to black identity. Whiteness is not a form of neurosis. "Whiteness is a lived experience. It is an ideology, a system of beliefs, policies and practices that enable white people to maintain social power and control." Through analysis she can uncover "the deep feelings of guilt and shame, the layers of melancholia, and then the experiences of acceptance and surrender" that accompany white privilege.[150] For Suchet, becoming cognizant of her white privilege in a world radically different world from the apartheid South Africa in which she was raised provides a means of recuperation. If there is a neurosis it is only in the form of "melancholia," that unconscious response to the loss of racism's stabilizing force, which needs to be examined through analysis in order to be understood.

The psychoanalyst and biographer Elizabeth Young-Bruehl, in her *The Anatomy of Prejudices*, creates a more differentiated set of subcategories for "prejudices," a social psychological category that she revitalizes in her work. She begins her book with a snapshot of the history of how "prejudice" develops as a category in American sociology and social psychology. She stresses that seeing prejudice as a single category masks the inherent psychological differences between antisemitism, racism, and sexism (and, marginally, homophobia). Thus antisemitism is rooted in a reality as well as a fantasy, as "the Jews are a birth group; they have a genealogical history, and they extend their identity as a group from generation to generation, debating as they do which laws of inclusion and descent will keep them defined by themselves and not by antisemites."[151] While "Jean-Paul Sartre once remarked that if the Jews did not exist the antisemites would have invented them—a remark which is quite untrue of the antisemites and the Jews, but which covers the situation of the homophobes and the homosexuals very well. The homophobes *have* invented the homosexuals."[152] The problems of classification make such distinctions necessary.

Her core argument makes a distinction between "ideologies of desire" and ethnocentrism or group identification.[153] The former she sees fulfilling individual needs and generating new subcategories; the latter reflect older, established group definitions. Ethnocentrism is thus historically driven, more visible and manipulatable, while ideologies of desire involve "layers of feeling . . . that are deeper" than those of ethnocentrism.[154] Thus antisemitism or anti-black racism "is expressed in xenophobic assertions that have at least a tangential relation to the characteristics of real groups or subgroups, especially to those living separately."[155] Ideologies of desire "are expressed in 'chimeras,' or fantasies that have irrational reference to real, observable, or verifiable characteristics of a group or marks of difference."[156] Earlier theories of prejudice focus on ethnocentrism while ignoring the equally powerful yet less visible ideologies of desire.

Whether racism (Kovel), hatred (Kernberg), difference (Gilman), ego disturbance (Holmes), whiteness (Suchet), ecological projection (Searles), or prejudices (Young-Bruehl), the debate about the psychological substructure of group antipathy remains unresolved as the classifications themselves remain unstable. Perhaps it is the case that the very question of what it means when such categories are defined as psychological lies at the core of their instability. Rather than a problem of methodology in and of itself, it becomes a question of defining interiority and the processes that relate the inner world to the world of experience and action.[157] Yet one does need to see such approaches as an answer to the claims that racism, hatred, difference in all of their forms are conscious and collective rather than unconscious and individual.[158] Claims of underlying structures that generated racism or prejudice were only compelling when the relationship between such structures (as in object relations theory) and their historical presentation were well articulated. Sigmund Freud understood the structure of dreams as multilayered: the symbolic language of dreams came from quotidian experience and the narrative of dreams from the desire to establish a coherent, if often confused, narrative out of the symbolic language. Yet the underlying structures of repression were not immediately visible in either of these aspects of the dream without complex analysis. The slippage between the analysis of individuals who are or are perceived as racist, antisemitic, xenophobic and a racist collective as the source of such beliefs not only absolved the individual of responsibility but also exempted the underlying structures of society that shield racism from further examination.

To conclude this chapter, let us consider how psychological theories of collective behavior have been absorbed and rearticulated among sociologists. Such a consideration returns us to our initial discussion of Le Bon and the significance of the crowd for understanding racism, including extreme, or violent, actions against members of another group. Where sociologists diverge, as we discuss below, is in their emphasis on the *mundanity* of crowd behavior (analogous perhaps to Arendt's emphasis on the *normality* of evil). That is, rather than seeing the crowd as abnormal, or primitive, among sociologists mob behavior serves an instrumental purpose in articulating social boundaries between groups, as well as confirming appropriate relations within an in-group, and between an in-group and out-group.

A significant branch of theorizing on race, racism, and group conflict focuses on what sociologist Michele Lamont has termed "boundary work," a concept rooted in social psychology and the emergent branch of cognitive sociology.[159] Lamont's thesis is that the basis of all social groups entails collective boundary-drawing between in-groups and out-groups, as well as the collective prescribing and proscribing of appropriate relations and practices within and between each. These boundaries are, of course, symbolic, and are accomplished through narrative practices that center on questions of the constitution of group identity.

Building upon Lamont's framework, others have suggested that events are significant for how social actors use cultural resources and symbolic categories to establish boundaries and appropriate relations both within and between groups.[160] Social events allow for social actors to "deploy cultural resources provided by group ideologies . . . and concretize themes interpretable within the emplotment of collective narratives."[161] To bring this full circle, we should consider how boundary work provides stability for the unstable concept of whiteness identified within psychoanalytic thought. Parallel, then, to Suchet's argument that whiteness is "a system of beliefs, policies and practices that enable white people to maintain social power and control," sociologist Mattias Smångs considers what historical practices have been used to lend stability to whiteness, subsequently engendering greater social control over in-group collective narratives, but also control over the lives of black Americans, as the referential out-group, or Other.

Smångs argues that the events most efficacious in establishing firm social group boundaries are "dramatic ones involving conflict in general and violence in particular. . . . [I]ntergroup violence may be understood as enacting symbolic group boundaries, categories, and identities."[162] Analyzing comprehensive lynching records from Georgia and Louisiana between 1882 and 1930, Smångs argues in part that *public* lynchings (those composed of mobs of fifty or more participants) should be understood not as instrumental means for immobilizing blacks, but rather as means for firming up boundaries between whites and blacks. Arguing that the Democratic Party played an important role in establishing white racial cohesion through its segregationist platform, Smångs shows with a great deal of precision that, prior to disenfranchisement, in communities with lower and intermediate levels of Democratic Party support (measured by the local Democratic vote percentage in election years) lynching incidents were more common, because they functioned to provide racial cohesion, articulated around the violent spectacle of the lynch mob.[163] In this model of intergroup violence as collective-identity building, the lynch mob is a performance staged by whites and for whites on the basis of its collective identity narrative. The effectiveness of the lynching

> depends on drawing participants into strong mutual focus of attention and high levels of emotional energy, commonly achieved by various ceremonial elements, for example, defilement and desecration of bodies—torture, mutilation, burning, decapitation, and flogging. Collective identity-building violence is enacted to uphold the integrity and sovereignty of the group as a whole by dramatizing symbolic boundaries and the extent of the group's mutual loyalties. Such violence defines the relationship among and between perpetrators (including adherents) and victims in terms of, on the one side, similarity, solidarity, and power, and, on the other, otherness, exclusion, and powerlessness. Thus, it may not be only expressive but also generative of the very social boundaries and collective identities that it invokes.[164]

In the pre-disenfranchisement South, where white supremacy had not quite been institutionalized, indicators of lower levels of white racial cohesion, measured by Democratic vote percentages, "influenced whites to enact community solidarity and empowerment through public lynchings." Meanwhile, communities with higher shares of the Democratic vote "were not similarly compelled to assert racial solidarity and power" through public lynchings.[165] Thus, Smångs returns us to where we began—with the crowd; albeit now the crowd is not abnormal, or a reflection of our society's most primitive or uncivilized collective self. Rather, the mob exemplifies *normative* collective behavior, in the sense that it articulates symbolic boundaries, and concretizes collective narratives, even in its most violent and abhorrent acts.

Conclusion

The Specter of Science in Twenty-First-Century Racial Discourse

Let us conclude our volume here with two brief stories that illustrate how the *idea* of racism is shaped in very contradictory ways by "cutting-edge" contemporary scientific discourses. In an essay that appeared in *The Lancet* in 1997, the Jewish cognitive neurophysiologist Itzhak Fried at the University of California, Los Angeles, and Tel Aviv University, recalling genocides from the murder of the Armenians through the Holocaust to more recent horrors in Bosnia and Rwanda, described this switch in behavior in terms of a medical syndrome, which he called "Syndrome E."[1] According to Fried the "E" stands for "evil." In a later interview he evoked a 1996 *Lancet* editorial that argued that at some point "an inquisitive scientist will come across evil, maybe from the preserved brains of those afflicted, and recognise it for what it is, something no-one has ever seen before. Should that happen, evil will be classifiable and may even prove reversible. If it does not, those specialising in the psychology of deviance will have to live with the notion that some horrors of human behaviour will forever elude them."[2] Fried observed, "I made a decision not to use the word 'evil,' as I thought it invited metaphors and biased the inquisitive mind. But I stuck with the 'E.'"[3] For the present project the reductive and constructed nature of the "E" is highly evocative of the "F" scale of *The Authoritarian Personality*.

While noting that there are radically different historical contexts to such actions, the question he asked is what are the symptoms that define such perpetrators. His analogy is telling: "Civil strife, extreme conditions, and ethnic conflicts have often had a role in these events, much as poverty and lack of hygiene lead to outbreaks of infectious disease."[4] The idea that poverty and hygiene is simply analogous to the context of genocide reduces prejudice to a limited and describable phenomenon. Indeed, even the use of the infectious disease model is highly problematic in and of itself. The symptoms come to be the common denominator of the perpetrators of genocide. He catalogues them as follows: "obsessive ideation, compulsive repetition, rapid desensitisation to violence, diminished affective reactivity, hyperarousal, environmental dependency, group contagion, and a failure to adapt to changing stimulus-reinforcement associations." Yet, he observes, "memory, language, planning, and problem-solving skills remain intact." He argues that this appears primarily in "males between 15 and 50" and is the result of a "cognitive fracture." He defines this as a failure of brain function: "hyperaroused orbitofrontal and medical prefrontal cortices tonically inhibit the amygdala and are no longer regulated by visceral and somatic homoeostatic controls ordinarily supplied by subcortical systems." Central to his argument is that such "individuals constitute a very small proportion of the population, and they often have a history of psychopathology."[5] That is, they are not "normal" in any way. And, as with most such approaches, he argues that there is the possibility of early intervention to prevent genocide, drawing again on the model of infectious disease: "Isolation of individuals with Syndrome E may offer hope of containing an outbreak, because the syndrome will not persist or propagate without contact with other individuals at risk or with potential victims. Prompt diagnosis would be of paramount importance as prevention may be effective only in the early stages. The signs and symptoms of the syndrome should be made widely known. Individuals in most societies know that a constellation of high fever and coughing may indicate pneumonia." Indeed, "early recognition of symptoms and signs could lead to presentation through education and isolation of affected individuals."[6] He even postulates a test to sort such individuals from "normals" as "individuals with Syndrome E should perform poorly on orbitofrontal tasks, such as rapid alteration of stimulus-reinforcement associations, but they should not differ from controls in performances on tests of dorsolateral frontal function, such as Wisconsin Card Sorting."[7] He imagines a test for prejudice and genocidal behavior that could predict even the potential for such beliefs and acts before they were fully formulated or acted upon.[8]

The response to Fried's essay in *The Lancet* was quite critical. One correspondent, John Fabre of the Institute of Child Health, University College London Medical School, argued the approach was a means of freeing the perpetrators from accountability: "to label such morally degenerate behavior with anodyne pseudoclinical labels such as syndrome E must represent the ultimate in our society's trend towards denial of personal responsibility. However admirable Fried's intentions, the soldier will be seen to be 'suffering' from Syndrome E."[9] Another noted that even if such clinical symptoms are present it is not "clear whether the brain alterations are causal or mediating."[10] Yet another reiterated that "the ethics of responsibility is at risk of being denied if the process is regarded as individual physiological impairment."[11] Fried's answer stressed the need to "rationally investigate [the psycho-physiological dimension] to increase the prospects of curbing such behavior" while stressing that the "intact intellectual domain . . . does not imply impunity from individual responsibility."[12] The play here is with the notion of legal rather than moral culpability. Such individuals would be legally responsible, Fried implies, because their impairment did not violate the McNaughton notion of being unable to distinguish right from wrong; this may provide a legal justification for conviction but still does allow a moral exculpation. This is a risk that Fried is willing to take: "The risk to the ethics of responsibility . . . may be the price that we have to pay for recognising a psychobiological dimension that offers a framework for systematic inquiry."[13]

In 2015 Fried hosted a major international conference in Paris on "Syndrome E." When interviewed about the basis for his approach, Fried again, as in his 1997 essay, evoked the questionable Milgram experiments discussed in Chapter Four as well as Christopher Browning's historical study of the Hamburg police, *Ordinary Men* (1992), which described those men who were drafted to become the first of the killing squads in the Holocaust. "In a short time, most became efficient killers, participating in the shooting of 38,000 Jews who had been rounded up by the Nazis, and herding 45,000 more into trains destined for the gas chambers. Their commander allowed the reservists to opt out, but only 10% or so decided not to kill. I felt that the transformation into repetitive killer had to have a biology behind it—all of our behaviour is guided by brain activity."[14] While social scientists present at the conference denounced what they saw as Fried's simple medicalization of the perpetrators, he said, "I don't see it as medicalizing the problem so much as formulating it in a way that I know is useful in the medical world. As a doctor, you always work with a degree of uncertainty, and you try to minimize that uncertainty by setting out the observable signs and symptoms in the hope that understanding will emerge. This seems a good way to provide a framework for interdisciplinary discussion." Yet Fried's intention is, over the long run, one of creating a world in which an "understanding things at a fundamental, biological level will encourage policy-makers to focus on the right sort of education about this. A small number of people don't make the transition to become killers in these critical situations. Early education might help to increase the number of those who are not susceptible." Early education rather than reeducation, in the post-1945 sense, would preclude any further genocide—a utopian goal to be achieved only through a concept of science that in complex ways replicates the biological determinism of racism itself.

If the problem is one of the shifting meanings of interiority, then the attempt to define hatred and prejudice has also been attempted within the neuropsychiatric discourse of the new brain science. According to a scholar examining the claims of social cognitive neuroscientist, "Researchers . . . have developed techniques for illuminating not only how but where in the brain race is processed."[15] Thus neuroscience will provide an "understanding [of] how race (and other stereotypes) function in the human mind."[16] Such views stress the unconscious production and function of racism as a reflex of normal brain structure and innate capacities such as memory. In other words racism consists of "normal cognitive processes related to categorization [that] might produce and perpetuate intergroup bias."[17] The alternative is to see racism as an aspect not of normal brain function, but as a pathological product of certain brains.[18]

Since the 1990s the Human Genome Project and parallel work on the International HapMap charting human genetic difference has exacerbated what Duana Fullwiley has called "the molecularization of race."[19] "Vanguard researchers" in human molecular genetics claim that they have found "the reality" of racial differences in the DNA's molecular structure, and *claim* to trace ancestry via patterns of single nucleotide polymorphisms. The resultant conjectures have attempted to explain virtually every pathology from diabetes to obesity, including a wide range of mental disorders. Race figures prominently in such discussions even though the real question of what geneticists mean by race is highly contested. The University of California geneticist Neil Risch stated that numerous studies over past decades have documented biological differences among the races with regard to susceptibility to and natural history of chronic diseases. Risch is comfortable using race as a category of analysis: "What is your definition of races? If you define it a certain way, maybe that's a valid statement. There is obviously still disagreement. . . . Scientists always disagree! A lot of the problem is terminology. I'm not even sure what race means, people use it in many different ways . . . but that doesn't preclude you from using it or the fact that it has utility."[20] Such utility masks the pitfall of uniformity.

The creation of a genetic cohort as a collective in the sense that race was used to unify and level groups is a specter in the machine of modern genetics. Lynn B. Jorde and Stephen P. Wooding noted that "[n]ew genetic data has enabled scientists to re-examine the relationship between human genetic variation and 'race.' . . . These [genetic] clusters are also correlated with some traditional concepts of race, but the correlations are imperfect because genetic variation tends to be distributed in a continuous, overlapping fashion among populations. Therefore, ancestry, or even race, may in some cases prove useful in the biomedical setting, but direct assessment of disease-related genetic variation will ultimately yield more accurate and beneficial information."[21] Francis Collins, head of the American Human Genome Project, does care, as "the downside of using race, whether in research or in the practice of medicine is that we are reifying it as if it has more biological significance than it deserves. Race is an imperfect surrogate for the causative information we seek. To the extent that we continue to use it, we are suggesting to the rest of the world that it is very reliable and that racial categories have more biological meaning than they do. We may even appear to suggest something that I know is not true: that there are bright lines between populations and that races are biologically distinct."[22] It is the bright line that defines heterogeneous groups that should be avoided in any modern reading of genetics.

The molecularization of racism is related to the new brain science in that it seeks what Deborah Lynn Steinberg calls a new faith in the science of categorization, a faith based on the affective claims of genetics in areas such as crime and personal identity.[23] Racism comes to be seen in the very evocation of such biological categories in the study of pathology. If you include blacks or women in a scientific study because of their claimed genetic difference are you not "foster[ing] the racism that its creators want to abrogate by establishing government-sponsored research on the basis of the belief that there are significant biological differences among the races"?[24] And why then these specific categories rather than others, such as the Jews, where genetically transmitted diseases are claimed to be a vital part of their collective genetic inheritance, if indeed the Jews can ever be defined as a homogenous genetic cohort?[25] What is not in question is the increased emphasis on the role of science to frame such problems as those of new collectives as an extension, as Troy Duster has argued, of the older concepts of race.[26] The application of the new genetics to racism has primarily been through the arena of evolutionary genetics, when it examines not-normal development by variations from a supposed norm. Evolutionary genetics, in the form of subdisciplines such as evolutionary psychology, stresses the evolution of human psychological traits as the functional products of natural selection, transmitted, as Steven Pinker has noted, through "adaptation, gene-level selection, and modularity."[27] Such an approach opens itself to providing an explanation of psychological phenomena such as racism.

Here one case to document such an approach to the psychopathology of racism must suffice, that of the self-described "evolutionary psychologist and . . . research[er] into Jewish-gentile relations" Kevin MacDonald, the author of a trilogy on Jewish reproductive strategies.[28] MacDonald is a retired professor of psychology at California State University, Long Beach. MacDonald had long argued for a close link between genetics and evolutionary biology: "Key advances in molecular genetics have also had a significant impact on personality research. New techniques are enabling researchers to identify specific alleles associated with personality traits."[29] But for the link "to be interesting to an evolutionist, genetic variation must be important to adaptation rather than simply adaptively neutral."[30] The question for MacDonald is what links can be made between group identity, such as that ascribed to the Jews (in particular from an antisemitic perspective), and individual traits, given that "genetic variation in personality and other valued traits serves to facilitate the production of a wide range of variation (within a delimited range) that facilitates the occupation of a wide range of possible niches in the human and nonhuman environment."[31] Indeed, it is a fundamental linkage, as "within this wide range of viable strategies, personality variation functions as a resource environment for individuals in the sense that personality variation is evaluated according to the interests of the evaluator (e.g., friendships, coalitions, or mate choice)."[32] Or, we may add, enmities.

To quote MacDonald (whose work is, in fact, highly derivative) on this linkage: "As indicated by the summaries of my books, my training as an evolutionist as well as the evidence compiled by historians leads me to conceptualize Judaism as self-interested groups whose interests often conflict with segments of the gentile community. Anti-Jewish attitudes and behavior have been a pervasive feature of the Jewish experience since the beginnings of the Diaspora well over 2000 years ago."[33] For MacDonald Judaism is less a religion than a biological strategy: "The basic proposal is that Judaism can be interpreted as a set of ideological structures and behaviors that have resulted in the following features: (1) the segregation of the Jewish gene pool from surrounding gentile societies; (2) resource and reproductive competition with gentile host societies; (3) high levels of within-group cooperation and altruism among Jews; and (4) eugenic efforts directed at producing high intelligence, high investment parenting, and commitment to group, rather than individual, goals." Moreover, "intellectual defenses of Judaism and of Jewish theories of anti-Semitism have throughout its history played a critical role in maintaining Judaism as a group evolutionary strategy." That is, antisemitism is a device used by Jews to maintain their social isolation and group cohesion. MacDonald's views are rather pure nineteenth-century biological antisemitism now cloaked in the rhetoric of an evolutionary biology driven by simplistic genetic models. Such evolutionary and genetic "just-so-stories" depend greatly on the definition of their components; science is, as has been recently remarked, always based on just-so-stories, but competent (not "good") science tests and retests its terms and assumptions so that it is dynamic in its processes and claims. MacDonald's work, like that of his predecessors, does not meet this test.

The problem with evoking such earlier racial models in the name of "evolutionary biology" is that it places you in odd political company. Thus MacDonald's self-descriptions quoted above begin his testimony given on Monday, January 31, 2000, as the sole "scientific" witness speaking for David Irving in the case of *Irving v. Penguin Books Ltd and Deborah Lipstadt*, in which Irving accused the American historian Deborah Lipstadt of libel for labeling him a "Holocaust denier" in her 1993 *Denying the Holocaust*. To quote Justice Gray's summary:

> Irving has for his own ideological reasons persistently and deliberately misrepresented and manipulated historical evidence; that for the same reasons he has portrayed Hitler in an unwarrantedly favourable light, principally in relation to his attitude towards and responsibility for the treatment of the Jews; that he is an active Holocaust denier; that he is anti-Semitic and racist, and that he associates with right-wing extremists who promote neo-Nazism.[34]

The upshot of the trial was that Irving, and by extension MacDonald, was declared by the British court to be antisemitic. That this is an accurate description can certainly be observed in MacDonald's response on a blog devoted to "white identity, interests, and culture" to the recent critiques of such claims: "No need to discuss the fact that Jewish genetic commonality discovered by (Jewish) population geneticists can only be explained ultimately by the fact that the Jews have always had a race mania."[35] The very notion that the Jews have a "mania" seems to locate racism as an intrinsic aspect of Jewish evolutionary patterns.

Such arguments in the early twenty-first century continue to call upon a reductive notion of what defines the human being as human. There is no question that "brain" and "mind" and "gene" are involved in such activities, yet reducing such complex behavior to a set of "symptoms" that could be ameliorated in advance builds upon earlier claims about the psychopathology of prejudice. Like the 2012 proposal of the Oxford investigators to find a pill against hatred, such attempts are bound to fail as the variety and complexity of the beliefs and actions involved put them beyond the therapeutic in this limited sense. The "tantalising possibility" alluded to by the researchers in the Oxford clinical trial refer to locating racism within the structures and functions of the brain. This would then provide the potential to treat the condition using the latest technologies—imaging, behavioral, and pharmaceutical—the medical and psychological sciences have to offer. Yet, on the other hand, these developments point to a broader trajectory in which the very *idea* of racism is produced by these technologies and developments. From the late eighteenth century to the present, various scientific minds have looked to *explain* racism. These explanations, when examined from a historical and sociological perspective, reflect a range of techniques that, within a given period, actually construct the object of inquiry. In the present period, however, the medicalization of various human conditions, including racism, is giving rise to an expansive repertoire of techniques meant to manage not only *what* we know about racism's causes and consequences, but also how best to practice this knowledge.

Race, Racism, and Biopower

Throughout this book, we have aimed to trace the shifting meanings of race and racism as parallel developments. Rather than treating racism as something to describe the practices enacted by medical and state authorities toward black Americans and Jews, we have instead focused on explaining meanings of race and racism alongside epistemic shifts in the medical and psychological sciences. The period beginning in the middle of the nineteenth century marked the genesis of a set of claims about the nature of scientific medicine, about the psychological and social sciences as empirical, indeed positivist disciplines, and even served to structure reactions to these claims. As a result, much of nineteenth- and early-twentieth-century scientific thought located the conditions of psychopathology within the "innate" properties belonging to distinct racial groups. Jews and black Americans were perceived as more susceptible to psychopathological conditions as the result of their *ontological* statuses.

In the post–World War II era, developments in the social, biological, and medical sciences produced a restatement of an empirical science of mind that parallels the emergence of a mental health governmentality. Deeply influenced by the public's exposure to, and subsequent condemnation of, the Third Reich's explicit doctrine of scientific racism and its horrific effects upon European Jewry, a shift occurred in the scientific understanding of race—from overwhelmingly a biological condition to a socially constructed category. This, in turn, produced a second shift in the perceived relationship between race, racism, and mental health among scientists, policymakers, and the public alike. As a result, the period following World War II through the present has been marked by two parallel claims that originate within science, and then are picked up and carried by policymakers and the public: the first claim is that continued exposure to racism has negative consequences for its targets. That is, enduring patterns of racism *produce* among black Americans and Jews a variety of clinical diagnoses, including depression, anxiety, and phobia. Racism *produces* pathology.

The second claim, arising from *within* the medical and psychological sciences in the post–World War II era, and then expanding to the domains of policy and the public, concerned the mental health status of individuals holding racist and bigoted beliefs and attitudes. Here, as overtly racist ideology was increasingly rejected, individuals who remained committed to now dated ideas about racial inferiority became the targets of expanding mental health governmentality. Racism *is* pathological. These two claims help construct the contemporary trend within health and medicine where new ground broken in biology and genetics is now co-opted as a form of *biopower*, and subsequently applied to develop treatment models for what previously were considered social and cultural problems.[36]

Increasingly, we find the "retrenchment" toward scientific racism, but in new form. The Human Genome Project and advancements in cognitive neuroscience provide promising new possibilities for identifying the origins of pathology, and psychopathology. Yet these projects and others also pose great challenges, most importantly the challenge of escaping the "black hole" that is race and racism's *interiority*. In attempting to locate the psychological and psychopathological origins of racism, we find the discussions summarized above extremely limiting in that they fail to provide any significant response to the mountain of empirical evidence demonstrating the pervasiveness of racism, including racial attitudes, among the larger population.

For example, the shifting meaning of racism to *extreme* attitudes and actions whose origins are located at the level of brain functioning, such as Fried's classification of "Syndrome E," ignores a mountain of empirical evidence that racial outcomes are not only pervasive throughout "normal" society, but mundane. For example, neo-Nazis may be a small proportion of the population, but beliefs that blacks and whites have different levels of intelligence persist across the broader population. Most recently, responses to questions about the intelligence of whites and blacks, taken from the General Social Survey, reveal the persistence of beliefs in the relationship between race and intelligence. Using a scale of 1 (unintelligent) to 7 (intelligent), respondents were asked to evaluate the intelligence of a variety of groups, including blacks and whites. Responses reveal that both whites *and* blacks perceive whites as more intelligent than blacks. Additionally, blacks' perceptions of superior white intellect were *greater* than whites'. In 2014, 46 percent of blacks perceived white intelligence to be at a 5 or above, compared to the 42 percent of blacks who perceived black intelligence to be at a 5 or above. Among whites, 40 percent in 2014 perceived white intelligence to be at a 5 or above, compared to the 28 percent of whites who perceived black intelligence to be at a 5 or above. Survey data such as this demonstrates just how pervasive the remnants of scientific racism remain, even among its targets.[37]

Now, the claim that these attitudes are manifested as psychopathological conditions is, in the strict sense, incorrect. Pathologies are, by definition, conditions of *abnormality*. As surveys like the GSS show, beliefs about the varied intelligence of racial groups are far from abnormal, but continue instead to be widely held. Yet even if these are not beliefs held by the majority of blacks *or* whites, classifying these beliefs as rooted in brain behaviors misses the larger point that while brain functions certainly shape perceptions of reality, our environment plays an equal, if not more important, role in shaping the "mental maps" that make sense of our reality. Furthermore, directing policy at the statistically insignificant amount of *extreme* racists, as suggested by Fried and his contemporaries, shifts attention away from policies directed at the social and structural level that have *proven* positive effects on reducing racial disparities, even if the reduction of racial prejudice is minimal or nonexistent. When taken as a whole, the *interiorizing* of the meaning of racism highlights the increasing medicalization of not just racism, but colorblind discourse. Here, emphasis is placed on extreme individual cases of explicit group-based prejudice, ideologies, and even neurological functions of the brain, while larger, structural features of racism that continue to shape the lives and outcomes of racial and ethnic minorities go unnoticed or unaddressed.

Certainly, racism operates at the unconscious level, and serves to structure outward beliefs among social actors, *even* among those who explicitly deny holding racist beliefs and may have many positive interracial interactions with minority groups.[38] Yet, this simple assertion is often translated, as we have seen above, into "racism *begins* at the unconscious level." We did not set out in this book to resolve the debates around this issue, but rather believe these debates are worth having, and have aimed throughout to describe the historical and contemporary practices of the epistemic culture that shape them.

What we know a body and brain to be capable of are the results of historically specific processes—social, cultural, and, of course, political. These processes establish the range of what *is*, as well as what *should be*.[39] Our book has aimed to describe the historical production, transformation, and diffusion of race and racism as ideas that shape the capabilities and capacities of members of racial categories, once defined as such. Our analysis has shown the deeply complex contingency of race and racism considered as psychopathological conditions and consequences, revealing the limits of the classificatory systems created and subsequently deployed to manage these categories.

Finally, to return to a point we first made in the Introduction, our analysis has privileged the arena of scientific inquiry as the arena for creating, maintaining, and contesting the boundaries and meanings of race, and subsequently racism. This is, as we noted previously, a departure from dominant theories of race and racial formation, including Omi and Winant's pathbreaking racial formation theory. Omi and Winant do note that the "the invocation of scientific criteria to demonstrate the natural basis of racial hierarchy was both a logical consequence of the rise of [scientific] knowledge and an attempt to provide a subtle and more nuanced account of human complexity in the new 'enlightened' age."[40] Yet, while their analysis centers the state as the arena governing, and shaping, scientific inquiry, the nineteenth, twentieth, and twenty-first centuries show quite the opposite: the scientific enterprise provides the very grounds through which an idea of a rational, bureaucratic state is born. Scientific techniques, including but not limited to population statistics, organizational and management theory, and the paradigm of *rationalism* increasingly dictate the scope and scale of state apparatuses meant to define the populations they then seek to manage. While the state is certainly a racial one, then, it is the result of an epistemic culture that provides racialization with its scientific, technical, and *rational* meaning in the first place.

At the beginning of the twenty-first century we can trace the contours and the implications of such debates. We also recognize that at some moments they resulted in horrors (such as the rise of a fascist regime of medical and eugenic control) but that at other moments they could be employed in a strategic overcoming of exactly such forces (as in the Civil Rights struggle in the United States). The tangled bank of the psychological and sociological "sciences" of race and their ongoing positions within the world of *biopower* remains a constant in our own world. Its outcome may be pernicious, as in the suggested prescription of drugs for racism to entire cohorts of society. Yet in raising such specters we come to be aware of the potential for such claims in other arenas of our daily life. Recognizing this is the first step in a form of *biopolitics* and may in the end have an unintended liberating effect.

NOTES

INTRODUCTION

1 Terbeck et al.,"Propranolol Reduces Implicit Negative Racial Bias."
2 Greenwald et al., "Measuring Individual Differences in Implicit Cognition."
3 Interested readers may find more information about the IAT at the *Project Implicit* website, a collaboration among researchers at Harvard, the University of Washington, and the University of Virginia. See https://implicit.harvard.edu.
4 Oxford UEHIRO Centre for Practical Ethics (2012), "Press Release," www.practicalethics.ox.ac.uk.
5 Bell and Dunbar, "Racism and Pathological Bias."
6 Soeter and Kindt, "An Abrupt Transformation," 881.
7 Ibid., 880.
8 Beecher-Monas and Garcia-Rill, "Genetic Predictions of Future Dangerousness."
9 Farah and Heberlein, "Personhood and Neuroscience."
10 Vedantam, "Psychiatry Ponders."
11 Lee, "'Murder and the Reasonable Man' Revisited"; Tesner, "Racial Paranoia as a Defense to Crimes of Violence."
12 Goddard, Kahn, and Adkins, "Racial Bias in Driver Yielding Behavior."
13 Reardon et al., "Brown Fades."
14 The question of scaling up from individual psychology to group dynamics is, of course, a fraught question. See Farhad Dalal, *Thought Paralysis: The Virtues of Discrimination* (London: Karnac Books, 2012), 88–91, for a discussion of S. H. Foulkes's approach to group psychotherapy, which assumes an inherent link between individual and group through the question of social communication.
15 Bartlett, *The Pathology of Man*, 33.
16 Young, *Colonial Desire*, 27:
> The question is whether the old essentializing categories of cultural identity, or of race, were really so essentialized, or have been retrospectively constructed as more fixed than they were. When we look at the texts of racial theory, we find that they are in fact contradictory, disruptive and already deconstructed. Hybridity here is a key term in that wherever it emerges it suggests the impossibility of essentialism.
17 Jackson and Weidman, *Race, Racism, and Science.*
18 On race and madness, see Summers, "'Suitable Care of the African'"; Metzl, *The Protest Psychosis*; Grob, *Mental Illness and American Society*; Keller, *Colonial*

Madness; Anderson, Jenson, and Keller, *Unconscious Dominions*. On the question of pathology and race, see also Wailoo, *Dying in the City of the Blues*; Molina, *Fit to Be Citizens?*; Roberts, *Infectious Fear*; Scott, *Contempt and Pity*; Holloway, *Confronting the Veil*; McKee, *Sociology and the Race Problem*.

19   Gilman, *Difference and Pathology*; *Jewish Self-Hatred*; *The Jew's Body*; *Freud, Race, and Gender*.

20   See recently Hart, ed., *Jews and Race*; Beller, "Solving Riddles"; Reitter, *On the Origins of Jewish Self-Hatred*; Efron, *A Chosen Calling*. The classic study remains Patai, *The Jewish Mind*.

21   We are aware that "prejudice" is not a neutral term. All of these concepts have long and complicated histories. The French philosopher Baron d'Holbach dismissed prejudice in the Enlightenment as harmful and incompatible with virtue. Kant too saw prejudice as violating the rule of judging without reflection and he simply dismissed it as it was opposed to true principles rather than true statements. However, the concept was partially recuperated in the work of Georg Friedrich Meier in Germany who argued though it was always an error it may be faulty only from the standpoint of its form and true in regard to its content. None think of it as having a psychopathological component, but its meaning and function is already debated in the eighteenth century. Werner Schneiders, *Aufklärung und Vorurteilskritik. Studien zur Geschichte der Vorurteilskritik* (Stuttgart: Frommann, 1983), 263–323.

22   On psychoanalytic theories of prejudice as a reflex of the identification with the aggressor in cases of internalized antisemitism, see Daniel Traub-Werner, "Towards a Theory of Prejudice," *International Review of Psycho-Analysis* 11 (1984): 407–412.

23   Lipphardt, "Das 'schwarze Schaf.'"

24   Mead, *Movements of Thought*, 176.

25   Omi and Winant, *Racial Formation in the United States*, 61.

26   Ibid.

27   Ibid., 64.

28   Thus the classic debate about whether what Jean-Jacques Rousseau first called "national character" is fixed, as David Hume in his essay "Of National Characters" (1748) stated specifically about blacks, or malleable, as Montesquieu states in *De l'esprit des lois* (1748). See Roberto Romani, *National Character and Public Spirit in Britain and France, 1750–1914* (Cambridge, UK: Cambridge University Press, 2004), 165ff.

29   Omi and Winant, *Racial Formation in the United States*, 71.

30   In addition to Omi and Winant's *Racial Formation in the United States*, readers could also consider as examples Feagin, *Systemic Racism*; Bonilla-Silva, *Racism without Racists*; Winant, *New Politics of Race*.

31   Omi and Winant, *Racial Formation in the United States*, 71.

32   Knorr Cetina, *Epistemic Cultures*, 7.

33 For an excellent sociological account for how knowledge is created within, and then shapes, society and social environments, see Knorr Cetina, *Epistemic Cultures*.

34 For "expert society," see Giddens, *The Consequences of Modernity*. For how society is permeated with knowledge culture, see Knorr Cetina, *Epistemic Cultures*.

35 See for example, Young, *Colonial Desire*, and McClintock, *Imperial Leather*.

36 Thomas, "Affect and the Sociology of Race."

37 One recent sign of the elision of "race" and "ethnicity" can be found within American biomedical literature dealing with the genetics of race. "Race" was employed for coherent genetic cohorts beginning with the first patent granted to BiDil on October 15, 2002, as a combined medication that is deemed to be most effective for a specific "race," African Americans, for a specific form of heart failure. (The term was first introduced in Peter Carson et al., "Racial Differences in Response to Therapy for Heart Failure.") The new genetics seemed to make "race" a category that is useful if not necessary; as the *New York Times* noted, "Race-based prescribing makes sense only as a temporary measure." ("Toward the First Racial Medicine" [editorial], November 13, 2004). After scholars such as one of the authors of the present volume questioned the unreflected reintroduction of the term "race," scientists began to employ an alternative for what had been labeled a "racial" cohort: "ethnicity." (As, for example, Anna Helgadottir et al., "A Variant of the Gene Encoding Leukotriene A4 Hydrolase.") See Gilman, "The New Genetics and the Old Eugenics" (and the entire special issue on the topic—*Patterns of Prejudice* 36), as well as Stevens, "Racial Meanings and Scientific Methods."

38 Indeed, it is equally problematic in its use in post-modern theory when in 1988 Jean-François Lyotard, published *Heidegger et "les juifs"* (Paris: Galilée, 1988), which was translated as *Heidegger and "the jews,"* trans. Andreas Michel and Mark S. Roberts (Minneapolis: University of Minnesota Press, 1990), with much discussion about the lower case "jews." (Lyotard was evoking the "jew" as the mark of ineffable alterity).

39 See Foucault, *The Birth of Biopolitics*.

40 See, for example, Bonilla-Silva, *Racism without Racists*, and Feagin, *Systemic Racism*.

41 Foucault, "The Confession of the Flesh."

42 Bröckling, Krasmann, and Lemke, "From Foucault's Lectures at the Collège de France," 1.

43 Foucault, *The History of Sexuality, Vol. 1*, 140.

44 Esposito, *Bíos*, 16–18.

45 Foucault, *The History of Sexuality, Vol. 1*, 143.

46 Foucault, "Truth and Power," 114–115.

47 Cooter, *Writing History in the Age of Biomedicine*, x.

48 Rabinow and Rose, "Biopower Today"; Rose, O'Malley, and Valverde, "Governmentality"; Rose, "The Human Sciences in the Biological Age."

49 Foucault, *The History of Sexuality, Vol. 1*, 144.
50 Rabinow and Rose, "Biopower Today," 195.
51 Weheliye, *Habeas Viscus*.
52 Hardt and Negri, *Empire*; Agamben, *Homo Sacer*. On Hardt and Negri, see Rabinow and Rose, "Biopower Today," 119.
53 Rabinow and Rose, 1"Biopower Today," 97.
54 Cooter, *Writing History in the Age of Biomedicine*, 196.
55 For Foucault, the original French for "apparatus" was *dispotif*. The English "apparatus" has become commonplace in translations of his work, and in subsequent writings by other scholars across disciplines. See Michel Foucault, *Power/Knowledge: Selected Interviews and Other Writings*, ed. Colin Gordon (New York: Random House, 1980).
56 See Morabia, ed., *A History of Epidemiologic Methods and Concepts*.
57 Fabrega, "Culture and History in Psychiatric Diagnosis and Practice."
58 Ibid., 393.
59 Ibid., 393–394.
60 Ibid., 401–402.
61 Ibid., 400.
62 Ibid., 401.
63 See Gilman, *Diseases and Diagnoses*.
64 William F. Bynum, "The Great Chain of Being after Forty Years: An Appraisal," *History of Science* 13 (1975): 1–28.

CHAPTER 1. PSYCHOPATHOLOGY AND DIFFERENCE FROM THE NINETEENTH CENTURY TO THE PRESENT

1 Burgle, *Die Hysterie*), 19.
2 Veronika Lipphardt, *Biologie der Juden: jüdische Wissenschaftler über "Rasse" und Vererbung 1900–1935* (Göttingen: Vandenhoeck & Ruprecht, 2008), and Céline Kaiser and Marie-Luise Wünsche, eds., *Die 'Nervosität der Juden' und andere Leiden an der Zivilisation: Konstruktionen des Kollektiven und Konzepte individueller Krankheit im psychiatrischen Diskurs um 1900* (Paderborn and München: Schönigh, 2003). See also Goldstein, "The Wandering Jew"; Efron, *Defenders of the Race*.
3 Charcot, *Leçons du Mardi*, vol. 2, 11–12. See the translation of the *Poliklinische Vorträge von Prof. J. M. Charcot*, trans. by Sigmund Freud (vol. 1) and Max Kahane (vol. 2), 2 vols. (Leipzig: Deuticke, 1892–95), vol. 2, 11.
4 Erb, *Über die wachsende Nervosität*.
5 Emil Kraepelin, "Zur Entartungsfrage," 748.
6 Jaspers, *General Psychopathology*, vol. 2, 670.
7 See the discussion of these concepts and phrases in Gilman, *Freud, Race, and Gender*, 100–103.
8 Brill and Karpas, "Insanity among Jews."
9 Ibid., 579.

10 Fishberg, *Materials for the Physical Anthropology*, 5.

11 Cartwright, "Report on the Diseases."

12 Olmstead, *A Journey in the Seaboard Slave States*, 226.

13 "The Accountability of Slavery," *North Star*.

14 See the discussion of the image of the "insane black" in Gilman, *Seeing the Insane*, 112–116.

15 Jarvis, "Insanity among the Coloured Population," 10.

16 Hughes, "Labeling and Treating Black Mental Illness"; Deutsch, "The First US Census of the Insane."

17 Hughes, "Labeling and Treating Black Mental Illness," 444–445.

18 Ibid., 445.

19 *Proceedings of the National Conference of Charities and Correction, 1887* (Ann Arbor: University of Michigan Library, 2005), 167.

20 Searcy, "Success in Life, Physiologically Considered"; Hughes, "Labeling and Treating Black Mental Illness," 459.

21 Barrows, ed., *Proceedings of the National Conference of Charities and Correction*, 397–398; also see Hughes, "Labeling and Treating Black Mental Illness," 436.

22 Williams, "Nineteenth Century Pan-Africanist John Henry Smyth,"; Barrows, ed., *Proceedings of the National Conference of Charities and Correction*, 470–473.

23 Jarvis, "On the Supposed Increase of Insanity," 335.

24 Ibid., 361.

25 Ibid., 363.

26 Gilman and Stepan, "Appropriating the Idioms of Science."

27 Galton, "Eugenics and the Jew," 16.

28 Babcock, "The Colored Insane"; Dawson, "Psychic Rudiments and Morality."

29 Billings, "Vital Statistics of the Jews," 70.

30 Bein, *The Jewish Question*, 594.

31 Zimmermann, *Wilhelm Marr*, 38ff.

32 Lombroso, *L'antisemitismo e la scienze moderne*, 83.

33 Interestingly, Lombroso holds a quite different opinion of blacks. Addressing rising homicide rates in the United States, and black criminality more generally, Lombroso writes:

> As regards the negroes, while we cannot say that they are irredeemable, since they have already made considerable progress, it will probably take a long time to infuse among them such a degree of intellectual culture as will refine them and develop their moral sense, for the impulsive and lower instincts are the last to disappear. These, in fact, have not been entirely eradicated even from the white race, as mobs frequently demonstrate. Societies have been formed for the promotion of negro emigration to Africa, and others for the purpose of relieving the congestion of the cities and spreading the surplus urban population over the country and away from large centers, all of which, if feasible, will tend to modify the evil I have referred to.
>
> Lombroso, "Why Homicide Has Increased in the United States," 10.

34 Engländer, *Die auffallend häufigen Krankheitserscheinungen*, 54.

35 Ibid., 123.

36 Ibid., 46.

37 Bein, *Theodor Herzl*, 173.

38 See Nirenberg, *Anti-Judaism*, 64–65.

39 Mantegazza, *The Sexual Relations of Mankind*, 99. On Mantegazza and antisemitism, see William I. Brustein, *Roots of Hate: Anti-Semitism in Europe before the Holocaust* (Cambridge, UK: Cambridge University Press, 2003), 164. Mantegazza's Italian Jewish readers saw this attack as an antisemitic one; see Derek Duncan, *Reading and Writing Italian Homosexuality: A Case of Possible Difference* (Aldershot, UK: Ashgate, 2006), 63, n. 22. Our summary is, of course, very cursory and the history of antisemitism is also dependent on context, even of the religious argument, rather than reductive classifications of anti-Judaism, antisemitism, xenophobia, etc. This is an argument that was made already in Sander L. Gilman and Steven T. Katz, eds., *Anti-Semitism in Times of Crisis* (New York: New York University Press, 1991).

40 Pinsker, *Auto-Emancipation*, 6.

41 Ibid., 3.

42 Ibid., 4.

43 James Walsh, "Richard Lalor Sheil," *Decies* 62 (2006): 95–117. For the general background see George Bornstein, *The Colors of Zion: Blacks, Jews, and Irish from 1845 to 1945* (Cambridge MA: Harvard University Press, 2011); Matthew Frye Jacobson, *Special Sorrows: The Diasporic Imagination of Irish, Polish and Jewish Immigrants in the United States* (Berkeley: University of California Press, 2002); Rory Miller, *Ireland and the Palestine Question* (Dublin: Irish Academic Press, 2005); Cormac Ó Grada. *Jewish Ireland in the Age of Joyce: A Socioeconomic History* (Princeton, NJ: Princeton University Press, 2006).

44 *A Collection of Speeches spoken by Daniel O'Connell, Esq. and Richard Sheil, Esq. on subjects connected with the Catholic question* (Dublin: John Cumming, 1828), iv.

45 Glos. RO, Hyett mss D6/F32/13, Maurice Frederick Fitzhardinge Berkeley to Charles Hyett, (25 June 1831). Quoted at ttp://www.historyofparliamentonline.org/volume/1820–1832/member/sheil-richard-1791–1851#footnote1_pm8fp06.

46 Justin McCarthy, *History of Our Own Times*, 4 vols. (New York and London: Harper Brothers, 1901), vol. 1, 34–35.

47 G.W.E. Russell, *Collections & Recollections*, rev. ed.. (London: Smith Elder & Co, 1899), 133. See also W. T .McCullagh, *Memoirs of the Rt. Hon. R. L Sheil*, 2 vols. (London: H. Colburn, 1855).

48 By the end of the nineteenth century it was widely anthologized, as in Chauncey Mitchell Depew, ed., *The Library of Oratory, Ancient and Modern: With Critical Studies of the World's Great Orators by Eminent Essayists*, Volume 5 (London: A. L. Fowle, 1902), 439–445, and William Jennings Bryan, ed., *Masterpieces of Eloquence: Famous Orations of Great World Leaders from Early Greece to the Present Time*, Volume 12 (New York: F. Collier & Son, 1905), 4949–4955. Ironically it was

not included in *The Speeches of the Right Honorable Richard Lalor Sheil, M.P with a Memoir, &c.,* ed. Thomas MacNevin (London: H. G. Bohn 1847).

49 All references are to *Hansard* HC DEB. (7 February 1848) 96 cols. 220–283, here cols. 272–278.

50 See, for example, Richard D. Hoblyn and L. M. Griffiths, *A Dictionary of Terms Used in Medicine and the Collateral Sciences* (London: Whittaker and Co., 1849).

51 From an extract in the *OED* from the *Columbian magazine, or monthly miscellany* 110/1 (November, 1786).

52 *Times* (November 20, 1855): "Baron Prokesch is . . . an 'Anglophobe'; so that it may safely be predicted that he and the British Ambassador will soon be on the very worst possible terms." Cited by the *OED*.

53 Ernest Cashmore, *Dictionary of Race and Ethnic Relations* (London: Routledge, 1996), 182.

54 Pinsker, *Auto-Emancipation*, 5, 12.

55 Friedrich Nietzsche, *An Spinoza,* in *Nachgelassene Fragmente 1884–1885,* Herbst 1884, 28 [49], *Kritische Studienausgabe,* Bd. 11, ed. Giorgio Colli und Mazzino Montinari, (München: dtv, 1988), 319; Andreas Sommer, "Nietzsche's Readings on Spinoza: A Contextualist Study, Particularly on the Reception of Kuno Fischer," *Journal of Nietzsche Studies* 43 (2012): 156–184.

56 Pinsker, *Auto-Emancipation*, 2.

57 Ibid., 2, 11.

58 Ibid., 9.

59 Sterling, *The Making of an Afro-American,* 122–136, 208–219.

60 Delany, *The Condition, Elevation, Emigration, and Destiny,* 45.

61 Pinsker, *Auto-Emancipation*, 4.

62 Delany, *The Condition, Elevation, Emigration, and Destiny,* 42.

63 Ibid., 175.

64 Gilman and Stepan, "Appropriating the Idioms of Science," 82.

65 Knorr Cetina, *Epistemic Cultures.*

66 Pinsker, *Auto-Emancipation*, 5; Delany, *The Condition, Elevation, Emigration, and Destiny,* 144.

67 Pinsker, *Auto-Emancipation*, 5.

68 Ibid., 11.

69 Delany, *The Condition, Elevation, Emigration, and Destiny,* 186.

70 Ibid., 217.

71 Delany, *The Condition, Elevation, Emigration, and Destiny,* 178.

72 Pinsker, *Auto-Emancipation*, 13.

73 Nordau, "Jewry of Muscle."

74 Wolfe, *At Home in Exile,* 14.

75 Kornberg, *Theodor Herzl,* 164.

76 Herzl, *Zionist Writings,* 166–167.

77 Quoted by Ben-Horin, *Max Nordau,* 180.

78 Herzl, "Neue Nasen." See also Hyöng, "A Dream of a White Vienna."

79 Joseph, "Über die operative Verkleinerung einer Nase." Translation from Joseph, "Operative Reduction of the Size of a Nose," 180.

80 Leo Strauss, "Anmerkung zur Diskussion über 'Zionismus und Antisemitismus,'" *Jüdische Rundschau* 28 (September 28, 1923): 501–502.

81 Lessing, *Der jüdische Selbsthaß*, 40.

82 Reitter, *On the Origins of Jewish Self-Hatred*, 23–24.

83 Kernis and Goldman, "A Multicomponent Conceptualization of Authenticity," 283.

CHAPTER 2. THE LONG, SLOW BURN FROM PATHOLOGICAL ACCOUNTS OF RACE TO RACIAL ATTITUDES AS PATHOLOGICAL

1 Martin Bulmer's *The Chicago School of Sociology* (1984) continues to be deeply influential in how the Chicago School perspective on race and race relations—the ecological model—is remembered. However, some scholars have issued rejections of the *centrality* of the Chicago School to a social-structural explanation of race and racism through an integration of Du Bois and his scholarship into the canon. See, for example, Anderson and Massey, *Problem of the Century*, 1–12.

2 The neglect of Du Bois's work, and the negative impact this had on the development of sociology as a discipline, has experienced a growing interest among academics in the past two decades. We would be doing a disservice to our readers, and to these contemporary scholars, if we did not make mention of some of works that cover this topic in-depth: McKee, *Sociology and the Race Problem*; Morris, *The Scholar Denied*; Hunter, *Black Citymakers*.

3 See Stocking, *Race, Color, and Evolution*; Barkan, *The Retreat of Scientific Racism*.

4 Pascoe, "Miscegenation Law," 47.

5 "Racialism" for Pascoe refers to racial ideologies that include, but are not limited to, scientific racism. See ibid., 48.

6 We want to distinguish here between what contemporary philosophers of race have described as the *social ontology* of race from the traditional use of ontology to describe an object's physical existence. Despite race having no biological-ontological basis, socially constructed meanings of race have become so saturated into the bodies of nonwhites that these meanings continue to be mistaken as natural/biological. As Lewis Gordon argues, we need to acknowledge that ontology, particularly when it comes to the study of race and racism, is not only a study of what "is" the case, but also a study of what is being treated as the case. Thus, the distinction between *social ontology* and *physical* ontology. See Gordon, *Bad Faith and Antiblack Racism*; also Lee, ed., *Living Alterities*.

7 Sypher, "The Rediscovered Prophet."

8 Hoffman, *Race Traits and Tendencies*.

9 Ibid., v–vi.

10 Ibid., v.

11 Ibid., viii.

12 For an exemplar, see Nobels, *Shades of Citizenship*.

13 Hoffman, *Race Traits and Tendencies*, 2.
14 Kerr, *Inebriety or Narcomania*, 131. Concerning the Jews, Kerr held exactly the opposite view, seeing them as genetically predisposed to temperance: "This extraordinary people has, amid wondrous vicissitudes, preserved a variety of distinctive characteristics; and I cannot help thinking that some inherited racial power of control as well as some inherited racial insusceptibility to narcotism, strengthened and confirmed by the practice of various hygienic habits, has been the main reason for their superior temperance" (146). See Gilman, "The Problem with Purim."
15 Robert Reyburn, *Type of Disease among Freed People*, 14, cited from Hoffman, *Race Traits and Tendencies*, 123–124.
16 Hoffman, *Race Traits and Tendencies*, 126.
17 Ibid., 128.
18 Ibid., 133.
19 Ibid., 143–144.
20 Bruce, *The Plantation Negro as a Free Man*, cited from Hoffman, 143.
21 Hoffman, *Race Traits and Tendencies*, 182.
22 Ibid., 184.
23 Ibid., 192.
24 Calkins, "Review of *Race Traits and Tendencies*," 754ff.
25 Ibid., 756.
26 Dawson, "Review of Race Traits and Tendencies of the American Negro."
27 O'Malley, "Psychoses in the Colored Race"; Tillinghast, "The Negro in Africa and America."
28 Du Bois left Atlanta University to become director of publications and research for the NAACP in New York, where he founded the organization's monthly magazine, *The Crisis*. Though he would not physically return to Atlanta University until 1934, where he would then chair their sociology department, Du Bois remained affiliated with the Atlanta University sociological incubator until 1914.
29 We are aware this may be a contentious statement, as the Chicago School under Albion Small and, later, Robert Park, would produce many important works on black life in America. However, no research center in the United States, including Chicago, did so with such consistency and clarity, and a focus *distinctly* on black Americans, as the Atlanta University center. According to Du Bois himself: "For twenty years Atlanta University was the only institution in the world that was making systematic and scientific study of the Negro race . . . it is fair to say that between 1910 and 1925 no book on the American Negro was written that was not at least in part based upon our studies in Atlanta University." See Du Bois, "The Atlanta University Studies of Social Conditions among Negroes."
30 Du Bois, "*Race Traits and Tendencies*" (review), 128ff.
31 Ibid., 132.
32 Ibid., 133.
33 Ibid.
34 "Social and Physical Condition of Negroes in Cities," 23ff.

35 Du Bois, *The Philadelphia Negro*, 148.

36 Ibid., 282.

37 Ibid., 284.

38 See Du Bois, "The Development of a People":

Any one looking the problem squarely in the face might conclude that it was un-just to expect progress, or the signs of progress, until many generations had gone by. Indeed, we must not forget that those people who claimed to know the Negro best, freely and confidently predicted during the abolition controversy—

1. That free Negroes would not, and could not, work effectively.

2. That the freedman who did work, would not save.

3. That it was impossible to educate Negroes.

4. That no members of the race gave signs of ability and leadership.

5. That the race was morally degenerate.

Not only was this said, it was sincerely and passionately believed, by honor-able men who, with their forefathers, had lived with the Negro three hundred years. And yet to-day the Negro in one generation forms the chief laboring force of the most rapidly developing part of the land. He owns twelve million acres of land, two hundred and fifty million dollars worth of farm property, and controls as owner or renter five hundred millions. Nearly three-fifths of the Negroes have learned to read and write. An increasing number have given evidence of ability and thoughtfulness—not, to be sure, of transcendent genius, but of integrity, large knowledge and common-sense. And finally there can be to-day no reasonable dispute but that the number of efficient, law-abiding and morally upright black people in this land is far larger than it ever was before, and is daily growing. (308–309)

Du Bois, ed., "Some Notes on Negro Crime": "[H]onest, intelligent, law-abiding black men are safer neighbors than ignorant, underpaid serfs, because it is the latter class that breeds dangerous crime" (66). Du Bois, ed., "The Health and Physique of the American Negro": "[There is no] adequate scientific war-rant for the assumption that the Negro race is inferior to other races in physical build or vitality. The present differences in mortality seem to be sufficiently explained by conditions of life; and physical measurements prove the Negro a normal human being capable of average human accomplishments" (110).

39 Dubois, *The Philadelphia Negro*, xiii.

40 Du Bois, *The Autobiography*, 175.

41 Bornstein, "W. E. B. Du Bois and the Jews."

42 Du Bois, *The Soul of Black Folks*, 12.

43 Ian Hacking, "Double Consciousness in Britain: 1815–1975," *Dissociation* 3 (1991): 134–146.

44 Appiah, *Lines of Descent*.

45 Ibid., 175.

46 Ibid., 171.

47 Ibid., 175.

48 Du Bois, "The Socialism of German Socialists," 192.
49 McKee, *Sociology and the Race Problem*, 29.
50 Ibid., 33.
51 Hinkle, *Founding Theory of American Sociology*, 300ff.
52 Glick, "Types Distinct from Our Own."
53 Adams, *The Philosophical Roots of Anthropology*, 303.
54 Boas, *Anthropology and Modern Life*, 34.
55 Park, *Race and Culture*. These perspectives are outlined in earlier works by Park, as well as the works of his students. *Race and Culture* represents an edited collection compiled by Everett C. Hughes, a former student of Park's. To truly understand Park's influence on the discipline, one should give less weight to his publication record, which, comparatively, is rather light. Instead, his perspective was often expressed in the introductions, prefaces, and forewords to his students' doctoral dissertations.
56 McKee, *Sociology and the Race Problem*, 111, See Park, *Race and Culture*, 138–153; Adams, *Interracial Marriage in Hawaii*.
57 Park, "Human Migration and the Marginal Man," 882ff.
58 Ibid., 882.
59 Ibid., 888.
60 Park, "Mentality of Racial Hybrids," 540ff.
61 Ibid., 542–547.
62 Hankins, *The Racial Bias of Civilization*, 347; cited from Teo, "The Historical Problematization of 'Mixed-Race,'" 92.
63 Reuter, "The Superiority of the Mulatto," *American Journal of Sociology*, 23 (1917): 83–106; cited from Teo, "The Historical Problematization of 'Mixed-Race,'" 92.
64 Reuter, "The Superiority of the Mulatto"; cited from Teo, 93.
65 Reuter, *The American Race Problem*, 17.
66 Ellwood, *Sociology and Modern Social Problems*, 262; see also McKee, *Sociology and the Race Problem*, 128.
67 The latter journal would change its name in 1954 to the current *Annals of Human Genetics*, a change reflecting a shift in perspective on the role of eugenics and scientific racism that the next chapter will touch upon.
68 Dawson, "Psychic Rudiments and Morality."
69 Ibid., 193.
70 Ibid., 199.
71 Mezes, "Review of Psychic Rudiments and Morality."
72 Bailey, "A Contribution to the Mental Pathology of Races."
73 Ibid., 188–189.
74 Ibid., 190.
75 Green, "Manic-Depressive Psychosis in the Negro," 619ff.
76 Green, "Psychoses among Negroes—A Comparative Study," 707ff. Also see Carter, *The Influence of Race and Racial Identity in Psychotherapy* 35.
77 Ferguson, "The Psychology of the Negro," 124ff.

78 Bevis, "Psychological Traits of the Southern Negro," 76ff.
79 Ibid., 74.
80 Ibid., 70; see also Babcock, "The Colored Insane."
81 Bevis, "Psychological Traits of the Southern Negro," 70.
82 Foster, "Paresis in the Negro," 632ff.
83 Mays, "Human Slavery as a Prevention of Pulmonary Consumption," 192ff.
84 Ibid., 192.
85 Ibid., 193.
86 Ibid., 194.
87 Samelson, "From 'Race Psychology' to 'Studies in Prejudice.'"
88 Hoffman, *Unwanted Mexican Americans in the Great Depression.*
89 Roger Daniels, Taylor, and Kitano, eds., *Japanese Americans.*
90 Richards, *Race, Racism, and Psychology,* xiv.
91 Taylor, "Remarks on the Health of the Colored People," 162.
92 Ibid.
93 See, for example, Feagin, *Systemic Racism*; and Feagin, *The White Racial Frame*; Bonilla-Silva, *Racism without Racists.*
94 Smith, "Mental Hygiene and the American Negro," 4–5.
95 Ibid., 5.
96 Ibid., 6.
97 Ibid. See also White, "Social Significance of Mental Disease," 877.
98 Brunner, "The Negro Health Problem in Southern Cities," 184.
99 Smith, "Mental Hygiene and the American Negro," 9.
100 Johnson and Bond, "The Investigation of Racial Differences," 337.
101 Dearborn and Long, "The Physical and Mental Abilities of the American Negro," 546.
102 See, for example, another contribution to the special issue: Smith, "A New Approach."
103 Rosenthal, "Racial Differences in the Incidence of Mental Disease," 493.
104 Thompson, "The Conclusions of Scientists Relative to Racial Differences."
105 Yoder, "Present Status of the Question of Racial Differences."
106 Dollard, *Class and Caste in a Southern Town.* For summaries and critiques of this work, see Richards, *Race, Racism, and Psychology*; McKee, *Sociology and the Race Problem.*
107 Richards, *Race, Racism, and Psychology,* 156; McKee, *Sociology and the Race Problem,* 160.
108 Richards, *Race, Racism, and Psychology,* 157.

CHAPTER 3. HATRED AND THE CROWD

1 Sighele, *La Folla delinquente.* See Mitchell, *Contagious Metaphor,* 71–74.
2 See Gilman, "Sexology, Psychoanalysis and Degeneration."
3 Tarde, "Les crimes des foules" and "Foules et sectes au point de vue criminal." See also his *L'opinion et la foule.*

4   Simmel, "The Metropolis and Mental Life" and "The Social and the Individual Level"; Borch, "Between Destructiveness and Vitalism."

5   Nye, *The Origins of Crowd Psychology*, 89ff.

6   Le Bon, *The Crowd*, 16, 17.

7   Gonen, *The Roots of Nazi Psychology*, 92–93.

8   Le Bon, *The Crowd*, 14–15.

9   Ibid., 39.

10 Ibid., 8.

11 See Barrows, *Distorting Mirrors*; McClelland, *The Crowd and the Mob*; Jonsson, *A Brief History of the Masses: Three Revolutions* and *Crowds and Democracy: The Idea and Image of the Masses from Revolution to Fascism.*

12 See, for example, Ratner-Rosenhagen, *American Nietzsche.*

13 Nietzsche, *The Will to Power*, 287. On the impact of the image of Nietzsche on the idea of contagious madness in the United States and in Germany see Gilman, "The Nietzsche Murder Case."

14 George Brandes, *Friedrich Nietzsche*, 9.

15 See Trotter, "Herd Instinct and Its Bearing on the Psychology of Civilized Man" and "Sociological Application of the Psychology of Herd Instinct." His definitive study was *Instincts of the Herd in Peace and War* (1916).

16 Wallace, *War and the Image of Germany*, 36–37; Pulzer, "Vorbild, Rivale und Unmensch"; Remus, *Germanophobia, Europhobia, Xenophobia.*

17 Trotter, *Instincts of the Herd in Peace and War*, 156.

18 Ibid., 156–157.

19 Ibid., 163.

20 Ibid., 176–177.

21 Ibid., 179.

22 Ibid., 59–60.

23 McDougall, *The Group Mind*, 38.

24 Ibid., 146.

25 Trotter, *Instincts of the Herd in Peace and War*, 70–71.

26 McDougall, *The Group Mind*, viii.

27 Freud, *Standard Edition of the Complete Psychological Works*, 18:117. Hereafter cited as *SE.*

28 Hyslop, *The Borderland*, 208.

29 Ibid., 225.

30 Dicks, *Clinical Studies in Psychopathology.*

31 See the discussion in Gilman, *Jewish Self-Hatred*, 219–221.

32 Gustav Jahoda, *Crossroads between Culture and Mind: Continuities and Change in Theories of Human Nature* (Cambridge, MA: Harvard University Press, 1993), 145.

33 Andrew D. Evans, *Anthropology at War: World War I and the Science of Race in Germany* (Chicago: University of Chicago Press, 2010).

34 Wundt, *Die Nationen und ihre Philosophie*. The quotes are taken from Baumgarten-Tramer, "German Psychologists and Recent Events." See also

Schwabe, *Wissenschaft und Kriegsmoral*; Danziger, "Origins and Basic Principles of Wundt's *Völkerpsychologie*."

35 Wundt, *Die Nationen und ihre Philosophie*, 117–119.

36 Ibid., 131–132.

37 Ibid., 144.

38 Scheler, *Der Genius des Krieges*.

39 Ibid., 79.

40 Ibid., 77–78.

41 Ibid., 170.

42 Ibid., 223.

43 Scheler, *Die Ursachen des Deutschenhasses*.

44 Ibid., 131.

45 Ibid., 138, 143.

46 Ibid., 153–158, 179.

47 Students of history and/or Freud may recall he was initially a strong supporter of the war as a citizen of the Imperial Austro-Hungarian state; only at the end of the war did his views shifted. As a citizen of the new and liberal Austrian Republic in the early 1920s, his views on the crowd continued to vacillate.

48 Freud, *SE* 18:69. In the 1920s there was some limited interest in antisemitism as a group phenomenon; see F. (Peretz) Bernstein, *Der Antisemitismus als Gruppenerscheinung: Versuch einer Soziologie des Judenhasses* (Berlin: Jüdischer Verlag, 1925), 81–134. Such an approach became more widely of interest, however, only in the early 1930s.

49 Ibid., 128.

50 Gilman, *Freud, Race, and Gender*.

51 Ibid., 100.

52 Barkan, *Retreat of Scientific Racism*; Duster, *Backdoor to Eugenics*.

53 Ludmerer, "American Geneticists and the Eugenics Movement," 352.

54 As recently as 2013, for example, Paul Campos, in *Time*, was commenting on the illegal sterilization of 148 women in California prisons. See Campos, "Eugenics Are Alive and Well." And, in 2012, University of Washington scientists were busy mapping entire genome of a fetus, which holds the promise of "herald[ing] an era in which parents might find it easier to know the complete DNA blueprint" of unborn children, including genetic diseases. See Pollack, "DNA Blueprint for Fetus"; also Douthat, "Eugenics, Past and Future."

55 Zenderland, *Measuring Minds*.

56 Benjamin, "The Birth of American Intelligence Testing."

57 Goddard, "The Binet and Simon Tests of Intellectual Capacity" and "The Grading of Backward Children."

58 Cravens, *Before Head Start*.

59 Goddard, *The Kallikak Family*.

60 Gould, *The Mismeasure of Man*.

61 Ibid., 166.

62 "Insanity and the Immigrant," *American Israelite* (November 28, 1912): 1.
63 Gibson and Lennon, *Historical Census Statistics*; American Jewish Historical Society, *American Jewish Desk Reference*.
64 Coolidge, *First Annual Message*.
65 Tchenm and Yeats, eds., *Yellow Peril!*
66 "Flashing Light Sign Used with Small Exhibits," *Philosophical Society*.
67 Jacobson, *Whiteness of a Different Color*; Roediger, *Working toward Whiteness*; Goldstein, *The Price of Whiteness*.
68 Pascoe, "Miscegenation Law"; Pascoe, *What Comes Naturally*.
69 Pascoe, "Miscegenation Law," 50.
70 Fowler, *Northern Attitudes towards Interracial Marriage*.
71 Grossberg, "Guarding the Altar."
72 Virginia Senate Bill 219, Racial Integrity Act.
73 Black, *War against the Weak*, 156.
74 Reilly, *The Surgical Solution*.
75 Trent, *Inventing the Feeble Mind*.
76 *Buck v. Bell* 274 (U.S. 200 1927).
77 Lombardo, *Three Generations, No Imbeciles*.
78 Josefson, "Oregon Governor Apologies."
79 Weiss, "Human Genetics and Politics."
80 Low, *Jews in the Eyes of the Germans*, 361.
81 Busch, *Graf Bismarck* I: 452 (January 10, 1871).
82 Tal, *Christians and Jews in the "Second Reich" (1870–1914)*, 223.
83 Efron, *Defenders of the Race*, 120–129; Rogoff, "Is the Jew White?," 206.
84 Ruppin, *The Jews of Today*, 227–228.
85 Ruppin, *Tagebuch*, cited by Bloom, *Arthur Ruppin*, 57.
86 Weindling, "Weimar Eugenics."
87 Kühl, *The Nazi Connection*, 40–42.
88 All references to Nazi documents are from Rabinbach and Gilman, eds., *The Third Reich Sourcebook*, here 338.
89 Ibid., 329.
90 Ibid., 209–210.
91 Koonz, *Mothers in the Fatherland*; Proctor, *Racial Hygiene*; Bridenthal, Grossmann, and Kaplan, *When Biology Became Destiny*; Stoltzfus, *Resistance of the Heart*.
92 Cited by Rabinbach and Gilman, *The Third Reich Sourcebook*, 392–393.
93 Friedlander, *The Origins of Nazi Genocide*.
94 Massin, "Anthropologie und Humangenetik im Nationalsozialismus," 23.
95 Freud, *SE* 23:91.
96 Assmann, *Moses the Egyptian*, 144–167.
97 Freud, *SE* 10:36. On the meaning given circumcision and its relationship to antisemitism within the psychoanalytic tradition, see Georges Maranz, "Les conséquence de la circoncision: Essai d'explication psychanalytique de

l'antisémitisme," *Psyché-Paris* 2 (1947): 731–745; B. Grunberger, "Circoncision et l'antisémitisme: En marge d'un article de Georges Maranz," *Psyché-Paris* 2 (1947): 1221–1228; Jules Glenn, "Circumcision and Anti-Semitism," *Psychoanalytic Quarterly* 29 (1960): 395–999.

98 Bennett and Peglau, "Nazi Denaturalization of German Emigrants," 44.

99 Wilhelm Reich, *Massenpsychologie des Faschismus: zur Sexualökonomie der politischen Reaktion und zur proletarischen Sexualpolitik* (Copenhagen: Verlag für Sexualpolitik, 1933). All quotations are from the translation: Reich, *Mass Psychology of Fascism*, here 88.

100 Reich, "Wilhelm Reich and Anna Freud."

101 Nitzschke, "Psychoanalyse im Nationalsozialismus."

102 Myron Sharaf, *Fury on Earth*, 163.

103 Reich, *Mass Psychology of Fascism*, 3.

104 Reich, *Mass Psychology of Fascism*, 294.

105 Freud, *SE* 21: 112.

106 Sharaf, *Fury on Earth*, 201.

107 Reich, *Mass Psychology of Fascism*, 294.

108 Ibid., 64.

109 Ibid., x.

110 Ibid., xv.

111 Perhaps in response to his being denounced as a wild analyst and a wild sociologist in Siegfried Bernfeld's "Die kommunistische Diskussion um die Psychoanalyse und Reichs 'Widerlegung des Todestriebhypothese,'" *Internationale Zeitschrift für Psychoanalyse* 18 (1932): 352–385.

112 Rabinbach, "Politicization of Reich," 91.

113 Reich, *Mass Psychology of Fascism*, 10.

114 Ibid., 13.

115 Ibid., 51.

116 "Joseph Sandler in Conversation with Anna Freud, Discussions in the Hampstead Index on *The Ego and the Mechanisms of Defence*: IV. The Mechanisms of Defence, Part 1," *Bulletin of the Anna Freud Centre* 4 (1981): 151–199, here 155. On the present status of these defense mechanisms, see McWilliams, "Primary (Primitive) Defensive Processes."

117 August Aichhorn, *Verwahrloste Jugend: Die Psychoanalyse in der Fürsorgeerziehung. Zehn Vorträge zur ersten Einführung.* (Vienna: Internationaler Psychoanalytischer Verlag, 1925). All quotations are from the translation: Aichhorn, *Wayward Youth*.

118 Aichhorn, *Wayward Youth*, 220.

119 Ibid., 5.

120 Ibid.

121 Ibid., 7.

122 Ibid., 30.

123 Freud, *Ego and the Mechanism of Defense*, 109ff.

124 Ibid., 119.

125 Ibid.

126 Cited by Appignanesi and Forrester, *Freud's Women*, 294.

127 "Joseph Sandler in Conversation with Anna Freud," 250.

128 Ibid.

129 Gilman, *Jewish Self-Hatred*. See, more recently, Reitter, *On the Origins of Jewish Self-Hatred*.

130 Wassermann, *My Life as German and Jew*, 156.

131 Ibid., 118–119.

132 Lewisohn, "Where Next . . ."

133 Chomsky, "The Synagogue and the School."

134 Theodor Reik, "Der Angstangriff," *Internationale Zeitschrift für Psychoanalyse* 23 (1937) 306–313. The translation is from Reik, "Aggression from Anxiety," 10.

135 Freud, "Comments on Aggression."

136 The psychiatric literature on obsessions does not cover racism, though Morton Prince's classic discussion of obsession reappears in his analysis of the obsessional quality in the Germans during the war; see his *The Psychology of the Kaiser* (1915) and *The American versus The German View of the War* (1915). Lennard Davis in his critical study *Obsessions* (2008) does not discuss racism at all.

137 Cartwright, "Contemporary Social Psychology in Historical Perspective," 84.

138 Lewin's collaborative relations with the Frankfurt School prior to Hitler's ascension to power led to him being asked to help guide the *Studies in Prejudice* series in 1944. While working on commissioning the series with the American Jewish Committee, Lewin was also collaborating with the state of Connecticut's Interracial Commission to set up "change experiment" workshops meant to combat religious and racial prejudices. These "change experiments" are considered the building blocks to what is contemporarily known as "sensitivity training." See Lasch-Quinn, *Race Experts*.

139 Lewin, "Self-Hatred among Jews. See also Marrow, *The Practical Theorist*; Schellenberg, *Masters of Social Psychology*; Stivers and Wheelan, eds., *The Lewin Legacy*.

140 Lewin, "Self-Hatred among Jews," 187.

141 Ibid.

142 This is a counterreading to that of Glenn, "The Vogue of Jewish Self-Hatred."

143 Lewin, "Self-Hatred among Jews," 188–189.

144 Ibid., 197–198.

145 Ibid., 198.

146 Ibid., 189.

147 Ibid., 198.

148 Horney, *Neurosis and Human Growth*, 20–23.

149 "Hitler Convicted of 'Crime against Civilization,'" *American Israelite*.

150 "Hitlerism Called Psychic Epidemic," *New York Times*.

151 Richard J. Evans, *The Third Reich in History and Memory* (Oxford: Oxford University Press, 2015), 142.

152 Pick, *The Pursuit of the Nazi Mind*.

153 See Gertzman, *Samuel Roth*.

154 Barzun, *Race*, 284.

155 Ibid., 284.

156 Rees, ed., *The Case of Rudolf Hess*, xiii.

157 We are noting here that these scientists were "Jewish," at least by Nazi legal terms, whether they saw themselves as Jewish or not.

158 Fromm, *Escape from Freedom*.

159 Ibid., 77, 92.

160 Ibid., 270–272.

161 Ibid., 207–208.

162 Erikson, "On Nazi Mentality."

163 Brickner, *Is Germany Incurable?*

164 See Davidoff, "Richard Brickner, M.D." "His one assay into semi-popular literature took the form of a book entitled *Is Germany Incurable?* While many people took issue with his conclusions and the book aroused a considerable amount of controversy, it served to stimulate a good deal of thinking about the psychology of the German people, which permitted the rise of a Hitler" (192).

165 Strecker, *Beyond the Clinical Frontiers*, 91. See Gerhardt, "The Medical Meaning of Re-Education for Germany."

166 Alexander, *Our Age of Unreason*, 520.

167 Gilkeson, *Anthropologists and the Rediscovery of America*, 137ff.

168 Brickner, *Is Germany Incurable?*, 234.

169 Ibid., 30.

170 Ibid., 93.

171 Ibid., 112.

172 Ibid., 93.

173 Ibid., 117.

174 Ibid., 163.

175 Ibid., 169.

176 Ibid., 175.

177 Ibid., 183.

178 Ibid., 184.

179 Ibid., 195.

180 Ibid., 196–197.

181 Ibid., 229–230.

182 Ibid., 231.

183 Fromm, "What Shall We Do with Germany?," 10.

184 Neiman, *Evil in Modern Thought*, 8–9.

185 Ibid., 251.

CHAPTER 4. THE HOLOCAUST AND POST-WAR THEORIES OF
ANTISEMITISM AND RACISM

1 Bettelheim, *The Informed Heart.*
2 Bettelheim, Testimony from Nuremberg Tribunal. There is a long and rather tedious debate about Bettelheim's veracity in regard to his therapeutic methods, theories, and even his biography that has colored much of the discussion of his importance as a public intellectual during the post-war period. See Pollak, *The Creation of Dr. B.* This is not reflected in this discussion. More relevant are Fisher, *Bettelheim*; Marcus, *Autonomy in the Extreme Situation.*
3 Here one can add the study by Bettelheim's fellow inmate at Buchenwald the psychoanalyst Ernst Federn, "The Terror as a System."
4 Bettelheim, "Individual and Mass Behavior."
5 Bettelheim, *The Informed Heart*, 420.
6 Garwood, "The Holocaust and the Power of Powerlessness"; Leys, "Die 'Über-lebensschuld' im psychoanalytischen Diskurs."
7 Viktor Frankl's *Man's Search for Meaning* (translated by Ilse Lasch) was first published in English under a different title in 1959, *From Death-Camp to Existentialism*; it originally appeared in 1946 as . . . *trotzdem Ja zum Leben sagen: Ein Psycholog erlebt das Konzentrationslager.* See Redsand, *Viktor Frankl*, 88–89.
8 Bettelheim, *The Informed Heart*, 419.
9 Ibid., 448.
10 Ibid., 425–426.
11 Bettelheim, *Freud's Vienna*, 109.
12 Christian Fleck and Albert Müller, "Bruno Bettelheim and the Concentration Camps," *Journal of the History of the Behavioral Sciences* 33 (1997): 1–37.
13 Sarnoff, "Identification with the Aggressor." There are many more similar studies in the time: Davidson, "An Interpretation of Antisemitism" (arguing that it is the identification with the Jew that reminds the antisemite 'continuously of his matriarchal dependence"); Loeblowitz-Lennard, "The Jew as Symbol" (arguing that it is Oedipal transference); Brenner, "Some Psychoanalytic Speculations on Antisemitism" (arguing an analogy between American white identification with the Negro and antisemite's identification with the Jew).
14 Bettelheim, *The Informed Heart*, 152.
15 Bettelheim, *Surviving*, 302.
16 Bettelheim, *The Informed Heart*, 157.
17 "Socially Fit—Asocial—Antisocial," *The Third Reich Sourcebook*, 343.
18 Bettelheim, *The Informed Heart*, 425.
19 Ibid., 447.
20 Bettelheim, "Eichmann, the System, the Victims," 25.
21 Bondy, "Problems of Internment Camps," 455.
22 Ibid., 457.
23 Ibid.

24 Bettelheim and Janowitz, *Dynamics of Prejudice*, 246. The book, originally published in 1950, was released in a retitled edition, prefaced with a long overview of the more recent social science literature on the psychology of prejudice, as *Social Change and Prejudice* (New York: Free Press of Glencoe, 1960).
25 Peck solidified his position as the defender of the outsider with this film, and it became part of the reason he was later cast as Atticus Finch in the 1962 film of Harper Lee's *To Kill a Mockingbird*.
26 Goldstein, *The Price of Whiteness*.
27 Bettelheim and Janowitz, *Dynamics of Prejudice*, 247
28 Reich, *The Mass Psychology of Fascism*, 53.
29 Richards, *Race, Racism and Psychology*, 269.
30 Bettelheim and Janowitz, *Dynamics of Prejudice*, 276.
31 Evans, ed., *The Making of Social Psychology*, 188.
32 Perry, *Behind the Shock Machine*.
33 Fermaglich, *American Dreams and Nazi Nightmares*, 88.
34 Blass, "The Milgram Paradigm after 35 Years," 955–956.
35 Katz, "The Jewish Chronic Disease Hospital Case."
36 "Hospital Accused on Cancer Study," *New York Times*; "State Broadens Cancer Inquiry," *New York Times*; "Test on Cancer to Need Consent," *New York Times*; "Many Scientific Experts Condemn Ethics of Cancer Injection," *New York Times*; "Experimental Ethics," *Time*.
37 On this debate see Krell and Sherman, *Medical and Psychological Effects of Concentration Camps*; Leys, *From Guilt to Shame*.
38 See Gilman, *Jurek Becker*, 26–33.
39 Bonhoeffer, "Beurteilung, Begutachtung und Rechtsprechung."
40 One of the authors has argued, separately, that the prototype for racialization and racial formation in the Western hemisphere was the Jewish body. See Thomas, "The Racial Formation of Medieval Jews."
41 Pross, *Paying for the Past*, 84ff. See also Durst, "Emotional Wounds That Never Heal."
42 Bienenfeld, "Justice, Aggression and Eros," 424.
43 Ibid., 423–424.
44 Kelsen, *Society and Nature*.
45 Rosenberg, *A Brief Stop on the Road from Auschwitz*, 234.
46 Tas, "Psychical Disorders." See Fuechtner, *Berlin Psychoanalytic*, 183.
47 Tas, "Psychical Disorders," 681.
48 Ibid., 684.
49 Ibid., 689.
50 Eissler, "Die Ermordung wie vieler seiner Kinder."
51 Leys, *Trauma*, 223–224.
52 Pross, *Paying for the Past*, 84ff.
53 Jones and Wessely, *Shell Shock to PTSD*.

54 William Helmreich, *Against All Odds: Holocaust Survivors and the Successful Lives They Made in America* (New York: Simon & Schuster, 1992), 221. See Judith M. Gerson and Diane L. Wolf, eds., *Sociology Confronts the Holocaust: Memories and Identities in Jewish Diasporas* (Durham, NC: Duke University Press, 2007).

55 Shoshana Feldman and Dori Laub, *Testimony: Crises of Witnessing in Literature, Psychoanalysis, and History* (New York: Routledge, 1992).

56 Boaz Kahana, Zev Harel, and Eva Kahana, "Predictors of Psychological Well-Being among Survivors of the Holocaust," in *Human Adaptation to Extreme Stress*, ed. John Preston Wilson, Zev Harel, and Boaz Kahana (New York: Plenum, 1988), 171–192. See also Zev Harel, Eva Kahana, Boaz Kahana, *Holocaust Survivors and Immigrants: Late Life Adaptations* (New York: Springer, 2005).

57 Robert Jay Lifton, *Death in Life: Survivors of Hiroshima* (New York: Random House, 1967), 508–509.

58 Gilman, *Freud, Race, and Gender*, 12–48.

59 Goldstein, *Capturing the German Eye*.

60 Freud, *SE* 19:271.

61 McGranahan and Janowitz, "Studies of German Youth."

62 Ibid., 3.

63 Ibid., 4.

64 Ibid., 5.

65 Ibid., 6.

66 Ibid., 12.

67 Jaspers, *General Psychopathology* II, 670.

68 Karl Jaspers, *Die Schuldfrage* (Heidelberg: Lambert Schneider, 1946). Quotations from the translation: *The Question of German Guilt*, here 34–35.

69 Jaspers, *The Question of German Guilt*, 10.

70 Weber, ed., *Max Weber*, 662. See also Rabinbach, "The German as Pariah."

71 Arendt, "On the Nature of Totalitarianism," 339.

72 Hannah Arendt, *The Jew as Pariah*, ed. Ron H. Feldman. (New York: Grove Press, 1978).

73 Von Klemperer, *German Resistance against Hitler*, 2.

74 Norberg, "Perspectives on Postwar Silence."

75 Mitscherlich and Mitscherlich, *Die Unfähigkeit zu trauern*; Mitscherlich and Mitscherlich, *The Inability to Mourn*. See Freimüller, ed., *Psychoanalyse und Protest*.

76 Mitscherlich, *Das Diktat der Menschenverachtung*.

77 Again we are not arguing whether this is true, only that this thesis captured the moment and became the focus of a national (indeed an international) debate about the psychopathology of the perpetrators. Tobias Freimüller, *Alexander Mitscherlich*, 305–307.

78 Ibid., 26.

79 Mitscherlich and Mitscherlich, *Die Unfähigkeit zu trauern*, 13.

80 Ibid., 63.

81 Ibid., 22.

82 Ibid., 27.

83 Ibid., 65.

84 Ibid., 113, 227.

85 Ibid., 228.

86 Ibid., 118.

87 Ibid., 114.

88 Anthony D. Kauders, "Drives in Dispute: The West German Student Movement, Psychoanalysis, and the Search for a New Emotional Order, 1967–1971," *Central European History* 44 (2011): 711–731.

89 Klaus Theweleit, *Männerphantasien* (Frankfurt am Main: Roter Stern, 1977); translated as Theweleit, *Male Fantasies*.

90 Mitscherlich-Nielsen, "Antisemitism—A Male Disorder?"

91 Herzog, *Sex after Fascism*.

92 Goldhagen, *Hitler's Willing Executioners*, 12.

93 Ibid., 14.

94 Newman, "'Social-Psychological' Account of Perpetrator Behavior?"

95 Goldhagen, *Hitler's Willing Executioners*, 322–323.

96 Ibid., 183. See also Herbert, "Academic and Public Discourses on the Holocaust"; Eley, "Ordinary Germans, Nazism, and Judeocide"; LaCapra, "Perpetrators and Victims."

97 Goldhagen, *Hitler's Willing Executioners*, 34.

98 Ibid., 397, 450, 140.

99 Ibid., 455.

100 Ibid., 398–399.

101 Ibid., 63.

102 Ibid., 68.

103 Ibid., 251.

104 Daniel J. Goldhagen, "Presentation on *Hitler's Willing Executioners*," in "The 'Willing Executioners'/"Ordinary Men" Debate," Daniel J. Goldhagen, Christopher R. Browning and Leon Wieseltier (with an introduction by Michael Berenbaum), *United States Holocaust Memorial Museum* (April 8, 1996), http://www.ushmm.org/m/pdfs/Publication_OP_1996-01.pdf. The quotation here is from 1–2.

105 Ibid., 2.

106 Ibid., 9.

107 Aschheim, "Archetypes and the German-Jewish Dialogue," 248–249.

CHAPTER 5. RACE AND MADNESS IN MID-TWENTIETH-CENTURY AMERICA AND BEYOND

1 Jerome and Taylor, eds., *Einstein on Race and Racism*, 9–20.

2 Ibid., 88.

3 Jackson, *Social Scientists for Social Justice*, 34.

4 Porter, *Black Child, White Child*, 22.
5 Lasker, "How to Correct Anti-Semitism among Jewish Children."
6 Davis and Dollard, *Children of Bondage*. See Scott, *Contempt and Pity*.
7 McKee, *Sociology and the Race Problem*; Steinberg, *Race Relations*.
8 Bridges, "Racial Identity Development"; Pickren, Dewsbury, and Wertheimer. *Portraits of Pioneers*, 141–144.
9 Horowitz and Horowitz, "Development of Social Attitudes in Children."
10 Ibid., 301.
11 Ibid., 308.
12 Gilman, *Seeing the Insane*.
13 Horowitz and Horowitz, "Development of Social Attitudes in Children," 312–313.
14 Horowitz and Murphy, "Projective Methods."
15 Ibid., 133.
16 Ibid., 134.
17 Horowitz, "Racial Aspects of Self-identification."
18 Ibid.
19 Jackson, *Gunnar Myrdal and America's Conscience*.
20 Myrdal, *An American Dilemma*, appendix 5, 1073–1078.
21 Ibid., 879–907.
22 Ibid., 76.
23 Ibid., 75.
24 Ibid., 77.
25 Aptheker, "The Negro People in America." See also Jackson, "The American Creed from a Swedish Perspective."
26 Myrdal, *An American Dilemma*, 61.
27 Ibid., 973.
28 LaCapra, *Emile Durkheim*; Kushner, *American Suicide*, 6–9.
29 Myrdal, *An American Dilemma*, 980.
30 Ibid., 1342.
31 Washington, *Up from Slavery*, 9–10.
32 Pietikäinen, *Madness: A History*, 93.
33 Myrdal, *An American Dilemma*, 981.
34 Baltzell, *The Protestant Establishment*, 168–170.
35 Boas, "Psychological Problems in Anthropology," 375.
36 Brickman, *Aboriginal Populations in the Mind*, 56, 222.
37 Blanchette, "Citizens and Savages," 289–302.
38 Havinghurst and Hilkevitch, "The Intelligence of Indian Children," 420.
39 Ibid., 432–433.
40 Havinghurst, Gunther, and Pratt, "Environment and the Draw a Man Test," 54.
41 Rigdon, *The Culture Facade*, 27.
42 Clark argues in 1954, the year of *Brown v. Board of Education*, that both anti-semitism and anti-black racism demand alliance building to form a bulwark for American democracy. See Kenneth B. Clark, "Jews in Contemporary America:

Problems in Identification," *Jewish Social Services Quarterly* 31 (1954): 12–22, as well as the discussion of this in Eric J. Sundquist, *Strangers in the Land: Blacks, Jews, Post-Holocaust America* (Cambridge, MA: Belknap Press/Harvard University Press), 53.

43 Stoetzler, ed., *Antisemitism and the Constitution of Sociology*; Amos Morris-Reich, *The Quest for Jewish Assimilation in Modern Social Science* (New York: Routledge, 2008).

44 Clark and Clark, "Racial Identification and Preference," 611.

45 Kenneth B. Clark and Mamie K. Clark, "Emotional Factors in Racial Identification and Preference in Negro Children," *Journal of Negro Education* 19 (1950): 341–350, here 348, 350.

46 Clark and Clark, "Segregation as a Factor"; Clark and Clark, "The Development of Consciousness of Self."

47 Cross, *Shades of Black*, 16–29.

48 Bernstein, *Racial Innocence*, 198, 239–240.

49 Clark and Clark, "Segregation as a Factor," 163.

50 See the recent monograph by Gabriel Mendes, *Under the Strain of Color* (2015).

51 Baldwin, *Notes of a Native Son*, 3. See Derek Charles Catsam, "Richard Wright and Black Resistance."

52 Doyle, "'A Fine New Child,'" 196. On Richard Wright and Frederick Wertham, see Zaretsky, *Political Freud*, 57–65.

53 Doyle, "'Where the Need Is Greatest,'" 751.

54 Kluger, *Simple Justice*, 444.

55 Ibid., 449.

56 Ibid., 440–441.

57 Beaty, *Frederic Wertham*.

58 Nyberg, *Seal of Approval*, 93.

59 *Brown v. Board of Education*, 347 U.S. 483. See, e.g., https://www.law.cornell.edu/supremecourt/text/347/483.

60 Wilkinson, *From Brown to Bakke*, 32.

61 For a recent discussion of the meanings of race in this context see also Feagin and Barnett, "Success and Failure."

62 Reprinted as Kenneth B. Clark, Isidor Chein, and Stuart W. Cook, "The Effects of Segregation and the Consequences of Desegregation. A (September 1952) Social Science Statement in the *Brown v. Board of Education of Topeka* Supreme Court Case," *American Psychologist* 59 (September 2004): 495–501.

63 Ibid., 496.

64 Ibid., 497.

65 Ibid.

66 Ibid., 498.

67 *Brown v. Board of Education*.

68 Again very much under the influence of the NAACP's mustering of the psychological literature. See Kenneth B. Clark, "Implications of Adlerian Theory for

an Understanding of Civil Rights Problems and Action," *Journal of Individual Psychology* 23 (1967): 181–190.

69 See Schiratzki, *Best Interests of the Child.*

70 Clark, *Prejudice and Your Child.*

71 "It should be noted that this is more about the image of the white child alongside the image of the black child, rather than actual physical bodies. Black children are taught to revere whiteness, not necessarily the white body, and black children are taught to fear/loathe/pity blackness as opposed to actual black bodies" (Clark, *Prejudice and Your Child*, 32). Gunnar Myrdal, referenced in Clark's book, explains how institutional segregation, a reality which forces blacks to value whiteness and see themselves as inferior, is antithetical to the "American Creed" (Myrdal, *An American Dilemma*, 579–581).

72 Clark, *Prejudice and Your Child*, 46.

73 Morrison, *Conversations with Toni Morrison*, 22. See De Lancey, "Sweetness, Madness, and Power."

74 See Strelka, "Politics and the Human Condition"; Müller-Funk, "Die Angst in der Kultur."

75 Kiss, "Does Mass Psychology Renaturalize Political Theory?"

76 See Jacobs, *The Frankfurt School.*

77 On the background to Simmel and interwar social theories, see Fuechtner, *Berlin Psychoanalytic*, 28–31.

78 "Social disease" was a euphemism for venereal disease coined by the New York public health official Prince Morrow at the beginning of the twentieth century, as such maladies were assumed to be transmitted by a "social evil," that is prostitution. See Brandt, *No Magic Bullet*, 32.

79 Wiggershaus, *Frankfurt School*, 358–359.

80 Simmel, "Anti-Semitism," 39–40.

81 Ibid., 47.

82 Ibid., 42–43.

83 Ibid., 46.

84 On Reich and the Frankfurt School as well as the legacy of Trotter, see Jaap van Ginneken, *Mass Movements in Darwinist, Freudian and Marxist Perspective: Trotter, Freud and Reich on War, Revolution and Reaction 1900–1933* (Apeldoorn: Het Spinhuis, 2007), 101–123.

85 Horkheimer, "Sociological Background," 6.

86 Ibid., 9.

87 Frenkel-Brunswik and Sanford, "Anti-Semitic Personality," 102.

88 Simmel, "Anti-Semitism," 66.

89 Adorno et al., *The Authoritarian Personality.*

90 Ibid., 39.

91 Ibid., 41.

92 Ibid., 52–53.

93 Ibid., 41.

94 On the question of the reliability of the TAT, see Phebe Cramer, "Future Directions for the Thematic Apperception Test," *Journal of Personality Assessment* 72 (1999): 74–92. There is a recent argument that abandoning the sort of visual testing used extensively in such studies in the 1930s and 1940s increases reliability; see N. Gruber and L. Kreuzpointner, "Measuring the Reliability of Picture Story Exercises Like the TAT," *PLOS ONE* 8 (2013), http://journals.plos.org/plosone.

95 Walter C. Kaufman, "Status, Authoritarianism, and Anti-Semitism," 381. See also Bergmann, ed., *Error without Trial*.

96 Martin, *The Dialectical Imagination*, 250.

97 Adorno et al., *The Authoritarian Personality*, 92–93.

98 McCandless and Holloway, "Race Prejudice and Intolerance of Ambiguity," 692.

99 Ackerman and Jahoda, *Anti-Semitism and Emotional Disorder*, 249.

100 One popular negative response to such a claim was a long essay by a neurologist at Temple University, Paul Sloane, "If We Would Prepare for the Struggle Ahead" (1948). He argues against "recent approaches to the problem of anti-Semitism [that study] the psychopathology of the anti-Semite. As the result a good deal has [admittedly] been learned about the psychological makeup of the anti-Semite, particularly that he is apt to be a maladjusted person who uses his hatred as an outlet and cloak for his personal frustrations. It was therefore natural to assume that anti-Semitism could be checked if personal maladjustments were eliminated. This was felt could be done by instituting a broad program of mental hygiene" (19). What Sloane argues is that such an approach is inherently fragmentary and that the self-worth of the Jewish community should not be dependent on the vagaries of the mental health of the antisemite.

101 Van Dijk, *Racism and Discourse*.

102 Silverman, ed., *Frantz Fanon's Black Skin, White Masks*, especially Bryan Cheyette, "Frantz Fanon and the Black-Jewish Imaginary," 74–99. See also Zaretsky, *Political Freud*, 68–75.

103 Wilder, *The French Imperial Nation-State*.

104 Judaken, *Jean-Paul Sartre and the Jewish Question*; Bernasconi, "The European Knows and Does Not Know," 100–111.

105 Fanon, *Black Skin, White Masks*, 17–18.

106 Ibid., 152–153. We should note that subsequent generations of scholars have built on Fanon and broadened the perspectives on where, and how, the root of, and identification with, the aggressor is located. One of the most fascinating revisions is in the emergent field of critical affect studies, where the links between Fanon's described *perception* of difference and the felt, or lived, corporeal effects of this perception of difference work in tandem to produce a *lived experience* of racialization. In her essay, "A Phenomenology of Hesitation: Interrupting Racializing Habits of Seeing," the philosopher Alia Al-Saji recalls Fanon's use of "affective ankylosis" (Fanon, *Black Skin, White Masks*, 121) to describe the condition of the

colonizer, but turns it around to describe the "rigidity, immobility, and numbing that characterize racializing affects" in the "epidermalized" bodies of racial Others. See Al-Saji, "A Phenomenology of Hesitation," 137, 140–141.

107 Fanon, *Black Skin, White Masks*, 151.
108 Bergner, "Who Is That Masked Woman?"
109 Sterba, "Some Psychological Factors."
110 Ibid., 411.
111 Ibid.
112 Ibid., 416.
113 Langlois, "The Bell Isle Bridge Incident."
114 Sterba, "Some Psychological Factors," 426.
115 Fanon, *The Wretched of the Earth*, 28ff.
116 Baugh, *French Hegel*, 93ff.
117 Crowley, "Albert Memmi."
118 Memmi, *The Colonizer and the Colonized*, 321–322.
119 Luhrmann, *The Good Parsi*, 11–12.
120 Wilkins's television interview is featured in "Awakenings (1954–1956)," the first episode of *Eyes on the Prize: America's Civil Rights Movement 1954–1985*, an award-winning fourteen-hour television series produced by Blackside (1987).
121 Marrow, "Psychology of Racial Prejudice," 63.
122 Steven J. Haggbloom et al., "The 100 Most Eminent Psychologists of the Twentieth Century," *Review of General Psychology* 6 (2002): 139–152.
123 See Marrow, *The Practical Theorist*.
124 Lasch-Quinn, *Race Experts*.
125 Rochefort, "Origins of the 'Third Psychiatric Revolution,'" 6ff.
126 Ibid., 11.
127 Hersch, "Social History, Mental Health," 749.
128 Ibid., 750.
129 Ibid., 751.
130 Ibid.
131 Rochefort, "Origins of the 'Third Psychiatric Revolution,'" 22.
132 Quoted in ibid., 23.
133 Kennedy, Remarks on Signing.
134 See Khanna, *Dark Continents*, 236–268.
135 See McCulloch, *Black Patients, White Psyches*.
136 Sachs, *Black Hamlet*, 177.
137 MacCrone, *Race Attitudes in South Africa*, 310. See Dubow, *Scientific Racism*, 197ff.
138 Sachs, *Black Hamlet*, 123.
139 Of obscure etymological origin, "Peruvian" was a derogatory term relating to the poor immigrants. See Mendelsohn and Shain, *The Jews in South Africa*, 45.
140 Sachs, *Black Hamlet*, 113.
141 Ibid., 170.

142 Ibid., 226.
143 Ibid., 130.
144 Ibid.
145 Ibid., 236.
146 Dubow, "Wulf Sachs's Black Hamlet," 523.
147 Edgar, ed., *An African American in South Africa*, 166.
148 Ibid., 189.
149 Crewe, "Black Hamlet."
150 Ibid., 280.
151 Arendt, *The Origins of Totalitarianism*, 205.
152 Malan, *My Traitor's Heart*, 195.
153 Ibid., 207.
154 Ibid., 212.
155 Ibid., 224.
156 Ibid.
157 Ibid., 181–235. See also Visser, "How to Live?"; Osinubi, "Abusive Narratives."
158 Sachs, *Black Hamlet*, 63.
159 Ibid., 254.
160 Malan, *My Traitor's Heart*, 151.
161 Ibid., 154.
162 Sachs, *Black Hamlet*, 132.
163 Ibid., 52.
164 Malan, *My Traitor's Heart*, 191.
165 Sachs, *Black Hamlet*, 296.
166 Arendt, *The Origins of Totalitarianism*, 430.
167 Arendt, "Race Thinking before Racism."
168 Arendt, *The Origins of Totalitarianism*, 159.
169 Gines, *Hannah Arendt and the Negro Question*, 128.
170 Arendt, *The Origins of Totalitarianism*, 85.
171 Ibid., 185.
172 Ibid., 191.
173 Ibid., 73.
174 Gilman and Stepan, "Appropriating the Idioms of Science."
175 Arendt, *The Origins of Totalitarianism*, vii.
176 Ibid., 412.
177 Ibid., 445.
178 Ibid., vii–ix.
179 Card, *The Atrocity Paradigm*, 3.
180 Neiman, *Evil in Modern Thought*, 2.
181 Pick, *The Pursuit of the Nazi Mind*. Historians still seem to be arguing for a model that sees the Nazi leadership, especially Hitler, as "insane"; see Caddick-Adams, *Snow and Steel*, 46–48.
182 Bernstein, "Are Arendt's Reflections on Evil Still Relevant?"

183 Arendt, *Eichmann in Jerusalem*, 25–26. This is an ongoing topic of scholarship. See Brunner, "Eichmann's Mind."

184 Robinson, *Wild Beasts and Idle Humors*.

185 Arendt, *Eichmann in Jerusalem*, 246–247. See Ezra, "The Eichmann Polemics." Most recently, see Stangneth, *Eichmann before Jerusalem*.

186 Neiman, *Evil in Modern Thought*, 271–272.

CHAPTER 6. THE MODERN PATHOLOGIZATION OF RACISM

1 Smith, "Treating the Disease of Racism."

2 Emery, "The Twin Battering Rams."

3 Akbar, "Mental Disorder among African-Americans"; Brown, "Critical Race Theory." See also Alexander Thomas and Samuel Sillen, "The Sickness of White Racism," in *Racism and Psychiatry* (with an introduction by Kenneth Clark) (New York: Brunner/Mazel, 1972), 112–121.

4 Conger, Dygdon, and Rollock, "Conditioned Emotional Responses."

5 According to the U.S. Census Bureau's American Community Survey five year estimates (2009–2013), the Philadelphia is now a majority black city, with blacks constituting approximately 43 percent of its 1.5 million residents, while whites now make up just over 41 percent. Of course, these proportions will not necessarily be reflected in the Eagles fan base. However, we're confident that, like most cities with major sports franchises, many residents of Philadelphia have moderate to strong ties to their football team, and this holds true across racial and class lines.

6 "On Radio, Comic Apologizes for Tirade," *Washington Post*.

7 "Mel Gibson's Apology to the Jewish Community," *Anti-Defamation League* (August 1, 2006), www.adl.org.

8 See Conrad, *The Medicalization of Society*.

9 "Letter to the Editor," *New York Times* (January 11, 2000).

10 "Letter to the Editor," *New York Times* (January 12, 2000).

11 Hall and Massey, "Interpreting the Crisis." Quoted from the version published in Richard S. Grayson and Jonathan Rutherford, eds., *After the Crash: Reinventing the Left in Britain* (London: Lawrence Wishart, 2010), 37.

12 Ibid., 38.

13 Rose, *Inventing Our Selves*.

14 Conrad, *The Medicalization of Society*.

15 Among the first generation of Chicago School researchers, Robert Park and Ernest Burgess were perhaps most central to demonstrating race as a "macro-level" social process, both in their own work and in the advising of their students' work, including Louis Wirth, Charles S. Johnson, and E. Franklin Frazier. See Mary Jo Deegan, "The Chicago School of Ethnography," in *Handbook of Ethnography*, ed. Paul Atkinson, Amanda Coffey, Sara Delamont, John Lofland, and Lyn Lofland (London: Sage, 2001), 11–25.

16 Kelly, Faucher, and Machery, "Getting Rid of Racism"; Terbeck et al., "Propranolol Reduces Implicit Negative Racial Bias."

17 Conrad, "Medicalization and Social Control."
18 Richards, *Race, Racism, and Psychology*, 157.
19 Allport, "Attitudes."
20 Horowitz, "Race Attitudes," 157.
21 Ibid., 216.
22 Ibid., 244.
23 Horowitz, "The Development of Attitude," 47; quoted from version published in Horowitz, "Race Attitudes," 167. Also see Horowitz and Horowitz, "Development of Social Attitudes in Children."
24 Horowitz, "Race Attitudes," 167.
25 Ibid.
26 Ibid., 183.
27 Ibid., 245–246.
28 Jay, *The Dialectical Imagination*.
29 Sanford, "The Approach of the Authoritarian Personality," 308, 312.
30 Wilson, "The Neuroses of Everyday Living," 395, 398.
31 Wilson and Lantz, "The Effect of Culture Change."
32 Ibid., 30.
33 Mead, *Cultural Patterns and Technical Change*, 4.
34 Jenkins, *Breaking Patterns of Defeat*, 85.
35 David Wilson and Edna M. Lantz, "Culture Change and Negro State Hospital Admissions," in *Mental Health and Segregation*, ed. Martin M. Grossack (Berlin: Springer, 1966): 139–149, here 148–149.
36 See, for example, Bach, "Father-Fantasies and Father-Typing"; Sclare, "Cultural Determinants in the Neurotic Negro"; Sears, Pintler, and Sears, "Effects of Father-Separation."
37 Quote from Pettigrew, "The Negro American Personality," 13. Also see Ausubel, "Ego Development"; Milner, "Some Hypotheses."
38 Pettigrew, "The Negro American Personality," 18; for similar positions from which Pettigrew drew, see Bacon, Child, and Barry, "A Cross-Cultural Study"; Kohn and Clausen, "Parental Authority Behavior."
39 Mumford, "Untangling Pathology," 56.
40 See ibid.
41 Ibid. See Clark, *The Dark Ghetto*.
42 Mumford, "Untangling Pathology," 59–60.
43 Ibid., 61. See "President Hails New Stage," *Washington Post*.
44 Patterson, "The Moynihan Future."
45 Mumford, "Untangling Pathology," 62; "New Crisis," *Newsweek*; "Moynihan Report," *New Republic*.
46 Ryan, "Savage Discovery." A shorter version of his commentary on the report would appear in *The Crisis*, under the title "The New Genteel Racism," that same year. See Ryan, "The New Genteel Racism."

47 Mumford, "Untangling Pathology," 62; Herbes, "Moynihan Hopeful"; "A Mother Can't Do a Man's Job," *Newsweek*; Meehan, "Moynihan of the Moynihan Report."

48 Rustin, "The Watts."

49 Mumford, "Untangling Pathology," 63; Meehan, "Moynihan of the Moynihan Report."

50 King, "The Role of the Behavioral Scientist."

51 William H. Grier and Price M. Cobbs, *Black Rage: Two Black Psychiatrists Reveal the Full Dimensions of the Inner Conflicts and the Desperation of Black Life in the United States* (New York: Basic Books, 1968). See John Hoberman, *Black and Blue: The Origins and Consequences of Medical Racism* (Berkeley: University of California Press, 2012), 173–181.

52 Grier and Cobbs, *Black Rage*, 207.

53 Ibid., 178.

54 Ibid., 162.

55 Ibid., 210.

56 Ibid., 206.

57 Ibid., 208.

58 Ibid., 34.

59 Kenneth B. Clark, "As Old as Human Cruelty," *New York Times* (September 22, 1968): 373.

60 As he notes in Clark, *Dark Ghetto*, 134. See also Kenneth B. Clark, "Empathy: A Neglected Topic in Psychological Research," *American Psychologist* 35 (1980): 187–190.

61 Rosalind Dymond Cartwright, "A Preliminary Investigation into the Relation of Insight and Empathy," *Journal of Consulting Psychology* 12 (1948): 228–233. This was quickly converted into a scale of empathy: Rosalind Dymond Cartwright, "A Scale for the Measurement of Empathic Ability," *Journal of Consulting Psychology* 13 (1949): 127–133.

62 William H. Grier and Price M. Cobbs, "Black Rage," *New York Times* (October 27, 1968): BR72.

63 Poussaint, "Interview with Alvin Poussaint" ("Dealing with the Black Psyche," video 7 of 10).

64 Poussaint, "Interview with Alvin Poussaint" ("My Career in Psychiatry," video 3 of 10).

65 Poussaint, "Interview with Alvin Poussaint" ("Beginning of the Black Power Movement," video 6 of 10).

66 For Poussaint's published statements on the rise of cultural shift in the Civil Rights Movement, see Poussaint, "How the 'White Problem' Spawned 'Black Power'"; Poussaint, "A Psychiatrist Looks at Black Power."

67 Poussaint, "Interview with John H. Johnson."

68 Poussaint, "Interview with Alvin Poussaint" ("Controversial Articles Written by Me," video 8 of 10).

69 Poussaint, "A Negro Psychiatrist Explains," 52.
70 Poussaint, "White Racism and Black Anger," F32.
71 Francis, *Saving Normal*.
72 Shenker, "Racism Is Called a Health Problem."
73 Bell, "Racism, Narcissism, and Integrity," 89.
74 Ibid.
75 Poussaint, "Interview with Alvin Poussaint" ("Controversial Articles Written by Me," video 8 of 10).
76 Poussaint, "They Hate. They Kill," 17.
77 "Response by Robert Spitzer, MD," *New York Times*.
78 "To the Editor," *New York Times*.
79 Daniel B. Borenstein, "Classifying Racism as Insanity Isn't That Easy," *New York Times* (August 31, 1999).
80 Poussaint, "What a Rorschach Can't Gauge."
81 Poussaint, "Interview with Alvin Poussaint" ("Controversial Articles Written by Me," video 8 of 10).
82 Skillings and Dobbins, "Racism as a Disease."
83 Dobbins and Skillings, "Racism as a Clinical Syndrome."
84 Asante, "Multiculturalism and the Academy." See also Cokley, "Testing Cross's Revised Racial Identity Model"; Neville et al., "Color-Blind Racial Ideology"; Taylor, Henderson, and Jackson, "A Holistic Model."
85 Guindon, Green, and Hanna, "Intolerance and Psychopathology."
86 The same Carl Bell who had claimed in the late 1970s and early 1980s that racism was a symptom of a narcissitic personality disorder.
87 Rubin, *Antisemitism*, 19.
88 Ibid., 23.
89 Masserman, *The Practice of Dynamic Psychiatry*, 654ff.
90 Ibid., 655.
91 Lewin, "Self-Hatred among Jews."
92 All references to Weltsch are to Rabinbach and Gilman, eds., *The Third Reich Sourcebook*, 636–638.
93 Scholem, *A Life in Letters*, 396.
94 Ibid., 399.
95 Glenn, "The Vogue of Jewish Self-Hatred," 98.
96 Ibid., 99.
97 Ibid., 101.
98 Rosenberg, "Jewish Identity in a Free Society," 509.
99 Shapiro, *A Time for Healing*, 206.
100 Bernstein, "Jewish Insecurity and American Realities," 125.
101 Ibid., 121.
102 Ibid., 127.
103 Ibid.
104 Diner, *We Remember with Reverence*.

105 Novick, *The Holocaust in American Life*, 146ff.
106 "Otto Dov Kulka," *Guardian*.
107 Elkana, "Biskhut Hashikhekha."
108 Rubin-Dorsky, "Philip Roth and American Jewish Identity."
109 Levin, "The Psychology of Populations under Chronic Siege."
110 Finlay, "Pathologising Dissent."
111 Mamet, *The Wicked Son*, 158.
112 Ibid., 160.
113 Friedman, "Jewish Self-Hatred."
114 Greenwald, "How Noam Chomsky Is Discussed."
115 Lerman, "Jewish Self-Hatred."
116 Rose, "The Myth of Self-Hated."
117 Falk, *Anti-Semitism*, 54.
118 Volkov, *Germans, Jews, and Antisemites*, 35.
119 Prince, "Psychoanalysis Traumatized," 183.
120 On the general question of classification, see Farhad Dalal, "Insides and Outsides: A Review of Psychoanalytic Renderings of Difference, Racism and Prejudice," *Psychoanalytic Studies* 3 (2001): 43–66, and, in more detail, his book *Race, Colour and the Process of Racialization: New Perspectives from Group Analysis, Psychoanalysis and Sociology* (Hove: Brunner-Routledge, 2002).
121 Kovel, *White Racism*. See Garcia, *Psychology Comes to Harlem*.
122 Kovel, *White Racism*, 211.
123 Ibid., 211–212.
124 Richards, *Race, Racism and Psychology*, 350–355.
125 Kovel, *White Racism*, 144.
126 See, for example, Assmann, *The Mosaic Distinction*.
127 Kovel, *Overcoming Zionism*, 8ff.
128 Gilman, *Difference and Pathology*, 15–36. See George Mosse, "Anatomy of a Stereotype," *New German Critique* 42 (1987): 163–168.
129 Gilman, *Difference and Pathology*, 18, 20.
130 Ibid., 20.
131 Ibid., 20–21.
132 Ibid., 23.
133 Kernberg, "The Psychopathology of Hatred."
134 Kernberg, "Aggression, Hatred, and Social Violence," 199.
135 Ibid., 196.
136 Ibid., 201.
137 Ibid., 201–202.
138 Harold F. Searles, "Scorn, Disillusionment and Adoration in the Psychotherapy Of Schizophrenia," *Psychoanalytic Review* 49 (1962): 39–60, here 39–40. See Neil Evernden, "Beyond Ecology: Self, Place, and the Pathetic Fallacy," in *The Ecocriticism Reader: Landmarks in Literary Ecology*, ed. Cheryll Glotfelty and Harold Fromm (Athens: University of Georgia Press, 1996), 92–104.

139 Harold F. Searles, *The Nonhuman Environment in Normal Development and in Schizophrenia* (New York: International Universities Press, 1960), 112.

140 Ibid., 16.

141 Zaretsky, *Political Freud: A History*, 7.

142 Holmes, "Race and Transference," 7–8. See also Salman Akhtar, ed., *The African American Experience: Psychoanalytic Perspectives* (Lanham, MD: Jason Aronson, 2012).

143 Holmes, "Race and Transference," 8.

144 Holmes, "Wrecking Effects of Race," 218.

145 First articulated by Peggy McIntosh, *White Privilege and Male Privilege: A Personal Account of Coming to See Correspondences through Work in Women's Studies* (Working Paper No. 189, Stone Center Work In Progress Papers) (Wellesley, MA: Wellesley College, Center for Research on Women, 1988).

146 This discussion among psychoanalysts does seem to begin with Neil Altman, "Black and White Thinking: A Psychoanalyst Reconsiders Race," *Psychoanalytic Dialogues* 10 (2000): 589–606, whose case presentations and summaries structure many of the later approaches.

147 Suchet, "Unraveling Whiteness," 867.

148 "According to Gilman, race is at the center of Freud's work. Categories of religious difference (Christian/Jewish) were changed into categories of racial difference (Aryan/Jew) in the late-19th-century Austro-German literature. Therefore, the 'dark' Jew was not considered 'white.' . . . In a very interesting hypothesis, Gilman suggested that Freud had transmuted the rhetoric of race into gender. In trying to overcome the pathological femininity and racialized inferiority of the male Jew, Freud shifted the burden of lack and inferiority onto woman; the Jewish body became the body of the woman." Suchet, "Relational Encounter," 423.

149 Suchet, "Whiteness Revisited," 453.

150 Suchet, "Unraveling Whiteness," 867.

151 Young-Bruehl, *The Anatomy of Prejudices*, 140.

152 Ibid., 141.

153 Ibid., 167, 185, 562 n.17.

154 Ibid., 97.

155 Ibid., 77.

156 Ibid.

157 David Wellman, "From Evil to Illness: Medicalizing Racism," *Journal of American Orthopsychiatry* 70 (2000): 28–32.

158 David Wellman, "Unconscious Racism, Social Cognition Theory and the Legal Intent Doctrine: The Neuron Fires Next Time," in *Handbook of Racial and Ethnic Relations*, ed. Hernán Vera and Joe R. Feagin (New York: Springer Science, 2007), 39–65.

159 Michele Lamont and Virag Molnar, "The Study of Boundaries in the Social Sciences," *Annual Review of Sociology* 28 (2002), 167–195. For cognitive sociology,

see Wayne Brekhus, *Culture and Cognition: Patterns in the Social Construction of Reality* (London: Polity, 2015).

160 Francesca Polletta, *It Was Like a Fever: Storytelling in Protest and Politics* (Chicago: University of Chicago Press, 2006).

161 Mattias Smångs, "Doing Violence, Making Race: Southern Lynching and White Racial Group Formation," *American Journal of Sociology* 121 (March 2006): 1329–1374, here 1334.

162 Ibid.

163 Ibid.

164 Ibid., 1335–1336.

165 Ibid., 1360.

CONCLUSION

1 Itzhak Fried, "Syndrome E," *Lancet* 350 (December 20–27, 1997): 1845–1848.

2 "Pandora and the Problem of Evil," *Lancet* 347 (January 6, 1996): 1.

3 Quoted in Alison Abbott, "What Makes Peaceful Neighbours Become Mass Murderers," *Nature* (May 11, 2015), www.nature.com.

4 Fried, "Syndrome E," 1845.

5 Ibid.

6 Ibid., 1846.

7 Ibid., 1848.

8 Such predictors had been imagined earlier with the development of fMRI brain scans that were claimed to be able to "detect people habouring racial prejudice." Adams, "Inside the Mind of a Racist."

9 "Correspondence," *Lancet* 351 (March 14, 1998): 829–830.

10 Ibid., 829.

11 Ibid.

12 Ibid., 830.

13 Ibid.

14 Quoted in Abbott, "What Makes Peaceful Neighbours."

15 Gary Blasi, "Advocacy against the Stereotype: Lessons from Cognitive Social Psychology," *UCLA Law Review* 49 (2002): 1241–1281, here 1243.

16 Ibid., 1245.

17 Linda Krieger, "The Content of Our Categories," *Stanford Law Review* 47 (1995): 1161–1223, here 1187.

18 Simon Williams, Stephen Katz, and Paul Martin, "Neuroscience and Medicalisation: Sociological Reflections on Memory, Medicine and the Brain," in *Sociological Reflections on the Neurosciences*, ed. Martyn Pickersgill and Ira Van Keulen (Bingley: Emerald, 2012), 231–254; Nikolas Rose, *Neuro: The New Brain Sciences and the Management of the Mind* (Princeton, NJ: Princeton University Press, 2013).

19 Duana Fullwiley, "The Molecularization of Race: Institutionalizing Human Difference in Pharmacogenetics Practice," *Science as Culture* 16 (2007): 1–30.

20 Neil Risch, "The Whole Side of It—An Interview with Neil Risch by Jane Gitschier," *PLOS Genetics* 1 (July 2005), http://journals.plos.org/plosgenetics.

21 Lynn B. Jorde and Stephen P. Wooding, "Genetic Variation, Classification and 'Race'" *Nature Genetics* 36 (2004): S28–S33.

22 "Not a Black and White Question," *Economist* (April 12, 2006): 80.

23 Deborah Lynn Steinberg, *Genes and the Bioimaginary: Science, Spectacle, Culture* (Farnham: Ashgate, 2015).

24 O. W. Brawley, Response to "Inclusion of Women and Minorities in Clinical Trials and the NIH Revitalization Act of 1993—The Perspective of the NIH Clinical Trialists," *Controlled Clinical Trials* 16 (1995): 293–295, here 293.

25 David B. Goldstein, *Jacob's Legacy: A Genetic View of Jewish History* (New Haven, CT: Yale University Press, 2008); Jon Entine, *Abraham's Children: Race, Identity, and the DNA of the Chosen People* (New York: Grand Central Publishing, 2007); Harry Ostrer, *Legacy: A Genetic History of the Jewish People* (Oxford: Oxford University Press, 2012); Nadia Abu El-Haj, *The Genealogical Science: The Search for Jewish Origins and the Politics of Epistemology* (Chicago: University of Chicago Press, 2012).

26 Troy Duster, "A Post-Genomic Surprise. The Molecular Reinscription of Race in Science, Law and Medicine," *British Journal of Sociology* 66 (2015): 1–27.

27 Archana Ruhela and Malini Sinha, *Recent Trends in Animal Behavior* (Oxford: Oxford Book Co., 2010), 36.

28 Kevin MacDonald, *A People That Shall Dwell Alone: Judaism as a Group Evolutionary Strategy* (Westport, CT: Praeger, 1994); *Separation and Its Discontents: Toward an Evolutionary Theory of Anti-Semitism* (Westport, CT: Praeger, 1998); *The Culture of Critique: An Evolutionary Analysis of Jewish Involvement in Twentieth-Century Intellectual and Political Movements* (Westport, CT: Praeger, 1998).

29 Nancy L. Segal and Kevin B. MacDonald, "Behavioral Genetics and Evolutionary Psychology: Unified Perspective on Personality Research," *Human Biology* 70 (1998): 159–184, here 179.

30 Ibid., 171.

31 Ibid., 172.

32 Ibid., 159.

33 "Statement of Professor Kevin MacDonald," *David Irving/International Campaign for Real History* (July 30, 1999), www.fpp.co.uk.

34 *Irving v. Penguin Books Ltd and Deborah Lipstadt* (2000), paragraph 13.167.

35 Kevin MacDonald, "Policing the Elites," *Occidental Observer* (September 4, 2010), http://theoccidentalobserver.net.

36 Governmentality here refers to its broad definition, "the art of government," from Foucault's lectures at the Collège de France from 1978–1979. These lectures are available in the volume *The Birth of Biopolitics* (New York: Picador, 2010). Importantly, "government" as Foucault defined it referred not only to state politics, but a wide range of techniques used to manage conduct, and, more specifically, the process of subjectification. Thus, as we use it in this chapter, a mental health gov-

ernmentality refers to the range of techniques—discursive, symbolic, corporeal—
that are used to manage our knowledge of self and society, and, subsequently, how
we practice that knowledge upon our selves and society.

37 James Allan Davis and Tom W. Smith, *General Social Survey* (Chicago: National
Opinion Research Center, 2010, 2012, 2014).

38 See, for example, Conger, Dygdon, and Rollock, "Conditioned Emotional Responses"; Matthew D. Lieberman, "An fMRI Investigation of Race-Related Amygdala Activity in African-American and Caucasian-American Individuals," *Nature
Neuroscience* 6 (2005): 720–722; Scott R. Vranna and David Rollock, "Physiological Response to a Minimal Social Encounter: Effects of Gender, Ethnicity, and
Social Context," *Psychophysiology* 35 (1998): 462–469.

39 Jason Lim, "Immanent Politics: Thinking Race and Ethnicity through Affect and
Machinism," *Environment and Planning A* 42 (2010): 2393–2409.

40 Omi and Winant, *Racial Formation in the United States*, 115.

BIBLIOGRAPHY

Abbott, Alison. "What Makes Peaceful Neighbors Become Mass Murders," *Nature* (May 11, 2015), www.nature.com.

"The Accountability of Slavery," *North Star* (October 12, 1849): 1.

Ackerman, Nathan, and Marie Jahoda. *Anti-Semitism and Emotional Disorder: A Psychoanalytic Interpretation.* New York: Harper, 1950.

Adams, David. "Inside the Mind of a Racist: Scans May Reveal the Brain's Hidden Centres of Prejudice," *Guardian* (November 7, 2003), www.theguardian.com.

Adams, Romanzo. *Interracial Marriage in Hawaii.* New York: Macmillan, 1937.

Adams, William Y. *The Philosophical Roots of Anthropology.* Stanford, CA: Stanford University Press, 1998.

Adorno, Theodor, Else Frenkel-Brunswik, Daniel Levinson, and Nevitt Sanford. *The Authoritarian Personality.* Studies in Prejudice, vol. 3. New York: Harper, 1950.

Agamben, Giorgio. *Homo Sacer: Sovereign Power and Bare Life*, trans. Daniel Heller-Roazen. Palo Alto, CA: Stanford University Press, 1998.

Aichorn, August. *Verwahrloste Jugend: Die Psychoanalyse in der Fürsorgeerziehung. Zehn Vorträge zur ersten Einführung.* Vienna: Internationaler Psychoanalytischer Verlag, 1925.

———. *Wayward Youth.* New York: Viking, 1935.

Akbar, Na'im. "Mental Disorder among African-Americans," in *Black Psychology*, ed. Reginald L. Jones. Berkeley, CA: Cobb & Henry Publishers, 1991, pp. 339–352.

Akhtar, Salman, ed. *The African American Experience: Psychoanalytic Perspectives.* Lanham, MD: Jason Aronson, 2012.

Alexander, Franz. *Our Age of Unreason: A Study of Irrational Forces in Social Life.* Philadelphia: J.B. Lippincott, 1942.

Allport, Gordon W. "Attitudes," in *A Handbook of Social Psychology*, ed. Carl Murchison. Worcester, MA: Clark University Press, 1935, p. 810.

Al-Saji, Alia. "A Phenomenology of Hesitation: Interrupting Racializing Habits of Seeing," in *Living Alterities: Phenomenology, Embodiment and Race*, ed. Emily S. Lee. Albany: SUNY Press, 2014, pp. 133–172.

Altman, Neil. "Black and White Thinking: A Psychoanalyst Reconsiders Race," *Psychoanalytic Dialogues* 10 (2000): 589–606.

American Jewish Historical Society. *American Jewish Desk Reference.* New York: Random House, 1999.

Anderson, Elijah, and Douglas Massey. *Problem of the Century: Racial Stratification in the United States.* New York: Russell Sage Foundation, 2001.

Anderson, Warwick, Deborah Jenson, and Richard C. Keller, *Unconscious Dominions: Psychoanalysis, Colonial Trauma, and Global Sovereignties.* Durham, NC: Duke University Press, 2011.

Appiah, Kwame Anthony. *Lines of Descent: W.E.B. Du Bois and the Emergence of Identity.* Cambridge, MA: Harvard University Press, 2014.

Appignanesi, Lisa, and John Forrester. *Freud's Women.* London: Verso, 1993.

Aptheker, Herbert. "The Negro People in America: A Critique of Gunnar Myrdal's *An American Dilemma,*" in *Herbert Aptheker on Race and Democracy: A Reader,* ed. Eric Foner and Manning Marable. Urbana: University of Illinois Press, 2006, pp. 184–197.

Arendt, Hannah. *Eichmann in Jerusalem: A Report on the Banality of Evil.* New York: Penguin, 1963.

———. *The Jew as Pariah,* ed. Ron H. Feldman. New York: Grove Press, 1978.

———. "On the Nature of Totalitarianism," in *Essays in Understanding,* ed. Jerome Kohn. New York: Harcourt Brace, 1994, pp. 328–360.

———. *The Origins of Totalitarianism.* New York: Harcourt, Brace & World, 1951.

———. "Race Thinking before Racism," *Review of Politics* 6 (1944): 36–73.

Asante, Molefi K. "Multiculturalism and the Academy," *Academe* 82 (1996): 20–23.

Aschheim, Steve. "Archetypes and the German-Jewish Dialogue: Reflections Occasioned by the Goldhagen Affair," *German History* 15 (1997): 240–250.

Assmann, Jan. *The Mosaic Distinction or The Price of Monotheism,* trans. Robert Savage. Palo Alto, CA: Stanford University Press, 2009.

———. *Moses the Egyptian: The Memory of Egypt in Western Monotheism.* Cambridge, MA: Harvard University Press, 1998.

Ausubel, D. P. "Ego Development among Segregated Negro Children," *Mental Hygiene* 42 (1958): 362–369.

Babcock, J. W. "The Colored Insane," *Alienist and Neurologist* 16 (1895): 423–447.

Bach, C. R. "Father-Fantasies and Father-Typing in Father-Separated Children," *Child Development* 17 (1946): 63–79.

Bacon, Margaret K., Irvin L. Child, and Herbert Barry. "A Cross-Cultural Study of Correlates of Crime," *Journal of Abnormal Social Psychology* 66 (1963): 291–300.

Bailey, Pearce. "A Contribution to the Mental Pathology of Races in the United States," *Archives of Neurology and Psychiatry* 7 (1922): 183–201.

Baldwin, James. *Notes of a Native Son.* Boston: Beacon Press, 1985.

Baltzell, Digby E. *The Protestant Establishment.* New York: Random House, 1964.

Barkan, Elazar. *The Retreat of Scientific Racism: Changing Concepts of Race in Britain and the United States between the Two World Wars.* Cambridge, UK: Cambridge University Press, 1992.

Barrows, Isabel C., ed. *Proceedings of the National Conference of Charities and Correction at the Twenty-Fifth Annual Session Held in the City of New York, May 18–25, 1898.* Boston: Geo. H. Ellis, 1899. https://archive.org/details/proceedingsnati111sessgoog.

Barrows, Susanna. *Distorting Mirrors—Visions of the Crowd in Late Nineteenth-Century France.* New Haven, CT: Yale University Press, 1981.

Bartlett, Steven James. *The Pathology of Man: A Study of Human Evil.* Springfield, IL: Charles C. Thomas, 2005.

Barzun, Jacques. *Race: A Modern Superstition.* London: Methuen, 1938.

Baugh, Bruce. *French Hegel: From Surrealism to Postmodernism.* New York: Routledge, 2003.

Baumgarten-Tramer, Franciska. "German Psychologists and Recent Events," *Journal of Abnormal and Social Psychology* 43 (1948): 452–465.

Beaty, Bart. *Frederic Wertham and the Critique of Mass Culture.* Jackson: University of Mississippi Press, 2005.

Beecher-Monas, Erica, and Edgar Garcia-Rill. "Genetic Predictions of Future Dangerousness: Is There a Blueprint for Violence?," *Law and Contemporary Problems* 69 (2006): 301–341.

Bein, Alex. *The Jewish Question: Biography of a World Problem,* trans. Harry Zohn. Rutherford, NJ: Fairleigh Dickinson University Press, 1990.

———. *Theodor Herzl: Biographie.* Wien: Selbstverl. der Österreichisch-Israelischen Gesellschaft, 1974.

Bell, Carl C. "Racism, Narcissism, and Integrity," *Journal of the National Medical Association* 70 (1978): 89–92.

Bell, Carl. C., and Edward Anthony Dunbar. "Racism and Pathological Bias as a Co-Occurring Problem in Diagnosis and Assessment," in *The Oxford Handbook of Personality Disorders,* ed. T. A. Widiger. New York: Oxford University Press, 2012, pp. 697–708.

Beller, Steven. "Solving Riddles: Freud, Vienna, and the Historiography of Madness," in *Journeys into Madness: Mapping Mental Illness in the Austro-Hungarian Empire,* ed. Gemma Blackshaw and Sabine Wieber. New York: Berghahn, 2012, pp. 27–42.

Ben-Horin, Meir. *Max Nordau: Philosopher of Human Solidarity.* New York: Conference of Jewish Social Studies, 1956.

Benjamin, Ludy T., Jr. "The Birth of American Intelligence Testing," *Monitor on Psychology* 40 (2009): 20–21.

Bennett, Philip, and Andreas Peglau. "The Nazi Denaturalization of German Emigrants: The Case of Wilhelm Reich," *German Studies Review* 37 (2014): 41–60.

Bergmann, Werner, ed. *Error without Trial: Psychological Research on Antisemitism.* Berlin and New York: de Gruyter, 1988.

Bergner, Gwen. "Who Is That Masked Woman? Or, the Role of Gender in Fanon's *Black Skin, White Masks,*" *PMLA: Publications of the Modern Language Association of America* 110 (1995): 75–88.

Bernasconi, Robert. "The European Knows and Does Not Know: Fanon's Response to Sartre," in *Frantz Fanon's Black Skin, White Masks: New Interdisciplinary Essays,* ed. Max Silverman. Manchester, UK: Manchester University Press, 2005, pp. 100–111.

Bernfeld, Siegfied. "Die kommunistische Diskussion um die Psychoanalyse und Reichs 'Widerlegung des Todestriebhypothese,'" *Internationale Zeitschrift für Psychoanalyse* 18 (1932): 352–385.

Bernstein, David. "Jewish Insecurity and American Realities: A Prescription against Mental Escapism," *Commentary* 5 (February 1948): 119–127.

Bernstein, F. (Peretz). *Der Antisemitismus als Gruppenerscheinung: Versuch einer Soziologie des Judenhasses*. Berlin: Jüdischer Verlag, 1925.

Bernstein, Richard J. "Are Arendt's Reflections on Evil Still Relevant?," *Review of Politics* 70 (Winter 2008): 64–76.

Bernstein, Robin. *Racial Innocence: Performing American Childhood from Slavery to Civil Rights*. New York: New York University Press, 2011.

Bettelheim, Bruno. "Eichmann, the System, the Victims," *New Republic* 148 (June 15, 1963): 23–33.

———. *Freud's Vienna and Other Essays*. New York: Knopf, 1990.

———. "Individual and Mass Behavior in Extreme Situations," *Journal of Abnormal and Social Psychology* 38 (1943): 417–452.

———. *The Informed Heart: Autonomy in a Mass Age*. Glencoe, IL: Free Press, 1960.

———. *Surviving and Other Essays*. New York: Knopf, 1979.

———. Testimony from Nuremburg Tribunal, in *Nazi Conspiracy and Aggression*, vol. VII, Office of United States Chief of Counsel for Prosecution of Axis Criminality. Washington, DC: U.S. Government Printing Office, 1946, pp. 818–839.

Bettelheim, Bruno, and Morris Janowitz. *Dynamics of Prejudice: A Psychological and Sociological Study of Veterans*. New York: Harper and Brothers, 1950.

Bevis, W. M. "Psychological Traits of the Southern Negro with Observations as to Some of His Psychoses," *American Journal of Pyschiatry* 78 (1921): 69–78.

Bienenfeld, F. R. "Justice, Aggression and Eros," *International Journal of Psycho-Analysis* 38 (1957): 419–427.

Billings, John S. "Vital Statistics of the Jews," *North American Review* 153 (1891): 70–84.

Black, Edwin. *War against the Weak: Eugenics and America's Campaign to Create a Master Race*. New York: Dialog Press, 2012.

Blanchette, Thad. "Citizens and Savages—Applied Anthropology and Indian Administration in the United States, 1880–1940." Ph.D. dissertation, Programa de Pós-Graduação em Antropologia Social do Museu Naciona, UFRJ, 2006.

Blasi, Gary. "Advocacy against the Stereotype: Lessons from Cognitive Social Psychology," *UCLA Law Review* 49 (2002): 1241–1281.

Blass, Thomas. "The Milgram Paradigm after 35 Years: Some Things We Know about Obedience to Authority," *Journal of Applied Social Psychology* 29 (1999): 955–978.

Bloom, Etan. *Arthur Ruppin and the Production of Pre-Israeli Culture*. Leiden: Brill, 2011.

Boas, Franz. *Anthropology and Modern Life*. New York: W.W. Norton, 1928.

———. "Psychological Problems in Anthropology. Lecture Delivered at the Celebration of the Twentieth Anniversary of the Opening of Clark University, September, 1909," *American Journal of Psychology* 21 (1910): 371–384.

Bondy, Curt. "Problems of Internment Camps," *Journal of Abnormal Psychology* 38 (October 1, 1943): 453–475.

Bonhoeffer, Karl. "Beurteilung, Begutachtung und Rechtsprechung bei den sogenannten Unfallsneurosen," *Deutsche Medizinische Wochenschrift* 52 (1926): 179–182.

Bonilla-Silva, Eduardo. *Racism without Racists: Color-Blind Racism and the Persistence of Racial Inequality in the United States*, 4th ed. Lanham, MD: Rowman & Littlefield, 2013.

Borch, Christian. "Between Destructiveness and Vitalism: Simmel's Sociology of Crowds," *Conserveries mémorielles* [En ligne], #8, mis en ligne le 25 septembre 2010, consulté le 26 juillet 2014. http://cm.revues.org/744.

Borenstein, Daniel B. "Classifying Racism as Insanity Isn't That Easy," *New York Times* (August 31, 1999).

Bornstein, George. *The Colors of Zion: Blacks, Jews and Irish from 1845 to 1945*. Cambridge, MA: Harvard University Press, 2011.

———. "W.E.B. Du Bois and the Jews: Ethics, Editing, and The Souls of Black Folk," *Textual Cultures* 1 (2006): 64–74.

Brandes, George. *Friedrich Nietzsche*, trans. A. G. Chater. London: W. Heinemann, 1914.

Brandt, Allan M. *No Magic Bullet: A Social History of Venereal Disease in the United States since 1880*. New York: Oxford University Press, 1987.

Brawley, O. W. "Response to 'Inclusion of Women and Minorities in Clinical Trials and the NIH Revitalization Act of 1993'—The Perspective of the NIH Clinical Trial Lists," *Controlled Clinical Trials* 16 (1995): 293–295.

Brekhus, Wayne. *Culture and Cognition: Patterns in the Social Construction of Reality*. London: Polity, 2015.

Brenner, Arthur B. "Some Psychoanalytic Speculations on Antisemitism," *Psychoanalytic Review* 35 (1948): 20–32.

Brickman, Celia. *Aboriginal Populations in the Mind: Race and Primitivity in Psychoanalysis*. New York: Columbia University Press, 2003.

Brickner, Richard M. *Is Germany Incurable?* Philadelphia: J.B. Lippincott, 1943.

Bridenthal, Renate, Atina Grossmann, and Marion A. Kaplan. *When Biology Became Destiny: Women in Weimar and Nazi Germany*. New Feminist Library. New York: Monthly Review Press, 1984.

Bridges, Eric M. "Racial Identity Development and Psychological Coping Strategies of African American Males at a Predominantly White University," *Annals of the American Psychotherapy Association* 13 (2010): 14–26.

Brill, A. A., and Morris J. Karpas. "Insanity among Jews," *Medical Record* 86 (1914): 577–579.

Bröckling, Ulrich, Susanne Krasmann, and Thomas Lemke. "From Foucault's Lectures at the Collège de France to Studies of Governmentality," in *Governmentality: Current Issues and Future Challenges*, ed. Ulrich Bröckling, Susanne Krasmann, and Thomas Lemke. New York: Routledge, 2011, p. 1.

Brown, Tony N. "Critical Race Theory Speaks to the Sociology of Mental Health: Mental Health Problems Produced by Racial Stratification," *Journal of Health and Social Behavior* 44 (2003): 292–301.

Bruce, Phillip A. *The Plantation Negro as a Free Man*. New York: G. P. Putnam, 1899.

Brunner, José. "Eichmann's Mind: Psychological, Philosophical, and Legal Perspectives," *Inquiries in Law* 1 (2000): 429–464.

Brunner, William F. "The Negro Health Problem in Southern Cities," *American Journal of Public Health* 5 (1915): 183–190.

Brustein, William I. *Roots of Hate: Anti-Semitism in Europe before the Holocaust*. Cambridge, UK: Cambridge University Press, 2003.

Bryan, William Jennings, ed. *Masterpieces of Eloquence: Famous Orations of Great World Leaders from Early Greece to the Present Time*, Volume 12. New York: F. Collier and Son, 1905.

Bulmer, Martin. *The Chicago School of Sociology*. Chicago: University of Chicago Press, 1984.

Burgle, Georg. *Die Hysterie und die Strafrechtliche Verantwortlichkeit der Hysterischen: Ein praktisches Handbuch für Ärzte und Juristen*. Stuttgart: Ferdinand Enke, 1912.

Busch, Moritz. *Graf Bismarck und seine Leute während des Kriegs mit Frankreich*. 2 vols. Leipzig: Grunow, 1878.

Bynum, William F. "The Great Chain of Being after Forty Years: An Appraisal," *History of Science* 13 (1975): 1–28.

Caddick-Adams, Peter. *Snow and Steel: The Battle of the Bulge, 1944–45*. Oxford: Oxford University Press, 2014.

Calkins, Gary N. "Review of Race Traits and Tendencies of the American Negro," *Political Science Quarterly* 11 (1896): 754–757.

Campos, Paul. "Eugenics Are Alive and Well in the United States," *Time* (July 10, 2013), http://ideas.time.com.

Card, Claudia. *The Atrocity Paradigm: A Theory of Evil*. Oxford: Oxford University Press, 2002.

Carson, Peter, S. Ziesche, G. Johnson, and J. N. Cohn. "Racial Differences in Response to Therapy for Heart Failure: Analysis of the Vasodilator-Heart Failure Trials," *Journal of Cardiac Failure* 5 (1999): 178–187.

Carter, Robert T. *The Influence of Race and Racial Identity in Psychotherapy: Toward a Racially Inclusive Model*. Hoboken, NJ: John Wiley & Sons, 1995.

Cartwright, Dorwin. "Contemporary Social Psychology in Historical Perspective," *Social Psychology Quarterly* 42 (1979): 82–93.

Cartwright, Rosalind Dymond. "A Preliminary Investigation into the Relation of Insight and Empathy," *Journal of Consulting Psychology* 12 (1948): 228–233.

———. "A Scale for the Measurement of Empathetic Ability," *Journal of Consulting Psychology* 13 (1949): 127–133.

Cartwright, Samuel A. "Report on the Diseases and Physical Peculiarities of the Negro Race," *New Orleans Medical and Surgical Journal* (May 1851): 691–715.

Cashmore, Ernest. *Dictionary of Race and Ethnic Relations*. London: Routledge, 1996.

Catsam, Charles. "Richard Wright and Black Resistance to White Supremacy: From Bigger Thomas to Henry Thomas," *Southern Studies* 17 (2010): 86–96.

Charcot, J. M. *Leçons du Mardi a la Salpêtrière*. 2 vols. Paris: Progrés médical, l889.

———. *Poliklinische Vorträge von Prof. J. M. Charcot, Volume 1*, trans. Sigmund Freud. Leipzig: Deuticke, 1892–1895.

————. *Poliklinische Vorträge von Prof. J. M. Charcot, Volume 2*, trans. Max Kahane. Leipzig: Deuticke, 1892–1895.

Chomsky, William. "The Synagogue and the School," *Jewish Exponent* (October 26, 1945): 5.

Clark, Kenneth B. "As Old as Human Cruelty," *New York Times* (September 22, 1968): 373.

————. *The Dark Ghetto: Dilemmas of Social Power*. New York: Harper and Row, 1965.

————. "Empathy: A Neglected Topic in Psychological Research," *American Psychologist* 35 (1980): 187–190.

————. "Implications of Adlerian Theory for an Understanding of Civil Rights Problems and Action," *Journal of Individual Psychology* 23 (1967): 181–190.

————. "Jews in Contemporary America: Problems in Identification," *Jewish Social Services Quarterly* 31 (1954): 12–22.

————. *Prejudice and Your Child*. Boston: Beacon, 1955.

Clark, Kenneth B., Isidor Chein, and Stuart W. Cook. "The Effects of Segregation and the Consequences of Desegregation. A (September 1952) Social Science Statement in the *Brown v. Board of Education of Topeka* Supreme Court Case," *American Psychologist* 59 (September 2004): 495–501.

Clark, Kenneth B., and Mamie K. Clark, "The Development of Consciousness of Self and the Emergence of Racial Identification in Negro Preschool Children," *Journal of Social Psychology* 10 (1939): 591–599.

————. "Emotional Factors in Racial Identification and Preference in Negro Children, "*Journal of Negro Education* 19 (1950): 341–350.

————. "Racial Identification and Preference in Negro Children," in *Readings in Social Psychology*, ed. Eleanor E. Maccoby, Theodore M. Newcomb, and Eugene L. Hartley. New York: Holt, 1958, p. 611.

————. "Segregation as a Factor in the Racial Identification of Negro Pre-School Children: A Preliminary Report," *Journal of Experimental Education* 8 (1939): 161–163.

Cokley, Kevin O. "Testing Cross's Revised Racial Identity Model: An Examination of the Relationship between Racial Identity and Internalized Racism," *Journal of Counseling Psychology* 49 (2002): 476–483.

A Collection of Speeches Spoken by Daniel O'Connell, Esq. and Richard Sheil, Esq. on Subject Connected with the Catholic Question. Dublin: John Cumming, 1828.

Conger, Anthony J., Judith A. Dygdon, and David Rollock. "Conditioned Emotional Responses in Racial Prejudice," *Ethnic and Racial Studies* 35 (2012): 298–319.

Conrad, Peter. "Medicalization and Social Control," *Annual Review of Sociology* 18 (1992): 209–232.

————. *The Medicalization of Society: On the Transformation of Human Conditions into Treatable Disorders*. Baltimore: Johns Hopkins University Press, 2007.

Coolidge, Calvin. *First Annual Message*, ed. Gerhard Peters and John T. Woolley. Washington, DC: American Presidency Project, 1923.

Cooter, Roger, with Claudia Stein. *Writing History in the Age of Biomedicine*. New Haven, CT: Yale University Press, 2013.

"Correspondence," *Lancet* 351 (March 14, 1998): 829–830.

Cramer, Phebe. "Future Directions for the Thematic Apperception Test," *Journal of Personality Assessment* 72 (1999): 74–92.

Cravens, Hamilton. *Before Head Start: The Iowa Station and America's Children*. Chapel Hill: University of North Carolina Press, 2002.

Crewe, Jonathan. "Black Hamlet: Psychoanalysis on Trial in South Africa," *Poetics Today* 22 (2001): 413–433.

Cross, William. *Shades of Black: Diversity in African American Identity*. Philadelphia: Temple University Press, 1991.

Crowley, Patrick. "Albert Memmi: The Conflict of Legacies," in *Postcolonial Thought in the French-Speaking World*, ed. Charles Forsdick and David Murphy. Liverpool: Liverpool University Press, 2009, pp. 126–135.

Dalal, Farhad. "Insides and Outsides: A Review of Psychoanalytic Renderings of Difference, Racism, and Prejudice," *Psychoanalytic Studies* 3 (2001): 43–66.

———. *Race, Colour, and the Process of Racialization: New Perspectives from Group Analysis, Psychoanalysis, and Sociology*. Hove: Brunner-Routledge, 2002.

———. *Thought Paralysis: The Virtues of Discrimination*. London: Karnac Books, 2012.

Daniels, Roger, Sandra C. Taylor, and Harry H. L. Kitano, eds. *Japanese Americans: From Relocation to Redress*. Salt Lake City: University of Utah Press, 1986.

Danziger, Kurt. "Origins and Basic Principles of Wundt's *Völkerpsychologie*," *British Journal of Social Psycholology* 22 (1983): 303–313.

Davidoff, Leo. "Richard Brickner, M.D 1896–1959," *American Journal of Psychiatry* 116 (1959): 191–192.

Davidson, G. "An Interpretation of Antisemitism," *Psychiatric Quarterly* 17 (1943): 123–134.

Davis, Allison, and John Dollard. *Children of Bondage*. Washington, DC: American Council of Education, 1940.

Davis, James Allan, and Tom W. Smith. *General Social Survey*. Chicago: National Opinion Research Center, 2012, 2012, 2014.

Davis, Lennard. *Obsessions*. Chicago: University of Chicago Press, 2008.

Dawson, George E. "Psychic Rudiments and Morality," *American Journal of Psychology* 11 (1900): 181–224.

Dawson, Miles Menander. "Review of Race Traits and Tendencies of the American Negro," *Publications of the American Statistical Association* 5 (1896): 142–148.

Dearborn, Walter F., and Howard H. Long, "The Physical and Mental Abilities of the American Negro: A Critical Summary," *Journal of Negro Education* 3 (1934): 530–547.

Deegan, Mary Jo. "The Chicago School of Ethnography," in *Handbook of Ethnography*, ed. Paul Atkinson, Amanda Coffey, Sara Delamont, John Lofland, and Lyn Lofland. London: Sage, 2011, pp. 11–25.

De Lancey, Dayle B. "Sweetness, Madness, and Power: The Confection as Mental Contagion in Toni Morrison's *Tar Baby*, *Song of Solomon*, and *The Bluest Eye*," *Process: A Journal of African American and African Diaspora Literature and Culture* 2 (2000): 25–47.

Delany, Martin Robinson. *The Condition, Elevation, Emigration, and Destiny of the Colored People of the United States*. Amherst, NY: Humanity Press, 2004.

Depew, Mitchell, ed. *The Library of Oratory, Ancient and Modern: With Critical Studies of the World's Great Orators by Eminent Essayists*, Volume 5. London: A. L. Fowle, 1902.

Deutsch, Albert. "The First US Census of the Insane (1840) and Its Use as Pro-Slavery Propaganda," *Bulletin of the History of Medicine* 15 (1944): 469–482.

Dicks, Henry V. *Clinical Studies in Psychopathology: A Contribution to the Aetiology of Neurotic Illness*. London: Edward Arnold, 1939.

Diner, Hasia. *We Remember with Reverence and Love: American Jews and the Myth of Silence after the Holocaust, 1945—1962*. New York: New York University Press, 2009.

Dobbins, James E., and Judith H. Skillings. "Racism as a Clinical Syndrome," *American Journal of Orthopsychiatry* 70 (2000): 14–27.

Dollard, John. *Class and Caste in a Southern Town*. New York: Doubleday, 1937.

Douthat, Ross. "Eugenics, Past and Future," *New York Times* (June 9, 2012): SR12.

Doyle, Dennis. "'A Fine New Child': The Lafargue Mental Hygiene Clinic and Harlem's African American Communities, 1946–1958," *Journal of the History of Medicine and Allied Sciences* 64 (2009): 173–212.

———. "'Where the Need Is Greatest': Social Psychiatry and Race-Blind Universalism in Harlem's Lafargue Clinic, 1946–1958," *Bulletin of the History of Medicine* 83 (2009): 746–777.

Du Bois, W.E.B. "The Atlanta University Studies of Social Conditions among Negroes, November 10, 1940." *W.E.B. Du Bois Papers (MS 312)*. Special Collections and University Archives, University of Massachusetts Amherst Libraries.

———. *The Autobiography of W.E.B. Du Bois: A Soliloquy on Viewing My Life from the Last Decade of Its First Century*. New York: International Publishers, 1968.

———. "The Development of a People," *International Journal of Ethics* 14 (April 1904): 92–311.

———. *The Philadelphia Negro*. Philadelphia: University of Pennsylvania Press, [1899]1996.

———. "Race Traits and Tendencies of the American Negro. By Frederick L. Hoffman, F.S.S." [review], *Annals of the American Academy of Political and Social Science* 9 (January 1897): 127–133.

———. "The Socialism of German Socialists," *Central European History* 31 (1898): 189–196.

———. *The Souls of Black Folk*. Rockville, MD: Arc Press, [1903]2008.

———, ed. "The Health and Physique of the American Negro," *Proceedings of the Eleventh Conference of the Study of Negro Problems*. Atlanta University, May 29, 1906.

———, ed. "Some Notes on Negro Crime Particularly in Georgia." *Proceedings of the Ninth Conference for the Study of the Negro Problems*. Atlanta University, May 24, 1904.

Dubow, Saul. "Wulf Sachs's *Black Hamlet*: A Case of 'Psychic Vivisection'?," *African Affairs*, 92 (October 1993): 519–556.

———. *Scientific Racism in Modern South Africa*. Cambridge, UK: Cambridge University Press, 1995.

Duncan, Derek. *Reading and Writing Italian Homosexuality: A Case of Possible Difference*. Aldershot, UK: Ashgate, 2006.

Durst, Nathan. "Emotional Wounds That Never Heal," *Jewish Political Studies Review* 14 (Fall 2002): 119–129.

Duster, Troy. *Backdoor to Eugenics*. New York: Routledge, 2003.

———. "A Post-Genomic Surprise: The Molecular Reinscription of Race in Science, Law, and Medicine," *British Journal of Sociology* 66 (2015): 1–27.

Edgar, Robert, ed. *An African American in South Africa: The Travel Notes of Ralph J. Bunche, 28 September 1937–1 January 1938*. Athens: Ohio University Press, 1992.

Efron, John. *Defenders of the Race: Jewish Doctors and Race Science in Fin-de-Siécle Europe*. New Haven, CT: Yale University Press, 1994.

Efron, Noah J. *A Chosen Calling: Jews in Science in the Twentieth Century*. Baltimore: Johns Hopkins University Press, 2014.

Eissler, K. R. "Die Ermordung wie vieler seiner Kinder muss ein Mensch symptomfrei ertragen, um eine normale Konstitution zu haben?," *Psyche* 17 (1963): 241.

Eley, Geoff. "Ordinary Germans, Nazism, and Judeocide," in *The "Goldhagen Effect": History, Memory, Nazism—Facing the German Past*, ed. Geoff Eley. Ann Arbor: University of Michigan Press, 2000.

El-Hag, Nadia Abu. *The Genealogical Science: The Search for Jewish Origins and the Politics of Epistemology*. Chicago: University of Chicago Press, 2012.

Elkana, Yehuda. "Biskhut Hashikhekha" ("A Plea for Forgetting"), *Ha'aretz* (March 2, 1988): 6.

Elkins, Stanley. *Slavery*. Chicago: University of Chicago Press, 1959.

Ellwood, Charles. *Sociology and Modern Social Problems*. New York: American Book Co., 1924.

Emery, Crystal Renee. "The Twin Battering Rams of Oppression: Racism and Capitalism and Their Children: Arrogance and Privilege," *Thedeadliestdisease's Blog* (November 19, 2010), http://thedeadliestdisease.wordpress.com.

Englander, Martin. *Die auffallend häufigen Krankheitserscheinungen der jüdischen Rasse*. Vienna: J. L. Pollak, l902.

Entine, Jon. *Abraham's Children: Race, Identity, and the DNA of the Chosen People*. New York: Grand Central Publishing, 2007.

Erb, Wilhelm. *Über die wachsende Nervosität unserer Zeit. Akademische Rede zum Geburtsfeste . . . Karl Friedrich am 22. November 1893*. Heidelberg: Universitäts-Buchdruckerei J. Höring, 1893.

Erikson, Erik H. "On Nazi Mentality" (1940), in *A Way of Looking at Things: Selected Papers from 1930 to 1980*, ed. Stephen Schlein. New York: W.W. Norton, 1987, pp. 341–345.

Esposito, Roberto. *Bíos: Biopolitics and Philosophy*, trans. and with an introduction by Timothy Campbell. Minneapolis: University of Minnesota Press, 2008.

Evans, Andrew D. *Anthropology at War: World War I and the Science of Race in Germany*. Chicago: University of Chicago Press, 2010.

Evans, Richard, ed. *The Making of Social Psychology*. New York: John Wiley & Sons, 1980.

Evans, Richard J. *The Third Reich in History and Memory*. Oxford: Oxford University Press, 2015.

Evernden, Neil. "Beyond Ecology: Self, Place, and the Pathetic Fallacy," in *The Ecocriticism Reader: Landmarks in Literary Ecology*, ed. Cheryll Glotfelty and Harold Fromm. Athens: University of Georgia Press, 1996.

"Experimental Ethics," *Time* (February 3, 1964): 48.

Ezra, Michael. "The Eichmann Polemics: Hannah Arendt and Her Critics," *Democratiya* 9 (Summer 2007): 141–165.

Fabrega, Horacio, Jr. "Culture and History in Psychiatric Diagnosis and Practice," *Psychiatric Clinics of North America* 24 (2001): 391–405.

Falk, Avner. *Anti-Semitism: A History and Psychoanalysis of Contemporary Hatred*. Westport, CT: Greenwood, 2008.

Fanon, Frantz. *Black Skin, White Masks*, trans. Richard Philcox. New York: Grove Press, 1967.

———. *The Wretched of the Earth*, trans. Constance Farrington. New York: Grove Press, 1968.

Farah, Martha J., and Andrea S. Heberlein. "Personhood and Neuroscience: Naturalizing or Nihilating?," *American Journal of Bioethics* 7 (2007): 37–48.

Feagin, Joe R. *Systemic Racism: A Theory of Oppression*. Boca Raton, FL: CRC Press, 2006.

———. *The White Racial Frame: Centuries of Racial Framing and Counter-Framing*, 2d ed. New York: Routledge, 2013.

Feagin, Joe R., and Bernice McNair Barnett. "Success and Failure: How Systemic Racism Trumped the Brown v. Board of Education Decision," *University of Illinois Law Review* 5 (2004): 1099–1130.

Federn, Ernst. "The Terror as a System: The Concentration Camp: Buchenwald as It Was," *Psychiatric Quarterly Supplement* 22 (1948): 52–86.

Feldman, Shoshana, and Dori Laub. *Testimony: Crises of Witnessing in Literature, Psychoanalysis, and History*. New York: Routledge, 1992.

Ferguson, George Oscar. "The Psychology of the Negro: An Experimental Study," *Archives of Psychology* 36 (1916): 1–158.

Fermaglich, Kirsten. *American Dreams and Nazi Nightmares: Early Holocaust Consciousness and Liberal America, 1957–1965*. Lebanon, NH: Brandeis University Press/ University Press of New England, 2007.

Finlay, W.M.L. "Pathologising Dissent: Identity Politics, Zionism and the "Self-Hating Jew," *British Journal of Social Psychology* 44 (2005): 201–222.

Fishberg, Maurice. *Materials for the Physical Anthropology of the Eastern European Jews*. Lancaster, PA: New Era, 1905.

Fisher, David James. *Bettelheim: Living and Dying*. Amsterdam and New York: Rodopi, 2008.

"Flashing Light Sign Used with Small Exhibits," Fitter Families Contest 1926, *American Philosophical Society, AES*, Am3,575.06,49.

Fleck, Christian, and Albert Müller. "Bruno Bettelheim and the Concentration Camps," *Journal of the History of the Behavioral Sciences* 33 (1997): 1–37.

Foster, Robert H. "Paresis in the Negro," *American Journal of Psychiatry* 82 (1926): 631–640.

Foucault, Michel. *The Birth of Biopolitics*. New York: Picador, 2010.

———. "The Confession of the Flesh," in *Power/Knowledge: Selected Interviews and Other Writings, 1972–1977*, ed. Colin Gordon, trans. C. Gordon et al. New York: Vintage, 1980, pp. 194–228.

———. *The History of Sexuality, Volume 1: An Introduction*, trans. Robert Hurley. New York: Vintage, 1990.

———. *Power/Knowledge: Selected Interviews and Other Writings*, ed. Colin Gordon. New York: Random House, 1980.

———. "Truth and Power," in *Power/Knowledge: Selected Interviews and Other Writings, 1972–1977*, ed. Colin Gordon, trans. C. Gordon et al. New York: Vintage, 1980, pp. 109–33.

Fowler, David H. *Northern Attitudes towards Interracial Marriage: Legislation and Public Opinion in the Middle Atlantic and the States of the Old Northwest 1780–1930*. New York: Garland, 1987.

Francis, Allen. *Saving Normal: An Insider's Revolt against Out-of-Control Psychiatric Diagnosis, DSM-5, Big Pharma, and the Medicalization of Ordinary Life*. New York: William Morrow, 2013.

Freimüller, Tobias. *Alexander Mitscherlich: Gesellschaftsdiagnose und Psychoanalyse nach Hitler*. Göttingen: Wallstein, 2007.

———, ed. *Psychoanalyse und Protest—Alexander Mitscherlich und die "Achtundsechziger."* Göttingen: Wallstein, 2008.

Frenkel-Brunswik, Else, and R. Nevitt Sanford. "The Anti-Semitic Personality: A Research Report," in *Anti-Semitism: A Social Disease*, ed. Ernst Simmel. New York: International Universities Press, 1946, pp. 96–125.

Freud, Anna. "Comments on Aggression," *International Journal of Psycho-Analysis* 53 (1972): 163–171.

———. *Ego and the Mechanism of Defense*, trans. Cecil Baines. New York: International Universities Press, 1946.

Freud, Sigmund. *Standard Edition of the Complete Psychological Works of Sigmund Freud*, ed. and trans. James Strachey, Anna Freud, Alix Strachey, and Alan Tyson. 24 vols. London: Hogarth, 1955–1974.

Fried, Itzhak. "Syndrome E," *Lancet* 350 (December 20–27, 1997): 1845–1848.

Friedlander, Henry. *The Origins of Nazi Genocide: From Euthanasia to the Final Solution*. Chapel Hill: University of North Carolina Press, 1995.

Friedman, Marilyn. "Jewish Self-Hatred, Moral Criticism, and Autonomy," in *Personal Autonomy and Social Oppression: Philosophical Perspectives*, ed. Marina A. L. Oshana. New York: Routledge, 2014, pp. 203–222.

Fromm, Erich. *Escape from Freedom*. New York: Farrar & Rinehart, 1941.

———. "What Shall We Do with Germany?" [review of *Is Germany Incurable?* by Richard M. Brickner], *Saturday Review* (May 29, 1943): 10.

Fuechtner, Veronika. *Berlin Psychoanalytic: Psychoanalysis and Culture in Weimar Germany and Beyond.* Berkeley: University of California Press, 2011.

Fullwiley, Duana. "The Molecularization of Race: Institutionalizing Human Difference in Pharmacogenetics Practice," *Sciences as Culture* 16 (2007): 1–30.

Galton, Francis. "Eugenics and the Jew," *Jewish Chronicle* (July 29, 1910): 16.

Garcia, Jay. *Psychology Comes to Harlem: Rethinking the Race Question in Twentieth-Century America.* Baltimore: Johns Hopkins University Press, 2012.

Garwood, Alfred. "The Holocaust and the Power of Powerlessness: Survivor Guilt an Unhealed Wound," *British Journal of Psychotherapy* 13 (1996): 243–258.

Gerhardt, Uta. "The Medical Meaning of Re-Education for Germany after World War II," *Paedagogica Historica, International Journal of the History of Education* 33 (l997): 135–155.

Gerson, Judith M., and Diane L. Wolf, eds. *Sociology Confronts the Holocaust: Memories and Identities in Jewish Diasporas.* Durham, NC: Duke University Press, 2007.

Gertzman, Jay A. *Samuel Roth: Infamous Modernist.* Gainesville: University Press of Florida, 2013.

Gibson, Campbell J., and Emily Lennon, *Historical Census Statistics on the Foreign-born Population of the United States: 1850–1990.* Washington, DC: Population Division, U.S. Bureau of the Census, 1999.

Giddens, Anthony. *The Consequences of Modernity.* Palo Alto, CA: Stanford University Press, 1991.

Gilkeson, John S. *Anthropologists and the Rediscovery of America, 1886–1965.* New York: Cambridge University Press, 2010.

Gilman, Sander L. *Difference and Pathology: Stereotypes of Sexuality, Race, and Madness.* Ithaca, NY: Cornell University Press, 1985.

———. *Diseases and Diagnoses: The Second Age of Biology.* New Brunswick, NJ, and London: Transaction Publishers, 2010.

———. *Freud, Race, and Gender.* Princeton, NJ: Princeton University Press, 1993.

———. *Jewish Self-Hatred: Anti-Semitism and the Hidden Language of the Jews.* Baltimore: Johns Hopkins University Press, 1986.

———. *The Jew's Body.* New York: Routledge, 1991.

———. *Jurek Becker: A Life in Five Worlds.* Chicago: University of Chicago Press, 2003.

———. "The New Genetics and the Old Eugenics: The Ghost in the Machine," *Patterns of Prejudice* 36 (2002): 3–4.

———. "The Nietzsche Murder Case," *New Literary History* 14 (1983): 349–372.

———. "The Problem with Purim: Jews and Alcohol in the Modern Period," *Leo Baeck Institute Year Book* 50 (2005): 215–231.

———. *Seeing the Insane: A Visual and Cultural History of Our Attitudes toward the Mentally Ill.* Brattleboro, VT: Echo Point Books, 2014.

———. "Sexology, Psychoanalysis and Degeneration: From a Theory of Race to a Race to Theory," in *Degeneration: The Dark Side of Progress*, ed. J. Edward Chamberlin and Sander L. Gilman. New York: Columbia University Press, 1985, pp. 72–96.

Gilman, Sander L., and Steven T. Katz, eds. *Anti-Semitism in Times of Crisis.* New York: New York University Press, 1991. Gilman, Sander L., and Nancy Stepan. "Appropriating the Idioms of Science: Some Strategies of Resistance to Biological Determinism," in *The Bounds of Race: Perspectives on Hegemony and Resistance,* ed. Dominick LaCapra. Ithaca, NY: Cornell University Press, 1991, pp. 72–103.

Gines, Kathryn T. *Hannah Arendt and the Negro Question.* Bloomington: Indiana University Press, 2014.

Glenn, Jules. "Circumcision and Anti-Semitism," *Psychoanalytic Quarterly* 29 (1960): 395–999.

Glenn, Susan A. "The Vogue of Jewish Self-Hatred in Post–World War II America," *Jewish Social Studies* 12 (2006): 95–136.

Glick, L. B. "Types Distinct from Our Own: Franz Boas on Jewish Identity and Assimilation," *American Anthropologist* 84 (1982): 545–565.

Goddard, Henry H. "The Binet and Simon Tests of Intellectual Capacity," *Training School* 5 (1908): 3–9.

———. "The Grading of Backward Children," *Training School* 5 (1908): 12–14.

———. *The Kallikak Family: A Study in the Heredity of Feeble-Mindedness.* New York: Macmillan, 1912.

Goddard, Tara, Kimberly Barsamian Kahn, and Arlie Adkins. "Racial Bias in Driver Yielding Behavior at Crosswalks" [report]. Portland: Oregon Transportation Research and Education Consortium, 2014.

Goldhagen, Daniel J. *Hitler's Willing Executioners. Ordinary Germans and the Holocaust.* New York: Knopf, 1996.

———. "Ordinary Men or Ordinary Germans?," in *The Holocaust and History: The Known, the Unknown, the Disputed, and the Re-examined,* ed. Michael Berenbaum and Abraham J. Peck. Washington, DC: United States Holocaust Memorial Museum/Indiana University Press, 1998, pp. 301–307.

———. "Presentation on *Hitler's Willing Executioners,*" in "The 'Willing Executioners' / 'Ordinary Men' Debate," Daniel J. Goldhagen, Christopher R. Browning, and Leon Wieseltier (with an introduction by Michael Berenbaum), *United States Holocaust Memorial Museum,* April 8, 1996.

Goldstein, Cora. *Capturing the German Eye: American Visual Propaganda in Occupied Germany.* Chicago: University of Chicago Press, 2009.

Goldstein, David B. *Jacob's Legacy: A Genetic View of Jewish History.* New Haven, CT: Yale University Press, 2008.

Goldstein, Eric L. *The Price of Whiteness: Jews, Race, and American Identity.* Princeton, NJ: Princeton University Press, 2006.

Goldstein, Jan. "The Wandering Jew and the Problem of Psychiatric Anti-Semitism in Fin-de-siécle France," *Journal of Contemporary History* 20 (1985): 521–552.

Gonen, Jay Y. *The Roots of Nazi Psychology: Hitler's Utopian Barbarism.* Lexington: University Press of Kentucky, 2000.

Gordon, Lewis R. *Bad Faith and Antiblack Racism.* Amherst, NY: Humanity Books, 1999

Gould, Stephen Jay. *The Mismeasure of Man.* New York: W.W. Norton, 1981.

Grada, Cormac Ó. *Jewish Ireland in the Age of Joyce: A Socioeconomic History*. Princeton, NJ: Princeton University Press, 2006.

Green, E. M. "Manic-Depressive Psychosis in the Negro," *American Journal of Psychiatry* 73 (1916): 619–626.

———. "Psychoses among Negroes—A Comparative Study," *Journal of Nervous and Mental Disease* 41 (1914): 697–708.

Greenwald, Anthony G., Debbie E. McGhee, and Jordan L. K. Schwartz. "Measuring Individual Differences in Implicit Cognition: The Implicit Association Test," *Journal of Personality and Social Psychology* 74 (1998): 1464–1480.

Greenwald, Glenn. "How Noam Chomsky Is Discussed," *Guardian* (March 23, 2013), www.theguardian.com.

Grier, William H., and Price M. Cobbs. "Black Rage," *New York Times* (October 27, 1968): BR72.

———. *Black Rage: Two Black Psychiatrists Reveal the Full Dimensions of the Inner Conflicts and the Desperation of Black Life in the United States*. New York: Basic Books, 1968.

Grob, Gerald N. *Mental Illness and American Society, 1875–1940*. Princeton, NJ: Princeton University Press, 1983.

Grossberg, Michael. "Guarding the Altar: Physiological Restrictions and the Rise of State Intervention in Matrimony," *American Journal of Legal History* 26 (July 1982): 221–224.

Gruber, N., and Kreuzpointner L. "Measuring the Reliability of Picture Story Exercises Like the TAT," *PLOS ONE* 8 (2013).

Grunberger, B. "Circoncision et l'antisémitisme: En marge d'un article de Georges Maranz," *Psyché-Paris* 2 (1947): 1221–1228.

Guindon, Mary H., Alan G. Green, and Fred J. Hanna. "Intolerance and Psychopathology: Toward a General Diagnosis for Racism, Sexism, and Homophobia," *American Journal of Orthopsychiatry* 73 (2003): 167–176.

Hacking, Ian. "Double Consciousness in Britain: 1815–1975," *Dissociation* 3 (1991): 134–146.

Hall, Stuart, and Doreen Massey. "Interpreting the Crisis: Doreen Massey and Stuart Hall Discuss Ways of Understanding the Current Crisis," *Soundings* 44 (2010): 57–71.

Hankins, Frank H. *The Racial Bias of Civilization: A Critique of Nordic Doctrine*. New York: Knopf, 1926.

Hardt, Michael B., ed. *Jews and Race: Writings on Identity and Difference, 1880–1940*. Brandeis Library of Modern Jewish Thought Series. Waltham, MA: Brandeis University Press, 2011.

Hardt, Michael B., and Antonio Negri. *Empire*. Cambridge, MA: Harvard University Press, 2001.

Harel, Zev, Eva Kahana, and Boaz Kahana. *Holocaust Survivors and Immigrants: Late life Adaptations*. New York: Springer, 2005.

Havinghurst, R. J., M. K. Gunther, and I. E. Pratt. "Environment and the Draw a Man Test: The Performance of Indian Children," *Journal of Abnormal and Social Psychology* 41 (1946): 50–63.

Havinghurst, R. J., and R. R. Hilkevitch. "The Intelligence of Indian Children as Measured by a Performance Scale," *Journal of Abnormal and Social Psychology* 39 (1944): 419–433.

Helgadottir, Anna, Andrei Manolescu, Agnar Helgason, Gudmar Thorleifsson, et al. "A Variant of the Gene Encoding Leukotriene A4 Hydrolase Confers Ethnicity-Specific Risk of Myocardial Infarction," *Nature Genetics* 38 (2006): 68–74.

Helmreich, William. *Against All Odds: Holocaust Survivors and the Successful Lives They Made in America*. New York: Simon and Schuster, 1992.

Herbers, John. "Moynihan Hopeful US Will Adopt a Policy of Promoting Family Stability," *New York Times* (December 12, 1965): 4.

Herbert, Ulrich. "Academic and Public Discourses on the Holocaust: The Goldhagen-Debate in Germany," *German Politics and Society* 17 (1999): 35–54.

Hersch, Charles. "Social History, Mental Health, and Community Control," *American Psychologist* 27 (1972): 749–754.

Herzl, Theodor. "Neue Nasen," in *Die treibende Kraft: Feuilltons*, ed. Markus G. Patka. Vienna: Picus, 2004, pp. 54–61.

——. *Zionist Writings, Essays and Addresses, I: January, 1896–June, 1898*, trans. Harry Zohn. New York: Herzl Press, 1973.

Herzog, Dagmar. *Sex after Fascism: Memory and Morality in Twentieth-Century Germany*. Princeton, NJ, and Oxford: Princeton University Press, 2005.

Hill, Herbert, and Jack Greenberg. *Citizen's Guide to Desegregation*. Boston: Beacon Press, 1955.

Hinkle, Roscoe C. *Founding Theory of American Sociology, 1881–1915*. Boston, MA: Routledge, 1980.

"Hitler Convicted of 'Crime against Civilization': Nazi Leaders Held Guilty, 20 Witnesses Indict Reich Regime as Threat to World Peace," *American Israelite* (March 15, 1934): 1.

"Hitlerism Called Psychic Epidemic," *New York Times* (March 8, 1934): 6.

Hoberman, John. *Black and Blue: The Origins and Consequences of Medical Racism*. Berkeley: University of California Press, 2012.

Hoblyn, Richard D., and L. M. Griffiths. *A Dictionary of Terms Used in Medicine and the Collateral Sciences*. London: Whittaker and Co., 1849.

Hoffman, Abraham. *Unwanted Mexican Americans in the Great Depression: Repatriation Pressures, 1929–1939*. Tucson, AZ: Tucson University Press, 1974.

Hoffman, Frederick L. *Race Traits and Tendencies of the American Negro*. New York: Macmillan, 1896.

Holloway, Jonathan Scott. *Confronting the Veil: Abram Harris, Jr., E. Franklin Frazier, and Ralph Bunche, 1919–1941*. Chapel Hill: University of North Carolina Press, 2002.

Holmes, Dorothy. "Race and Transference in Psychotherapy and Psychoanalysis," *International Journal of Psycho-Analysis* 73 (1992): 1–11.

——. "The Wrecking Effects of Race and Social Class on Self and Success," *Psychoanalytic Quarterly* 75 (2006): 215–235.

Horkheimer, Max. "Sociological Background of the Psychoanalytic Approach," in *Anti-Semitism: A Social Disease*, ed. Ernst Simmel. New York: International Universities Press, 1946, pp. 1–11.

Horney, Karen. *Neurosis and Human Growth*. New York: W.W. Norton, 1950.

Horowitz, Eugene L. "The Development of Attitude toward the Negro," *Archives of Psychology* 194 (1936): 1–45.

———. "Race Attitudes," in *Characteristics of the American Negro*, ed. Otto Klineberg. New York: Harper and Row, 1944, pp. 141–247.

Horowitz, Eugene L., and Ruth E. Horowitz, "Development of Social Attitudes in Children," *Sociometry* 1 (1938): 301–338.

Horowitz, Ruth E. "Racial Aspects of Self-identification in Nursery School Children," *Journal of Psychology* 7 (1939): 91–99.

Horowitz, Ruth E., and Lois Barclay Murphy, "Projective Methods in the Psychological Study of Children," *Journal of Experimental Education* 7 (December 1938): 133–140.

Hughes, John S. "Labeling and Treating Black Mental Illness in Alabama, 1861–1910," *Journal of Southern History* 58 (August 1992): 435–460.

Hunter, Marcos Anthony. *Black Citymakers: How the Philadelphia Negro Changed Urban America*. New York: Oxford University Press, 2013.

Hyöng, Peter. "A Dream of a White Vienna after World War I: Hugo Bettauer's *The City without Jews* and *The Blue Stain*," in *At Home and Abroad: Historicizing Twentieth-Century Whiteness in Literature and Performance*, ed. La Vinia Delois Jennings. Knoxville: University of Tennessee Press, 2009, pp. 29–60.

Hyslop, Theo B. *The Borderland: Some of the Problems of Insanity*. London: Philip Allan and Co, 1925.

"Insanity and the Immigrant," *American Israelite* (November 28, 1912): 1.

Jackson, John P., Jr. *Social Scientists for Social Justice: Making the Case against Segregation*. New York: NYU Press, 2005.

Jackson, John P., Jr., and Nadine M. Weidman. *Race, Racism, and Science: Social Impact and Interaction*. New Brunswick, NJ: Rutgers University Press, 2006.

Jackson, Walter. "The American Creed from a Swedish Perspective: The Wartime Context of Gunnar Myrdal's 'An American Dilemma,'" in *The Estate of Social Knowledge*, ed. Joanne Brown and David K. van Keuren. Baltimore: Johns Hopkins University Press, 1991, pp. 209–227.

———. *Gunnar Myrdal and America's Conscience: Social Engineering and Racial Liberalism, 1938–1987*. Chapel Hill, NC: University of North Carolina Press, 1990.

Jacobs, Jack. *The Frankfurt School, Jewish Lives, and Antisemitism*. New York: Cambridge University Press, 2014.

Jacobson, Matthew Frye. *Special Sorrows: The Diasporic Imagination of Irish, Polish, and Jewish Immigrants in the United States*. Berkeley: University of California Press, 2002.

———. *Whiteness of a Different Color: European Immigrants and the Alchemy of Race*. Cambridge, MA: Harvard University Press, 1999.

Jahoda, Gustav. *Crossroads between Culture and Mind: Continuities and Change in Theories of Human Nature*. Cambridge, MA: Harvard University Press, 1993.

Jarvis, Edward. "Insanity among the Coloured Population of the Free States," *American Journal of the Medical Sciences* (January 1844): 3–15.

———. "On the Supposed Increase of Insanity," *American Journal of Psychiatry* 8 (April 1, 1852): 333–364.

Jaspers, Karl. *Die Schuldfrage*. Heidelberg: Lambert Schneider, 1946.

———. *General Psychopathology*, trans. J. Hoenig and Marian Hamilton. 2 vols. Baltimore: Johns Hopkins University Press, 1997.

———. *The Question of German Guilt*, trans. E. B. Ashton. New York: Dial Press, 1947.

Jay, Martin. *The Dialectical Imagination: A History of the Frankfurt School and the Institute of Social Research, 1923–1950*. Berkeley: University of California Press, 1996.

Jenkins, Richard L. *Breaking Patterns of Defeat*. Philadelphia: J.B. Lippincott, 1954.

Jerome, Fred, and Rodger Taylor, eds. *Einstein on Race and Racism*. New Brunswick, NJ: Rutgers University Press, 2006.

Johnson, Charles S., and Horace M. Bond, "The Investigation of Racial Differences prior to 1910," *Journal of Negro Education* 3 (1934): 328–339.

Jones, Edgar, and Simon Wessely. *Shell Shock to PTSD: Military Psychiatry from 1900 to the Gulf War*. Hove and New York: Psychology Press, 2005.

Jonsson, Stefan. *A Brief History of the Masses: Three Revolutions*. New York: Columbia University Press, 2008.

———. *Crowds and Democracy: The Idea and Image of the Masses from Revolution to Fascism*. New York: Columbia University Press, 2013.

Jorde, Lynn B., and Stephen P. Wooding. "Genetic Variation, Classification, and 'Race,'" *Nature Genetics* 36 (2004): S28–S33.

Josefson, Deborah. "Oregon Governor Apologies for Forced Sterilizations," *British Medical Journal* 325 (2002): 1380.

Joseph, Jacques. "Über die operative Verkleinerung einer Nase (Rhinomiosis)," *Berliner klinische Wochenschrift* 40 (1898): 882–885. Translation from Jacques Joseph, "Operative Reduction of the Size of a Nose (Rhinomiosis)," trans. Gustave Aufricht, *Plastic and Reconstructive Surgery* 46 (1970): 178–181.

"Joseph Sandler in Conversation with Anna Freud, Discussions in the Hampstead Index on *The Ego and the Mechanisms of Defense*: IV. The Mechanisms of Defense, Part 1," *Bulletiin of the Anna Freud Centre* 4 (1981): 151–199.

Judaken, Jonathan. *Jean-Paul Sartre and the Jewish Question: Anti-Antisemitism and the Politics of the French Intellectual*. Lincoln: University of Nebraska Press, 2006.

Kahana, Boaz, Sev Harel, and Eva Kahana. "Predictors of Psychological Well-Being among Survivors of the Holocaust," in *Human Adaptation to Extreme Stress*, ed. John Preston Wilson, Zev Harel, and Boaz Kahana. New York: Plenum, 1988, pp. 171–192.

Kaiser, Céline, and Marie-Luise Wünsche, eds. *Die 'Nervosität der Juden' und andere Leiden an der Zivilisation: Konstruktionen des Kollektiven und Konzepte indivi-*

dueller Krankheit im psychiatrischen Diskurs um 1900. Paderborn and München: Schönigh, 2003.

Kardiner, Abraham, and Lionel Ovesey. *The Mark of Oppression: A Psychosocial Study of the American Negro.* New York: W.W. Norton, 1951.

Katz, Jay. "The Jewish Chronic Disease Hospital Case," in *Experimentation with Human Beings.* New York: Russell Sage Foundation, 1972, pp. 9–65.

Kauders, Anthony D. "Drives in Dispute: The West German Student Movement, Psychoanalysis, and the Search for a New Emotional Order, 1967–1971," *Central European History* 44 (2011): 711–731.

Kaufman, Walter C. "Status, Authoritarianism, and Anti-Semitism," *American Journal of Sociology* 62 (1957): 379–382.

Keller, Richard C. *Colonial Madness: Psychiatry in French North Africa.* Chicago: University of Chicago Press, 2007.

Kelly, Daniel, Luc Faucher, and Edouard Machery. "Getting Rid of Racism: Assessing Three Proposals in Light of Psychological Evidence," *Journal of Social Philosophy* 41 (2010): 293–322.

Kelsen, Hans. *Society and Nature.* London: Kegan Paul, 1946.

Kennedy, John F. Remarks on Signing Mental Retardation Facilities and Community Health Centers Construction Bill, October 31, 1963. Presidential Papers. President's Office Files. Speech Files.

Kernberg, Otto F. "Aggression, Hatred, and Social Violence," *Canadian Journal of Psychoanalysis* 6 (1998): 191–206.

———. "The Psychopathology of Hatred," *Journal of the American Psychoanalytic Association* 39S (1991): 209–238.

Kernis, Michael, and Brian M. Goldman, "A Multicomponent Conceptualization of Authenticity: Theory and Research," *Advances in Experimental Social Psychology* 38 (2006): 283–357.

Kerr, Norman. *Inebriety or Narcomania: Its Etiology, Pathology, Treatment, and Jurisprudence.* London: H. K. Lewis, 1894.

Khanna, Ranjana. *Dark Continents: Psychoanalysis and Colonialism.* Durham, NC: Duke University Press, 2003.

King, Martin Luther, Jr. "The Role of the Behavioral Scientist in the Civil Rights Movement," *Journal of Social Issues* 24 (1968): 180–186.

Kiss, Endre. "Does Mass Psychology Renaturalize Political Theory? On the Methodological Originality of *Crowds and Power*," *European Legacy: Toward New Paradigms* 9 (2004): 725–738.

Kluger, Richard. *Simple Justice: The History of Brown v. Board of Education and Black America's Struggle for Equality.* New York: Alfred A. Knopf, 1976.

Knorr Cetina, Karen. *Epistemic Cultures: How the Sciences Make Knowledge.* Cambridge, MA: Harvard University Press, 1999.

Kohn, M. L., and J. A. Clausen, "Parental Authority Behavior and Schizophrenia," *American Journal of Orthopsychiatry* 26 (1956): 297–313.

Koonz, Claudia. *Mothers in the Fatherland: Women, the Family, and Nazi Politic*. New York: St. Martin's Press, 1987.

Kornberg, Jacques. *Theodor Herzl: From Assimilation to Zionism*. Bloomington: Indiana University Press, 1993.

Kovel, Joel. *Overcoming Zionism: Creating a Single Democratic State in Israel/Palestine*. London: Pluto, 2007.

———. *White Racism: A Psychohistory*. New York: Columbia University Press, [1970]1984.

Kraepelin, Emil. "Zur Entartungsfrage," *Zentralblatt für Nervenheilkunde und Psychiatrie* 19 (1908): 745–751.

Krell, Robert, and Marc I. Sherman. *Medical and Psychological Effects of Concentration Camps on Holocaust Survivors*. New Brunswick, NJ: Transaction, 1977.

Krieger, Linda. "The Content of our Categories," *Stanford Law Review* 47 (1995): 1161–1223.

Kuhl, Stefan. *The Nazi Connection: Eugenics, American Racism, and German National Socialism*. New York: Oxford University Press, 1994.

Kushner, Howard I. *American Suicide: A Psychocultural Exploration*. New Brunswick, NJ: Rutgers University Press, 1989.

LaCapra, Dominick. *Emile Durkheim: Sociologist and Philosopher*. Ithaca, NY: Cornell University Press, 1972.

———. "Perpetrators and Victims: The Goldhagen Debate and Beyond," in *Writing History, Writing Trauma*, ed. Dominick LaCapra. Baltimore: Johns Hopkins University Press, 2001, pp. 114–140.

Lamont, Michele, and Virag Molnar. "The Study of Boundaries in the Social Sciences," *Annual Review of Sociology* 28 (2002): 167–195.

Langlois, Janet L. "The Bell Isle Bridge Incident: Legend, Dialectic, and Semiotic System in the 1943 Detroit Race Riots," *Journal of American Folklore* 118 (1983): 219–236.

Lasch-Quinn, Elizabeth. *Race Experts: How Racial Etiquette, Sensitivity Training, and New Age Therapy Hijacked the Civil Rights Revolution*. New York: W.W. Norton, 2001.

Lasker, Bruno. "How to Correct Anti-Semitism among Jewish Children," in *Jewish Experiences in America: Suggestions for the Study of Jewish Relations with Non-Jews*, ed. Bruno Lasker. New York: Inquiry, 1930, pp. 111–120.

Le Bon, Gustave. *The Crowd: A Study of the Popular Mind*. New York: Macmillan, 1896.

Lee, Cynthia. "'Murder and the Reasonable Man' Revisited: A Response to Victoria Nourse." *Ohio State Journal of Criminal Law* 3 (2003): 301–306.

Lee, Emily S., ed. *Living Alterities*. Albany: SUNY Press, 2014.

Lerman, Antony. "Jewish Self-Hatred: Myth or Reality," *Jewish Quarterly* 210 (2008): 46–51.

Lessing, Theodor. *Der jüdische Selbsthaß*. Berlin: Jüdischer Verlag, 1930.

Levin, Kenneth. "The Psychology of Populations under Chronic Siege," *Post Holocaust and Antisemitism* 46 (Jerusalem Center for Public Affairs, July 2, 2006), www.jcpa.org.

Lewin, Kurt. "Self-Hatred among Jews," *Contemporary Jewish Record* 4 (1941): 219–232.

Lewisohn, Ludwig. "Where Next . . . ," *Jewish Exponent* (February 4, 1938): 1.

Leys, Ruth. "Die 'Überlebensschuld' im psychoanalytischen Diskurs—Ein kurzer historischer Überblick," *Tel Aviver Jahrbuch fur Deutsche Geschichte* 39 (2011): 86–115.

———. *From Guilt to Shame: Auschwitz and After.* Princeton, NJ: Princeton University Press, 2007.

———. *Trauma: A Genealogy.* Chicago: University of Chicago Press, 2000.

Lieberman, Matthew D. "An fMRI Investigation of Race-Related Amygdala Activity in African-American and Caucasian-American Individuals," *Nature Neuroscience* 6 (2005): 720–722.

Lifton, Robert Jay. *Death in Life: Survivors of Hiroshima.* New York: Random House, 1967.

Lim, Jason. "Immanent Politics: Thinking Race and Ethnicity through Affect and Machinism," *Environment and Planning A* 42 (2010): 2393–2409.

Lipphardt, Veronika. *Biologie der Juden: jüdische Wissenschaftler über "Rasse" und Vererbung 1900–1935.* Göttingen: Vandenhoeck and Ruprecht, 2008.

———. "Das 'schwarze Schaf' der Biowissenschaften. Marginalisierungen und Rehabilitierungen der Rassenbiologie im 20. Jahrhundert," in *Pseudowissenschaft : Konzeptionen von Nichtwissenschaftlichkeit in der Wissenschaftsgeschichte*, ed. Dirk Rupnow, Veronika Lipphardt, Jens Thiel, and Christina Wessely. Frankfurt am Main: Suhrkamp, 2008, pp. 223–250.

———. *Die 'Nervosität der Juden' und andere Leiden an der Zivilisation : Konstruktionen des Kollektiven und Konzepte individueller Krankheit im psychiatrischen Diskurs um 1900.* Paderborn and München: Schönigh, 2003.

Loeblowitz-Lennard, Henry. "The Jew as Symbol. II. Antisemitism and Transference," *Psychiatric Quarterly* 21 (1947): 253–260.

Lombardo, Paul A. *Three Generations, No Imbeciles: Eugenics, the Supreme Court, and Buck v. Bell.* Baltimore: Johns Hopkins University Press, 2010.

Lombroso, Cesare. *L'antisemitismo e la scienze moderne.* Turin: L. Roux, 1894.

———. "Why Homicide Has Increased in the United States. II. Barbarism and Civilization," *North American Review* 166 (January 1898): 1–11.

Low, Alfred D. *Jews in the Eyes of the Germans.* Philadelphia: Institute for the Study of Human Issues, 1979.

Ludmerer, Kenneth. "American Geneticists and the Eugenics Movement, 1905–1935," *Journal of the History of Biology* 2 (1969): 337–362.

Luhrmann, Tanya M. *The Good Parsi: The Fate of a Colonial Elite in a Postcolonial Society.* Cambridge, MA: Harvard University Press, 1996.

Lyotard, Jean-François. *Heidegger et "Les Juifs."* Paris: Galilée, 1988.

MacCrone, I. D. *Race Attitudes in South Africa: Historical, Experimental, and Psychological Studies.* Oxford: Oxford University Press, 1937.

MacDonald, Kevin. *The Culture of Critique: An Evolutionary Analysis of Jewish Involvement in Twentieth Century Intellectual and Political Movements.* Westport, CT: Praeger, 1998.

———. *A People That Shall Dwell Alone: Judaism as Group Evolutionary Strategy.* Westport, CT: Praeger, 1994.

————. "Policing the Elites," *Occidental Observer* (September 4, 2010): http://theocci-dentalobserver.net

————. *Separation and Its Discontents: Toward an Evolutionary Theory of Anti-Semitism.* Westport, CT: Praeger, 1998.

MacNevin, Thomas, ed. *The Speeches of the Right Honorable Richard Lalor Sheil, M.P. with a Memoir.* London: H.G. Bohn 1847.

Malan, Rian. *My Traitor's Heart: A South African Exile Returns to Face His Country, His Tribe and His Conscience.* New York: Vintage, 1991.

Mamet, David. *The Wicked Son: Anti-Semitism, Self-Hatred and the Jews.* New York: Nextbook/Schocken, 2006.

Mantegazza, Paolo. *The Sexual Relations of Mankind*, trans. Victor Robinson. New York: Eugenics Pub. Co., 1935.

Maranz, Georges. "Les consequences de la circoncision: Essai d'explication psychanaly-tique de l'antisémitisme," *Psyché-Paris* 2 (1947): 731–745.

Marcus, Paul. *Autonomy in the Extreme Situation. Bruno Bettelheim, the Nazi Concen-tration Camps and the Mass Society.* Westport, CT: Praeger, 1999.

Marrow, Alfred J. *The Practical Theorist: The Life and Work of Kurt Lewin.* New York: Teachers College Press, 1977.

————. "Psychology of Racial Prejudice: An Aspect of Mental Health," in *Annual Conference of the National Urban League.* New York: Commission on Intergroup Relations, 1958, pp. 163–168.

Martin, Jay. *The Dialectical Imagination: A History of the Frankfurt School and the Insti-tute of Social Research, 1923–1950.* Berkeley: University of California Press, 1996.

Masserman, Jules. *The Practice of Dynamic Psychiatry.* Philadelphia and London: W.B. Saunders, 1955.

Massin, Benoit. "Anthropologie und Humangenetik im Nationalsozialismus oder: Wie schreiben deutsche Wissenschaftler ihre eigene Wissenschaftsgeschichte?," in *Wissenschaftlicher Rassismus. Analysen einer Kontinuität in den Human- Naturwis-senschaften*, ed. Heidrun Kaupen-Haas and Christian Saller. Frankfurt am Main: Campus, 1999.

Mays, Thomas J. "Human Slavery as a Prevention of Pulmonary Consumption," *Trans-actions of the American Clinical and Climatological Association* 20 (1904): 192–197.

McCaffrey, James P. "Hospital Accused on Cancer Study," *New York Times* (January 21, 1964): 31.

McCandless, Boyd R., and Harold D. Holloway. "Race Prejudice and Intolerance of Ambiguity in Children," *Journal of Abnormal and Social Psychology* 51(1955): 692–693.

McCarthy, Justin. *History of Our Own Times*, 4 Vols. New York and London: Harper Brothers, 1901

McClelland, J. S. *The Crowd and the Mob: From Plato to Canetti.* London: Unwin Hy-man, 1988.

McClintock, Anne. *Imperial Leather: Race, Gender, and Sexuality in the Colonial Con-test.* London: Routledge, 1995.

McCullagh, W.T. *Memoirs of the Rt. Hon. R.L. Sheil*, 2 Vols. London: H. Colburn, 1855.

McCulloch, Jock. *Black Patients, White Psyches, Colonial Psychiatry and "The African Mind."* Cambridge, UK: Cambridge University Press, 1995.

McDougall, William. *The Group Mind: A Sketch of the Principles of Collective Psychology with Some Attempt to Apply Them to the Interpretation of National Life and Character.* Cambridge, UK: Cambridge University Press, 1920.

McGranahan, D. V., and Morris Janowitz, "Studies of German Youth," *Journal of Abnormal and Social Psychology* 41 (1946): 3–14.

McIntosh, Peggy. *White Privilege and Male Privilege: A Personal Account of Coming to See Correspondences through Work in Women's Studies* (Working Paper No. 189, Stone Center Work in Progress Papers). Wellesley, MA: Wellesley College, Center for Research on Women, 1988.

McKee, James B. *Sociology and the Race Problem: The Failure of a Perspective.* Urbana: University of Illinois Press, 1993.

McWilliams, Nancy. "Primary (Primitive) Defensive Processes," in *Psychoanalytic Diagnosis.* New York: Guilford Press, 1994, pp. 96–115.

Mead, George H. *Movements of Thought in the Nineteenth Century.* Chicago: University of Chicago Press, 1936.

Mead, Margaret. *Cultural Patterns and Technical Change.* New York: New American Library, 1955.

Meehan, Thomas. "Moynihan of the Moynihan Report," *New York Times Magazine* (July 31, 1966): 173.

"Mel Gibson's Apology to the Jewish Community," *Anti-Defamation League*, August 1, 2006. www.adl.org.

Memmi, Albert. *The Colonizer and the Colonized*, trans. Howard Greenfield. Boston: Beacon Press, 1965.

Mendelsohn, Richard, and Milton Shain. *The Jews in South Africa: An Illustrated History.* Johannesburg and Cape Town: Jonathan Ball, 2008.

Mendes, Gabriel N. *Under the Strain of Color: Harlem's Lafargue Clinic and the Promise of Antiracist Psychiatry.* Ithaca, NY: Cornell University Press, 2015.

Metzl, Jonathan. *The Protest Psychosis: How Schizophrenia Became a Black Disease.* Boston: Beacon Press, 2009.

Mezes, S. E. "Review of Psychic Rudiments and Morality," *Psychological Review* 8 (1901): 320–323.

Miller, Rory. *Ireland and the Palestine Question.* Dublin: Irish Academic Press, 2005.

Milner, Esther. "Some Hypotheses Concerning the Influence of Segregation on Negro Personality Development," *Psychiatry* 16 (1953): 291–297.

Mitchell, Peta. *Contagious Metaphor.* London: Bloomsbury Academic, 2012.

Mitscherlich, Alexander. *Das Diktat der Menschenverachtung: Der Nürnberger Ärzteprozeß und seine Quellen.* Heidelberg: Lambert Schneider, 1947.

Mitscherlich, Alexander, and Margarete Mitscherlich. *Die Unfähigkeit zu trauern: Grundlagen kollektiven Verhaltens.* München: R. Piper, 1967.

——. *The Inability to Mourn: Principles of Collective Behavior*, trans. Eric Mosbachs. New York: Grove, 1974.

Mitscherlich-Nielsen, Margarete. "Antisemitism—A Male Disorder?," *Psyche* 37 (1983): 41–54.

Molina, Natalia. *Fit to Be Citizens?: Public Health and Race in Los Angeles, 1879–1939*. Berkeley: University of California Press, 2006.

Morabia, Alfreda, ed. *A History of Epidemiologic Methods and Concepts*. New York: Springer, 2004.

Morris, Aldon. *The Scholar Denied: W.E.B. DuBois and the Birth of American Sociology*. Berkeley: University of California Press, 2015.

Morrison, Toni. *Conversations with Toni Morrison*, ed. Danille Taylor-Guthrie. Oxford: University Press of Mississippi, 1994.

Morris-Reich, Amos. *The Quest for Jewish Assimilation in Modern Social Science*. New York: Routledge, 2008.

"A Mother Can't Do a Man's Job," *Newsweek* (August 22, 1966): 41.

"Moynihan Report," *New Republic* (September 11, 1965): 8–9.

Müller-Funk, Wolfgang. "Die Angst in der Kultur: Hermann Brochs Massenwahntheorie im historischen Kontext," *Trans: Internet-Zeitschrift für Kulturwissenschaften* 16 (March 2006): 54.

Mumford, Kevin J. "Untangling Pathology: The Moynihan Report and Homosexual Damage," *Journal of Policy History* 24 (2012): 53–73.

Myrdal, Gunnar. *An American Dilemma: The Negro Problem and Modern Democracy*. New Brunswick, NJ: Transaction, [1940]1996.

Neiman, Susan. *Evil in Modern Thought: An Alternative History of Philosophy*. Princeton, NJ: Princeton University Press, 2002.

Neville, Helen A., M. Nikki Coleman, Jameca W. Falconer, and Deadre Holmes. "Color-Blind Racial Ideology and Psychological False Consciousness among African Americans," *Journal of Black Psychology* 31 (2005): 27–45.

"New Crisis: The Negro Family," *Newsweek* (August 9, 1965): 32–35.

Newman, Leonard S. "What Is a 'Social-Psychological' Account of Perpetrator Behavior? The Person versus the Situation in Goldhagen's *Hitler's Willing Executioners*," in *Understanding Genocide. The Social Psychology of the Holocaust*, ed. Leonard S. Newman and Ralph Ebner. Oxford: Oxford University Press, 2002, pp. 43–67.

Nietzsche, Friedrich. "An Spinoza," in *Nachgelassene Fragmente 1884–1885, Herbst 1884, 28 [49]*, *Kritische Studienausgabe*, Bd. 11, ed. Giorgio Colli und Mazzino Montinari. München: dtv, 1988, 319.

——. *The Will to Power*, trans. Walter Kaufmann and R. J. Hollingdale. New York: Vintage, 1968.

Nirenberg, David. *Anti-Judaism: The Western Tradition*. New York: Norton, 2013.

Nitzschke, Bernd. "Psychoanalyse im Nationalsozialismus: Aktuelle Konsequenzen einer historischen Kontroverse: der 'Fall' Wilhelm Reich," *Psychotherapie, Psychosomatik, medizinische Psychologie* 49 (1999): 131–138.

Nobels, Melissa. *Shades of Citizenship: Race and the Census in Modern Politics*. Palo Alto, CA: Stanford University Press, 2001.

Norberg, Jakob. "Perspectives on Postwar Silence: Psychoanalysis, Political Philosophy, and Economic Theory," *German Politics & Society* 29 (2011): 1–20.

Nordau, Max. "Jewry of Muscle (June 1903)," excerpted in *The Jew in the Modern World: A Documentary History*, ed. Paul R. Mendes-Flohr and Jehuda Reinharz. New York: Oxford University Press, 1980, pp. 547–548.

"Not a Black and White Question," *Economist* (April 12, 2006): 80.

Novick, Peter. *The Holocaust in American Life*. Boston: Houghton Mifflin, 1999.

Nyberg, Amy Kiste. *Seal of Approval: The History of the Comics Code*. Jackson: University of Mississippi Press, 1998.

Nye, Robert. *The Origins of Crowd Psychology: Gustave Le Bon and the Crisis of Mass Democracy in the Third Republic*. London: Sage, 1975.

Olmstead, Friedrich L. *A Journey in the Seaboard Slave States; with Remarks on Their Economy*. New York and London: Dix and Edwards/Sampson Low, Son & Co., 1856.

O'Malley, Mary. "Psychoses in the Colored Race," *American Journal of Psychiatry* 71 (1914): 309–337.

Omi, Michael, and Howard Winant. *Racial Formation in the United States from the 1960s to the 1980s*. New York: Routledge, 1986.

"On Radio, Comic Apologizes for Tirade," *Washington Post* (November 26, 2006), www.washingtonpost.com.

Osinubi, Taiwo Adetunji. "Abusive Narratives: Antjie Krog, Rian Malan, and the Transmission of Violence," *Comparative Studies of South Asia, Africa and the Middle East* 28 (2008): 109–123.

Osmundsen, John A. "Many Scientific Experts Condemn Ethics of Cancer Injection," *New York Times* (January 26, 1964): 70.

Ostrer, Harry. *Legacy: A Genetic History of the Jewish People*. Oxford: Oxford University Press, 2012.

"Otto Dov Kulka: 'Every One of Us Had His or Her Own Story of Survival. But We Never Talked about It,'" *Guardian* (March 7, 2014), www.theguardian.com.

"Pandora and the Problem of Evil," *Lancet* 347 (January 6, 1996): 1.

Park, Robert E. "Human Migration and the Marginal Man," *American Journal of Sociology* 23 (1928): 881–893.

———. "Mentality of Racial Hybrids," *American Journal of Sociology* 36 (1931): 534–551.

———. *Race and Culture*. New York: Free Press, 1950.

Pascoe, Peggy. "Miscegenation Law, Court Cases, and Ideologies of 'Race' in 20th-Century America," *Journal of American History* 83 (June 1996): 44–69.

———. *What Comes Naturally: Miscegenation Law and the Making of Race in America*. New York: Oxford University Press, 2010.

Patai, Raphael. *The Jewish Mind*. New York: Jason Aronson, 1977.

Patterson, James T. "The Moynihan Future," *New York Times* (May 28, 2010): 25.

Perry, Gina. *Behind the Shock Machine: The Untold Story of the Notorious Milgram Psychology Experiments*. New York: New Press, 2012.

Pettigrew, Thomas F. "The Negro American Personality: Why Isn't More Known?," *Journal of Social Issues* 20 (1964): 4–23.

Pick, Daniel. *The Pursuit of the Nazi Mind: Hitler, Hess, and the Analysts.* Oxford: Oxford University Press, 2012.

Pickren, Wade E., Donald A. Dewsbury, and Michael Wertheimer. *Portraits of Pioneers in Developmental Psychology.* New York: Psychology Press, 2012.

Pietikäinen, Peteri. *Madness: A History.* London and New York: Routledge, 2015.

Pinsker, Leon. *Auto-Emancipation*, trans. D. S. Blondheim. New York: Maccabean Publishing Co., 1906.

Polk, Hugh. "Letter to the Editor," *New York Times* (January 12, 2000).

Pollack, Andrew. "DNA Blueprint for Fetus Built Using Tests of Parents," *New York Times* (June 6, 2012): 1.

Pollak, Richard. *The Creation of Dr. B: A Biography of Bruno Bettelheim.* New York: Simon & Schuster, 1997.

Polletta, Francesca. *It Was Like a Fever: Storytelling in Protest and Politics.* Chicago: University of Chicago Press, 2006.

Porter, Judith D. R. *Black Child, White Child: The Development of Racial Attitudes.* Cambridge, MA: Harvard University Press, 1971.

Poussaint, Alvin F. "How the 'White Problem' Spawned 'Black Power,'" *Ebony Magazine* 22 (1967): 88–93.

———. "A Negro Psychiatrist Explains the Negro Psyche," *New York Times Magazine* (August 20, 1967): 52.

———. "A Psychiatrist Looks at Black Power," *Ebony Magazine* 24 (1969): 142–152.

———. "They Hate. They Kill. Are They Insane?," *New York Times* (August 26, 1999): 17.

———. "What a Rorschach Can't Gauge," *New York Times* (January 9, 2000): sec. 4, 19.

———. "White Racism and Black Anger," *Boston Globe* (April 21, 1968): F32.

Poussaint, Renee. "Interview with Alvin Poussaint," *National Visionary Leadership Project*, www.visionaryproject.org/poussaintalvin.

———. "Interview with John H. Johnson," *National Visionary Leadership Project*, www.visionaryproject.org/johnsonjohn.

"President Hails New Stage in Negro Battle for Justice," *Washington Post* (June 5, 1965).

Prince, Morton. *The American versus the German View of the War.* London: T. Fisher Unwin, 1915.

———. *The Psychology of the Kaiser: A Study of His Sentiments and His Obsession.* Boston: R.G. Badger 1915.

Prince, Robert. "Psychoanalysis Traumatized: The Legacy of the Holocaust," *American Journal of Psychoanalysis*, 69 (2009): 179–194.

Proceedings of the National Conference of Charities and Corrections, 1887. Ann Arbor: University of Michigan Library, 2005.

Proctor, Robert. *Racial Hygiene.* Cambridge, MA: Harvard University Press, 1988.

Pross, Christian. *Paying for the Past: The Struggle over Reparations for Surviving Victims of the Nazi Terror*, trans. Belinda Cooper. Baltimore: Johns Hopkins University Press, 1998.

Pulzer, Peter. "Vorbild, Rivale und Unmensch. Das sich wandelnde Deutschlandbild in England 1815–1945," in *Deutschlandbilder in Dänemark und England, in Frankreich und den Niederlanden*, ed., H. Süssmuth. Baden-Baden: Nomos, 1996, pp. 235–250.

Rabinbach, Anson. "The German as Pariah: Karl Jaspers and the Question of German Guilt," *Radical Philosophy* 75 (1996): 15–25.

———. "The Politicization of Reich: An Introduction to Wilhelm Reich's 'The Sexual Misery of the Working Masses,'" *New German Critique* 1 (1974): 90–97.

Rabinbach, Anson, and Sander L. Gilman, eds. *The Third Reich Sourcebook*. Berkeley: University of California Press, 2013.

Rabinow, Paul, and Nikolas Rose. "Biopower Today," *BioSocieties* 1 (2006): 195–217.

Ratner-Rosenhagen, Jennifer. *American Nietzsche: A History of an Icon and His Ideas*. Chicago: University of Chicago Press, 2011.

Reardon, Sean F., Elena Tej Grewal, Demetra Kalogrides, and Erica Greenberg. "Brown Fades: The End of Court-Ordered School Desegregation and the Resegregation of American Public Schools," *Journal of Policy Analysis and Management* 31 (2012): 876–904.

Redsand, Anna. *Viktor Frankl: A Life Worth Living*. New York: Houghton Mifflin, 2006.

Rees, John R., ed. *The Case of Rudolf Hess: A Problem in Diagnosis and Forensic Psychiatry*. London: Wm. Heinemann, 1947.

Reich, Lore Rubin. "Wilhelm Reich and Anna Freud: His Expulsion from Psychoanalysis," *International Forum of Psychoanalysis* 12 (2003): 109–117.

Reich, Wilhelm. *Massenpsychologie des Faschismus: zur Sexualökonomie der politischen Reaktion und zur proletarischen Sexualpolitik*. Copenhagen: Verlag für Sexualpolitk, 1933.

———. *The Mass Psychology of Fascism*, 3d rev. ed., trans. Theodore P. Wolf. New York: Orgone Press, 1946.

Reik, Theodor. "Aggression from Anxiety," *International Journal of Psycho-Analysis* 22 (1941): 7–16.

———. "Der Angstangriff," *Internationale Zeitschrift für Psychoanalyse* 23 (1937): 306–313.

Reilly, Philip R. *The Surgical Solution*. Baltimore: Johns Hopkins University Press, 1991.

Reitter, Paul. *On the Origins of Jewish Self-Hatred*. Princeton, NJ: Princeton University Press, 2012.

Remus, Thérèse. *Germanophobia, Europhobia, Xenophobia—About Stereotypes in Anglo-German Relations*. München: Grin Verlag, 2012

Reuter, Edward B. *The American Race Problem: A Study of the Negro*. New York: Thomas Cromwell, 1927.

———. "The Superiority of the Mulatto," *American Journal of Sociology* 23 (1917): 83–106.

Reyburn, Robert. *Type of Disease among Freed People of the United States, Consolidated reports of sick and wounded freed people and white refugees under treatment from 1865 to June 30, 1872, by medical officers on duty in Bureau of Refugees, Freedmen and Abandoned Lands*. Washington, DC: Gibson Bros., 1891.

Richards, Graham. *Race, Racism, and Psychology: Towards a Reflective History*, 2d ed. New York: Routledge, 2011.

Rigdon, Susan M. *The Culture Facade: Art, Science, and Politics in the Work of Oscar Lewis*. Champaign: University of Illinois Press, 1988.

Risch, Neil. "The Whole Side of It—An Interview with Neil Risch by Jane Gitschier," *PLOS Genetics* 1 (July 2005).

Roberts, Samuel. *Infectious Fear: Politics, Disease, and the Health Effects of Segregation*. Chapel Hill: University of North Carolina Press, 2009.

Robinson, Daniel. *Wild Beasts and Idle Humors: The Insanity Defense from Antiquity to the Present*. Cambridge, MA: Harvard University Press, 1998.

Rochefort, David. "Origins of the 'Third Psychiatric Revolution': The Community Mental Health Centers Act of 1963," *Journal of Health Politics, Policy, and Law* 9 (1984): 1–30.

Roediger, David R. *Working toward Whiteness: How America's Immigrants Became White*. New York: Basic Books, 2006.

Rogoff, Leonard. "Is the Jew White?: The Racial Place of the Southern Jew," *American Jewish History* 85 (1997): 195–230.

Romani, Roberto. *National Character and Public Spirit in Britain and France, 1750–1914*. Cambridge, UK: Cambridge University Press, 2004.

Rose, Jacqueline. "The Myth of Self-Hated," *Guardian* (February 8, 2007), www.the-guardian.com.

Rose, Nikolas. "The Human Sciences in the Biological Age," *Theory, Culture, and Society* 30 (2013): 3–34.

———. *Inventing Our Selves: Psychology, Power, and Personhood*. Cambridge, UK: Cambridge University Press, 1998.

———. *Neuro: The New Brain Sciences and the Management of the Mind*. Princeton, NJ: Princeton University Press, 2013.

Rose, Nikolas, Pat O'Malley, and Mariana Valverde. "Governmentality," *Annual Review of Law and Social Science* 2 (2006): 83–104.

Rosenberg, Goran. *A Brief Stop on the Road from Auschwitz*, trans. Sarah Death. New York: Other Press, 2015.

Rosenberg, Harold. "Jewish Identity in a Free Society: On Current Efforts to Enforce 'Total Commitment,'" *Commentary* 9 (June 1950): 509.

Rosenthal, Solomon P. "Racial Differences in the Incidence of Mental Disease," *Journal of Negro Education* 3 (1934): 484–493.

Rubin, Theodore Isaac. *Antisemitism: A Disease of the Mind—A Psychiatrist Explores the Psychodynamics of a Symbol Sickness*. New York: Continuum, 1990.

Rubin-Dorsky, Jeffrey. "Philip Roth and American Jewish Identity: The Question of Authenticity," *American Literary History* 13 (2001): 79–107.

Ruhela, Archana, and Malini Sinha. *Recent Trends in Animal Behavior*. Oxford: Oxford Book Co., 2010.

Ruppin, Arthur. *The Jews of Today*. London: G. Bell and Sons, 1913.

———. *Tagebuch*, August 26, 1898, Central Zionist Archive, A107/217.

Rustin, Bayard. "The Watts," *Commentary* (March 1, 1966): 29–35.

Ryan, William. "The New Genteel Racism," *Crisis* (December 1965): 623–631.

———. "Savage Discovery: The Moynihan Report," *Nation* (November 22, 1965): 380–384.

Sachs, Wulf. *Black Hamlet*, with an introduction by Saul Dubow. Baltimore: Johns Hopkins University Press, 1996.

Samelson, Franz. "From 'Race Psychology' to 'Studies in Prejudice': Some Observations on the Thematic Reversal in Social Psychology," *Journal of the History of the Behavioral Sciences* 14 (1978): 265–278.

Sandler, Joseph, and Anna Freud, "Discussions in the Hampstead Index on The Ego and the Mechanisms of Defence: IV. The Mechanisms of Defence, Part 1," *Bulletin of the Anna Freud Centre* 4 (1981): 151–199.

Sanford, Nevitt. "The Approach of the Authoritarian Personality," in *Psychology of Personality: Six Modern Approaches*, ed. J. L. McCary. New York: Logos, 1956, pp. 253–319.

Sarnoff, Irving. "Identification with the Aggressor: Some Personality Correlates of Antisemitism among Jews," *Journal of Personality* 20 (1951–1952): 199–218.

Scheler, Max. *Der Genius des Krieges und der Deutsche Krieg*. Leipzig: Verlag der "Weissen Buecher," 1915.

———. *Die Ursachen des Deutschenhasses—Eine national-paedagogische Eroerterung*. Leipzig: Wolff, 1917.

Schellenberg, James. *Masters of Social Psychology: Freud, Mead, Lewin, Skinner*. New York: Oxford University Press, 1978.

Schiratzki, Johanna. *Best Interests of the Child*. New York: Oxford University Press, 2013.

Schneiders, Werner. *Aufklärung und Voruteilskritik. Studien zur Gesichichte der Vorurteilskritik*. Stuggart: Fromman, 1983.

Scholem, Gershom. *A Life in Letters: 1914–1982*, ed. and trans. Anthony David Skinner. Cambridge, MA: Harvard University Press, 2002.

Schwabe, Klaus. *Wissenschaft und Kriegsmoral: Die deutschen Hochschullehrer und die politischen Grundfragen des Ersten Weltkrieges*. Göttingen: Musterschmidt, 1969.

Sclare, A. B. "Cultural Determinants in the Neurotic Negro," *British Journal of Medical Psychology* 26 (1953): 278–288.

Scott, Daryl Michael. *Contempt and Pity: Social Policy and the Image of the Damaged Black Psyche, 1880–1996*. Chapel Hill: University of North Carolina Press, 1997.

Searcy, James T. "Success in Life, Physiologically Considered," *Transactions of the Medical Association of the State of Alabama* (1885): 357–359.

Searles, Harold F. *The Nonhuman Environment in Normal Development and in Schizophrenia*. New York: International Universities Press, 1960.

———. "Scorn, Disillusionment, and Adoration in the Psychotherapy of Schizophrenia," *Psychoanalytic Review* 49 (1962): 39–60.

Sears, R. R., Eleanor Pintler, and Pauline S. Sears. "Effects of Father-Separation on Preschool Children's Doll Play Aggression," *Child Development* 17 (1946): 219–243.

Segal, Nancy L., and Kevin B. MacDonald. "Behavioral Genetics and Evolutionary Psychology: Unified Perspective on Personality Research," *Human Biology* 70 (1998): 159–184.

Shapiro, Edward S. *A Time for Healing: American Jewry since World War II*. Baltimore: Johns Hopkins University Press, 1992.

Sharaf, Myron. *Fury on Earth: A Biography of Wilhelm Reich*. New York: Da Capo Press, 1994.

Shenker, Israel. "Racism Is Called a Health Problem," *New York Times* (May 9, 1969): 12.

Sighele, Scipio. *La Folla delinquente*. Torino: Fratelli Bocca, 1892.

Silverman, Max, ed. *Frantz Fanon's Black Skin, White Masks: New Interdisciplinary Essays*. Manchester, UK: Manchester University Press, 2005.

Simmel, Ernst, "Anti-Semitism and Mass Psychopathology," in *Anti-Semitism: A Social Disease*, ed. Ernst Simmel. New York: International Universities Press, 1946, pp. 33–79.

———, ed. *Anti-Semitism: A Social Disease*, with an introduction by Gordon Allport. New York: International Universities Press, 1946.

Simmel, Georg. "The Metropolis and Mental Life," in *The Sociology of Georg Simmel*, ed. Kurt H. Wolff. New York: Free Press, 1950, pp. 409–424.

———. "The Social and the Individual Level: An Example of General Sociology," in *The Sociology of Georg Simmel*, ed. Kurt H. Wolff. New York: Free Press, 1950, pp. 26–39.

Sirota, Milton. "Letter to the Editor," *New York Times* (January 11, 2000).

Skillings, Judith H., and James E. Dobbins. "Racism as a Disease: Etiology an Treatment Implications," *Journal of Counseling and Development* 70 (1991): 206–212.

Sloane, Paul. "If We Would Prepare for the Struggle Ahead: Psychological Views on Jewish Problems," *Jewish Exponent* (December 10, 1948): 19–20.

Smångs, Mattias. "Doing Violence, Making Race: Southern Lynching and White Racial Group Formation," *American Journal of Sociology* 121 (March 2016): 1329–1374.

Smith, Alan P. "Mental Hygiene and the American Negro," *Journal of the National Medical Association* 23 (1931): 1–10.

Smith, C. E. "A New Approach to the Problem of Racial Differences," *Journal of Negro Education* 3 (1934): 523–529.

Smith, Linell. "Treating the Disease of Racism," *Johns Hopkins Medicine: Diversity &Inclusion* (2010), www.hopkinsmedicine.org/diversity.

"Social and Physical Condition of Negroes in Cities: Report of an Investigation under the Direction of Atlanta University." *Proceedings of the Second Conference for the Study of Problems Concerning Negro City Life*, Atlanta University, May 25–26, 1897, 1–85.

"Socially Fit—Asocial—Antisocial," *Kölnische Zeitung* 64 (December 10, 1937), in *The Third Reich Sourcebook*, ed. Anson Rabinbach and Sander L. Gilman. Berkeley: University of California Press, 2013, p. 343.

Soeter, Marieke, and Merel Kindt. "An Abrupt Transformation of Phobic Behavior after a Post-Retrieval Amnesic Agent," *Biological Psychiatry* 78 (December 15, 2015): 880–886.

Sommer, Andreas. "Nietzsche's Readings on Spinoza: A Contextual Study, Particularly on the Reception of Kuno Fischer," *Journal of Nietzsche Studies* 43 (2012): 156–184.

Spiegel, David. "To the Editor," *New York Times* (August 30, 1999).

Spitzer, Robert. "Response by Robert Spitzer, MD," *New York Times* (August 30, 1999).

Stangneth, Bettina. *Eichmann before Jerusalem: The Unexamined Life of a Mass Murderer*, trans. Ruth Martin. New York: Knopf, 2014.

"State Broadens Cancer Inquiry," *New York Times* (January 22, 1964): 38.

"Statement of Professor Kevin MacDonald," *David Irving/International Campaign for Real History* (July 30, 1999), www.fpp.co.uk

Steinberg, Deborah Lynn. *Genes and the Bioimaginary: Science, Spectacle, Culture*. Farnham: Ashgate, 2015.

Steinberg, Stephen. *Race Relations: A Critique*. Palo Alto, CA: Stanford University Press, 2007.

Sterba, Richard. "Some Psychological Factors in Negro Race Hatred and in Anti-Negro Riots," *Psychoanalysis and the Social Sciences* 1 (1947): 411–427.

Sterling, Dorothy. *The Making of an Afro-American: Martin Robison Delany*. Boston: Da Capo Press, 1996.

Stevens, Jacqueline. "Racial Meanings and Scientific Methods: Changing Policies for NIH-Sponsored Publications Reporting Human Variation," *Journal of Health Policy* 28 (2003): 1033–1044.

Stivers, Eugene, and Susan Wheelan, eds. *The Lewin Legacy: Field Theory in Current Practice*. Berlin and New York: Springer-Verlag, 1986.

Stocking, George, Jr. *Race, Color, and Evolution: Essays in the History of Anthropology*. Chicago: University of Chicago Press, 1968.

Stoetzler, Marcel, ed. *Antisemitism and the Constitution of Sociology*. Lincoln: University of Nebraska Press, 2014.

Stoltzfus, Nathan. *Resistance of the Heart: Intermarriage and the Rosenstrasse Protest in Nazi Germany*. New York: W.W. Norton, 1996.

Straus, Leo. "Anmerkung zur Diskussion über 'Zionismus und Antisemitismus,'" *Jüdische Rundschau* 28 (September 28, 1923): 501–502.

Strecker, Edward A. *Beyond the Clinical Frontiers: A Psychiatrist Views Crowd Behavior*. New York: W.W. Norton, 1940.

Strelka, Joseph. "Politics and the Human Condition: Broch's Model of a Mass Psychology," in *Hermann Broch: Literature, Philosophy, Politics*, ed. Stephen D. Dowden. Columbia, SC: Camden House, 1988.

Suchet, Melanie. "A Relational Encounter with Race," *Psychoanalytic Dialogues* 14 (2004): 423–438.

———. "Unraveling Whiteness," *Psychoanalytic Dialogues* 17 (2007): 867–886.

———. "Whiteness Revisited: Reply to Commentary," *Psychoanalytic Dialogues* 14 (2004): 453–456.

Summers, Martin. "'Suitable Care of the African When Afflicted with Insanity': Race, Madness, and Social Order in Comparative Perspective," *Bulletin of the History of Medicine* 84 (2010).

Sundquist, Eric J. *Strangers in the Land: Blacks, Jews, Post-Holocaust America*. Cambridge, MA: Belknap Press/Harvard University Press, 2009.

Sypher, Francis J. "The Rediscovered Prophet: Frederick L. Hoffman (1865–1946)," *Cosmos Journal* (2000), www.cosmosclub.org.

Tal, Uriel. *Christians and Jews in the "Second Reich" (1870–1914): A Study in the Rise of German Totalitarianism*. Jerusalem: Magnes, 1985.

Tarde, Gabriel. "Foules et sectes au point de vue criminel," *Revue des Deux Mondes* 332 (1893): 349–387.

———. "Les crimes des foules," *Archives de l'Anthropologie Criminelle* 7 (1892): 353–386.

———. *L'opinion et la foule, Introduction par Dominique Reynié*. Paris: Presses Universitaires de France, 1989.

Tas, J. "Psychical Disorders among Inmates of Concentration Camps and Repatriates," *Psychiatric Quarterly* 25 (1951): 679–690.

Taylor, Jerome, Delores Henderson, and Beryl B. Jackson. "A Holistic Model for Understanding and Predicting Depressive Symptoms in African-American Women," *Journal of Community Psychology* 19 (1991): 306–320.

Taylor, J. Madison. "Remarks on the Health of the Colored People," *Journal of the National Medical Association* 7 (1915): 160–163.

Tchen, John Kuo Wei, and Dylan Yeats, eds. *Yellow Peril!: An Archive of Anti-Asian Fear*. London and New York: Verso, 2014.

Teo, Thomas. "The Historical Problematization of 'Mixed-Race' in Psychological and Human-Scientific Discourses," in *Defining Difference: Race and Racism in the History of Psychology*, ed. Andrew Winston. Washington, DC: American Psychological Association, 2004.

Terbeck, Sylvia, Guy Kahane, Sarah McTavish, Julian Savulescu, Philip J. Cowen, and Miles Hewstone. "Propranolol Reduces Implicit Negative Racial Bias," *Psychopharmacology* 222 (2012): 419–424.

Tesner, Michael A. "Racial Paranoia as a Defense to Crimes of Violence: An Emerging Theory of Self Defense or Insanity?," *Boston College Third World Law Journal* 11 (1991): 307–334.

"Test on Cancer to Need Consent," *New York Times* (January 23, 1964): 28.

Theweleit, Klaus. *Male Fantasies*, trans. Stephen Conway. Minneapolis: University of Minnesota Press, 1987.

Thomas, Alexander, and Samuel Sillen, "The Sickness of White Racism," in *Racism and Psychiatry*. New York: Brunner/Mazel, 1972.

Thomas, James M. "Affect and the Sociology of Race: A Program for Critical Inquiry," *Ethnicities* 14 (2014): 72–90.

———. "The Racial Formation of Medieval Jews: A Challenge to the Field," *Ethnic and Racial Studies* 33 (2010): 1737–1755.

Thompson, Charles H. "The Conclusions of Scientists Relative to Racial Differences," *Journal of Negro Education* 3 (1934): 494–512.

Tillinghast, Joseph A. "The Negro in Africa and America," *Publications of the American Economic Association, 3rd Series* 3 (1902): 1–231.

Traub-Werner, Daniel. "Towards a Theory of Prejudice," *International Review of Psycho-Analysis* 11 (1984): 407–412.

Trent, James W., Jr. *Inventing the Feeble Mind: A History of Mental Retardation in the United States.* Berkeley: University of California Press, 1994.

Trotter, Wilfred. "Herd Instinct and Its Bearing on the Psychology of Civilized Man," *Sociological Review* (1908): 227–248.

———. *Instincts of the Herd in Peace and War.* New York: Macmillan, 1916.

———. "Sociological Application of the Psychology of Herd Instinct," *Sociological Review* (January 1909): 36–54.

United States Senate Subcommittee on Health of the Committee on Labor and Public Welfare, *Hearings on S. 755 and S. 756, 88th Congress, 1st Session, 1963.* Washington, DC: U.S. Government Printing Office, 1963.

United States Supreme Court. *Brown v. Board of Education*, 347 U.S. 483 (1954).

van Dijk, Teun Adrianus. *Racism and Discourse in Spain and Latin America.* Amsterdam and Philadelphia: John Benjamins, 2005.

van Ginnekan, Jaap. *Mass Movements in Darwinist, Freudian, and Marxist Perspective: Trotter, Freud, and Reich on War, Revolution, and Reaction 1900–1933.* Apeldoorn: Het Spinhuis, 2007.

Vedantam, Shankar. "Psychiatry Ponders Whether Extreme Bias Can Be an Illness," *Washington Post* (December 10, 2005), www.washingtonpost.com.

Virginia Senate Bill 219, Racial Integrity Act (1924), *DNA Learning Center*, www.dnalc.org.

Visser, Irene. "How to Live? Guilt and Goodness in Rian Malan's *My Traitor's Heart*," *Research in African Literatures* 39 (2008): 149–163.

Volkov, Shulamit. *Germans, Jews, and Antisemites: Trials in Emancipation.* Cambridge, UK: Cambridge University Press, 2006.

von Klemperer, Klemens. *German Resistance against Hitler, 1938–1945.* Oxford: Clarendon Press, 1992.

Vranna, Scott R., and David Rollock. "Physiological Response to a Minimal Social Encounter: Effects of Gender, Ethnicity, and Social Context," *Psychophysiology* 35 (1998): 462–469.

Wailoo, Keith. *Dying in the City of the Blues: Sickle Cell Anemia and the Politics of Race and Health.* Chapel Hill: University of North Carolina Press, 2001.

Wallace, Stuart. *War and the Image of Germany: British Academics, 1914–1918.* Edinburgh: J. Donald, 1988.

Walsh, James. "Richard Lalor Sheil," *Decies* 62 (2006): 95–117.

Washington, Booker T. *Up from Slavery.* Oxford: Oxford University Press, 1995.

Wassermann, Jacob. *My Life as German and Jew.* London: George Allen and Unwin, 1933.

Weber, Marianne, ed. *Max Weber, ein Lebensbild.* Tübingen: JCB Mohr, 1926.

Weheliye, Alexander. *Habeas Viscus: Racializing Assemblages, Biopolitics, and Black Feminist Theories of the Human.* Durham, NC: Duke University Press, 2014.

Weindling, Paul. "Weimar Eugenics: The Kaiser Wilhelm Institute for Anthropology, Human Heredity and Eugenics in Social Context," *Annals of Science* 42 (1985): 303–318.

Weiss, Sheila Faith. "Human Genetics and Politics as Mutually Beneficial Resources: The Case of the Kaiser Wilhelm Institute for Anthropology, Human Heredity and Eugenics During the Third Reich," *Journal of the History of Biology* 39 (2006): 41–88.

Wellman, David. "From Evil to Illness: Medicalizing Racism," *Journal of American Orthopsychiatry* 70 (2000): 28–32.

———. "Unconscious Racism, Social Cognition Theory, and the Legal Intent Doctrine: The Neuron Fires Next Time," in *Handbook of Racial and Ethnic Relations*, ed. Hernán Vera and Joe R. Feagin. New York: Springer, 2007.

White, William A. "Social Significance of Mental Disease," *Archives of Neurology and Psychiatry* 22 (1929): 877.

Wiggershaus, Rolf. *The Frankfurt School: Its History, Theories, and Political Significance*, trans. Michael Robertson. Cambridge, MA: MIT Press, 1995.

Wilder, Gary. *The French Imperial Nation-State: Negritude and Colonial Humanism between the Two World Wars*. Chicago: University of Chicago Press, 2005.

Wilkinson, Harvie, III. *From Brown to Bakke: The Supreme Court and School Integration, 1954–1978*. New York: Oxford University Press, 1979.

Williams, Simon, Stephen Katz, and Paul Martin. "Neuroscience and Medicalisation: Sociological Reflections on Memory, Medicine, and the Brain," in *Sociological Reflections on the Neurosciences*, ed. Martyn Pickersgill and Ira Van Keulen. Bingley: Emerald, 2012, 213–254.

Williams, Walter L. "Nineteenth Century Pan-Africanist John Henry Smyth, United States Minister to Liberia, 1878–1885," *Journal of Negro History* 63 (January 1978): 18–25.

Wilson, David C. "The Neuroses of Everyday Living," *Psychiatric Quarterly* 26 (1952): 387–398.

Wilson, David C., and Edna M. Lantz. "Culture Change and Negro State Hospital Admissions," in *Mental Health and Segregation*, ed. Martin M. Grossack. Berlin: Springer, 1966, 139–149.

———. "The Effect of Culture Change on the Negro Race in Virginia, as Indicated by a Study of State Hospital Admissions," *American Journal of Psychiatry* 114 (1957): 25–32.

Winant, Howard. *New Politics of Race: Globalism, Difference, Justice*. Minneapolis: University of Minnesota Press, 2004.

Wolfe, Alan. *At Home in Exile: Why Diaspora Is Good for the Jews*. Boston: Beacon Press, 2014.

Wundt, Wilhelm. *Die Nationen und ihre Philosophie—Ein Kapitel zum Weltkrieg* [*The Nations and Their Philosophy—A Contribution to the World War*]. Leipzig: Alfred Kroener Verlag, 1915.

Yoder, Dale. "Present Status of the Question of Racial Differences," *Journal of Educational Psychology* 19 (1928): 463–470.

Young, Robert J. *Colonial Desire: Hybridity in Theory, Culture, and Race*. New York: Routledge, 1994.

Young-Bruehl, Elizabeth. *The Anatomy of Prejudices*. Cambridge, MA: Harvard University Press, 1996.

Zaretsky, Eli. *Political Freud: A History*. New York: Columbia University Press, 2015.

Zenderland, Leila. *Measuring Minds: Henry Herbert Goddard and the Origins of American Intelligence Testing*. New York: Cambridge University Press, 1998.

Zimmermann, Mosche. *Wilhelm Marr: The Patriarch of Anti-Semitism*. New York: Oxford University Press, 1986.

INDEX

acculturation: Arendt on, 211; Bettelheim on, 126; Charcot on, 22; as identification with oppressor, 42, 43; Lombroso on, 31; Pinsker on, 37, 211; unacculturated Jews flee Russia, 21
Ackerman, Nathan, 189
Adams, John Quincy, 26
Adams, Romanzo, 60
Adams, William, 59
Adenauer, Konrad, 147
Adlerian psychology, 180
Adorno, Theodor: *Authoritarian Personality*, 131, 179, 186–89, 196, 197, 228, 242, 273; on class and racism, 188; at Institute of Social Research (Frankfurt School), 182–83; Marrow collaborates with, 197; on mass culture, 178; on pathology of Nazi racism, 182
Against All Odds: Holocaust Survivors and the Successful Lives They Made in America (Helmreich), 141
Agamben, Giorgio, 15
aggression, 119–20
Aichhorn, August, 106, 142–43
alcoholism, 49, 63, 64, 97
Alexander, Franz, 119
Aliens Act of 1937 (South Africa), 206
Allport, Gordon, 226
Alpha Tests, 169
Al-Saji, Alia, 312n106
Altman, Neil, 266
American Breeders Association, 93

American Dilemma, An (Myrdal), 165–70, 175–76, 180–81, 253, 311n71
American Eugenics Society, 92
American Hospital Association, 199
American Jewish Committee, 131, 186, 189, 196, 197, 303n138
American Jewish Congress, 115, 197
American Journal of Orthopsychiatry, 247
American Journal of Psychiatry, 64, 242
American Journal of Psychology, 63
American Journal of Sociology, The, 58, 60, 62
American Medical Association, 69
American Orthopsychiatric Association, 247
American Psychiatric Association, 70, 199, 234, 240–47, 251
American Race Problem, The (Reuter), 62
Anatomy of Prejudices, The (Young-Bruehl), 267–68
Anglophobia, 36
Annals of Eugenics, 63, 297n67
Annals of Human Genetics, 297n67
anthropology: biomedical terminology in, 5; Chicago School, 46, 58; cultural, 169; race as seen in, 161; racial science in, 19; in sciences of man, 23; Thompson's survey of anthropologists, 72–73
anti-immigrant sentiment, 67
anti-miscegenation laws, 92–93, 97–98, 166

Babcock, J. W., 65
Bailey, Pearce, 64
Baldwin, James, 177
Barker, Lewellys F., 115–16
Barthes, Roland, 13
Bartlett, Stephen, 4
Barzun, Jacques, 117
Bataille, Georges, 195
Becker, Ernest, 123–24
Bell, Carl, 2, 242–43, 247, 251, 318n86
Bell, Carrie, 94
Berlin Psychoanalytic Society, 185, 201
Bernfeld, Siegfried, 302n11
Bernstein, David, 252–53, 254
Bertillon, Jacques, 241
Bettelheim, Bruno: at American Jewish
    Committee conference on antisemi-
    tism, 131; on "anti-socials," 128; debate
    over veracity of, 305n2; Elkins influ-
    enced by, 230; on Holocaust victims,
    123–29; on identification with the
    aggressor, 124–25, 127, 128; "Individual
    and Mass Behavior in Extreme Situ-
    ations," 124; The Informed Heart, 123,
    124, 126; on "musselmann," 127; on
    Nazi behavior in camps, 128–29; on
    social scientist observers, 130
Bevis, William M., 65
Beyond the Clinical Frontiers (Strecker),
    119
bias: implicit, 1; intergroup, 276; patho-
    logical, 2, 247. See also prejudice
Bienenfeld, F. R., 138
Billings, Joshua, 30
Binet, Alfred, 89, 162
"Binet and Simon Tests of Intellectual
    Capacity, The" (Goddard), 89
biocultural dialectic, 18
bio-logic, 18
biology: biological antisemitism, 180, 209,
    279; biomedical approach to race, 5–6,
    9, 43, 45, 47, 61, 62, 145, 161; discursive
    split between culture and, 46; first and

second ages of, 18–19, 225; genetics
    and evolutionary, 278; in post–World
    War II era, 281–82; race as reflex of, 7;
    in sciences of man, 23; techniques of
    governance in, 30. See also genetics
biopolitics, 13, 15, 285
Bio-Politics: An Essay in the Physiology,
    Pathology and Politics of the Social
    (Roberts), 13
biopower, 13–14, 15–16, 19, 285
Bishop, Shelton Hale, 176
Bismarck, Otto von, 95
Black Anger (Sachs), 205–6
Black Hamlet: The Mind of an African Ne-
    gro Revealed by Psychoanalysis (Sachs),
    201–5, 207–8, 209
Black Like Me (Griffin), 132
Black Power Movement, 238
Black Rage (Grier and Cobbs), 235–37
blacks: American anti-black racism
    versus antisemitism, 133–35; Au-
    thoritarian Personality's on anti-black
    racism, 186–87, 188; black physicians,
    38, 69, 71; black psychiatry, 237–41;
    black psychoanalysts, 266; Boas on,
    58, 59; the Clarks' studies of, 173–76;
    crime rates among, 230; Delany on
    emigration of, 38–40; Du Bois's The
    Philadelphia Negro, 52, 54–55; in Du
    Bois's The Souls of Black Folks, 56–
    57; family structure, 229–30, 231–34;
    Fanon on, 190–92; German attitudes
    toward, 133; ghettoes, 232; Hoffman
    on, 48–55; hypersexuality attributed
    to, 133, 134; increasing rates of hos-
    pitalization for mental illness, 229;
    increasing rates of insanity in freed
    slaves claimed, 27; innate properties
    attributed to, 281; Jewish scientists
    focus on prejudice against, 161–70;
    Kovel on anti-black prejudice, 259;
    Lombroso on, 291n33; Marrow on
    effects of racism on, 196–98;

Chomsky, William, 109, 256
Citizen's Guide to Desegregation (Greenberg and Hill), 229
Civilization and Its Discontents (Freud), 102
"Civilized Sexual Morality and Modern Nervousness" (Freud), 101
Civil Rights Movement: activists shift to Black Power Movement, 238; antifascist discourse in, 189, 228; *The Authoritarian Personality* study and, 196–200; doll studies cited by, 176; early successes of, 18; individual psychopathology approach to racism and, 226; on Moynihan Report, 234; new science of measurement and, 30; Poussaint provides treatment for workers, 237; on psychological damage caused by racism, 189–90, 217; special German psychopathology and, 157. *See also* NAACP
Clark, Kenneth Bancroft: on alliance of anti-antisemitism and anti-black racism movements, 309n42; on best interests of the child, 180; *The Dark Ghetto*, 232; on desegregation, 175, 180; doll studies with black children, 173–76; "Effects of Prejudice on Personality Development," 180; Elkins's work compared with that of, 230; on Grier and Cobbs's *Black Rage*, 235–37; Moynihan influenced by, 232; *Prejudice and Your Child*, 181, 311n71; work used in *Brown v. Board of Education*, 169, 176, 179
Clark, Mamie Phipps, 131, 173–76, 179, 180, 181, 230
Class and Caste in a Southern Town (Dollard), 73–74
Cobbs, Price M., 235–37
cognitive neuroscience, 218, 282
Colby, Bainbridge, 115
Cold Spring Harbor eugenics laboratory, 93
Cold War, 124, 137, 147, 190, 213
Coles, Robert, 232

collective behavior, psychological and sociological approaches to, 268–71
collective consciousness (mind), 76–77, 80, 81–82, 84, 85
collective guilt, 145, 146, 147
Collier, John, 170
Collins, Francis, 277
Colonizer and the Colonized, The (Memmi), 195–96
"Colored Insane, The" (Babcock), 65
comic books, 177–78
community attitudes, 164
community influence, 162
Community Mental Health Centers Act (CMHCA) of 1963, 199–200
compensation neurosis, 138
Condition, Elevation, Emigration, and Destiny of the Colored People of the United States, The (Delany), 38–40
conflict resolution, 67
conjunctural crises, 223–24
Conrad, Joseph, 157, 211
Conrad, Peter, 225
Contact with America (Myrdal and Myrdal), 165
Coolidge, Calvin, 91
Cooper, Riley, 220
Cooter, Roger, 14, 16
cosmetic surgery, 42
Cottrell, Leonard, 236
criminology, 31, 75
critical race studies, 260
Crowd, The: A Study of the Popular Mind (Le Bon), 76–77
Crowds and Power (Canetti), 182
crowd theories, 75–122; Arendt on, 250; in Bettelheim's account of camp behavior, 125, 128; "crowd" becomes real entity in late-nineteen-century psychology, 75; crowd's origin as forensic concept, 75–76; in Kernberg's account of racism, 263; in Klemperer's view of German support for Nazis, 147;

ABOUT THE AUTHORS

Sander L. Gilman is Distinguished Professor of the Liberal Arts and Sciences, as well as Professor of Psychiatry, at Emory University. A cultural and literary historian, he is the author or editor of more than ninety books, most notably *Seeing the Insane* and *Jewish Self-Hatred*.

James M. Thomas is Assistant Professor of Sociology at the University of Mississippi. He is the author of *Working to Laugh: Assembling Difference in American Stand-Up Comedy Venues* and co-author of *Affective Labour: (Dis)Assembling Distance and Difference*.